MW01225752

EXPLORING IBM AS/400 COMPUTERS

Eighth Edition

Other titles of interest from Maximum Press

Exploring IBM Technology & Products: edited by Hoskins
   1-885068-29-8

Exploring IBM's Bold Internet Strategy: Hoskins, Lupiano,
   1-885068-16-6

Building Intranets with Lotus Notes & Domino: Krantz,
   1-885068-10-7

Marketing on the Internet, Second Edition: Mathiesen,
   1-885068-09-3

Real World Client/Server: Krantz, 0-9633214-7-1

Exploring IBM Personal Computers, Ninth Edition: Hoskins,
   Wilson, 1-885068-12-3

Exploring IBM RS/6000 Computers, Eighth Edition:
   Hoskins, Davies, 1-885068-20-4

Exploring the IBM AS/400 Advanced 36, Second Edition:
   Hoskins, Dimmick; 1-885068-11-5

Exploring IBM's New Age Mainframes, Fifth Edition:
1-885068-05-0, Davies

For more information, visit our World Wide Web site at:
http://www.maxpress.com
or e-mail us at *moreinfo@maxpress.com*

EXPLORING IBM AS/400 COMPUTERS

Eighth Edition

Roger Dimmick

Jim Hoskins

MAXIMUM PRESS
605 Silverthorn Road
Gulf Breeze, FL 32561
(850) 934-0819
www.maxpress.com

Publisher: Jim Hoskins

Manager of Finance/Administration: Donna Tryon

Production Manager: ReNae Grant

Cover Design: Lauren Smith Designs

Compositor: PageCrafters Inc.

Copyeditor: Andrew Potter

Proofreader: Julie Cameron

Indexer: Janis Paris

Printer: Malloy Lithographing

This publication is designed to provide accurate and authoritative information in regard to the subject matter covered. It is sold with the understanding that the publisher is not engaged in rendering professional services. If legal, accounting, medical, psychological, or any other expert assistance is required, the services of a competent professional person should be sought. ADAPTED FROM A DECLARATION OF PRINCIPLES OF A JOINT COMMITTEE OF THE AMERICAN BAR ASSOCIATION AND PUBLISHERS.

Copyright 1998 by Maximum Press.

All rights reserved. Published simultaneously in Canada.

Reproduction or translation of any part of this work beyond that permitted by Section 107 or 108 of the 1976 United States Copyright Act without the permission of the copyright owner is unlawful. Requests for permission or further information should be addressed to the Permissions Department, Maximum Press.

Recognizing the importance of preserving what has been written, it is a policy of Maximum Press to have books of enduring value published in the United States printed on acid-free paper, and we exert our best efforts to that end.

Library of Congress Cataloging-in-Publication Data

Hoskins, Jim.

   Exploring IBM AS/400 computers / Jim Hoskins and Roger Dimmick.

-- 8th ed.

   p. cm.

Dimmick's name appears first in the 7th edition.

 Includes bibliographical references and index.

  ISBN 1-885068-19-0 (pbk.)

   1. IBM AS/400 (Computer) I. Dimmick, Roger, 1932- II. Title. III.

Title: Exploring IBM AS/four hundred computers

  QA76.8.I25919 D56 1998

  004.1'45--ddc21

               98-8960

               CIP

Acknowledgments

Many "IBMers" assisted us in preparing the eighth edition of the book despite their demanding schedules. Some provided information about their products. Others read the manuscript and provided helpful comments. To all those who assisted, we thank you. We would especially like to thank John Plansky for helping coordinate this edition.

We would also like to thank Dick O'Dell, Len Kludtke, John Rush, Larry Pederson, George Weaver, Deb Landon, Kim Greene, Carol Woodbury, Mark McKelvey, Dave Marshik, Pete Cornell, Chuck Miller, Carol Miner, and Kathy Cook.

Disclaimer

The purchase of computer software or hardware is an important and costly business decision. While the author and publisher of this book have made reasonable efforts to ensure the accuracy and timeliness of the information contained herein, the author and publisher assume no liability with respect to loss or damage caused or alleged to be caused by reliance on any information contained herein and disclaim any and all warranties, expressed or implied, as to the accuracy or reliability of said information.

This book is not intended to replace the manufacturer's product documentation or personnel in determining the specifications and capabilities of the products mentioned in this book. The manufacturer's product documentation should always be consulted, as the specifications and capabilities of computer hardware and software products are subject to frequent modification. The reader is solely responsible for the choice of computer hardware and software. All configurations and applications of computer hardware and software should be reviewed with the manufacturer's representatives prior to choosing or using any computer hardware and software.

Trademarks

The words contained in this text which are believed to be trademarked, service marked, or otherwise to hold proprietary rights have been designated as such by use of initial capitalization. No attempt has been made to designate as trademarked or service marked any personal computer words or terms in which proprietary rights might exist. Inclusion, exclusion, or definition of a word or term is not intended to affect, or to express judgement upon, the validity of legal status of any proprietary right which may be claimed for a specific word or term.

Table of Contents

Chapter 1:
What Is An AS/400 System?   1

Chapter 2:
Options and Peripherals 95

Chapter 3:
AS/400 Software   183

Chapter 4:
Operating Systems   244

Chapter 5:
AS/400 and Communications—An Introduction   347

Chapter 6:
Application Systems and Your Business   387

Introduction

What This Book Is

This book is dedicated to IBM's midsize business computers, namely, the **Application System/400 (AS/400)** family and the **AS/400 Advanced 36**. Together, these computers make up IBM's strategic direction in midsized business computing. For convenience, the AS/400 family and the AS/400 Advanced 36 are collectively referred to as IBM's **Application Systems.**

First, the Application Systems are introduced. The features of these new computers are compared with those of the earlier System/36 and System/38 family in a way understandable to the business user. The AS/400 family was introduced in 1988, and the first edition of this book, which described the AS/400 family, was published in 1989. IBM has refreshed the AS/400 family in performance, capacity, and/or application support each year since 1988, and on an average of every three years has evolved the systems areas of applicability. Each of those changes has resulted in a new edition of this book to maintain currency with the existing hardware and software directions of the system family.

Second, to help you with software buying decisions, the different types of software necessary to do "real work" are also described.

Finally, we discuss ways to apply Application Systems to improve business operations. Proper selection and use of Application Systems products is impossible unless you understand how you can use these components to fill business needs. Specific Application Systems hardware and software configurations for typical environments are offered. Many important computer automation planning issues are also discussed.

What This Book Is Not

Many computer books try to be all things to all people, covering everything from checkbook balancing to the Space Shuttle's redundant flight computer complex. This book is not a general overview of computers.

It is specific to IBM's Application Systems (a broad enough subject for any single book). This book is neither a technical reference manual (IBM will sell you that) nor a guide to computer programming. It does, however, provide a good understanding of IBM's Application Systems and how to use them in the business environment.

Finally, this book does not expect you to be an engineer. Business people are typically short on time and patience as far as technical matters are concerned. Although some technical discussions are necessary, we have tried to keep these as simple and concise as possible while still conveying necessary and useful information.

How To Use This Book

Chapter 1 introduces the entire AS/400 family and the AS/400 Advanced 36, including the Model 150, an AS/400 System/server priced in the range of a PC server but including full OS/400 capabilities. Nine new models—four general purpose and five servers—are introduced, plus three special-purpose derivative models. Each of these models offers significantly increased performance (up to 6.5 times the performance) in both hardware and software over the equivalent model being replaced.

Another important difference is that the operating system (OS/400) is now bundled with the hardware; it is not possible to buy the hardware without getting the OS/400 operating system with it. The latter part of the chapter examines the elements (built-in database, multiprocessor architecture, etc.) that make up AS/400 computers and separate them from the competition's offerings. These elements of the AS/400 family are contrasted to those of the System/3X computers.

A section on performance and benchmarks is included to assist in comparing the AS/400 family computers against competitive computers that also might be under consideration. The benchmarks section in particular should be helpful in understanding the workloads used to measure the systems and how those workloads relate to your particular business. This section was changed to reflect IBM's continuing effort to measure their systems in a manner that reflects the best understanding of how the customers are using those systems.

Chapter 2 surveys the many hardware options available for Application Systems, including terminals, printers, disk expansion, and communications. Included are the network station, referred to in early literature as the Thin Client, which introduces a new concept in work-stations, and pen-enabled mobile computers, including 200 MHz performance. The FSIOP has been renamed as the Integrated PC Server and the performance has been improved sufficiently to allow its use as a Windows NT Server under the covers. The largest models of the AS/400 can provide up to 16 parallel Windows NT Servers without need to be concerned about "blue screen failure." This section on I/O devices and adapters is provided primarily as a reference to help you identify and select the proper options for your Application System.

Chapter 3 describes the workings of the three types of programs necessary to do productive work with AS/400 computers: application programs, operating systems, and System Licensed Internal Code (SLIC), and continues with a discussion of application programs. Some Application Systems application programs useful to most businesses are discussed. New with this edition is a discussion of Lotus Notes, which has been split into two parts–a server portion called Domino and a client portion that retains the name Lotus Notes. Notes provides collaborative computing support while Domino runs on the Integrated PC server and also executes natively on the AS/400. Many applications have been refreshed with Operations Navigator to provide a GUI interface. OfficeVision and Job Scheduler have been improved to provide many of the functions requested by the customers. We also address an emerging application area–Neural Networks–which has been moved into the Intelligent Miner product for data mining. Industry-specific application programs are introduced with an example. Finally, the question of "prewritten" vs. "custom" application programs is addressed.

Chapter 4 continues the discussion on operating systems. First, basic operating system concepts such as "multiuser" and "interactive processing" are defined in terms of their usefulness in the business environment. Then the Application System's operating system products are described. New for this edition, Client Access/400 has been split into Client Access Family for Windows for AS/400 and Client Access Family for AS/400. Included in this chapter is a section on developing application programs from a host perspective. This is then extended to include migration of host-based applications to the client/server environment. Many of the communications functions only available previously on SNA and APPC are protocol-based networks now available on TCP/IP. Kernel threads have been added to increase performance for many of the Windows- and Lotus-based functions. The potential impacts to be expected upon host and client/server program migration as a result of the emergence of object-oriented programming are then surveyed, including an introduction to Java and frameworks.

Chapter 5 shows how specific AS/400 options and software products are used to participate in the computer communications environments commonly found in businesses. New security services for APPN and TCP/IP are discussed, networks are discussed, along with AS/400 support for Internet services. With the advent of the new security services discussed in Chapter 6, the emphasis of the AS/400 has been shifted to one of network computing, particularly leaning toward the electronic business (e-biz) environment.

Chapter 6 discusses issues related to the selection of Application Systems hardware and software for small, medium, and large businesses. Hypothetical businesses are outfitted with the appropriate Application Systems. Important topics such as user training, ergonomics, security, maintenance, leasing vs. buying, and cost justification are then discussed. In particular, AS/400 online education and security and its importance in an Internet environment has been expanded upon. The expansion includes the addition of firewalls with proxy and sockets servers and the secure sockets layer with 40-, 56-, and 128-bit encryption capabilities to the previously available security available for the Internet. Charts are provided to allow comparison of previous AS/400 system models to the current standard for measuring system performance.

To provide for reference, the appendices list (1) user groups who have significant experience with the AS/400 family and (2) the various service offerings available from IBM on the AS/400.

To help you better understand the topics covered in this book, key terms and phrases are defined and **highlighted**. These key terms are also listed in the index at the back of this book. If, while reading, you forget the definition of a key term or phrase, the index will quickly provide the page(s) on which the term was originally discussed.

A Glance Backward At The System/3X Family

On July 30, 1969, IBM executives from the entire company joined 1200 IBMers at their plant site in Rochester, Minnesota, to announce the System/3 computer shown in Figure I.1. This system was the first computer totally developed in Rochester. Although only of historical interest today, the System/3 represented some significant advances in the

Figure I.1. IBM System/3.

technology of its time. For example, it introduced Monolithic Systems Technology, which allowed engineers to package more circuitry in a smaller space, as well as a punch card one-third of normal size that held 20 percent more information. This was the first advancement in punch-card technology in over 40 years. To celebrate the announcement of the System/3, Rochester IBMers held a dance featuring Ralph Marterie and his orchestra in a newly constructed building. The Rochester plant, which became a full IBM division in November of that year, was tasked to develop a "low-end" computer family. One System/3, fondly named "Old Reliable," ran faithfully until it was shut down in September 1973. When it was finally retired, its meter showed that it had run for 15,377.97 hours, representing more run time than any other system in existence.

The System/32, shown in Figure I.2, was the next member of the family. It was announced in January 1975 and featured direct keyboard data entry and a display that could present up to 6 rows of text 40 characters long. The System/32 had up to 32K of memory and up to 13 MB of fixed disk storage.

The System/34 computer, announced in April 1977, was the first system truly designed to manage multiple (local and remote) worksta-

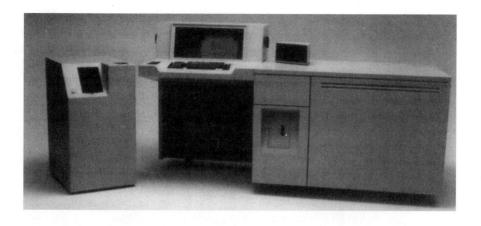

Figure I.2. IBM System/32.

tions (i.e., terminals and printers), each being up to 5000 feet away from the computer. This allowed it to perform tasks for up to eight local users simultaneously. The System/34, shown in Figure I.3, provided up to 256K of memory and 13 MB of fixed disk.

Next came the System/38, announced in October 1978. This represented a divergence from its S/3X predecessors, offering a new architecture optimized for application development productivity. The System/38, shown in Figure I.4, could support up to 32 MB of memory, 14 GB of disk storage, and 256 local workstations.

Once again, building on the architectural base of the System/34, the first System/36 was announced in May 1983 (Figure I.5). It grew to support up to 7 MB of main memory, 1.4 GB of disk storage, and 72 local workstations. Other models of the System/36 varying in processing power and capacity were announced over time. Collectively the System/3, System/32, System/34, System/36, and System/38 are known as the **System/3X** family of computers.

The last S/36 model (the 5363) was enhanced and renamed the **IBM AS/Entry** system. IBM has announced its intentions to provide future enhancements to the AS/Entry products. This means that they are vital to IBM's midrange product strategy, as we will see later in the book.

On June 20, 1988, IBM unveiled the AS/400 family of products. The AS/400 has close architectural ties with System/38 while in most cases providing application program compatibility with both the System/36 and the System/38. Since the original announcement of the AS/400

Figure I.3. IBM System/34.

Figure I.4. IBM System/38.

Figure I.5. IBM System/36.

family, IBM has regularly announced new AS/400 hardware and software products—a trend that shows no signs of slowing.

How AS/400 Computers Differ from System/3X Computers

What characteristics make IBM AS/400 computers different from the System/3X family of computers? The answer lies in the areas of compatibility, performance, expansion capability, and usability.

The AS/400 computers offer more **compatibility** across the product line than did the System/3X computers. Two operating systems and a single architecture are used consistently across the entire AS/400 family. This means that programs and data can be freely exchanged among AS/400 systems and used without any changes. This was not possible in the System/3X family, in which different architectures and operating systems prevented the System/36 from running System/38 programs without change (and vice versa). Further, the AS/400 operating system was the first "midsize computer" operating system to participate in IBM's

Systems Application Architecture (SAA), which allows programs to be exchanged among PS/2s, AS/400s, and System/390s.

AS/400 computers can also run programs written for the System/3X family. Many of those written for the System/38 will need little or no change, and many of those written for the System/36 can be migrated to AS/400 systems using available tools. In fact, the AS/400 Advanced 36 allows coexistence of the System 36 SSP operating system and applications with the OS/400 operating system and applications. When coexisting, the two operating systems share a common file system and can make calls to use each other's I/O functions. This means that System/3X users can move their custom-written System/3X application programs to AS/400 computers. Also, many of the System/3X software companies have migrated their application program offerings to the AS/400 systems, allowing users to choose from a vast array of software to solve business problems. Chapter 3 looks more closely at AS/400 compatibility.

AS/400 computers can also run programs written for other computers, both from IBM and from selected competitors. (This capability is referred to as portability.)

The **performance** of a computer is the speed at which it can work. The higher the performance, the better. For example, the largest AS/400 computers offer performance several thousand times that of the largest System/38. The performance advantage of the AS/400 family is afforded primarily by a combination of faster processors, more efficient architectures, more storage, and improved disk units. With the addition of server models, performance is affected by the tuning provided within the operating system to the applications that are executing on the system. We look more closely at performance in Chapter 1.

The AS/400 computers offer more **expansion capability** to support growing needs. First, because the AS/400 computers are fully compatible from the smallest system to the largest, users can grow without the disruption of conversion that used to accompany moving from a System/36 to the larger System/38 family. In the AS/400 family, there is a much wider range of growth between the largest and smallest systems. The integrated approach with expansion towers used in the new AS/400 systems better lends itself to configuration flexibility and modular expansion than did the rack-mounted approach used in the older AS/400 B through F models or the older box approach of the System/38. The largest AS/400 systems can span several of these towers and accommodate up to 1546.1 GB of disk storage in a single system, compared with the 165.4 GB of the rack-mounted F models or the 14-GB maximum of the largest System/38. Furthermore, the AS/400 system can support up to 250 communications lines, surpassing the maximum of 12 lines with the System/38.

Each AS/400 computer also offers expansion slots that can accept various controllers and adapters to add function and performance. For example, main storage can be expanded from 128 MB to 20,480 MB in the largest AS/400 computer through the addition of storage expansion adapters. As necessary, additional expansion slots can be added to the Advanced Systems by installing additional I/O card units in AS/400 towers. Chapter 2 describes many optional controllers and adapters that can be installed to add capability to AS/400 computers.

Not only do AS/400 computers offer more advanced capabilities, they are **easier to use** than comparable System/3X systems. The operating system required for normal operation comes preloaded on all systems, eliminating the tedious installation process. The user interface of this operating system conforms to IBM's **Common User Access (CUA)** method, providing online help and consistency with other SAA environments (e.g., Operating System/2 on the Personal System/2). Those used to System/3X computers will also see many similarities when interacting with the operating system for AS/400 computers. Also, most of the familiar System/3X devices (terminals, printers, etc.) can be used with the new family of computers. IBM's Electronic Customer Support offered for all AS/400 systems is another way to get help when you have a question. Every AS/400 system also comes with computer-based education programs that teach new users about many aspects of the new AS/400 computers. Some authoring tools are also available on AS/400 computers that allow you to design your own courses to meet specialized training needs.

1

What Is An AS/400 System?

This chapter provides an overview of the IBM AS/400 family of computers, covering the highlights of these systems and then moving in for a closer look at the details. The characteristics of the AS/400 computers are compared with those of the IBM System/3X family.

The IBM Application System/400 (AS/400) family of products represents IBM's newest generation of midsize business computing systems. Like their predecessors, the System/3X family, they are **multiuser** computer systems, meaning a single computer can interact with more than one user at a time. In developing the AS/400 systems, designers drew from the ease-of-use features of the System/36, combined these with the advanced architecture and productivity of the System/38, and then added new functions. In addition to the many application programs developed directly for execution on the AS/400, many of the application programs developed for the System/36 and System/38 computers can be migrated to and used on AS/400 systems by applying the migration tools available.

Many users have no conception of what equipment makes up the computer system they use daily. Fortunately, it is not necessary for them to, just as it is not necessary to understand the inner workings of a carburetor to drive a car. However, it is helpful to have a fundamental view of what general elements make up an AS/400. Figure 1.1 shows

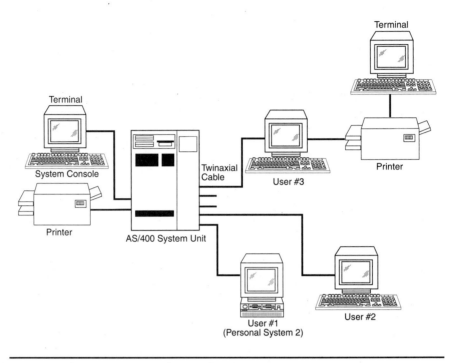

Figure 1.1. Components of a simple AS/400 system.

the components of a very simple AS/400 system configuration. The heart of the system is the system unit, which contains the "brain" that runs the computer programs and controls all activities. People interact with the computer system through terminals (or personal computers [PCs] acting as terminals) that display computer information and allow for keyboard entry. The terminal shown on the left side of the figure is the **system console**. The system console is a specially designated terminal used by the system operator to manage the day-to-day operations of the computer system. The other terminals are for general-purpose use. The printers shown in the figure are used to generate reports, documents, graphs, and the like. A printer can be a workstation used to fill the needs of specific user(s), or it can be shared by all users. Both terminals and printers were initially attached to the system unit via twinaxial cable (or twinax), typically laid in the building's walls or ceiling. In today's environment, the terminals (or PCs) and printers are attached through many other media including radio communications and telephone wiring. Figure 1.2 shows the AS/400 Advanced System 400 packaging used for the Advanced System 36 mentioned above. This packaging is typical of the AS/400 system line in that it encompasses the primary components of the computer system including everything necessary to comprise an entry system except the terminal functions identified above. Figure 1.2 also shows the packaging for a typical AS/400 system. Among the elements which distinguish the system from other systems available in the mid-range marketplace are the rounded rear cover which allows it to be placed against walls, and the air intake scoops at the bottom and mid-area of the unit's front. The rounded rear cover allows air ex-

Figure 1.2. AS/400 Advanced System 400 and Advanced Server 40S.

haust and cabling to exit from the rear, and the fact that all air intake is through the front cover allows the unit to be placed against walls and desks at either side.

Application-Centric Computing

As a result of recent releases, the AS/400 system has been transformed from a host-centric computing system to an application-centric computing system. This transformation has been accomplished while supporting and expanding the host-centric applications that execute on the AS/400 system. Those host-centric applications constitute the core of the 350,000 installed systems. The system configuration shown in Figure 1.1 is an example of what constitutes a host-centric computing system: All the computational capability resides in a centralized processor called the host, and that host is surrounded by non-intelligent terminals that provide data input to the application programs, which both reside and execute on the host.

An application-centric computing system is one that will execute and support an application's data and programs on the operating system, regardless of the operating system of origin, (Windows, Macintosh, UNIX, Lotus, Java, etc.). The support may include network-centric computing systems, in which case the data and/or programs may reside on separate computing systems, some of which may be Internet servers, and the application, which is the composite of the data and program, may execute on a different system. In an application-centric computing system, the application itself may have been defined on one vendor's computing system and be executing on a different vendor's computing system.

Consider the system configuration shown in Figure 1.1. If the terminals were replaced randomly by both AS/400 systems and PCs, with the vendors of the PCs selected at random, and the terminal connection interface were replaced by a Local Area Network (LAN), then the hardware portion of the application-centric paradigm would have been met. If in addition the applications to be executed within the configuration of LAN-interconnected systems could be developed on any of the systems, regardless of the vendor source, and would still execute on any other of the systems (regardless of the vendor source), then the software part of the application-centric paradigm would have been met.

Within the context of this description of application-centric computing, not only is host-centric computing included, *open systems computing, client/server computing,* and *distributed computing* are also included. The AS/400 Advanced Series achieved the transformation to an application-centric computing system by supporting all of these forms of computing system structures. Host-centric computing was defined earlier. Open systems computing, client/server computing, and distributed computing will be defined in the following paragraphs and are described in greater detail in Chapters 4, 5, and 6. The AS/400 Advanced Series achieved the transformation to an application-centric computing system by supporting all of these forms of computing system structures. Figure 1.3 illustrates the architecture implemented to achieve the open and client/server portions from what was previously a host-centric base with distributed computing.

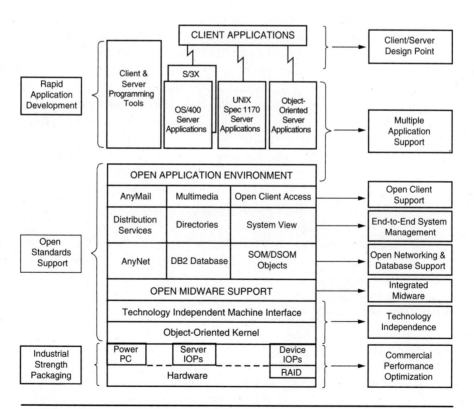

Figure 1.3. Advanced Applications Architecture.

Open Systems Computing

Open systems computing has in the minds of some people come to mean UNIX. In reality, open systems computing means that applications developed on an open system will provide the two characteristics of interoperability and portability. **Interoperability** means that both programs and people can exchange information in a meaningful way. **Portability** means that it is possible to move applications, data, and users from one vendor or computer architecture to another. Together, interoperability and portability mean that an application will achieve the same results from the same data and present the users with the same interfaces at the system level no matter what vendor's system is executing the application.

Businesses should perceive four benefits from the achievement of the open systems computing capability: freedom of choice, flexibility and change management over time, lasting value, and investment protection. *Freedom of choice* means that the business can select from among many vendors the hardware and software needed. *Flexibility and change management over time* mean that businesses can recombine and redeploy their open systems applications and information technology infrastructure as business needs dictate without requiring perfect foresight, knowing that the application can be moved to several different platforms over its useful life. *Lasting value* means the business is not locked into a single vendor's hardware or software. *Investment protection* is provided to the business because new software and retraining are not required if the hardware base is changed. The AS/400 has achieved open system computing by providing an open application environment, which supports interoperability and portability not only for nearly all of the other vendors' de facto standard application interfaces, but also for most UNIX applications. How this was accomplished will be described in a later paragraph on the AS/400 Advanced Series Architecture.

Client/Server Computing Systems

Client/server computing systems are those in which applications or resources (programs, data, and sometimes both) are spread across more than one intelligent system. Usually, the client is a workstation or a PC, and the server(s) is a larger system that controls resources such as data or hardware. The outboard intelligence is called the **client**, and the centralized intelligence is called the **server**. Most of today's LAN-connected client/server computing environments include PCs or network stations and any or all of the following: file servers, fax servers, database servers, application servers, print servers, communications servers, and Internet servers.

In many of the PC-based client/server computer systems, each of the server functions is performed by a separate PC and the user's problem is one of management to keep all of this separate activity in synchronization with the application. In the AS/400, all of the server functions are integrated and come under the control of a single operating system. As a result, performance is optimized, connectivity issues that arise from the presence of multiple servers are avoided, and when more performance is needed users can easily add memory or other features to the AS/400e systems.

The AS/400e series supports over 1600 different client/server applications under the many languages that are available. A listing of abstracts from those applications is available from the Internet at *http://www2.software.ibm.com/solutions/isv/igssg.nsf/as400searchgui*. The client/server environment for the AS/400 has been extended with the support for Novell NetWare 4.10 on the **Integrated PC Server** (formerly called the **File Server Input/Output Processor**, or **FSIOP**), including file serving, print serving, and data sharing with NetWare Loadable Modules (NLMs) while preserving NetWare commands to install, configure, and control the environment. In addition, Novell's **Internet Packet Exchange (IPX)** protocol is now available as a native protocol in the AS/400 suite of communications protocols, enabling AS/400 to be plugged into existing Novell networks with fewer problems and administrative changes.

Distributed Computing Systems

Distributed computing systems at first glance look like client/server computing systems, but instead of a full copy of all data and programs residing on the server, the data may be segmented and reside across many system boundaries in the network of systems, and each application program may reside on the computer at which it is normally executed. Although this is the normal situation, the programs may be called and executed at any computer in the network. Ideally, which computer in the distributed system network of computers is actually executing the program is unknown to the user. Except in the case of some very short programs with limited data sets, the ideal has not yet been achieved in most distributed computing system networks. In "AS/400 System Clustering" in Chapter 5, the positioning of the AS/400 relative to other distributed computing systems will be discussed in greater detail.

AS/400 Advanced Application Architecture

Figure 1.3 illustrates the Advanced Application Architecture, which was implemented on the AS/400 system to achieve the open client/server computing system capabilities described in the preceding paragraphs. The following paragraphs will introduce the layers of this architecture, with Chapters 3, 4, and 5 providing additional detail for the reader who wishes to understand in greater depth.

There are seven layers in the Advanced Application Architecture for client/server and distributed computing. The top layer is the client application layer. This primarily consists of Client Access Family for Windows for /400 and Client Access Family for AS/400, the PC-resident offering that allows the widest variety of clients to take advantage of the AS/400 server resources. This includes support for both the Microsoft ODBC interface and the Java DBC interface at both the client and at the server, as well as Apple's DAL. Client operating systems supported are:

- Extended DOS

- 32-bit Windows

- Macintosh SNA*ps

- Novell NetWare 4.10 with NLM

- Microsoft Windows 3.1

- IBM Connection

- 16-bit OS/2

- Windows NT

- Windows 95

- Windows 3.1

- Program/400 for RS/6000

- Base DOS

- UNIX (SUN or HP)

- 32-bit OS/2

The second layer is the server layer, which supports client and server programming tools, OS/400 server applications, PC server applications, A-OPEN (UNIX Spec 1170) server applications, and object-oriented server applications. In general, this layer enables the distributed computing function, whereby the client application might also execute at the server in whole or in part. This layer in combination with the next layer down (the open application environment) enables the AS/400 to support more than 80 percent of the most commonly used commercial APIs in UNIX applications.

The fact that these server functions are equivalent to each other allows them to share data through the integrated file system including the DB2 for AS/400 relational database, which, along with Data Propagator/400, allows flat files and relational files to coexist and PC applications to readily access data, change it, and put it back again, as well as replicate it in whole or in part to a different application. Thus, legacy applications, client/server applications, and object-oriented applications can coexist in one AS/400.

Implemented within the third layer as part of the integrated file system are triggers, stored procedures, declarative referential integrity, two-phase commit, and long file names. These functions are available not only for the client/server and open systems interconnect file structures but for all of the file structures supported, improving the total function of the AS/400 including legacy applications.

The fourth layer is the integrated midware layer, which allows the AS/400 to reduce the system management headaches associated in general with both client/server computing and with distributed computing. The integrated midware layer reduces complexity in the following areas:

- Network protocols

- Database management

- Security

- Access to coded and noncoded data (open file system)

- Enablers for advanced applications such as multimedia

- Enablers for mail and directory services

This midware is integrated and tested before it is delivered on the system as part of OS/400.

Among the tools available in the midware are Systems Manager, Managed Systems Services, OS/2 Warp server, and ADSM/400. Systems Manager and Managed Systems Services allow the AS/400 to deliver new releases of PC applications to all authorized users; OS/2 Warp Server for AS/400 allows the AS/400 and Novell networks to share resources such as printers and storage devices and allows central administration of the networks; and ADSM/400 allows the backup and recovery services of the AS/400 to be extended to PC users.

The fifth layer is the technology-independent machine interface, which allows the AS/400 to change major hardware and software components of the system without affecting your business applications. This allows the AS/400 to change the functions and hardware below this interface without causing customers to rewrite or recompile their applications.

The sixth layer is the System Licensed Internal Code (SLIC), now designed in C++, which runs on 64-bit microprocessors. This layer allows new hardware to be introduced without affecting the applications above the machine interface layer until those applications are ready to exploit the new functions provided.

The final layer, the seventh, is the hardware layer. In the August 1997 release of this layer integrated DASDs were continued, and a RAID (**Redundant Array of Independent DASDs**) capability for the MultiFunction I/O Processor (MFIOP)–attached integrated DASDs were introduced, the Integrated PC Server (IPCS) now includes a firewall function, and new systems packaging, a family of PCI IOPs and controllers. Because RISC is the new evolving technology for the AS/400 family main processor, before discussing the remainder of the hardware, we will spend a few paragraphs briefly explaining what RISC technology is and the PowerPC AS implementation of that technology. Then we will point out the differences from other RISC implementations necessitated by the commercial processing nature of the AS/400 family.

Why RISC?

Although additional improvements could have been achieved with the **CISC (Complex Instruction Set Computer)**–based microprocessor family, which constituted the base for all of the pre-1995 AS/400 systems, the AS/400 was moved to a **RISC (Reduced Instruction Set Computer)** base because RISC provides extended future growth, is mainstream and strategic, can be optimized for commercial usage, and offers several advantages at a complete system level, which involves more than chips. RISC also better enables an optimizing compiler and simplifies the instruction decode function.

Before discussing those driving elements, let's define CISC and RISC somewhat more fully. CISC as implemented in the IMPI (Integrated Micro Programmed Interface) microprocessor had 392 instructions 2, 4, or 6 bytes in length, including a group of 8 different complex operations. The RISC PowerPC AS (PowerPC AS is the specific implementation of the PowerPC RISC architecture implemented for the AS/400) has 250 instructions, all of which are 4 bytes in length and require only two move-assist complex operations. The net result is that the RISC PowerPC AS allows for growth to a larger address space, improved performance from 64-bit data and instructions, more than 20 GB (gigabytes, or billion bytes) of main storage, including a larger page size (4 KB), and significant I/O growth (greater than 4-GB addressability, more I/O busses, and three times faster bus performance). What this all means is you get more processing power with RISC and that power will be needed as the computing paradigm moves toward emerging technologies such as object-oriented programming, multimedia computing, network computing, and distributed computing.

The RISC PowerPC AS technology for the AS/400 provides synergy with the remainder of IBM and is strategic to the long-term direction of the AS/400. The question was never whether the AS/400 would move to RISC, but when the move would be made. The RISC PowerPC AS was determined to be compatible with commercial applications if some things could be added, including a Tags Active mode for single-level storage, decimal assist functions, move-assist operations for fast memory management, and vectored supervisor calls. The PowerPC AS with a wider I/O bandwidth allowed the implementation of a larger number of I/O busses, each of which could have a greater functional bandwidth. This allows systems to grow in I/O capacity commensurate with the performance capabilities of the processor and memory components.

RISC PowerPC AS Microprocessors

A microprocessor is a computer chip containing millions of microscopic transistors that work together to form the "brain" of a computer system. The internal structure of a microprocessor is called its architecture, and many different architectures are in use today. Current AS/400 systems (and other computers, such as the IBM RS/6000 family) use one or more PowerPC microprocessors as the basis for their computing engines. These microprocessors are special implementations of the PowerPC architecture, which is based on the Reduced Instruction Set Computer (RISC) concept. The idea behind RISC (pronounced "risk") is to gain a performance advantage by utilizing a simple set of instructions executed very quickly to do all work.

The PowerPC architecture enables high levels of performance through its superscalar design, using pipelining, hardwired operations, new op codes, and formats for optimal decoding and branch prediction to improve superscalar scheduling and cycle times. The op code is the portion of the instruction which tells the microprocessor what operations to perform on the data to be manipulated by the instruction. **Superscalar** means that more than one instruction can be executed in a single cycle of the processor. **Pipelining** allows instructions to be processed as if they were on an assembly line. **Optimal decoding** adds a structure to the instruction layout that makes interpretation (within the microprocessor) faster. **Branch prediction** means that (during the compiling activity) potential jumps from one section of a program to another have been inspected to predict if they will be taken, in order to minimize the delay caused by the need to empty the pipeline if the branch requirements are met. Many compiler optimization techniques have been implemented to minimize design bottlenecks while maximizing parallelism.

AS/400 PowerPC microprocessors have on-chip cache memory. These very high-speed memory areas serve as temporary storage and reduce the amount of time the microprocessor spends waiting for information to be pulled in from main storage, where access speed may be as much as 35 times slower. There are separate instruction and data cache areas to help streamline information flow through the microprocessor.

The AS/400 versions of PowerPC microprocessors (called RISC PowerPC AS microprocessors) have several unique features not found in the base PowerPC architecture (decimal support, move assist, vectored supervisory calls, tagged operations, etc.). These extensions help RISC-based AS/400 systems maintain and enhance commercial transaction performance. Commercial computing workloads have different characteristics than engineering/scientific computing workloads (a traditional strength of RISC). The commercial environment typically has an increased number of concurrent users, longer instruction path lengths in both application code and the operating system, decreased predictability in branches, mostly fixed point arithmetic functions, and randomly organized I/O activity. These differences are illustrated in Figure 1.4.

Commercial Workloads	Scientific/Engineering Workloads
• Many concurrent users	Few concurrent users
• Longer path length over larger set of instructions	Smaller instructions working sets
• More execution time in operating system code	More execution time spent in application work
• Fewer loop iterations—more branches	Tight loops
• Extensive manipulation of data structures through integer arithmetic and string operations	Extensive use of floating point arithmetic
• Random I/O activity	Sequential I/O activity

Figure 1.4. Commercial vs. engineering/scientific workloads.

The RISC PowerPC AS systems also have a wider I/O bandwidth, allowing for AS/400 systems with more I/O busses. This makes for AS/400 systems with greater I/O capacity, which are necessary to maintain balance with the higher levels of performance the RISC PowerPC AS microprocessors enable. Three PowerPC AS microprocessors used in current AS/400 systems are the A10 Microprocessor, the A30 Microprocessor, and the A35 Microprocessor.

The A10 Microprocessor

The A10 Microprocessor is a single-chip CMOS (Complementary Metal-Oxide Semiconductor) technology implementation that performs at a 77-MHz cycle rate as a pipelined superscalar design with separate fixed point, floating point, load/store, condition register, and branch units. In entry and midsize AS/400 systems, the A10 Microprocessor has about 4.7 million transistors. It can execute up to three instructions per cycle at a peak rate of 231 Million Instructions Per Second (MIPS). There are two on-chip caches, a 4-KB (1 KB is about 1000 bytes) instruction cache and an 8-KB data cache, and the A10 can support an optional 1-MB (1 MB is about 1 million bytes) off-chip cache. Figures 1.5 and 1.6 illustrate the interconnection paths for the memory and I/O for the various processors using the A10 Microprocessor chip as their base.

In Figure 1.5, one additional chip is used to generate the copper I/O bus used in the system unit that houses the processor, one additional chip is used to generate each pair of external optical busses used to house I/O in the external expansion towers, and the memory is driven directly by the A10 Microprocessor chip. In Figure 1.6, the I/O is driven in the same way as in Figure 1.5, but the memory bus is partitioned into two busses, each of which is supported by a separate storage control chip that manages the main storage accesses, and up to 0.5 MB of intermediate-level cache can be supported.

The A30 Microprocessor

The A30 Microprocessor is a 154-MHz implementation in BiCMOS (Bipolar Complementary Metal-Oxide Semiconductor) technology that contains about 24 million transistors. The implementation is a pipelined, low-latency, superscalar design for the top of the midsize AS/400 systems. The microprocessor can execute up to four instructions per cycle and has a peak rate of 616 MIPS. There is an 8-KB on-chip in-

Processor Models: 2110, 2130–2132, 2140–2142

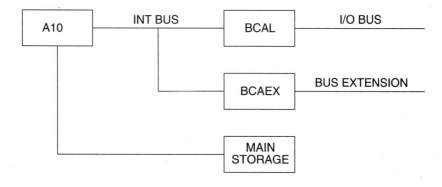

Figure 1.5. A10 Microprocessor I/O and main storage interconnect for entry and midrange processors.

Processor Models: 2120, 2121, 2143, 2144

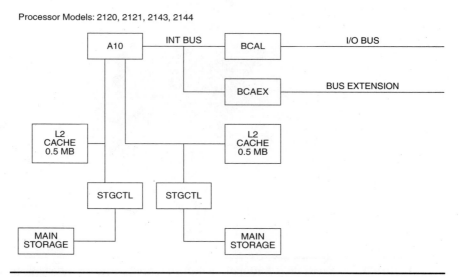

Figure 1.6. A10 Microprocessor I/O and main storage interconnect for midrange and high-end processors.

struction cache and a 256-KB data cache. The design supports 1-, 2-, and 4-way tightly coupled Symmetric MultiProcessor (SMP) configurations.

The A30 Microprocessor comprises two of the seven chips that reside on the multichip module, shown in Figure 1.7, together with the heat sink necessary to contain the power dissipated on the multichip module.

Figure 1.8 illustrates and identifies the seven chips used to build the multichip module and the interconnection between them. The seven chips are the fixed point processor (PU) chip, which contains an 8-KB instruction cache; a Floating Point Unit (FPU), which can process at least some of its operations in parallel with the PU; four Main Storage Control Units (MSCUs), which each contain 64 KB of data cache; and the Processor Interface Unit (PIU), which resides on the main storage data bus and generates an intermediate-level bus to work with the I/O func-

Figure 1.7. Seven-chip A30 module for Advanced Series 53X systems with cover off and impingement cooling heat sink mounted.

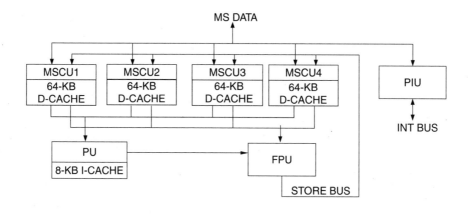

Figure 1.8. A30 Microprocessor multichip module, chip content, and interconnect.

tions of the systems. The A30 Microprocessor really consists of the two chips constituting the fixed point unit and the floating point unit.

The A35 Microprocessor

The A35 Microprocessor is a single-chip **CMOS** (Complementary Metal-Oxide Semiconductor) technology implementation of the RISC PowerPC AS that performs at a 125-MHz cycle rate as a pipelined superscalar design with separate fixed point, floating point, load/store, condition register, and branch units for entry-level to midsize AS/400 machines. The A35 Microprocessor has about 4.7 million transistors. It can execute up to three instructions per cycle at a peak rate of 375 Million Instructions Per Second (MIPS). There are two on-chip caches, a 64-KB (1 KB is 1000 bytes) instruction cache and an 64-KB data cache, and the A35 can support an optional 1-MB or 4-MB (1 MB is about 1 million bytes) off-chip cache. Because the caches are separate, they can be accessed in parallel, increasing performance.

In midsize AS/400 systems, the A35 Microprocessor is connected to main storage through a storage control chip and to the I/O interfaces through a Bus Control Adapter Logic (BCAL) chip. The BCAL chip creates an intermediate interface from which other chips create either a

PCI bus interface or a SPD bus interface. The base system unit in these systems always contains a PCI bus interface. The SPD bus is a private internal bus to which I/O adapters attach. The SPD bus is used in the high mid-range systems and the high-end systems to attach I/O. All expansion and extension units containing I/O adapter cards contain an SPD bus.

In the high-end symmetrical multiprocessor system units, the main storage is again managed through storage control chips but the storage cards are arranged in either two or four banks and the I/O interface is driven across a high-speed serial/parallel interface bus referred to as a SCIL (Serial Control Interface Logic) bus. The implementation of the SCIL bus allows the I/O devices to be packaged in a unit separate from the system processor/memory unit. The separate unit contains a SPD bus. The Model 640/S30 systems do not take advantage of this possible separation. The Models 650/S40 do use the separation to package the I/O in a separate tower.

As stated above, in high-end AS/400e systems, the I/O is driven from a SCIL bus (the SCIL bus is an ultra-high-speed serial interface), which drives up to three optical interface cards to which can be connected up to 18 optical busses and one copper bus. The copper bus connects to an I/O tower, which can be populated with disk units, tape units, and I/O interface cards. The main storage bus is partitioned into two busses, each of which is supported by a separate storage control chip (STGCTL) that manages the main storage accesses and up to 0.5 MB of intermediate-level cache. This dual-memory bus architecture helps improve the performance of these systems. Figures 1.9, 1.10, and 1.11 illustrate the connection of the A35 Microprocessor in uniprocessor, 8-way processor, and 12-way processor configurations.

Meet the AS/400 Family

Seven basic computers form the core of the IBM AS/400e series family: the Entry Model 150, available in both general-purpose and server configurations, the Advanced 36, the Model 170 with five processor options, which also is available as a server, the Model 600 with four processor options, the Model 620 with five processor options, the Model 640 with three processor options, and the Model 650 with two processor op-

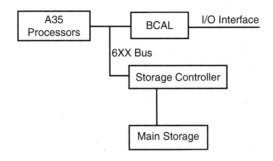

Figure 1.9. A35 Microprocessor/main storage and I/O interface for 2136 and 2119 Processors.

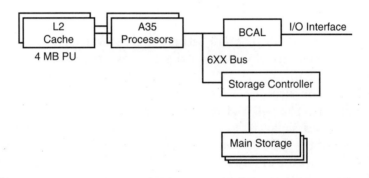

Figure 1.10. A35 Microprocessor/main storage and I/O interface for 2179, 2180, 2181, 2182, 2161, 2163, and 2165 Processors.

tions. In addition, there are six server models structured from the core set: the entry-level server Model 150, the Model 170 server versions, the S10 with two processor options, the S20 with four processor options, the S30 with four processor options, and the S40 with 8-way and 12-way processor options. There are also three special server models structured from the S20, S30, and S40. The S20-ISV and S30-ISV models provide improved interactive performance running the specific software packages provided by J. D. Edwards and Software Systems Associates, Intentia International's Movex V10.5, and International Busi-

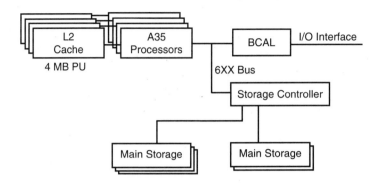

Figure 1.11. A35 Microprocessor/main storage and I/O interface for Processors 2239, and 2166.

ness Systems' IBS. The S40-SB1 is a main storage, DASD, and other-I/O-device constrained version of the 12-way processor version of the S40 server specifically tuned to provide high performance in the compute-intensive environment required by many multitiered computing environments. The S40-SB1 is intended to be used as a SAP R3 application server to a separate second-tier server. Figure 1.12 contains a photograph of the AS/400e series family. Let us briefly look at each of these. The "e" in the AS/400e series names for these systems is intended to signify that the systems are capable of supporting the electronic business environment, which means that the user may establish a storefront on the World Wide Web and conduct business with the assurance for both the user and the customer that any and all transactions are secure and private.

The Entry Model 150 is the smallest, lowest-performing version of the AS/400 system. It is available in a general processing version and a server version, each of which come in two configurations, entry and growth. The general processing version can attach up to 28 twinaxial workstations plus a single LAN connection on the MFIOP to support PC users. The server version can support up to about 150 PC-based clients and allows 28 interactive workstations to be attached via twinaxial cable. Both models are available with up to 192 MB of main storage and 29.9 GB of disk storage, and can have up to 5 communications lines. The software integrated with the system includes support for im-

Figure 1.12.   AS/400 V4R1 Family showing left to right, Models 600/620/640/650 and S40/S30/S20/S10/S150.

proved performance, new Internet functions, new versions of Client Access Family for Windows, support for Windows NT Server, new encryption and security capabilities, and wireless capabilities for a small business.

The Advanced 36 is the successor to what previously was called AS/Entry. It was the first of the AS/400 Advanced Series systems to receive a RISC processor. The Advanced 36 is discussed in greater detail in a separate book titled *Exploring the IBM AS/400 Advanced 36* by Jim Hoskins and Roger Dimmick, published by Maximum Press. What is important to the reader interested in the AS/400 is that coexistence of the AS/400 operating system (OS/400) capability and the System 36 SSP operating system within a single system at one and the same time, has been achieved. In fact, multiple copies of the SSP may coexist with OS/400. This coexistence allows the System 36 SSP to make simple calls to the OS/400 I/O functions that do not exist on the System 36 in order to use those I/O functions within the SSP. This makes available to the SSP user the I/O capabilities of the AS/400 such as wireless LAN, fax, and token-ring LAN, as well as all the communications interfaces that the SSP does not support. The new activity with the Advanced 36 is that the SSP operating system will be enabled to function on all of the RISC based AS/400 models. The Advanced 36 is the only AS/400 system that can execute the SSP operating system without having OS/400 also resident.

The AS/400e server 170 comes in a new footprint and is intended to fulfill the function of a department server. Five processor options are allowed, ranging in performance from about twice the performance of the Model 150 processor to approximately equal to the performance of the lowest processor in the AS/400e system 620. It is not possible to upgrade to the Model 170 from the Model 600 or the Model S10. Main storage feature cards are not customer installed; if the customer orders additional main storage, IBM will install the main storage and any other features also ordered.

Like its predecessors, the Model 170 is packaged into a small desk-side unit, which is then cabled to the necessary AS/400 workstations and printers. Like the predecessor 600 and S10 models, the processor performance within the AS/400e series models can be upgraded without having to change any other element of the system. The primary difference relative to the previous Advanced System 600 and S10 models is the much improved performance offered and the total I/O capacity of the systems. The 170 model uses the same OS/400 operating system as the rest of the AS/400 family. This means that application programs and data on a 9406 Model 170 system can be used unchanged on larger AS/400e systems as a business grows. All of the server models described here now support up to 28 twinaxial workstations versus the 7 previously supported.

The AS/400e system 170 and server 170 are differentiated from each other by the fact that the processor and operating system for the server model are optimized for server applications (sharing resources with other computers) and are not optimized for interactive applications, whereas the processor and operating system for the general-purpose processing Model 170 is optimized for the interactive processing environment. The foregoing statement regarding optimization is true in each case where a server and general-purpose processing system use a common packaging base.

The IBM AS/400e system 600 and server S10 are packaged in a chassis that is approximately the height and length of the base model 170 without the bolt-on expansion side car. The Model 600 and the S10 can use the normal 110-V electrical power found in every office.

The AS/400e system 600 and server S10 feature customer install of feature I/O cards and DASD devices, concurrent maintenance of disk/tape devices; and hardware checksum/mirroring data protection. A UPS (Universal Power Supply) can be installed to provide protection against power failures.

The IBM AS/400e system 620 and the server S20 are packaged in a chassis that looks like the Model 600 discussed in the previous paragraph mounted on a raised platform. The raised platform includes batteries and UPS electronics, and sometimes additional power supplies and disk unit support (depending upon the processor contained in the system). Like the Model 600, the Model 620 and S20 use 240-V electrical power.

The AS/400e system 620 and server S20 can be ordered from the factory in high-availability versions (referring to the ability to continue operation in the event of component failures). The high-availability features on these models include redundant power supplies; internal battery backup with up to 2 days of Continuously Powered Main Storage (CPM), which will be explained in a later section; concurrent maintenance of disk/tape devices; and hardware checksum/mirroring data protection.

The AS/400e system 640 and server S30 make up the high end of the middle range of the AS/400e series family. The Model 640 and S30 include the 1-way, 2-way and 4-way versions of AS/400 computers using the most powerful of the A35 Microprocessors, thereby providing for higher performance, more users, more communications, more storage, and greater expandability than either the Model 600 or the Model 620. The Model S30 includes the 8-way version of the processor. The Model 640 and Model S30 use a common package approximately the size of the 1.6-meter rack in the previous B through F 9406 models and operate from a 240-V line source.

The AS/400e system 650 and server S40 make up the high end of the AS/400 family. Both the Model 650 and S40 include the 8-way and 12-way versions of AS/400 computers. Both use the more powerful A35 Microprocessor, thereby providing for higher performance, more users, more communications, more storage, and greater expandability than either the Model 640 or the Model 620. The AS/400e system 650 and server S40 use a common package approximately the size of the 1.6-meter rack in the previous B through F 9406 models plus a separate I/O function tower the size of the previous Model 500 system unit. Both the processor unit and the I/O function tower operate from a 240-V line source. The I/O function tower connects to the processor unit tower by means of a new technology interface cable called SCIL (Serial Control Interface Logic), which allows a separation between these two units of up to 100 meters. The processor unit for these systems consists of a tower the same size as the total system unit in the Model 640. The Model 640 and S30 also use a SCIL bus for connecting to the I/O function, the base portion of which is totally contained within the system unit tower. With this introduction to the members of the AS/400 family, we will describe in greater detail each of the system unit members in the following paragraphs.

To accommodate users with the previous 19-inch rack-mounted equipment, the new 6X0- and SX0-based models can interface compatibly with that equipment. It is also possible to perform processor performance upgrades within the new models. These models use the same OS/400 operating system as the rest of the AS/400 family; in fact, the operating system is now bundled with the hardware, which means that when one of the e systems, whether it is a server or general-purpose system, is ordered, the operating system is included with that order. For previous hardware models, an operating system license was ordered separately from the hardware. For clarity, we will refer to all AS/400e systems and servers, and AS/400 Advanced 36 systems as Application Systems. When we discuss a specific product, the specific name will be used.

In addition, a set of custom e-business servers are constructed from the S20, S30, and S40 base servers. These servers come preloaded with software from a specific set of IBM business partners, and can only be ordered with prior licensing agreements in place. IBM intends to expand the number of Independent Software Vendors (ISVs) included in this custom server set. A Business Partner is a company (like J. D. Edwards) which has an agreement in place with IBM to develop products to a set of standards which IBM has established, and also agrees to allow IBM to test the agreed to product for compliance with those standards.

AS/400 Advanced Entry Model 150 Specifics

The AS/400 Advanced Entry Model 150 has been enhanced with a larger main storage capacity, a higher-capacity tape drive, a higher performance CD-ROM, an improved-performance Integrated PC Server (IPCS), and larger disk units. The Model 150 is targeted for the 2- to 20-user environment, including distributed locations and small businesses. The package, the smallest of the AS/400 systems described in the following paragraphs, is shown in Figure 1.13. Restraints on positioning the system unit against walls or desks do not apply unless the user removes the rounded rear cover. Air intake is entirely from the front, and exhaust is

Figure 1.13.   AS/400 Advanced Entry Model 150.

entirely through the rounded rear cover. The rounded rear cover allows for both cable exit and air exhaust independent of system positioning. The control panel on the front of the system unit is used by the system operator and service personnel to control the Model 150. From this panel, power can be turned on or off, the system can be initialized, and system problems can be analyzed. Many of these functions, including turning on the system power, can be performed remotely through communications lines.

The standard tape unit and CD-ROM can also be seen from the front of the system unit. The Model 150 can be plugged into a standard electrical outlet (90–140 VAC) or a high-voltage outlet (180–260 VAC) and meets "quiet office" guidelines (under 5.5 dB) for operational noise.

Utility power failure protection can be added via a 9910 UPS, which will hold the system up in the presence of a utility power failure for 5 minutes while data from main storage is being written to disk. This, along with its attractive appearance, allows the Model 150 to fit easily beside a desk or in a corner.

The package includes a 12/20× CD-ROM, a 8-GB ¼-inch cartridge tape unit, one 4-GB DASD unit, and up to three 8-GB DASD units, a 64-bit PowerPC Advanced System Microprocessor, a 32-bit PowerPC-603 I/O Microprocessor, and an industry-standard 72-pin, 4-byte Single In-line Memory Module (SIMM) with **Error Correction Code** (ECC), and may feature a 133-MHz Intel Pentium coprocessor (standard on the "Growth Server" version), and slots for 3 **Portable Computer Interface** (PCI) I/O adapters. The system is available both as a commercial processing–based unit, in which case some of the workstations must be twinax based, and as a server, in which case some of the workstations must be PCs and LAN connected, and a Communications Console must be present. A port is provided for an external UPS.

The system capacities and performance capabilities of the Model 150 are summarized in Figure 1.14. As shown in the figure, the Model 150 system has both entry- and growth-level models. The entry-level system has a constrained processor performance rating of 13.8 CPW (constrained performance means that the amount of memory and disk limit the performance), 64 MB of main storage, 4 GB of DASD, 1 communications line, and either a twinaxial adapter (twinaxial version), which can support up to 7 users (the 0185 Processor can support 14 workstations), or a LAN (server version), which can support up to 28 PC users. One modem is provided for support of the Establishment Communications System (ECS) connection.

The main storage of the Model 150 may be increased to 192 MB in three steps of 32 or 64 MB each, and three additional disk units may be provided for a total capacity of 29.9 GB. When the memory and disk capacity are at the maximum, the unconstrained processor performance is 27.0 CPW (unconstrained performance means that the processor is the first limit on performance). There are five PCI adapter slots.

The Entry Model 150 is also available in a growth model, which changes the processor to have a unconstrained CPW rating of 35 with the maximum main storage and disk drives. The growth model supports up to 28 workstations addresses in addition to what is used in the three expansion slots. A software modem function is available for the growth model. The Entry Server is also available in a growth model,

Packages	Twinax Entry (0191)	Twinax Growth (0192)	Server Entry (0193)	Server Growth (0194)
Software	BasePak	BasePak	BasePak	BasePak
Performance				
Constrained CPW Rating	13.8	20.2	13.8	20.2
Unconstrained CPW Rating	27.0	35.0	27.0	35.0
Main Storage (MB) min/max	64/192	128/192	64/192	128/192
Disk Storage (GB) min/max	4.194/29.9	4.194/29.9	4.194/29.9	4.194/29.9
Tape and Internal Optional Attachments (max/system)				
¼-inch Cartridge Tape	1	1	1	1
CD-ROM	1	1	1	1
Physical Packaging				
PCI I/O Card Slots	5	5	5	5
Integrated PC Server and Bridge Card Slots	2	2	2	2
Workstation Attachments (max)				
Twinaxial Controllers	1	1	0/1	0/1
Twinaxial Devices	1/7	1/28	0 std 7 opt	0 std 28 opt
Communications Lines (max)	5	5	5	5
Integrated PC Server	0/1	0/1	0/1	1
Lan IOA	0/2	0/2	1/2	1/2
Integrated PC Server LAN (max)	2	2	2	2
MFIOP LAN (max)	1	1	1	1

Figure 1.14. Model 150 capacities chart.

which has an unconstrained performance rating of 35.0. Both growth models have a starting main storage of 128 MB.

The software provided with the Model 150 includes OS/400, Query, Client Access, DB2/400 Query and SQL Development Toolkit, Performance Manager, and FAX Support/400. See Chapter 4, "Software Solution Packages," for a more detailed description of Entry Model 150 BasePak software. The hardcopy publications provided with the system have been minimized to include only system planning (backup communications), customizing environments (sign-on, passwords, etc.) and customized universal installation instructions. All other publications are delivered on a CD-ROM, and if hardcopy is desired it must be printed on the user's equipment.

AS/400 Advanced 36 Model 436 Specifics

The AS/400 Advanced 36 is the next smallest deskside system in the Application Systems product line. Figure 1.2 shows a photograph of the AS/400 Advanced 36 Model 436. The Model 436 is packaged in the same package as the previous Advanced System 200, which offered several improvements over the 9402 F model package. The previous F model restraints on positioning the system or the expansion unit against walls or desks are removed. Air intake is entirely from the front, and exhaust is entirely through the rounded rear cover. The rounded rear cover allows for both cable exit and air exhaust independent of system positioning.

The control panel on the front of the system unit is used by the system operator and service personnel to control the Model 436. From this panel, power can be turned on or off, the system can be initialized, and system problems can be analyzed. The key-lock on the control panel can be used to secure the system from unauthorized operation. Many of these functions, including turning on the system power, can be performed remotely through communications lines. The standard tape unit can also be seen from the front of the system unit. The Model 436 can be plugged into a standard electrical outlet (90–140 VAC) or a high-voltage outlet (180–260 VAC) and meets "quiet office" guidelines (under 5.5 dB) for operational noise. Utility power failure protection can be added via a 9910 UPS, which will keep the system operating in the presence of a utility power failure for 5 minutes. If the optional OS/400 operating system is present, data recovery is provided with a UPS by writing the data from main storage to disk. This, along with its attractive appearance, allows the Model 436 to fit easily beside a desk or in a corner.

Capability within the mechanical package includes one to four disk devices, one tape device, one CD-ROM, main storage capacities of up to 256 MB, and up to two feature I/O processors. To support this range of growth, two power supplies are offered. The first power supply is a 175-watt supply capable of supporting the processor, the MultiFunction

Processor Feature Code	2102/2104/2106
CPW Performance Rating SSP-OS400	1.0–14.4/1.3–18.3/2.4–24.5
Main Storage, min–max (MB)	32–224/32–224/64–256
Disk storage, min–max	1.03–23.6
Communications Lines	20
Local Area Networks (LANS)	2
Twinaxial Workstations	280
Remote Workstations	192
Diskette	2 (External)
¼-Inch Tape Cartridge	1
½-Inch Tape	4
UPS	1

Figure 1.15. AS/400 Advanced 36 Model 436 capacities.

IOP, two disk devices, one CD-ROM, one tape device, and one feature IOP (see Figure 1.15 for a summary of the Model 436 configuration offerings). As performance needs increase, processors may be exchanged to achieve performance somewhat greater than the previous Model F50. The processor features provide Commercial Processing Workload (CPW, described later in this chapter) values of 14.4, 18.3, and 24.5 in OS/400 mode, and 1.0, 1.3, and 2.4 in SSP mode. The second power supply supports the addition of the third and fourth disk devices. The achievable maximum capacities within the base system package are 23,600 MB of disk space, 256 MB of main storage, 28 GB of uncompacted tape cartridge space, the MultiFunction IOP with two communications lines and an external diskette interface, and two feature I/O processors. The main storage expansion options used on these models attach directly to the processor card, so no expansion slots are consumed.

The disk units exploit **thin-film** technology, which allows for high-density recording. The standard 2.5-GB ¼-inch cartridge tape unit can be used to load programs, to exchange data between systems, or as a disk backup device. Also offered is an 8-mm tape cartridge that with compaction can store up to 14 GB of disk backup data. Up to 280 workstations can be attached via the twinaxial connection path, and up to 20 communications lines can be supported, with up to two LAN lines on the Model 436.

Figure 1.16. AS/400e server 170.

AS/400e server 170 Specifics

The AS/400e server 170 is shown in Figure 1.16. The Model 170 comes in a base unit and can be expanded by attaching a bolt-on expansion sidecar. In appearance, the Model 170 looks like a Model 600 but is slightly wider when the expansion sidecar is attached. The Model 170 is a desk-side system. It reuses the mechanical package of the Model 600 and comes standard with a PowerPC A35 RISC Microprocessor (CPW performance rating 73.0), 64 MB of main storage, a MultiFunction I/O Processor (MFIOP), a 4.19-GB 3½-inch disk drive, a CD-ROM drive, a communications adapter, and a Local Area Network (LAN) port. The LAN port can be either Ethernet or token ring. The base system can also include a workstation adapter.

The Model 170 performance can be increased by selecting one of four processor upgrades (feature codes 2160, 2164, 2176, or 2183) with CPW performance ratings of 114, 125.0, 125, and 125 constrained and

114, 210, 319, and 319 unconstrained, respectively. Each of these processors is a uniprocessor. Processors 2164, 2176, and 2183 contain a base main storage of 256 MB.

The Model 170 base structure can house up to ten disk drives in two disk cage assemblies (one base, and one featured) for a maximum disk capacity of 85.8 GB. It can also house one tape drive, one CD-ROM, and an operator panel. The internal tape, disk, and CD-ROM drives are all supported via an Ultra-SCSI interface. The 64 MB of base main storage supported by the base processor and the 2160 Processor can be grown to 832 MB. The main storage with processors 2164, 2176, and 2183 can be grown to 1024 MB. The main storage expansion options used on these models attach within the processor cage so that they don't consume expansion slots. It is also possible to attach up to 228 twinaxial workstations spread across 6 controllers, 12 communications lines, and 5 LANs. A total of 3 high-speed Portable Computer Interface (PCI) adapters may be used (either ATM or 10/100 Ethernet). System capacities are summarized in Figure 1.17. One tape library, either ½-inch cartridge or 8-mm tape, and one optical library can be attached. The maximum number of twinaxial workstations can be attached only to the general-purpose configuration of the system, not to the server version of system unit. The server version of the system unit can accommodate 28 twinaxial workstations.

To achieve the maximum system capacities noted in the previous paragraph, it is necessary to attach the bolt-on system expansion unit, which can increase the total number of disk drives by five, housed in one disk drive cage. The Model 170 system unit expansion also can house an additional PCI card cage, which can house up to 14 PCI cards. The additional expansion towers can be either storage expansion towers or I/O expansion towers.

The Model 170 system unit and the system unit expansion option can be individually plugged into standard electrical outlets (110–260 VAC). Base utility power failure protection is provided with an external CPM/UPS and Continuously Powered Main Storage (CPM), described later in this chapter.

AS/400e system 600 Specifics

The AS/400e system 600, shown in Figure 1.18, comes standard with a PowerPC A10 RISC microprocessor (CPW performance rating 22.7),

Uniprocessor Feature Number	2159/2160/2164/2176/2183
Relative System Performance (CPW)	
Constrained Rating	
Client/Server	73/114/125/125/125
Interactive	16/23/29/40/ 67
Unconstrained Rating	
Client/Server	73/114/210/319/319
Interactive	16/23/29/40/67
Main Storage (MB)	
Minimum	64/128/256/256/256
Maximum	832/832/1GB/1GB/1GB
Disk Capacity (GB)	
Minimum	4.19
Maximum	85.8
Communication Lines	1–12
FSIOA2 (with 1 or 2 LANs)	0–2
LAN Ports	1–6
High-Speed PCI slot (ATM, 10/100 Ethernet)	0–3
Twinaxial Controllers	0–5
Maximum Twinaxial Workstations	28
CD-ROM	1
¼-Inch 8mm Cartridge Tape	0–1
½-Inch Tape	
9348	0–1
3XXX (except 3480/3490/3490E-C10)	0–1
Uninterruptible Power Supply (w/CPM)	0–1
8-mmCartridge Tape (External)	0–1

Notes: Relative system performance measurements (CPW values) are based on AS/400 environment, commercial processing workload (CPW). The CPW workload is representative of commercial applications, particularly those that do significant database processing in conjunction with journaling and commitment control. The CPW workload is measured on maximum configurations. CPW values may not be realized in all environments.

Figure 1.17. AS/400e server 170 capacities and performance summary.

64 MB of main storage, a MultiFunction I/O Processor (MFIOP), a communications adapter, a 4.19-GB 3½-inch disk drive, a CD-ROM drive, and either a workstation controller or a console adapter.

The Model 600's performance can be increased by selecting one of three processor upgrades (feature codes 2134, 2135, and 2136). The

Figure 1.18. AS/400e system 600.

2134 and 2135 are uniprocessor versions of the A10 RISC Microprocessor; the 2136 is a uniprocessor version of the A35 Microprocessor.
The CPW performance ratings of these processors are 32.5, 45.4, and
73.1 respectively.

The Model 600 base structure can house up to ten disk drives for a
total system capacity of 175.4 GB in two disk cage assemblies (one
base, and one featured), one tape drive, one CD-ROM, an operator
panel, up to 384 MB of main storage (512 MB on the 2136 Processor),
and a Portable Computer Interface (PCI) I/O card cage. All of the disk
units are attached to the MFIOP and can have their data protected by
either RAID or mirroring algorithms. The main storage expansion options used on these models attach directly to the processor card so that
they don't consume expansion slots, and they must be installed in pairs,
except for systems using the 2136 Processor, in which case the main
storage cards must be installed in groups of four. It is also possible to
attach up to 188 twinaxial workstations, 9 communications lines, and
3 **local area networks** (LANs). The PCI card cage can accommodate a
total of 8 PCI adapters. In addition, one tape library, either ½-inch cartridge or 8-mm tape, can be attached.

The Model 600 can be plugged into a standard electrical outlet (90–140 VAC) or a high-voltage outlet (180–260 VAC) and meets quiet office guidelines (under 5.5 dB) for operational noise. Utility power failure protection can be added via a UPS, which will keep the system operating in the presence of a utility power failure for 5 minutes or longer while data from main storage is being written to disk. Figure 1.19 summarizes the Model 600 system capacities and performance capabilities.

Uniprocessor Feature number	2,129/2,134/2,135/2,136
Performance Rating (CPW)	22.7/32.5/45.4/73.1
Main Storage (MB)	
Minimum	64/64/64/128
Maximum	384/384/384/512
Disk Capacity (GB)	
Minimum	4.19
Maximum	175.4
Communication Lines	1–9
LAN Ports	0–3
Twinaxial Controllers	0–5
Maximum Twinaxial Workstations	188
¼-Inch 8-mm Cartridge Tape	0–1
½-Inch Tape	
9348	0–1
3XXX (except 3480/3490/3490E-C10)	0–1
8-mm Cartridge Tape (External)	0–2

Notes: Relative system performance measurements (CPW values) are based on AS/400 environment, commercial processing workload (CPW). The CPW workload is representative of commercial applications, particularly those that do significant database processing in conjunction with journaling and commitment control. The CPW workload is measured on maximum configurations. CPW values may not be realized in all environments.

Capacities shown are for models shipped from the plant and include any prerequisite expansion features. Some combinations of devices may be subject to configuration restrictions.

Figure 1.19. AS/400e system 600 capacities and performance capabilities summary.

AS/400e server S10 Specifics

The AS/400e server S10 is a desk-side server in the AS/400 product line (Figure 1.18). The Model S10 package is based on the Model 600 package and comes standard with a PowerPC A10 RISC Microprocessor (CPW performance rating 45.4 client/server, 16.2 interactive), 64 MB of main storage, a MultiFunction I/O Processor (MFIOP), a 4.19-GB 3½-inch disk drive, a CD-ROM drive, a communications adapter, a local area network adapter (either Ethernet or token ring), and a console adapter.

Model S10 performance can be increased by selecting one processor upgrade (feature code 2119), a uniprocessor version of the A35 RISC Microprocessor with CPW performance ratings of 73.1 client/server and 24.3 interactive.

The Model S10 base structure can house up to ten disk drives for a total system capacity of 175.4 GB in two disk cage assemblies (one base, and one featured), one tape drive, one CD-ROM, an operator panel, up to 384 MB of main storage (512 MB on the 2119 Processor), and an 8-adapter Portable Computer Interface (PCI) I/O card cage. All of the disk units are attached to the MFIOP and can have their data protected by either RAID or mirroring algorithms. The main storage expansion options used on these models attach directly to the processor card so that they don't consume expansion slots, and they must be installed in pairs, except for systems using the 2119 Processor, in which case the main storage cards must be installed in groups of four. It is also possible to attach up to 28 twinaxial workstations, 8 communications lines, and 3 local area networks (LANs). One tape library, either ½-inch cartridge or 8-mm tape, can also be attached. Figure 1.20 summarizes the capacities and performance capabilities of the S10 system.

The Model S10 can be plugged into a standard electrical outlet (90–140 VAC) or a high-voltage outlet (180–260 VAC) and meets quiet office guidelines (under 5.5 dB) for operational noise. Utility power failure protection can be added via a UPS, which will keep the system operating in the presence of a utility power failure for 5 minutes or longer while data from main storage is being written to disk.

The Model S10 replaces the Model 40S, which replaced the 20S server. Both the Model 600 and the Model S10 support the Integrated PC Server (IPCS) function through a combination of PCI cards, which will be discussed in Chapter 2. The wireless local area network func-

Uniprocessor Feature number	2118/2119
Relative System Performance (CPW)	
Client/Server Environment	45.4/73.1
Interactive Environment	16.2/24.3
Main Storage (MB)	
Minimum	64/128
Maximum	384/512
Disk Capacity (GB)	
Minimum	4.19
Maximum	175.4
Communication Lines	1–8
LAN Ports	1–3
Twinaxial Controllers	0–1
Maximum Twinaxial Workstations	28
¼-Inch 8-mm Cartridge Tape	0–1
½-Inch Tape	
9348	0–1
3XXX (except 3480/3490/3490E-C10)	0–1
8-mm Cartridge Tape (External)	0–1

Notes: Relative system performance measurements (CPW values) are based on AS/400 environment, commercial processing workload (CPW). The CPW workload is representative of commercial applications, particularly those that do significant database processing in conjunction with journaling and commitment control. The CPW workload is measured on maximum configurations. CPW values may not be realized in all environments.

Capacities shown are for models shipped from the plant and include any prerequisite expansion features. Some combinations of devices may be subject to configuration restrictions.

Figure 1.20. AS/400e server S10 capacities and performance capabilities summary.

tion, although not available as a PCI card, is now supported from any local area network by the addition of an access point and a software addition to OS/400. Certain hardware functions are not available in the PCI card form factor at this time, including facsimile support and encryption. However, encryption is available as part of a software offering, the Internet Connection Secure Server for AS/400. (For additional information on Internet security see "Security" in Chapter 6.) None of the I/O cards or main storage cards from any previous release AS/400 model may be migrated to the Models 600 or S10.

AS/400e system 620 Specifics

The AS/400e system 620 system unit is shown in Figure 1.21. In appearance, the Model 620 looks like a Model 600 placed upon a platform. The platform in this case houses additional power components and disk units. The Model 620 is a desk-side system. It reuses the mechanical package of the Model 600 and comes standard with a PowerPC A35 RISC Microprocessor (CPW performance rating 85.6), 256 MB of main storage, a MultiFunction I/O Processor (MFIOP), a 4.19-GB 3½-inch disk drive, a CD-ROM drive, a communications adapter, and a workstation controller.

The Model 620's performance can be increased by selecting one of three processor upgrades (feature codes 2180, 2181, 2182) with CPW performance ratings of 113.8, 210.0, and 464.3 respectively. The 2182 processor is a 2-way processor; the other processors in the model line are uniprocessors.

The Model 620 base structure can house up to ten disk drives in two disk cage assemblies with the 2179 and 2180 Processors, and up to 15 disk drives in three disk cage assemblies with processors 2181 and

Figure 1.21. AS/400e system 620 and server S20 with expansion.

2182 (one base, and two featured). It can also house one tape drive, one CD-ROM, an operator panel, and an 8-adapter PCI I/O card cage. Up to 4096 MB of main storage can be packaged with the 2182 Processor, whereas the maximum main storage with the other processors available for the model is 2048 MB. The main storage expansion options used on these models attach within the processor cage so that they don't consume expansion slots. All main storage cards must be installed in matched pairs of either 32 MB or 128 MB. It is also possible to attach up to 2392 twinaxial workstations, or 1044 ASCII workstations, 96 communications lines, 32 fax lines, and 16 local area networks (LANs). The ASCII workstation attachment requires the bolt-on 9364 System Expansion unit with the 9331 SPD Card Cage option. System capacities are summarized in Figure 1.22. Four tape libraries, either ½-inch cartridge or 8-mm tape, and 14 optical libraries can be attached.

To achieve the maximum system capacities enumerated in the previous paragraph, it is necessary to attach the bolt-on system expansion unit, which can increase the total number of disk drives by 15 (housed in three disk drive cages), and use the system expansion and storage expansion towers identified later. The Model 620 system unit expansion also can house either an additional SPD card cage or an additional Portable Computer Interface (PCI) card cage. The SPD card cage can house seven SPD I/O cards, one of which is the optical bus controller, which can generate up to four optical busses for attachment of an additional four expansion towers. The PCI I/O Card Cage can house up to 14 PCI cards and 2 optical bus adapter cards to generate attachments for two expansion towers. The additional expansion towers can be either storage expansion towers or I/O expansion towers.

The Model 620 system unit and the system unit expansion option can be individually plugged into standard high-voltage electrical outlets (180–260 VAC). Utility power failure protection is via internal battery backup and Continuously Powered Main Storage (CPM), described later in this chapter.

The bus expansion towers (feature codes 5073 and 5072) and the disk storage expansion units (feature codes 5051 and 5052) will be described in greater detail in Chapter 2. The SPD bus I/O card slots identified earlier may take any of the non-PCI IOP controllers described in Chapter 2, including the FAX IOP, the Wireless LAN IOP, the RAID-5 DASD storage controller, and the Integrated PC Server (IPCS).

Processor Feature Number	2179/2180/2181/2182
Processor Configuration	Uni-/Uni-/Uni-/2-Way
Relative System Performance (CPW)	85.6/113.8/210.0/464.3
Main Storage (MB)	
Minimum	256/256/256/256
Maximum	2,048/2,048/2,048/4,096
Disk Capacity (GB)	
Minimum	4.19
Maximum	944.8
Communication Lines	1–96
LAN Ports	0–16
Twinaxial Controllers	0–60
Maximum Twinaxial Workstations	2,392
ASCII Controllers	0–58
Maximum ASCII Workstations	1,044
Maximum Workstation Controllers	1–60
¼-Inch 8-mm Cartridge Tape	0–17
½-Inch Tape	
2440/9348	0–4
9347	0–2
3XXX	0–4
8-mm Cartridge Tape (External)	0–4
Diskette (8- or 5¼-Inch)	0–2
Optical Libraries	0–14
Fax IOPs	0–32

Notes: Relative system performance measurements (CPW values) are based on AS/400 environment, commercial processing workload (CPW). The CPW workload is representative of commercial applications, particularly those that do significant database processing in conjunction with journaling and commitment control. The CPW workload is measured on maximum configurations. CPW values may not be realized in all environments.

Capacities shown are for models shipped from the plant and include any prerequisite expansion features. Some combinations of devices may be subject to configuration restrictions.

Figure 1.22. AS/400e system 620 capacities and performance capabilities summary.

AS/400e server S20 Specifics

The AS/400e server S20 is a desk-side system (Figure 1.21). It uses the Model 620 mechanical package and comes standard with a PowerPC A35 RISC Microprocessor (CPW performance rating 113.8), 256 MB of main storage, a MultiFunction I/O Processor (MFIOP), a 4.19-GB 3½-inch disk drive, a CD-ROM drive, a communications adapter, a workstation controller, and a LAN adapter.

The Model S20's performance can be increased by selecting one of three processor upgrades (feature codes 2163, 2165, 2166) with CPW performance ratings of 210.0, 464.3, and 759.0 respectively. The 2165 Processor is a 2-way Symmetrical MultiProcessor (SMP) implementation, and the 2166 is a 4-way SMP implementation.

The Model S20 base structure can house up to 10 disk drives in two disk cage assemblies with the 2161 Processor, and up to 15 disk drives in three disk cage assemblies (one base and two featured) with the 2163, 2165, and 2166 Processors. It can also house one tape drive, one CD-ROM, an operator panel, and an 8-adapter Portable Computer Interface (PCI) I/O card cage. Up to 4096 MB of main storage can be packaged with the 2165 and 2166 Processors, and 2048 MB of main storage can be packaged with the 2161 and 2163 Processors. The main storage expansion options used on these models attach within the processor cage so that they don't consume expansion slots. Main storage must be added in matched pairs using either 32-MB or 128-MB storage cards. It is also possible to attach up to 28 twinaxial workstations, or 6 ASCII workstations, 96 communications lines, 32 fax lines, and 16 local area networks (LANs). In addition, four tape libraries (either ½-inch cartridge or 8-mm tape) and 14 optical libraries can be attached. Figure 1.23 illustrates the maximum system capacities and performance capabilities for the Model S20.

To achieve the maximum system capacities, it is necessary to attach the bolt-on expansion unit, which can increase the total number of disk drives by 15, housed in three disk drive cages. The Model S20 expansion unit also can house either an additional SPD card cage or an additional PCI card cage. The 9331 SPD card cage has space for 7 SPD I/O cards, one of which is the optical bus controller, which can generate up to 4 optical busses for attachment of an additional four expansion towers. The PCI card cage in the expansion unit can house up to 14 PCI

Processor Feature Number	2161/2163/2165/2166
Processor Configuration	Uni-Uni-/2Way/2-Way
Relative System Performance (CPW)	
Client/Server environment	113.8 /210.0/464.3/759.0
Interactive environment	31.0/35.8/49.7/56.9
Main Storage (MB)	
Minimum	256/256/256/256
Maximum	2,048/2,048/4,096/4,096
Disk Capacity (GB)	
Minimum	4.19
Maximum	944.8
Communication Lines	1–96
LAN Ports	1–16
Twinaxial Controllers	0–1
Maximum Twinaxial Workstations	28
ASCII Controllers	0-1
Maximum ASCII Workstations	6
Maximum Workstation Controllers	1
¼-Inch 8-mm Cartridge Tape	0-17
½-Inch Tape	
2440/9348	0–4
9347	0–2
3XXX	0–4
8-mm Cartridge Tape (External)	0–4
Diskette (8- or 5¼-Inch)	0–2
Optical Libraries	0–4
Fax IOPs	0–32

Notes: Relative system performance measurements (CPW values) are based on AS/400 environment, commercial processing workload (CPW). The CPW workload is representative of commercial applications, particularly those that do significant database processing in conjunction with journaling and commitment control. The CPW workload is measured on maximum configurations. CPW values may not be realized in all environments.

Capacities shown are for models shipped from the plant and include any prerequisite expansion features. Some combinations of devices may be subject to configuration restrictions.

Figure 1.23. AS/400e server model S20 capacities and performance summary.

cards, among which can be two optical bus adapter cards to generate attachments for two expansion towers, which can be either storage expansion towers or I/O expansion towers. The maximum capacities of the Model S20 system can only be attained by using these expansion towers.

The Model S20 system unit can be plugged into standard high-voltage electrical outlets (180–260 VAC). Utility power failure protection is via internal battery backup and Continuously Powered Main Storage (CPM). The internal battery backup is capable of retaining main storage content for up to 24 hours using CPM. Longer periods of retention may be attained by attaching the external battery backup feature.

AS/400e system 640 Specifics

The Model 640 is a tall-tower system (Figure 1.24) approximately the same size as the older AS/400 B through F model white rack systems. The Model 640 comes standard with a PowerPC A35 RISC Microprocessor (CPW performance rating 319.0), 512 MB of main storage, a

Figure 1.24. AS/400e system 640 and server S30.

MultiFunction I/O Processor (MFIOP), a 4.19-GB 3½-inch disk drive, a CD-ROM drive, a communications adapter, a workstation controller, a six-bus-capable optic controller, one SPD bus, and a logic cage capable of containing one additional feature card and two additional optic controller cards.

The Model 640's performance can be increased by selecting one of two processor upgrades (feature codes 2238 and 2239) with CPW performance ratings of 583.3 and 998.6, respectively. The 2238 Processor is a 2-way and the 2239 is a 4-way Symmetrical MultiProcessor (SMP) configuration.

The Model 640 base structure can house up to 12 disk drives, one tape drive, one CD-ROM, an operator panel, and up to 12,288 MB of main storage. Up to 18 optical busses can be generated for the attachment of expansion towers. The main storage expansion options used on these models attach within the processor cage so that they don't consume expansion slots. Main storage cards, available in 128-, 256-, 512-, and 1024-MB sizes, must be added in matched pairs. It is also possible to attach up to 7000 twinaxial workstations or 3150 ASCII workstations, 200 communications lines, 64 fax lines, and 32 local area networks (LANs). Twenty-two optical libraries can be attached. Whenever the second disk cage is added, the feature power supply must be added. Figure 1.25 summarizes the capacities and performance capabilities of the Model 640. To achieve the maximum system capacities it is necessary to attach expansion towers to each of the 18 possible optical busses.

The Model 640 system unit can be plugged into standard high-voltage electrical outlets (180–260 VAC). Base utility power failure protection is provided by internal battery backup and Continuously Powered Main Storage (CPM). The internal battery backup is capable of retaining main storage content for up to 24 hours using CPM. Longer periods of retention may be attained by attaching the external battery backup feature.

AS/400e server S30 Specifics

The AS/400e server S30 (Figure 1.24) shares the package of the Model 640 and as a result is a tall-tower system. The Model S30 comes standard with a PowerPC A35 RISC Microprocessor (CPW performance rating 319.0), 512 MB of main storage, a MultiFunction I/O Processor

Processor Feature Number	2237/2238/2239
Processor Configuration	Uni-/2-Way/4-way
Relative System Performance (CPW)	319.0/583.3/998.6
Main Storage (MB)	
Minimum	512
Maximum	12,288
Disk Capacity (GB)	
Minimum	4.19
Maximum	1,340.0
SPD Busses	1–19
Communication Lines	1–200
LAN Ports	0–32
Twinaxial Controllers	0–175
Maximum Twinaxial Workstations	7,000
ASCII Controllers	0–175
Maximum ASCII Workstations	3,150
Maximum Workstation Controllers	175
¼-Inch 8-mm Cartridge Tape	0–17
½-Inch Tape	
2440/9348	0–2
9347	0–4
3XXX	0–8
8-mm Cartridge Tape (External)	0–4
Diskette (8- or 5¼-Inch)	0–2
Optical Libraries	0–22
Fax IOPs	0–32

Notes: Relative system performance measurements (CPW values) are based on AS/400 environment, commercial processing workload (CPW). The CPW workload is representative of commercial applications, particularly those that do significant database processing in conjunction with journaling and commitment control. The CPW workload is measured on maximum configurations. CPW values may not be realized in all environments.

Capacities shown are for models shipped from the plant and include any prerequisite expansion features. Some combinations of devices may be subject to configuration restrictions.

Figure 1.25.   AS/400e system 640 capacities and performance capabilities summary.

(MFIOP), a 4.19-GB 3½-inch disk drive, a CD-ROM drive, a communications adapter, a workstation controller, a LAN adapter, an optic controller capable of controlling up to six optical busses, one SPD bus, and a logic cage capable of containing three additional feature cards.

The Model S30's performance can be increased by selecting one of three processor upgrades (feature codes 2258, 2259, and 2260) with CPW performance ratings of 583.3, 998.6, and 1794 respectively. The 2258, 2259, and 2260 are respectively 2-way, 4-way, and 8-way Symmetrical MultiProcessors (SMPs). The base main storage on the 2260 processor is 1024 MB.

The Model S30 base structure can house up to 12 disk drives, one tape drive, one CD-ROM, an operator panel, up to 12,288 MB of main storage , and an 8-card SPD I/O card cage. Up to 18 optical busses can be generated for the attachment of expansion towers. The main storage expansion options used on these models attach within the processor cage so that they don't consume expansion slots. Main storage cards must be installed in matched pairs. Main storage card sizes available are 128, 256, 512, and 1024 MB. It is also possible to attach up to 28 twinaxial workstations, or 6 ASCII workstations, 200 communications lines, 64 fax lines, and 32 local area networks (LANs). Twenty-two optical libraries can be attached. Whenever the second disk cage is added, the feature power supply must be added. The system capacities and performance capabilities are summarized in Figure 1.26. To achieve the maximum system capacities, it is necessary to attach expansion towers to each of the 19 possible optical busses.

The Model S30 system unit can be plugged into standard high-voltage electrical outlets (180–260 VAC). Base utility power failure protection is provided by internal battery backup and Continuously Powered Main Storage (CPM). When the second disk cage is added, the feature power supply must also be added.

AS/400e system 650 Specifics

The AS/400e system 650 (Figure 1.27) is a tall-tower system connected by a cable to the base system unit I/O tower (similar to the Model 530 I/O Tower except not bolted to the processor system unit). The Model 650 package approximates the size of the B through F model white

Processor Feature Number	2257/2258/2259
Processor Configuration	Uni-/2-Way/4-Way
Relative System Performance (CPW)	
Client/Server Environment	319.0/ 583.3/ 998.6
Interactive Environment	51.5/64.0/64.0
Main Storage (MB)	
Minimum	512
Maximum	12,288
Disk Capacity (GB)	
Minimum	4.19
Maximum	1,340.0
SPD Busses	1–19
Communication Lines	1–200
LAN Ports	1–32
Twinaxial Controllers	0–1
Maximum Twinaxial Workstations	28
ASCII Controllers	0–1
Maximum ASCII Workstations	6
Maximum Workstation Controllers	2
¼-Inch 8-mm Cartridge Tape	0–17
½-Inch Tape	
2440/9348	0–4
3XXX	0–8
8-mm Cartridge Tape (External)	0–4
Diskette (8- or 5¼-Inch)	0–2
Optical Libraries	0–22
Fax IOPs	0–32

Notes: Relative system performance measurements (CPW values) are based on AS/400 environment, commercial processing workload (CPW). The CPW workload is representative of commercial applications, particularly those that do significant database processing in conjunction with journaling and commitment control. The CPW workload is measured on maximum configurations. CPW values may not be realized in all environments.

Figure 1.26. AS/400e server S30 capacities and performance capabilities summary.

Figure 1.27. AS/400e system 650 and server S40.

racks and comes standard with an 8-way PowerPC A35 RISC Microprocessor (CPW performance rating 1794.0), 1024 MB of main storage, a MultiFunction I/O Processor (MFIOP), a 4.19-GB 3½-inch disk drive, a CD-ROM drive, a six-bus-capable optical controller, a communications adapter, a workstation controller, one SPD bus, and a logic cage capable of containing five additional feature cards and three additional disk units.

The Model 650's performance can be increased by selecting one 12-way processor upgrade (feature code 2243) with a CPW performance rating of 2340.0. Both the 8-way base processor and the 12-way upgrade processor are Symmetrical MultiProcessors (SMPs).

The Model 650 base structure can house up to four 3½-inch disk drives, one tape drive, one CD-ROM, an operator panel, up to 20,480 MB of main storage, and a 16-slot SPD I/O card cage. The SPD I/O card cage contains the disk units, the MFIOP, the optical bus adapters, and up to three SPD bus feature cards. Up to 18 optical busses and two feature optical controllers for the attachment of expansion towers can be generated from the base. The main storage expansion options used on these models attach within the processor tower so that they don't consume expansion slots. It is also possible to attach up to 7000 twinaxial workstations, or 3150 ASCII workstations, 250 communications lines, 64 fax lines and 48 local area networks (LANs). Twenty-two optical libraries can be attached. The 5052 Storage Expansion Unit may be added to the base I/O tower to increase the total number of 3½-inch disk drives to 20. The system capacities and performance capabilities of the Model 650 are summarized in Figure 1.28. To achieve the maximum system capacities, it is necessary to attach expansion towers to each of the 18 possible optical busses.

The Model 650 system unit processor tower and the base I/O tower must be plugged individually into standard high-voltage electrical outlets (180–260 VAC). Base utility power failure protection is provided by internal battery backup and Continuously Powered Main Storage (CPM). The internal battery backup is capable of retaining 16 GB of main storage content using CPM for 24 hours. To extend the retention interval to 48 hours or to support greater than 16 GB of main storage, the external battery backup feature must be installed.

AS/400e server S40 Specifics

The AS/400e server S40 uses the same package as the Model 650 (Figure 1.27). The Model S40 package is approximately the same physical size as the older B through F model white racks. It comes standard with an 8-way PowerPC A35 RISC Microprocessor (CPW performance rating 1794.0), which is a Symmetrical MultiProcessor (SMP), 1024 MB of main storage, a MultiFunction I/O Processor (MFIOP), a 4.19-GB 3½-inch disk drive, a CD-ROM drive, a 6-bus-capable optical controller, a communications adapter, a workstation controller, a LAN, one SPD bus, and a logic cage capable of containing five additional feature cards and three additional 3½-inch disk units.

The Model S40 can be upgraded to a 12-way PowerPC A35 RISC Microprocessor (CPW performance rating 2340.0) by inserting processor 2261.

The Model S40 base structure can house up to four 3½-inch disk drives, one tape drive, one CD-ROM, an operator panel, up to a maximum of 20,480 MB of main storage in increments of four main storage cards each, and a 16-slot SPD I/O card cage. The SPD I/O card cage

Processor Feature Number	2240/2243
Processor Configuration	8-Way/12-Way
Relative System Performance (CPW)	1,794.0/2340.0
Main Storage (MB)	
Minimum	1,024
Maximum	20,480
Disk Capacity (GB)	
Minimum	4.19
Maximum	1,546.1
SPD Busses	1–19
Communication Lines	1–250
LAN Ports	0–48
Twinaxial Controllers	0–175
Maximum Twinaxial Workstations	7,000
ASCII Controllers	0–175
Maximum ASCII Workstations	3,150
Maximum Workstation Controllers	175
¼-Inch 8-mm Cartridge Tape	0–17
½-Inch Tape	
2440/9348	0–4
9347	0–2
3XXX	0–8
8-mm Cartridge Tape (External)	0–4
Diskette (8- or 5¼-Inch)	0–2
Optical Libraries	0–22
Fax IOPs	0–32

Notes: Relative system performance measurements (CPW values) are based on AS/400 environment, commercial processing workload (CPW). The CPW workload is representative of commercial applications, particularly those that do significant database processing in conjunction with journaling and commitment control. The CPW workload is measured on maximum configurations. CPW values may not be realized in all environments.

Figure 1.28. AS/400e system 650 capacities and performance capabilities summary.

contains the disk units, the optical adapter cards, the MFIOP, and up to three feature cards. Up to 18 optical busses and two feature optical controllers for the attachment of expansion towers can be generated from the base. The main storage expansion options used on these models attach within the processor tower so that they don't consume I/O expansion slots. Main storage must be plugged in groups of four cards. Main storage card sizes are 128, 256, 512, and 1024 MB. It is also possible to attach up to 28 twinaxial workstations, or 6 ASCII workstations, 250 communications lines, 64 fax lines, and 48 local area networks (LANs). Twenty-two optical libraries can be attached. The 5052 Storage Expansion Unit may be added to the base I/O tower to increase the total number of 3½-inch disk drives to 20. The total system capacities and performance capabilities of the Model S40 are summarized in Figure 1.29. To achieve the maximum system capacities, it is necessary to attach expansion towers to each of the 18 possible optical busses. The S40 server supports up to 48 LANs with up to 12,288 PC workstations attached.

The Model S40 system unit processor tower and the base I/O tower must be plugged individually into standard high-voltage electrical outlets (180 260 VAC). Base utility power failure protection is provided by internal battery backup and Continuously Powered Main Storage (CPM). The internal battery backup is capable of retaining 16 GB of main storage content using CPM for 24 hours. To extend the retention interval to 48 hours, or to support more than 16 GB of main storage, the external battery backup feature must be installed.

Custom e-business Servers

Currently the vendors participating in the custom e-business server environment are J. D. Edwards and Software Systems Associates, Intentia International's Movex V10.5, International Business System's (IBS) and SAP AG. The J. D. Edwards, Movex V10.5, IBS, and SSA software products execute on specialized versions of the Advanced Server Models S20 and S30; the SAP AG software executes on a specialized version of the Model S40 server. IBM intends to expand this approach of packaged vendor software solutions and AS/400 hardware to include other top Independent Software Vendors (ISVs), which will increase the opportunities for both AS/400 and ISV software based on the commitment of the vendors to a business case for those products.

Processor Feature Number	2256/2261
Processor Configuration	8-Way/12-Way
Relative System Performance (CPW)	
Client/Server Environment	1,794.0/2,340
Interactive Environment	64.0/64.0
Main Storage (MB)	
Minimum	1,024
Maximum	20,480*
Disk Capacity (GB)	
Minimum	4.19
Maximum	1,546.1
SPD Busses	1–19
Communication Lines	1–250
LAN Ports	1–48
Twinaxial Controllers	0–1
Maximum Twinaxial Workstations	28
ASCII Controllers	0–1
Maximum ASCII Workstations	6
Maximum Workstation Controllers	2
¼-Inch 8-mm Cartridge Tape	0–17
½-Inch Tape	
2440/9348	0–4
3XXX	0–8
8-mm Cartridge Tape (External)	0–4
Diskette (8- or 5¼-Inch)	0–2
Optical Libraries	0–22
Fax IOPs	0–32

Notes: Relative system performance measurements (CPW values) are based on AS/400 environment, commercial processing workload (CPW). The CPW workload is representative of commercial applications, particularly those that do significant database processing in conjunction with journaling and commitment control. The CPW workload is measured on maximum configurations. CPW values may not be realized in all environments.

Capacities shown are for models shipped from the plant and include any prerequisite expansion features. Some combinations of devices may be subject to configuration restrictions.

Maximum main storage is achieved by field upgrade only. Maximum main storage for systems shipped from the plant is 17,408 MB.

Figure 1.29. AS/400e server S40 capacities and performance capabilities summary.

AS/400e server S20-ISV Specifics

The AS/400e server S20-ISV processor models are for users considering ISV software that needs a single server configuration that complies with a mixed workload environment with a high volume of interactive processing. These solutions combine IBM hardware with ISV software to provide a packaged total solution. The hardware has been specially balanced to react specifically to the ISV software solutions.

The server S20-ISV is a selected processor version of the S20 server (Figure 1.21). The Model S20-ISV comes standard with a 4-way PowerPC A35 RISC Microprocessor (CPW client/server performance rating 759.0, interactive performance rating 110.7), 256 MB of main storage, a MultiFunction I/O Processor (MFIOP), a 4.19-GB 3½-inch disk drive, a CD-ROM drive, a communications adapter, and a LAN adapter.

The Model S20-ISV performance can be increased by one processor upgrade (feature code 2178), also a 4-way, with CPW performance ratings of 759.0 client/server, 211.4 interactive. Both the base processor and the upgrade 4-way processor configuration are Symmetrical MultiProcessors (SMPs).

Disk storage on the S20-ISV can be increased to 944.8 GB using the system expansion unit and optically connecting 5082 Storage Expansion Units to the four available optical buses. Optically connected 5073 System Expansion Units may also be used to increase the other I/O functions on the system. Figure 1.30 summarizes the maximum capacities of devices by type that may be supported on the S20-ISV.

The Model S10-ISV system unit is plugged into a standard high-voltage electrical outlets (180–260 VAC) and meets quiet office guidelines (under 5.5 dB) for operational noise. Utility power failure protection is provided using internal battery backup and Continuously Powered Main Storage (CPM).

AS/400e server S30-ISV Specifics

The AS/400e server S30-ISV processor models are for users considering ISV software that needs a single e-server configuration that complies with a mixed workload environment with a high volume of interactive processing. These solutions combine IBM hardware with ISV software to provide a packaged total solution. The hardware has been specially balanced to react specifically to the ISV software solutions.

Processor Feature Number	2177/2178
Processor Configuration	4-Way/4-Way
Relative System Performance (CPW)	
Client/Server Environment	759.0/759.0
Interactive Environment	110.7/211.4
Main Storage (MB):	Min: 256/256 / Max: 4096/4096
Disk Capacity (GB)	Min: 4.19 / Max: 944.8
Communication Lines	1–96
LAN Ports	1–16
Twinaxial Controllers	0–1
Maximum Twinaxial Workstations	28
ASCII Controllers	0–1
Maximum ASCII Workstations	6
Maximum Workstation Controllers	1
¼-Inch 8-mm Cartridge Tape	0–17
½-Inch Tape	
2440/9348	0–4
9347	0–2
3XXX	0–4
8-mm Cartridge Tape (External)	0–4
Diskette (8- or 5¼-Inch)	0–2
Optical Libraries	0–14
Fax IOPs	0–32

Notes: Relative system performance measurements (CPW values) are based on AS/400 environment, commercial processing workload (CPW). The CPW workload is representative of commercial applications, particularly those that do significant database processing in conjunction with journaling and commitment control. The CPW workload is measured on maximum configurations. CPW values may not be realized in all environments.

Performance measurements for AS/400e server models S20 and S30 with ISV processors running J. D. Edwards' software can be obtained through IBM/J. D. Edwards' International Competence Center in Denver. Additional performance data based on standard J. D. Edwards' benchmarks can be obtained through IBM/J. D. Edwards' competence centers or through J. D. Edwards' Web page *(http://www.jdedwards.com/).*

Performance measurements for AS/400e server models S20 and S30 with ISV processors running SSA software can be obtained through IBM/SSA international competence center in Chicago. Additional performance data based on standard SSA benchmarks can be obtained through IBM/SSA competence centers or SSA's Web page *(http://www.ssax.com/).*

Capacities shown are for models shipped from the plant and include any prerequisite expansion features. Some combinations of devices may be subject to configuration restrictions.

Figure 1.30. AS/400 custom server model S20-ISV capacities and performance capabilities summary.

The Model S30-ISV is a selected processor version of the S30 server (Figure 1.24). The Model S30-ISV comes standard with a 4-way PowerPC A35 RISC Microprocessor (CPW client/server performance rating 998.6, interactive performance rating 215.1), 512 MB of main storage, a MultiFunction I/O Processor (MFIOP), a 4.19-GB 3½-inch disk drive, a CD-ROM drive, a communications adapter, and a LAN adapter.

The Model S30-ISV's performance can be increased by two processor upgrades. One of the processor upgrades uses feature code 2321, which is an 8-way processor providing CPW performance ratings of 1794.0 client/server, 386.4 interactive. The other processor upgrade, feature code 2322, is also an 8-way processor providing the same client/server CPW performance rating of 1794.0, but with a higher interactive performance rating of 579.6. All of the processor configurations for the Model S30-ISV are Symmetrical MultiProcessors (SMPs). These processor-based models start with 1024 MB of main storage, which is allowed to grow to 12,288 MB.

Disk storage on the S30-ISV can be increased to 1340.0 GB, and other I/O capacities can be increased by optically connecting 5082 Storage Expansion Units and 5073 System Expansion Units to the 18 available optical buses. Figure 1.31 summarizes the maximum capacities of I/O devices and functions that may be supported on the S30-ISV

The Model S30-ISV system unit is plugged into standard high-voltage electrical outlets (180–260 VAC). Utility power failure protection is provided using internal battery backup and Continuously Powered Main Storage (CPM).

AS/400e server S40-SB1 Specifics

The AS/400e server S40-SB1 is intended to be used as the second-tier server in a compute-intensive environment. Because of its intended use as a compute-intensive server, the model has a large main storage with tight restrictions on the other I/O functions available.

The Model S40-SB1 is a tall-tower system connected by a cable to the base system unit I/O tower (similar to the Model 530 I/O tower except not bolted to the processor system unit). The mechanical package (Figure 1.27) approximates the size of the B through F model white racks and comes standard with a 8-way PowerPC A35 RISC Microprocessor (125,888 normalized FI Dialog Steps per hour at 65% CPU utilization), 4096 MB of main storage, a MultiFunction I/O Processor (MFIOP), two 8.58-GB 3½-inch disk drives, a CD-ROM drive, a

Processor Feature Number	2320/2321/2322
Processor Configuration	4-Way/8-Way/8-Way
Relative System Performance (CPW)	
Client/Server Environment	998.6/1794.0/1794.0
Interactive Environment	215.1/ 386.4/ 579.6
Main Storage (MB)	Min: 512/ 1024/ 1024
	Max: 8704/12288/12288*
Disk Capacity (GB)	Min: 4.19 / Max: 1,340.0
Communication Lines	1–200
LAN Ports	1–32
Twinaxial Controllers	0–1
Maximum Twinaxial Workstations	28
ASCII Controllers	0–1
Maximum ASCII Workstations	6
Maximum Workstation Controllers	1
¼–Inch 8-mm Cartridge Tape	0–17
½–Inch Tape:	
2440/9348	0–4
3XXX	0-8
8-mm Cartridge Tape (External)	0–4
Diskette (8- or 5¼-Inch)	0–2
Optical Libraries	0–22
Fax IOPs	0–32

Notes: Relative system performance measurements (CPW values) are based on AS/400 environment, commercial processing workload (CPW). The CPW workload is representative of commercial applications, particularly those that do significant database processing in conjunction with journaling and commitment control. The CPW workload is measured on maximum configurations. CPW values may not be realized in all environments.

Performance measurements for AS/400e server models S20 and S30 with ISV processors running J. D. Edwards' software can be obtained through IBM/J. D. Edwards' International Competence Center in Denver. Additional performance data based on standard J. D. Edwards' benchmarks can be obtained through IBM/J. D. Edwards' competence centers or through J. D. Edwards' Web page (*http://www.jdedwards.com/*).

Performance measurements for AS/400e server models S20 and S30 with ISV processors, running SSA software can be obtained through IBM/SSA International Competence Center in Chicago. Additional performance data based on standard SSA benchmarks can be obtained through IBM/SSA competence centers or SSA's Web page (*http://w.ssax.com/*).
Capacities shown are for models shipped from the plant and include any prerequisite expansion features. Some combinations of devices may be subject to configuration restrictions.

Maximum main storage is achieved by field upgrade only. Maximum main storage for systems shipped from plant is 9216 MB.

Figure 1.31. AS/400e custom server model S30-ISV capacities and performance capabilities summary.

6-bus-capable optical controller, a communications adapter, a workstation controller, a LAN, and one SPD bus.

The Model S40-SB1's performance may be increased by swapping the 8-way processor with a 12-way processor (feature code 2311) for 185,533 normalized FI Dialog Steps per hour at 65% CPU utilization. Both of the processor configurations supported on the Model S40-SB1 are Symmetrical MultiProcessors (SMPs).

The Model S40-SB1 base structure can house up to four 3½-inch disk drives to achieve a maximum disk capacity of 34.35 GB to enable mirroring of the disk data, one tape drive, one CD-ROM, an operator panel, and a 16-slot SPD I/O card cage. Main storage may not be increased beyond the base 4096 MB. Up to 5 optical busses can be generated for the attachment of expansion towers or to attach to other processors. It is also possible to attach up to 7 twinaxial workstations, or 6 ASCII workstations, 16 communications lines, 2 fax lines, and 5 local area networks (LANs). Two optical libraries can be attached, as can one cryptographic card. The Model S40-SB1 capacities are summarized in Figure 1.32.

Two I/O expansion towers may be optically attached, expanding the total number of I/O cards to 29. The Model S40-SB1 system unit processor tower and the base I/O tower must be plugged individually into standard high-voltage electrical outlets (180–260 VAC). Base utility power failure protection is provided by internal battery backup and Continuously Powered Main Storage (CPM). The internal battery backup is capable of retaining 16 GB of main storage content using CPM for 24 hours. To extend the retention interval to 48 hours, it is necessary to install the external battery backup feature.

To assist in the understanding of the discussions for the Model 640 and the S30 servers, the 1-way, 2-way, and 4-way processor/memory and I/O bus connections are shown in Figures 1.33 through 1.35, respectively.

AS/400 Upgrades

There are two methods available for upgrading within the AS/400e series product line:

1. *Upgrading within a model.* This method is used if the need is for more performance or input/output device functionality and

Processor Feature Number	2310/2311
Processor Configuration	8–Way/12–Way
Relative System Performance (CPW) normalized FI Dialog Steps/hr @ 65% CPU utilization	125,888/185,533
Main Storage (MB)	
Minimum	4,096
Maximum	4,096
Disk Capacity (GB)	
Minimum	16.77
Maximum	34.35
SPD Busses	1–5
Communication Lines	1–10
LAN Ports	1–5
Twinaxial Controllers	1
Maximum Twinaxial Workstations	28
ASCII Controllers	1
Maximum ASCII Workstations	6
Maximum Workstation Controllers	1
¼-Inch and/or 8-mm Cartridge Tape	0–3
½-Inch Tape	
2440/9348	0–4
8-mm Cartridge Tape (External)	0–4
Optical Libraries	0–2
Cryptographic Cards	0–1
Fax IOPs	0–2

Notes: AS/400e custom server model S40-SB1 performance measurements when used as a SAP R/3 application server. FI (financial) Dialog Steps per hour is a workload derived from SAP-defined benchmark testing. This workload calculated at 65% CPU utilization can be used to size AS/400 configurations for specific customer situations. FI Dialog Steps per hour may not be realized in all environments.

Results can be obtained through the IBM/SAP International Center of Competence in Walldorf, Germany. Additional performance data from SAP-defined benchmarks that demonstrate AS/400 scalability in a multitier environment can also be obtained through IBM/SAP competence centers and/or SAP's Web page *(http://www.sap.com)*.

Capacities shown are for models shipped from the plant and include any prerequisite expansion features. Some combinations of devices may be subject to configuration restrictions.

Figure 1.32.   AS/400e custom server model S40-SB1 capacities and performance capabilities summary.

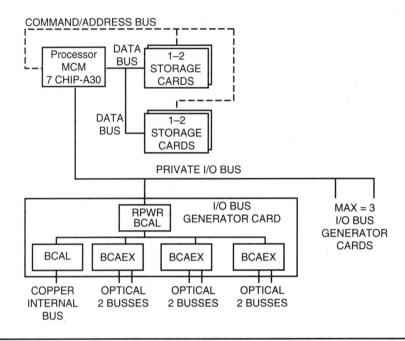

Figure 1.33. AS/400e series 1-way processor/memory and I/O interconnection.

the current system is not using the maximum performance processor, main storage size, attachable I/O device capability, or disk storage size available within that specific AS/400 model. In this situation, within a model, performance can be upgraded by swapping processors, adding additional main storage, or adding disk storage or additional IOPs without having to swap system units. In general, the system should be upgraded within the model until those maximums are reached. This method of growth is referred to as *horizontal growth*.

2. *Upgrading through a system unit swap.* Another way to upgrade within the AS/400 family is to replace the current AS/400 system unit with a more powerful model (e.g., you upgrade a Model 600 to a Model 620, 640, or 650 by changing the system unit). This method is used if the current system is at its processor and storage maximums or the number of users has increased

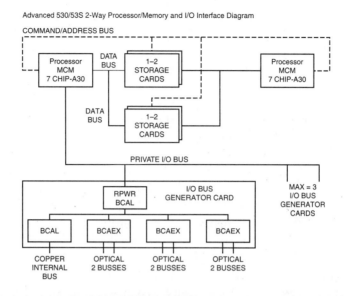

Figure 1.34. AS/400e series 2-way processor/memory and I/O interconnection.

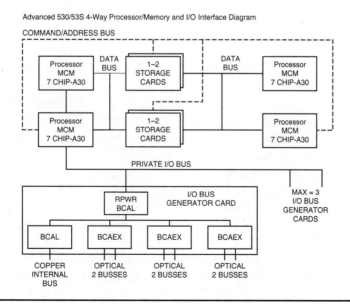

Figure 1.35. AS/400e series 4-way processor/memory and I/O interconnection.

beyond the capabilities of the current model. This method would also be used if there is a need for application programs that only run on newer RISC-based AS/400 models or if you are upgrading from an older AS/400 model. This method of growth is referred to as *vertical growth*.

No upgrades between Models 150, 170, 600, 620, 640, or 650 or between the server versions of the 150 or 170 or the S10, S20, S30, and S40 servers may be accomplished without the exchange of the system unit. You can continue to use all the same workstations, modems, etc., but if your upgrade is to a Model 600, or an S10, it is not possible to move any existing I/O processors. Also, if your upgrade is to a Model 620 or S20, it will be necessary to use either the attached expansion unit with the SPD bus feature or an external 5072 System Unit Expansion Tower to accommodate your previous model's IOP features. The non-support of existing IOPs on the Models 600/S10 results in the nonsupport of all external DASD units, diskette drives, and non-SCSI external tape drives on these models.

You cannot upgrade to or from either the Model 150 or the Advanced 36 Model 436 without changing the system unit.

Upgrades from the older AS/400 F Models to the new AS/400e systems are fully supported with the following exceptions in devices or adapters: 9406 stage 1 B level hardware, including 5030 and 5031 I/O Card Units; early 9404 hardware, including 315-MB, 5¼-inch disk storage, 3½-inch disk storage units (feature codes 1105, 1107, and 1109), and 120-MB tape; some early stage 2 hardware, including DASD/TAPE (feature codes 2600, 2622, 2647); communications adapters (most 615X, 617X and standard ECS adapters); and LAN attachments (feature codes 2625, 2636, and 6160). The following 9402 and 9404 hardware won't fit or work with the new system units: integrated diskette units, battery backup units, and previous release 9402/9404 Expansion Units. The following 9406 disk storage devices will not work because the interface is no longer supported: 9332 and 9335 Disk Storage Units. Main storage exchanges from the CISC Advanced System 200 and 300 sequence numbered models to the RISC Advanced System 400 and 500 sequence numbered models are not supported. No B, C, D, or E Model upgrades are supported. Main storage exchanges to the new 6XX and SXX are offered from the 9404/9406 F models and the 3XX models until January 1998, and from the 4XX and 5XX models until September 1998. Figures 1.36 through 1.40 identify the recommended migration paths between older AS/400 system/server models and the new system/server models.

Continuously Powered Main Storage (CPM)

With the exception of the Entry Model 150, the Advanced 36, the Advanced System 600, and the S10 models, which use an Uninterruptible Power Supply (UPS), the AS/400e systems and servers all use Continuously Powered Main Storage (CPM) to provide protection against utility failures. It becomes impractical to provide batteries as a backup

From:	To:							
Model/ Processor	Model 600				Model 620			
	2129	2134	2135	2136	2179	2180	2181	2182
F02/2414	X	X	X					
F04/2586	X	X	X	X				
F06/2582	X	X	X	X				
F10/2587	X	X	X	X	X			
F20/2588	X	X	X	X	X	X		
F25/2583	X	X	X	X	X	X		
F35/2592	X	X	X	X	X	X		
F45/2593		X	X	X	X	X		
F50/2594					X	X	X	
F60/2595					X	X	X	X
F70/2596						X	X	X
F80/2597							X	X
F90/2598							X	X
236/2100			X	X	X	X		
436/2102			X	X	X	X		
/2104			X	X	X	X	X	
/2106						X	X	
200/2030	X	X	X	X	X			
/2031	X	X	X	X	X	X		
/2032			X	X	X	X		
300/2040	X	X	X	X	X	X		
/2041	X	X	X	X	X	X		
/2042		X	X	X	X	X	X	

Figure. 1.36. Migration from previous release AS/400 systems to V4R2 AS/400e system models 600 and 620. *(continued on next page)*

From: Model/ Processor	To: Model 600				Model 620			
	2129	2134	2135	2136	2179	2180	2181	2182
310/2043					X	X	X	X
/2044						X	X	X
320/2050						X	X	X
/2051							X	X
400/2130	X	X	X	X	X	X		
/2131		X	X	X	X	X	X	
/2132			X	X	X	X	X	
/2133				X	X	X	X	
500/2140					X	X	X	
/2141					X	X	X	X
/2142					X	X	X	X
510/2143							X	X
/2144							X	X
600/2129		X	X	X	X	X	X	
/2134			X	X	X	X	X	
/2135				X	X	X	X	X
/2136						X	X	X
620/2179						X	X	X
/2180							X	X
/2181								X

Figure 1.36. Migration from previous release AS/400 systems to V4R2 AS/400e system models 600 and 620. *(continued from previous page)*

methodology for systems with up to 4 GB of main storage and expect the data resident to be dumped to the available disk storage. The required dump interval is greater than 2 hours, during which time the entire system must be kept operating, because all the facilities of the system unit are required. To counteract the impracticality of not having adequate battery or UPS availability, CPM is provided.

Here is how CPM works: After a utility power failure is detected by the power system of the system unit, a signal is sent to the operating system, which alerts the processor of an impending shutdown. The operating system allows continued operation for 45 seconds to determine if the utility failure is permanent. During the first 30 seconds, the processor executes to a place to stop at a machine interface boundary. After the 45 seconds have elapsed without utility recovery, the AS/400 system

From: Model/ Processor	To: Model 640			Model 650	
	2237	2238	2239	2240	2243
F60/2595	X				
F70/2596	X	X			
F80/2597	X	X			
F90/2598	X	X	X		
F95/2599	X	X	X		
F97/2528	X	X	X	X	
310/2043	X				
/2044	X	X			
320/2050	X	X	X		
/2051	X	X	X	X	
500/2141	X				
/2142	X	X			
510/2143	X	X	X		
/2144	X	X	X		
530/2150	X	X	X	X	
/2151	X	X	X	X	
/2152		X	X	X	X
/2153			X	X	X
/2162			X	X	X
620/2179	X	X			
/2180	X	X	X		
/2181	X	X	X	X	
/2182			X	X	X
640/2237		X	X	X	X
/2238			X	X	X
/2239				X	X
650/2240					X

Figure 1.37. Migration from previous release AS/400 systems to V4R2 AS/400e system models 640 and 650.

begins preparations for CPM, during which time the MFIOP assists the processor in writing internal register contents to memory. At 90 seconds the AS/400 power-off occurs. In CPM power-off, no power is supplied to any system units except main storage, which, though still powered, has switched to a low-power state in which its refresh clock is slowed way down to preserve power.

From:	To:					
Model/	Model S10		Model S20			
Processor	2118	2119	2161	2163	2165	2166
40S/2109	X	X	X	X		
/2110		X	X	X		
/2111			X	X	X	
/2112				X	X	X
50S/2120				X	X	X
/2121				X	X	X
/2122				X	X	X
S10/2118		X	X	X	X	
/2119			X	X	X	X
S20/2161				X	X	X
/2163					X	X
/2165						X

Figure 1.38. Migration from previous release AS/400 servers to V4R2 AS/400e server models S10 and S20.

From:	To:					
Model/	Model S30				Model S40	
Processor	2257	2258	2259	2260	2256	2261
50S/2120	X	X				
/2121	X	X	X			
/2122	X	X	X			
53S/2154	X	X	X	X		
/2155		X	X	X	X	X
/2156			X	X	X	X
/2157			X	X	X	X
S20/2161	X	X	X			
/2163	X	X	X			
/2165			X	X	X	X
/2166			X	X	X	
S30/2257		X	X	X	X	X
/2258			X	X	X	X
/2259				X	X	X
S40/2256						X

Figure 1.39. Migration from previous release AS/400 servers to V4R2 AS/400e server models S30 and S40.

From:	To:			
Model/	Model S20	Model S30		
Processor	2178	2320	2321	2322
S20/2177	X	X	X	X
/2178			X	X
S30/2320			X	X
/2321				X

Figure 1.40. Migration path for V4R2 e-server models.

Once utility power is restored, the system automatically powers on and begins an Initial Program Load (IPL) (if previously enabled by the user). Main store refresh is restored on any system power on. The operating system detects that the system was previously powered off into CPM. It then writes all changed pages from the preserved main storage to DASD and initiates a re-IPL to perform any required error recovery operations.

Performance Overview

One important aspect of a computer system is the speed at which the computer can perform work, or the **performance** of the computer. The higher the performance, the more work the computer can do. Many things—such as the processor, main storage, disk storage, I/O bandwidth, and program design—affect the performance of a computer system. It is difficult and often misleading to predict the overall performance of a computer system by looking at selected specifications of the individual components that make up the computer system. Although things such as disk unit seek times and raw processor speed (usually measured in Millions of Instructions Per Second, or MIPS) are important, they do not provide the whole picture in terms of overall system performance.

In addition to these considerations, in the case of the AS/400 Advanced Series computers, performance must be considered in relation to the environment in which the computer system is executing. The AS/400 may operate in a general-purpose (batch and interactive processing) environment or in a client/server environment. What makes a computer function well in one of these environments may be an inhibitor in the other environment. (A computer that has been tuned for the client/server environment will perform weakly in an interactive environment and vice versa.) As a result, different methodologies are used to measure computer performance for those different environments.

When choosing a multiuser computer system, it is important to understand that the maximum number of active users is different from the maximum number of workstations that can be attached to a system. History has shown that when the active number of users is greater than 40 percent of the maximum number of workstations allowed, there is a strong probability that some of the users will start to experience a decrease in response. The maximum number of users is not a system configuration limitation but rather a system performance limitation for the benchmark used. Therefore, if occasional users are among the user population, it is normally desirable to put more workstations on a system than can be simultaneously supported.

Response time of a computer system is at least as important as throughput. The satisfaction and productivity of users can be drastically affected by a computer's sluggish response after the user hits the enter key. As was mentioned earlier, response time is related to the workload on the computer system. This is not intended to imply that every workload will see subsecond response time.

The AS/400's System/36 environment allows a program originally written for a System/36 architecture to be migrated to and used on an AS/400 system. With the capability of running SSP-based programs on all AS/400 Advanced Series RISC processor–based models concurrently with the OS/400 operating system, there should no longer be any performance degradation when running old System/36 applications on an AS/400.

Benchmark Testing Overview

Benchmark testing has evolved as the best way to compare the overall performance of different computers. Benchmark testing involves loading the computer system with various programs designed to simulate a workload and then measuring how the system behaves under the load. Through this benchmark testing, all elements of the computer system come into play and the overall performance of selected computer systems can be meaningfully compared.

To perform benchmark testing, the test group must make assumptions about the kind of work being done and the behavior of the users at each workstation. For this reason, the performance measurements derived from a benchmark may vary significantly from what users will get if their business environment does not match the assumptions made in the testing. For example, word processing users typically load a system down more heavily than users performing business transactions. Therefore, a system with heavy word processing activity will usually not be able to support as many users as a system performing order entry. However, because all assumptions are the same for all computers included in the benchmark testing, it is possible to get a good idea of the relative performance of the computer systems. IBM has conducted benchmark testing on AS/400 systems using the CPW benchmark, which is designed to simulate a typical business workload (e.g., order entry, accounts payable, and accounts receivable).

CPW Benchmark Test Results

In 1996, IBM introduced a new benchmark testing parametric called **Commercial Processing Workload** (CPW), which replaced the RAMP-C benchmark previously used. IBM chose to make the change to CPW because RAMP-C was driven by the increased performance levels of current AS/400 models and the recognition that users are now utilizing more OS/400 software function. (Contention, queuing, and journaling are examples of software functions that RAMP-C did not test.) In today's environment, IBM feels that CPW benchmarks provide a more representative result than RAMP-C. Tables 6.13 through 6.17 in Chapter 6 are provided to facilitate comparing the old RAMP-C values to CPW performance values for CISC and RISC models for the systems available prior to Version 4 Release 1. The tables also contain a column titled Relative Performance Ratings Internal Processor, which may be used to compare different throughput ratios of system processors in a computation-intensive environment (less I/O activity). Figure 1.41 shows the CPW performance ratings of the general-purpose processing RISC-based models of AS/400 systems. Additional information on other benchmark results on the AS/400 and other vendors' general-purpose commercial processing systems' performance may be obtained from the Transaction Performance Council (TPC, *http://www.tpc.org*), which publishes test results on a wide variety of systems.

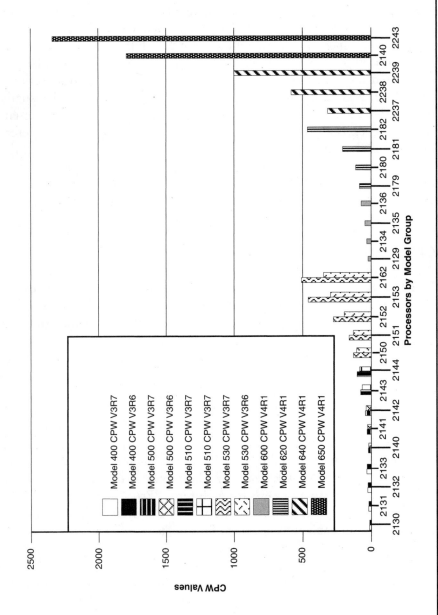

Figure 1.41. CPW/Values for AS/400 RISC-based processors in V3R7 and V4R2.

Symmetrical MultiProcessing (SMP)

Some of the models use Symmetrical MultiProcessing (SMP), meaning they use more than one processor in a single system. ("Hardware Architecture Overview" contains additional discussion on how the use of multiple processors achieves this performance increase.) With SMP, the performance rating increases with each new processor added. For example, if you compare a single processor system to an SMP system with two processors of identical power, you get a performance increase of about 70%. The reason you don't get a 100% improvement is that the two system processors must spend some of their processing power coordinating activities with one another. They must also share the same main storage, I/O bus(ses), disk storage, and so on. For these reasons, adding a second system processor does not result in doubling the performance of the system. However, you do get significant performance improvements with SMP configurations. Figure 1.41 shows the performance advantage afforded by the use of 2- and 4-way processors in the Model 640, and 8-way (2240) and 12-way (2243) processors in the Model 650 SMP configurations.

Server Performance

Client/Server Labs measures server performance on systems for many companies, using a benchmark suite specially tailored for servers. The server environment evolved as a result of two nearly coincident events: (1) the personal computer (PC) penetration into the generalized business world, and (2) the natural desire to share the information contained on those PCs. The PC put the power of computers into the hands of each critical individual within a business.

The need to share the results on one PC with the users on several PCs resulted in the definition of the Local Area Network (LAN). An example of an application across a LAN would be this: If one secretary at a business location reserved a conference room for 1:00 P.M. on Tuesday, when other secretaries accessed that conference room for Tuesday, they would see that the conference room was reserved at 1:00 P.M. and by whom it was reserved. As identified by our example, a LAN should be used to connect together groups of users with some common interest. The first LAN to be defined was Ethernet, which eventually became IEEE 803.2, followed later by the token ring, which became IEEE 803.5. LAN definitions, speeds, and protocols that could not talk to each other proliferated until the distributed computing environment evolved, which settled upon TCP/IP and APPC as the LAN access method and management structure.

The other problem of only networking PCs is that if one user wants a specific piece of information and the PC that has that information is turned off at the time the information is needed, the information cannot be accessed. Also, since PCs have limited disk storage space, individual users were asking why they should spend money and time creating a repository for data that, once created, might be of no further interest. Finally, the question of controlling access to the information on the network was begging for an answer because the **privacy issue** and **need to know** relative to company business still existed. An answer that evolved was to create the **client/server** relationship, in which the PCs were the **clients** and the **server** was a large centralized repository of information. In this environment, the client requested either programs or data from the server, which checked the authorization of the client to receive that information and sent the data to the client. The client then processed the data and sent the results back to the server repository for long-term storage. It was found that in order to check the authorization, find the programs and data, and provide enough storage repository to be useful, the server required the processing characteristics of the client. In fact, in the case of certain long-running applications, it would be preferable to execute the application at the server and send only the results of the application to the client, who could then decide whether the data generated should reside on the server or at the client. The fact that the long-running application executed on the server freed the client resources for execution of short-running applications during the long application's execution time.

It follows, then, that minimizing paths in the server for APPC and TCP/IP, and minimizing database search structures (via good search algorithms, improved base structures, some capability for parallel I/O processing, efficient file serving, and efficient batch processing capability) are the characteristics of a good server. The performance of the server models is shown in Figure 1.42, with the tallest column showing the server batch processing performance at Version 4 Release 2, and the lower column for the same processor showing the interactive performance that results from tuning to the server environment. The S20-ISV, S30-ISV, and S40-SB1 models have been tuned by limiting the configuration and the available application set to provide improved interactive performance. It has been found that when the system has been tuned to

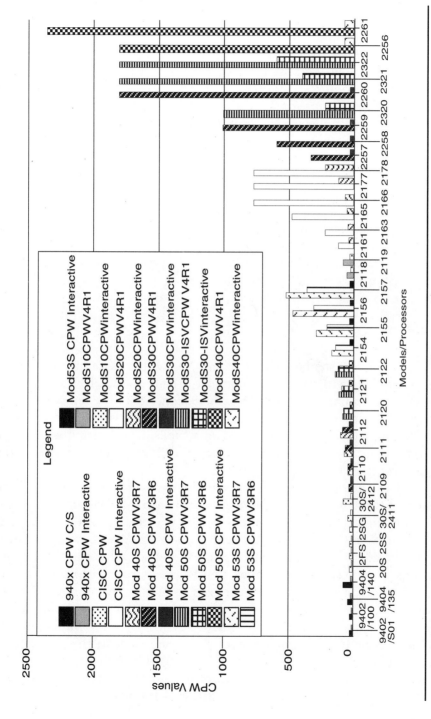

Figure 1.42. CPW values for AS/400 servers including V4R1 and V4R2 processors. Interactive values are only for V3R7 and V4R2.

maximize performance in the server environment, if the interactive work-load increases much beyond 8 to 10% processor utilization, the server performance and the interactive response time for the S10 and S20 models slow down. On the S30 and S40 models if the interactive workload increases beyond 2%, the server performance slows down as well as the interactive performance. Figure 1.42 illustrates the performance ratings for the server models in the AS/400 product line.

RPMark95

The Workplace Server Benchmark has been acquired and altered by Client Server Labs to become RPMark95. Client Server Labs maintains an Internet home page that, in addition to AS/400 server performance, includes data from other vendors comparing to the AS/400 Server systems. Please refer to *http://www.cslinc.com/rpmark/rpmark.htm* on the Internet for the latest information.

Opticonnect Performance

The AS/400e system 6XX and server SXX models (with the exception of the 600 and S10) support a high-performance optical bus connection called Opticonnect. Through this connection, AS/400 systems can be connected together and cooperate (exchange programs and data) without suffering the performance degradation typically associated with system interconnection via other methods (e.g., TCP/IP, Ethernet, or token-ring networks).

Measured performance capacity increases of from 1.5 to 1.7 times the performance of a single system (results vary depending upon application efficiency) have resulted from connecting two AS/400 systems together via Opticonnect. Currently, up to 32 AS/400 systems can be connected via Opticonnect to provide loosely coupled distributed computing. Loosely coupled computing is an environment in which data and programs are exchanged between computers over a serial communications line and the only thing shared from a hardware aspect of the systems is the communications line. The coupling is referred to as loose because the potential processing which can occur in the system from which the information is being moved is significant during the period of the transfer, and because of the problems involved as a result in keeping the information in the sharing systems synchronized.

Version 4 Release 2 (V4R2) Performance-Related Actions

In Version 4 Release 2, OS/400 has been enhanced to provide broad-based performance improvements through changes to improve the operating system code. The improvements ranged from rewriting key components of the operating system to using Feedback Directed Programming Restructuring technology on the System Licensed Internal Code (SLIC). Other optimizations enabled by the transition to RISC technology have been continued. The changes made to improve performance were focused in the following areas:

- IPL times have been improved by up to 50% depending upon the size of the system, the hardware configuration, system management procedures, and the selection of IPL options.

- On a typical system, assuming a mix of object types varying in size, saves can be performed up to 10% faster.

- Save while active is effective in more application environments, which reduces the time the system is not available during save operations. To a large degree the locking conflicts while an object is being saved have been eliminated. Many of the save operations no longer require the system to be in restricted mode, and as a result, the system is available to execute application programs.

- It is now possible to perform a save of multiple objects from a single library utilizing multiple tape drives during save operations. With two tape drives, the save will occur in about half the time needed with only one tape drive.

- APPC communications have been enhanced in the starting and stopping of an interface, and the logging and recovery of errors have been streamlined.

All maximum percentage performance improvements were achieved with maximum system hardware configurations.

The range of performance improvement when running the V4R2 operating system on V3R6 and V3R7 hardware varies from 5 to 35% for traditional commercial transaction processing applications that have many users, much contention, and do significant data base processing in conjunction with journaling and commitment control. The amount of improvement varies by processor model and by the characteristics of a given application.

A Closer Look

Many elements provide the functions and performance of IBM AS/400 computers. The remainder of this chapter provides a closer look at the following aspects of the IBM AS/400 systems:

- Hardware Architecture

  - Clustering Technology

  - OptiConnect/400

- Main Storage

  - Storage Management

  - Virtual Storage

  - Auxiliary Storage

  - Diskette Storage

  - Disk Storage

- Disk Unit Performance

  - Optical Libraries

  - Tape Storage

  - Packaging Technology

  - Fiber Optic Bus

Before the AS/400 systems are examined more closely, it should be mentioned that many of the concepts used in the AS/400 system were built on those of IBM's System/38 computer. This fact is a testimonial to the rich function and growth capability built into the original System/38.

Hardware Architecture Overview

The underlying arrangement and interconnection of a computer system's electrical components is called its **hardware architecture**. This architecture is the fundamental structure upon which all system functions are built and has the largest effect on how the computer system will behave. A basic understanding of the AS/400 system architecture (Figure 1.43) makes it possible to compare AS/400 computers with other systems and to understand important aspects of system performance and capacity.

The core of the AS/400 computer (as in all computers) is the **system processor** (shown near the center of the figure). The system processor is

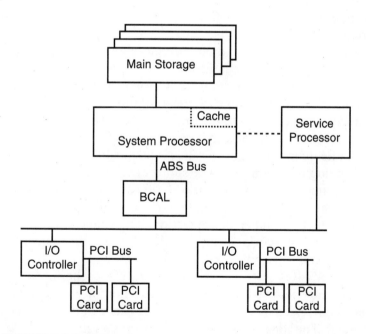

Figure 1.43. Block diagram of AS/400 hardware used in all PCI-based models (150, 170, 600, 620, S10, S20).

the circuitry that actually executes a computer program's instructions and does all the mathematical calculations. The smallest piece of information (data) in the computer is called a **bit**. Bits are grouped into bytes (8 bits), half words (16 bits), full words (32 bits), and double words (64 bits) inside the computer. These groupings form the computer's representation of numbers, letters of the alphabet, and instructions in a program. AS/400 system processors move information around one double word (64 bits) at a time. Since much of a computer's time is spend moving information around, the double-word organization helps improve overall system performance.

Other bits inside the system processor are used to uniquely identify or **address** storage and input/output devices (e.g., a disk unit) within the computer system. AS/400 system processors group 64 bits together to form a unique address. This 64-bit addressing provides 18,446,744 trillion (2^{64}) unique addresses, which is more than any other IBM computer system from PCs to the largest System/390 computers. This is more than enough addresses for today's midsize computer environment (and even for the foreseeable future). In fact, the largest AS/400 systems and servers today have not even needed to use one trillion of those addresses. This shows the kind of growth potential inherent in the AS/400 architecture.

The "memory" or **main storage** (shown at the top of the figure) provides a work space for the system processor. Since much of a computer's time is spent moving information to and from main storage, the speed of main storage can be a limiting factor to the overall performance of any computer system. The speed of storage is measured by the time it takes to respond to a request to store or recall information, or the **cycle time**. The main storage cycle time for AS/400 computers varies depending on the model. The shorter the cycle time, the better the system performance. The largest AS/400 computers can have up to 20,480 MB of main storage. The main storage in all AS/400 systems provides **error detection** and **error correction**. This main storage error detection and correction works to protect the all-important integrity of user information in the computer system.

All AS/400 system processors also use cache memory to help increase the effective cycle time of main storage. A cache is a small and very-high-speed memory area that sits between the processor and main storage. The idea is to keep the information most likely to be needed next in cache to avoid the time delay associated with main storage.

AS/400 systems have data and instruction caches on the processor to accelerate performance when accessing information/program instructions (respectively).

Another important part of the AS/400 architecture is the **System Licensed Internal Code (SLIC)**. SLIC is a set of extremely simple instructions (never seen by the computer programmer or user) that are directly performed by the electronic circuits within the system processor. All user program instructions are automatically converted into a series of these SLIC instructions, which are then executed by the system processor.

The input/output (I/O) processors (shown at the bottom of the figure) are responsible for managing any devices attached to the AS/400 system. Each of these specialized processors has independent responsibilities and performs tasks in coordination with the system processor. A computer that has multiple processors working together with the system processor like this has a **multiprocessor architecture**. The advantage of having multiple processors performing work simultaneously is simply that more work can be done in a given period of time. For example, the workstation I/O processor manages the detailed processing associated with the multiple terminals and printers attached to the system, allowing the system processor to concentrate on doing more productive work for the user. The same is true of the other specialized I/O processors such as the storage I/O processor, which manages disk, diskette, and tape devices attached to the AS/400 system. The I/O processors communicate with the system processor over an I/O bus (called the SPD bus), a group of wires that carry information very quickly from one area to another inside the computer system. As indicated in the figure, some AS/400 systems have a single I/O bus whereas others have multiple I/O busses. Because only one information transfer can occur on any one bus at any one time, systems with multiple busses have the advantage of allowing overlapping transfers between I/O processors and the system processor or main storage. Therefore, multiple busses contribute to the overall system performance advantages of larger AS/400 systems.

Various controllers and adapters plug into physical slots in each of the packages used to provide electrical connections to the bus. In addition to I/O processors, a service processor (shown in the upper right of the figure) is built into every AS/400. It is responsible for starting the system and constantly monitoring the health of the entire computer. It interacts with the system operator through the control panel and helps with such things as system fault isolation, error detection, and error reporting. It is the equivalent of having a built-in service person who watches over things with relentless consistency.

All AS/400 systems employ a multiprocessor architecture in that they have a system processor and multiple specialized processors (e.g., workstation and I/O processors) to handle specific tasks. However, larger AS/400 models (e.g., Models 620, 640, S20, S30, S40, and 650) employ multiple **system** processors to cooperatively execute a single copy of the operating system (OS/400), thus appearing to be a single large processor. This multiple system processor architecture is called the **N-way multiprocessor** architecture (where N is replaced by the number of processors), also referred to as the Symmetric MultiProcessor (SMP) architecture. Figure 1.44 shows how N-way models are organized. (*Note:* All system processors share the same I/O busses, I/O processors, and main storage.) Symmetric multiprocessors process in parallel, sharing a task list. Each processor in a symmetric multiprocessor set has its own data and instruction cache, and its own virtual storage view of the system. In the case of a query, each processor in the SMP group will process in parallel against a segment of disk storage to resolve the query. Figure 1.45 illustrates the memory and I/O connections for the 8-way and 12-way processor models.

AS/400 Clustering Technology

What Is OptiConnect/400?

OptiConnect/400 is the system-to-system interconnection fabric that allows distributed functions and applications to operate at high speed. It can be used to form a high-performance, multisystem, loosely coupled cluster.

Two things differentiate OptiConnect from traditional communications-based distributed operations. The first is a system bus connection between multiple systems using high-speed fiber optic technology. The second is an I/O driver embedded in the operating system that streamlines the application access to data on a remote system. To accomplish this, OptiConnect provides a shared bus on which systems communicate using a peer-to-peer protocol. Once OptiConnect establishes sys-

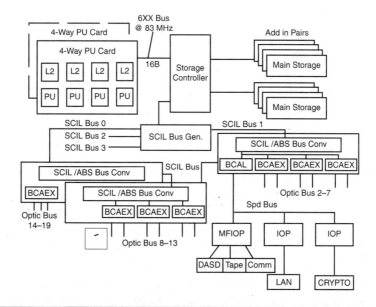

Figure 1.44. Model 640 and S30 hardware architecture block diagram.

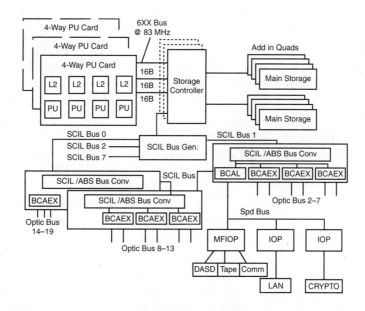

Figure 1.45. Model 650 and S40 8-way and 12-way hardware architecture block diagram.

tem connections on the shared bus, much of the APPC (Advanced Peer to Peer Communication) protocol stack is bypassed. The OptiConnect fast-path connection for database transactions provides DDM (Distributed Data Management) access to databases anywhere in the OptiConnect cluster at a fraction of the standard communications code path. Data warehouse, DRDA, and data propagation functions can use this technology.

Traditional communication protocol overhead is too impractical for heavy workload distributed applications. To minimize latency, or the time it takes to send a message and receive a response, the protocol chosen must be efficient in the number of code steps required. To maximize bandwidth, or the amount of data that can be transferred in a unit of time, high-performance hardware must be used. The OptiConnect channel is very efficient and the best solution for both latency and bandwidth. The length of the cable affects how low latency can get. As distance increases, the speed of light becomes a limiting factor for a given bandwidth. OptiConnect is limited to 500 meters over the 1063-Mbps (megabit-per-second) link used on RISC models and 2 kilometers over the 220-Mbps link supported on CISC models.

OptiConnect/400-Enabled Functions

An OptiConnect cluster can consist of up to 14 systems with full system-to-system connectivity and up to 32 systems in complex structures where all satellite systems must communicate with one or two hub systems. Figure 1.46 illustrates the clustering of three systems through an expansion unit hub. The OptiConnect for OS/400 software provides a streamlined communications path across the dedicated system buses. Together with the hardware the following functions can utilize the high-speed system-bus-level connections between AS/400 systems:

- All Distributed Data Management (DDM) operations for supported object types can run across OptiConnect, including data files, data areas, and data queues.

- All Structured Query Language (SQL) support provided by Distributed Relational Database Architecture (DRDA) will run across OptiConnect, including distributed unit of work and remote unit of work.

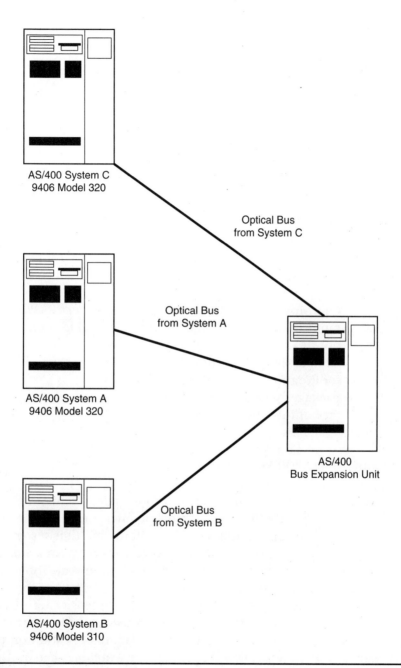

AS/400 System C
9406 Model 320

Optical Bus
from System C

Optical Bus
from System A

AS/400 System A
9406 Model 320

AS/400
Bus Expansion Unit

Optical Bus
from System B

AS/400 System B
9406 Model 310

Figure 1.46.   Three-system cluster with one bus given up in each system to connect to the expansion tower.

- DB2 Multisystem with its DB2/400 support for multinode files will run across OptiConnect, providing data warehouse functions of Query/400 support and two-phase commit.

- ObjectConnect/400 will operate over OptiConnect to provide high-speed system-to-system save/restore functions.

- Standard APPC Conversations are available over OptiConnect with an OptiConnect communication controller. This allows for System Network Architecture Distribution Services (SNADS), display station pass-through, network printer pass-through, and other functions.

- OptiConnect has an Application Program Interface (API) to which business partner software packages can code.

- OptiMover for OS/400 is a special, low-cost PRPQ version of OptiConnect for OS/400 software. It enables non-DDM functions to utilize the OptiConnect high-speed link, allowing system-bus-level connections between AS/400 systems. PRPQ stands for Programming Request Per Quote. Business partner software packages written to these APIs allow customers to take advantage of this lower-priced option.

OptiConnect/400 Environment

There are two primary uses for the OptiConnect technology. Horizontal growth is the traditional and most popular use. Separating database operations from application workload allows multiple systems to operate as a cluster to grow computing power beyond what a single system can provide. It is important to understand that not all applications are conducive to this type of workload distribution. The horizontal growth scalability is dependent on the database I/O intensity. The best implementation is the separation of the interactive application from the corresponding data while maintaining the batch application on the same system as the batch data. Techniques are available that transparently manage the batch job submission to the database server system.

The second use for OptiConnect technology is high availability. When used in conjunction with business partner applications such as those offered by Lakeview Technology and Vision Solutions, efficient high-availability solutions can be achieved. The OptiConnect technology provides the most efficient use of CPU resources to allow fast replication of data between systems.

Main Storage

The "memory" or **main storage** is the set of electronic circuits within an AS/400 system that provides a "workspace" for the system processor. Data and programming instructions are moved from disk storage to main storage for the programs and the processing of data. After execution or processing, modified data are moved back to main storage and kept there until no longer needed. At that point, the data are typically written back to disk storage for safekeeping.

AS/400 systems spend much time moving information between the system processor and main storage. There are two major reasons that this is so. First, all programs currently being executed by the system processor reside in main storage. Therefore, the system processor must (at some point) retrieve every instruction from main storage. Second, main storage holds the data to be acted on by the system processor. Since the information traffic between the system processor and main storage is heavy, the speed of main storage is important to overall system performance. That is why high-speed cache memory, which increases the effective speed of main storage, is included in the system design.

As we have seen, every main storage location in AS/400 main storage consists of 64 pieces of information, or bits. All information in main storage is encoded using these 64-bit groupings, called double words. In addition to the 64 bits of information, each word in main storage has several additional bits (called **check bits**) that are generated based on the value of that particular 64-bit word. In the event that one or two of the 64-bit words is somehow corrupted, the check bits notify the AS/400 computer that the error exists. If only one of the 64 bits is corrupted, as is usually the case, the check bits actually restore the corrupted bit and correct the error. This main storage error detection and correction works to protect the all-important integrity of user information in the computer system.

In earlier days of computing, the main storage size limited the amount of work a computer could manage at any one time. This limitation capped the size of programs, the number of programs that could be run concurrently, the number of users that could share the system, and so on. In modern computers a technique called **virtual storage** alleviates the need to squeeze all active programs and data into main storage.

Storage Management

The methods used within a computer system to manage main storage and disk storage, called the computer's **storage management**, are fundamental to the capabilities of the computer. Understanding the basics of storage management provides insight into one of the unique features of AS/400 computers as compared with traditional computer systems.

Figure 1.47 shows conceptually what the storage in AS/400 computers looks like. All programs and information currently being used by the computer system must be contained in main storage, which resides inside the computer's system unit. Main storage is relatively expensive and responds at very high speeds (compared to disk storage) when called on to provide or store information. Because main storage loses all information when the computer system is turned off, it is called **volatile** storage.

Disk storage is less expensive but cannot provide or store information as quickly as main storage. Disk storage is said to be **nonvolatile** because it does not lose its information when the power is turned off (or lost owing to a power failure). As a result of this nonvolatility and relatively low cost, disk storage is commonly used to hold all information that must be readily available to the computer. Disk storage may reside either inside the system unit or inside a separate box cabled to the system unit (as depicted in the figure).

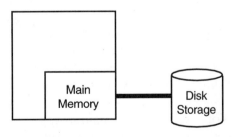

Figure 1.47. AS/400 main storage and fixed disk storage.

When the AS/400 computer is first turned on, information vital to an orderly startup and smooth operation is automatically copied from the disk to main storage. Once normal system operation is established, users can begin to do their work. During the course of this work, users will start various computer programs. As each program is started, it is copied from the disk to main storage and then executed. Depending on the work being done, the computer programs manipulate various sets of data that are also loaded from the disk as needed. It does not take long to realize that the main storage in a computer can quickly become filled up with programs and data as the system is called upon to do more and more work.

In earlier days, the main storage size limited the amount of work a computer could manage at any one time. This limitation capped the size of programs, the number of programs that could be run concurrently, the number of users that could share the system, and so on. In today's environment, a technique called **virtual storage** (discussed more fully in the next section) alleviates the need to squeeze all active programs and data into main storage. In computers that support virtual storage, the computer basically "fakes out" the computer programs and users and appears to have much more main storage than it actually has. (The AS/400 allows a virtual storage size of 18 million terabytes. Virtual storage therefore allows more programs, data, and users to be simultaneously active on the system than could be supported in real main storage without virtual storage.

Although virtual storage is a powerful system feature, the "swapping" between disk and main storage is processing overhead that can reduce the overall system performance. A little swapping does not appreciably hurt performance, but increased swapping does. When the swapping performed by a virtual storage system becomes excessive, the system is said to be **thrashing**, or spending too much time swapping information between disk and main storage. Thrashing can be reduced by increasing the amount of main storage in the AS/400 system through the installation of main storage expansion options. Increasing the main storage in the system provides more room for programs and data, reducing the amount of virtual storage swapping. Thrashing can also be reduced through system management means such as rescheduling work for off-peak periods.

The virtual storage concept is implemented in many of today's computer systems to one degree or another. AS/400 systems implement their virtual storage scheme through a concept called **single-level storage**. This simply means that in AS/400 systems, no distinction is made between disk storage and main storage. All storage appears to be one homogeneous sea of main storage accessed in exactly the same way. This consistency provides for a simple and efficient virtual storage implementation that is the same for programs, data, temporary holding areas, and so forth. The simplicity of single-level storage results in a consistent and more complete virtual storage system than most other implementations.

Another difference between AS/400 storage management and that of conventional computer systems is **object-oriented access**. With this concept, all programs, databases, documents, and so on stored in AS/400 computers are stored as independent entities called **objects**. The AS/400's object-oriented access again provides the user and the programmer with a simple and consistent way of managing all programs and information in the system. Users can access an object by simply referring to its name. The AS/400 security system will check to make sure that the user has authorization to use the object and that it is being used properly. This is called **capability-based addressing**. The AS/400 system manages the complexities associated with the physical location and addressing of the information.

AS/400's implementation of single-level storage and capability-based addressing spreads information through various disk units in a way that optimizes storage efficiency. Objects provide consistency in the areas of security, usage, and systems management for all items stored on AS/400 systems. Objects can be organized into groups called **libraries**. A library (which is also an object) is analogous to a drawer in a file cabinet (or a subdirectory, for those familiar with PC disk management). A library might contain all programs related to the accounting function of a business to keep things organized. Because access to libraries can be restricted by the AS/400 security system, a payroll database, for example, might be kept in a library separate from other business information for security reasons

Virtual Storage

Virtual storage is a technique for using main storage that alleviates the need to squeeze all active programs and data into main storage. In computers that support virtual storage, the computer basically "fakes out" the computer programs and users and appears to have much more main storage than it actually has. The virtual storage supported by AS/400 systems is over a whopping 18 million terabytes (TB) in size (over 18 quintillion [18,000,000,000,000,000 or 18×10^{15}] unique addresses). This 18 million TB of addressing capability is enough to keep track of the information contained on over 9 quintillion pages of single-spaced computer output—a stack of paper over 800 billion miles high that could stretch between the earth and the moon 3 million times. Virtual storage therefore allows more programs, data, and users to be simultaneously active on the system than could be supported in real main storage without virtual storage.

Virtual storage works as follows: A user tells the computer to start a word processing program. The computer first attempts to load the needed portion of the word processing program into main storage. If there is no space left in main storage, some space is made available by overwriting an inactive portion of some program or by "swapping" out some inactive data to a temporary space on the disk. The needed portion of the word processing program can then be loaded in the available space, and the user can then begin typing the memo. If the program that was overwritten or the data that were "swapped" out are again needed, they are reloaded from a disk unit to some other available main storage area. Therefore, a virtual storage computer system is constantly swapping programs and information between main storage and disk storage, robbing Peter to pay Paul and vice versa.

Virtual storage allows the maximum size program or combination of all programs and data to be limited only by the combined amount of main storage and disk storage space rather than by the amount of main storage alone. The advantage of virtual storage is that neither the programmer nor the user of any AS/400 system needs to be concerned with main storage size. To them, the system seems to have as much main storage as they need, and they are never made aware that information is constantly being swapped from main storage to disk storage and back again. The computer system manages this "swapping" automatically.

Auxiliary Storage

Auxiliary storage, commonly used to keep data and program information in all computers, is an inexpensive way to retain and later access information. Information kept on auxiliary storage can be easily modified or kept unchanged over long periods of time as an archive. Because all auxiliary storage is nonvolatile, the information stored remains intact whether the computer is turned on or off. The AS/400 systems use four types of auxiliary storage: **diskette, disk, optical libraries,** and **tape.**

Diskette Storage

Diskettes are a portable magnetic storage medium that can be used to record and later retrieve computer information via a diskette unit. The diskettes consist of a flexible disk with a magnetic surface permanently enclosed in a square, protective outer jacket, as shown in Figure 1.48.

One of the primary functions of diskettes is to provide portable storage, allowing for the transfer of programs and data between computers. To this end, all similarly configured AS/400 computer systems can freely exchange programs and data via diskettes. Also, information on System/3X diskettes can be freely exchanged with a properly configured AS/400 computer.

Disk Storage

Earlier in the chapter we introduced another kind of auxiliary storage used with AS/400 systems called disk storage units or **Direct Access Storage Devices (DASDs).** These are high-capacity magnetic storage devices commonly used in all types of computers from PS/2s to large

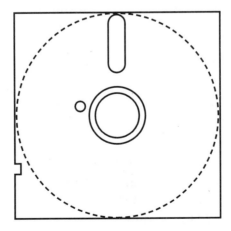

Figure 1.48. Diskette used with application systems.

mainframe computer systems. The basic anatomy of a disk unit is shown in Figure 1.49. Disks consist of a drive mechanism with permanently installed metallic disks often called **platters** (because they are shaped like a dinner plate). These platters have a magnetic surface that can store information. Disk units will be described in greater detail later in this chapter and in Chapter 2 under "Disk Storage."

Disk Unit Performance Overview

Disk unit performance is important to the overall performance of a computer system in most applications. This is particularly true in virtual storage and/or multiuser environments, in which there is heavy transfer of information between disk storage and main storage.

The performance of a disk unit refers to the rate at which information can be located and transferred between the disk unit and the main storage. The speed at which a disk unit can position the read/write head over the proper region of the platter is the **average seek time,** usually expressed in milliseconds (1/1000 second). After the read/write head is properly positioned, the system must wait as the platter spins until the needed data begins to pass under the read/write head. The average time it takes for the platter to rotate to the proper position is called the **average latency** (also expressed in milliseconds). Finally, once the read/write head is positioned and the data begin to pass by on the spinning platter, the information is transferred from the disk unit to the computer system. The speed at which this is done is called the **data transfer rate** and is usually expressed in millions of bytes per second (MBps). The shorter

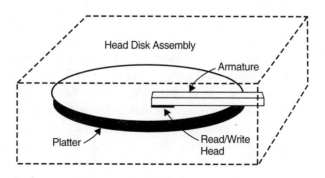

Figure 1.49. The anatomy of a disk unit.

the average seek time and the average latency, and the higher the transfer rate, the better the performance of the disk storage subsystem and the overall computer system. Figure 1.50 shows the average seek times, average latency, and data transfer rates for some internal disk units that are provided as standard equipment on AS/400 systems.

In addition to the disk unit specifications, there are other performance considerations when configuring the disk storage subsystem of an AS/400 system. Some disk units have multiple actuators whereas others only have one. Often, each actuator in a disk unit can perform independently, so the more actuators you have for a given amount of disk storage, the better the performance. In fact, choosing disk storage configurations that have more **actuators** for a given amount of storage can result in higher performance than selecting disk units with faster specifications but fewer actuators. (The actuator is the accessing mechanism of the disk unit, which carries the read/write head and flies over the surface of the disk detecting or imprinting the magnetic bits.) This is particularly true with AS/400 systems because single-level storage tends to spread information over many areas of the disk units. This spreading of information produces more efficient operation because the actuators can all share the load, but it does emphasize the need to follow proper backup procedures.

Optical Libraries

Optical libraries consist of arrays of optical disks associated with one or more optical disk read/write units. In some cases, the optical storage read/write units also have one or more conventional magnetic disk storage units associated with them to improve the write performance from a system perspective. The optical disks may be **CD-ROM**, **WORM**, or **WMRM** technology, each of which imposes different requirements upon the read/write unit and upon the controller within the system. **CD-ROM** is an abbreviation for **Compact Disk–Read Only Memory**, and the technology presents digital data in a continuous serpentine path across the surface of the optical disk. **WORM** is an abbreviation for **Write Once, Read Many**. This technology presents data in circumferential paths across the surface of the optical disk. Because the data will only be written once, this technology generally has the header embedded on the raw media, and a sector corresponds to the data content that can fit in the shortest circumferential track. **WMRM**, sometimes referred to as erasable optical disk technology, is an abbreviation for **Write Many, Read**

Computer System	Standard Configuration	Fixed-Disk Devices Used	Average Seek Time	Data Transfer Rate	Latency	Number of Actuators
AS/400e Entry	4,194 MB	One 3.5-inch 4194-MB disk unit	8.6 ms	20 MB/sec	5.56ms	1/drive
Advanced 36	1,030 MB	One 3.5-inch 1030-MB disk unit	8.6 ms	5 MB/sec	5.56 ms	1/drive
	1,960 MB	One 3.5-inch 1960-MB disk unit	8.6 ms	5 MB/sec	5.56 ms	1/drive
AS/400e 600, 620, 640, 650, S10, S20, S30, S40, 170	4,194 MB	One 3.5-inch 4,194-MB disk unit	8.6 ms	40 MB/sec	5.56 ms	1/drive
AS/400e 600, 620, 640, 650, S10, S20, S30, S40, 170, 150	8,580-MB	One 3.5-inch 8580 MB disk unit	8.6 ms	40 MB/sec	5.56 ms	1/drive
AS/400e 600, 620, 640, 650, S10, S20, S30, S40	17,500 MB	One 3.5-inch 17,500-MB disk unit	8.6 ms	40 MB/sec	5.56 ms	1/drive

Figure 1.50. Performance characteristics of internal fixed disks provided as standard in AS/400 systems.

Many and also presents data in circumferential paths across the surface of the optical disk but, because the data written at one time must be erased before new data may be written to replace the erased data, must follow the sectoring, header, trailer, and error correction rules of magnetic disk technology, including bad track recovery and directory management.

Tape Storage

The last type of auxiliary storage to be covered is magnetic tape or simply "tape." One primary purpose of tape is to provide a backup storage medium for information on the computer's disk storage. The low cost and high recording densities inherent in tape make it ideal for archiving information. Tape is also very useful in distributing programs and transferring information from one computer system to another. Diskettes can be used for these same functions, but the higher storage capacity of tapes is preferred if you are dealing with a large amount of information. Tape storage consists of a long flexible strip coated with magnetic material and rolled on a reel or into a cartridge.

Packaging Technology

Most of the circuitry in AS/400 systems was built using IBM's version of **Very Large Scale Integration (VLSI)** technology called **Complementary Metal-Oxide Semiconductor (CMOS)**. This packaging technology builds circuits with 0.25-micron-sized elements, allowing up to 25 million high-speed transistors in a single chip. Main storage is implemented using IBM's 16-Mb and 64-Mb (16-million-bit) memory chip technology. Sixteen-megabit chips are used on all except the largest-capacity memory cards, which use 64-Mb chips to achieve an improved packaging density.

Seven basic mechanical designs are used in AS/400 computer system units. The sizes range from the deskside tower of the Model 150 to the dual tall-tower racks that house the Model 650. The system unit package contains the system processor, main storage, tape, disk units, a CD-ROM, and some number of I/O controllers.

The main storage for the A10 Microprocessor–based processors is contained on a card that measures about 7 × 3 inches and plugs directly to the processor card. Main storage for Models 600/620/S10/S20 is packaged on standard DIMM form factor cards. Main storage for the A35 Microprocessor–based processors for Models 640/650/S30/S40 is contained on separate 9 × 15-inch cards contained in a separate metal container called a book. Other circuitry is packaged on 9 × 11-inch cards that are plugged into an internal card chassis (called a **cage**), allowing for electrical connections to the bus. The design is modular, and the various elements can be easily added or replaced without the need for IBM service personnel.

All AS/400 systems use the **cable-thru** wiring scheme. Cable-thru allows multiple displays or printers (i.e., workstations) to be attached together in a **daisy-chain** fashion as shown in Figure 1.51. With cable-thru, it is not necessary to run a separate cable from the computer to each workstation. Instead, a single cable from the computer can be used to attach up to seven workstations over a distance of up to 5000 feet.

Fiber Optic Bus

The **fiber optic bus** design continued from the D, E, and F models allows the larger Advanced Series systems to add additional I/O busses to an AS/400 system, which allows the system to accommodate more I/O devices without loading down existing I/O busses. The fiber optic cable that attaches these additional SPD I/O busses (i.e., system unit expansion features) uses laser light rather than electrical signals to exchange information with the rest of the AS/400 system. Using light allows the additional I/O busses to operate at full speed over greater distances and eliminates the electrical interference inherent in electrical cables carrying high-speed signals. The fiber optic cables can carry light signals at a

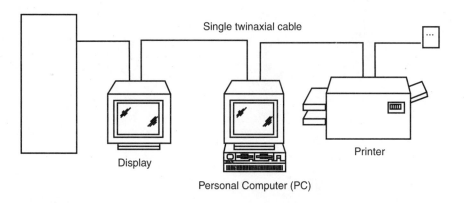

Figure 1.51. All Application Systems use the cable-thru approach to attach to local workstations.

rate of 1063 Mbps. Except for the rack-mounted 5042 units, V4R2 upgrades that contain the older 266-Mbps fiber optic cables must be upgraded to the 1063-Mbps type. With these optical cables, the various towers of an AS/400 system can be located up to 100 meters apart rather than within the 12-foot limit imposed by earlier electrical I/O bus cables. Furthermore, optical cable configurations are available that will allow intertower distances of up to 2 kilometers in some situations.

2

Options and Peripherals

Application Systems are likely to be found in many diverse environments—from fish markets to insurance companies. The activities performed by people in these environments vary widely, and so do their computing needs. Application Systems can be customized to many environments by selecting the appropriate optional equipment. This includes **feature cards, internal options,** and **peripherals**. Feature cards are circuit boards containing electronics that provide some additional capacity or function(s) to Application Systems. They can be installed in one of the I/O expansion slots provided in all Application System computers. Peripherals are devices that attach to Application System computers, usually via a cable, and perform functions under the computer's control. This chapter covers

- Workstations

- Main Storage Expansion Options

- Auxiliary Storage Options

- Communications Options

- Other Options

Although this chapter does not provide comprehensive coverage of all the optional equipment that can be used with Application Systems, it does introduce the reader to many devices that are representative of those most commonly used in the business environment.

Workstations

The devices used to interact with Application Systems are known as **workstations**, which can be either terminals or printers. A **computer terminal** (also called a display station) is the TV-like device that converts the computer's electrical signals into light images that convey information to the user. Terminals also come equipped with a keyboard that allows the user to send information back to the computer. **Printers** are electro-mechanical devices that print the computer's electronically encoded information onto paper. If a workstation is near the computer system—for example, in the same building—it can be **locally** attached to the computer system via a cable. If the workstation is not near the computer—for example, in another state—it can be **remotely** attached over communications lines. Either way, the function provided to the workstation user is the same. Some type of workstation is required to allow the user to interact with the Application Systems. Many types of workstations can be used with Application Systems. In this chapter, we look at the following:

- InfoWindow II 3486/3487 Display Stations

- InfoWindow II 3488/3489 Modular Display Station

- Personal Computer (PC) Terminal Emulation

- Retail Workstations

- Network Computer Workstations

- Printers

  - Impact Printers

- Dot-Matrix Printers

- Band Printers

- Nonimpact Printers

  - Thermal Printers

  - Inkjet Printers

  - Laser Printers

- Workstation Controllers

  - Twinaxial Controllers

  - ASCII Controllers

- Protocol Converters

InfoWindow II 3486/3487 Display Stations

The 3486 and 3487 Display Stations (Figure 2.1) are members of the InfoWindow II family of text-only display stations (also called terminals) for use with the Application Systems. The 3486 is the entry member of the InfoWindow II family of displays. It is compatible with the earlier 3476 and 3196 displays while providing some additional features. First, the 3486 supports an enhanced user interface that employs a mouse and special graphical characters (e.g., scroll bars, radio buttons, pushbuttons, check boxes, and continuous window frames) to ease the user's interaction with application programs. This enables AS/400 applications (specially written or used in conjunction with the IBM WindowTool/400 product [5798-RYF]) to provide pop-up menus and help screens popular with personal computer (PC) users.

Also provided by the 3486 is support for two display sessions and one printer, split-screen viewing of new 32×8 and 49×8 screen formats, and a built-in calculator. As with all InfoWindow II displays, the image presented on the 3486 Display screen has been improved (new

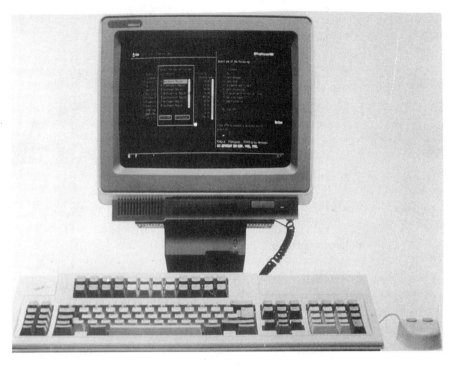

	Model 3486	Model 3487
Display:	14" Monochrome	15" Monochrome 14" Color
Features:	Tilt/swivel printer port	Tilt/swivel printer port

Figure 2.1.   Info WindowII 3486/3487 Modular Display Station.

character fonts, reduced flicker, etc.) to comply with emerging display-quality standards (ISO 9241 part 3). Finally, the 3486 can support a PC-type printer (for example, an IBM Personal Printer Series II), which can be cabled directly to a port provided on the rear of the 3486. This printer can be used as a system printer, just like other printers attached to the Application System, or it can be used to print an image of whatever is on the 3486's screen. Printers supported now include laser printers such as the IBM 4019 and 4029 or the Hewlett-Packard LaserJet III.

The 3486 displays are monochrome only and have 14-inch display screens. The displays can be either green on black (BG models) or amber/gold on black (BA models). Which you choose is purely a matter of individual taste. Either version can display 24 lines of text 80 characters in length while still leaving a row at the bottom to display status messages. The display comes with a tilt/swivel base to allow a comfortable viewing angle. The record/play mode feature of the 3486 displays includes the ability to store up to 1500 often-used keystroke sequences that are recalled by pressing a single command key. The display can be set up to go blank after a specified time of keyboard inactivity to protect the display's **phosphors**, which, like those used in a television, are deposited on the inside surface of the display and glow, when excited by electronic signals generated by the display station, to create an image. When a display station is left on but unattended, an image can be permanently "burned" into the phosphors. The blanking feature prevents this. A blanked image is automatically restored when any key is pressed. This feature can be adjusted through operator setup functions, as can the alarm volume, keyboard clicker volume, cursor shape, and other items.

The provided key-lock disables the keyboard and display, helping to prevent unauthorized entering or viewing of information. You also have the choice of either a 102-key keyboard (IBM Enhanced Keyboard) like those used with Personal System/2 computers or a 122-key typewriter keyboard. Either keyboard has an adjustable slope (6- or 12-degree tilt). The primary difference in keyboards is that the 122-key keyboard has more programmable function keys. The InfoWindow II 3487 Display Stations are compatible with the older InfoWindow 3477 and 3179 Display Stations. They are functionally the same as the 3486 Display Stations described earlier but offer larger display screens on all models and a color display on one model:

- 14-inch color display (HC models)

- 15-inch green-on-black display (HG models)

- 15-inch amber/gold-on-black display (HA models)

Color can be used to effectively highlight and associate information on a display, making the information clearer. Some highlighting capability is provided on most monochrome displays, but color provides additional flexibility in this area while providing a more pleasing image. The 15-inch display offers larger characters, which is especially helpful when operating the 3487 in its 27 lines of 132 characters mode.

The image presented on the display screen of all InfoWindow II displays has been improved (new character fonts, reduced flicker, etc.) to comply with emerging display-quality standards (ISO 9241 part 3). Finally, an optional barcode/magnetic badge reader (i.e., the 7695 Model 250) can be attached to the 3487 to allow data entry through bar codes or magnetic badges in addition to normal keyboard entry.

InfoWindow II 3488/3489 Modular Display Station

The InfoWindow II 3488 Modular Display Station (Figure 2.2) and the InfoWindow II 3489 Modular Display station embody a modular design that allows the user to attach a Personal System/2 display (any VGA or VGA-compatible display) to the 3488/3489 display logic module. That is, the user has the flexibility to customize the display station to suit his or her needs by selecting from any PC-type monitor. As user needs change, the monitor can be upgraded. Conversely, if the user moves up to a PC workstation, he or she can retain the monitor and use it with the PC. Functionally, the 3488 provides the same functions as the 3486/3487 Display Stations discussed earlier, including light pen, color, and mouse functions.

Personal Computer (PC) Terminal Emulation

With the proper feature card and software (e.g., Client Access Family for AS/400 for Windows or Client Access Family for AS/400), a PC (Figure 2.3), a Personal System/2, or any other vendor's PC can also be used as a terminal for Application Systems. In this case, the PC is said to be acting like or **emulating** a terminal. In the simplest case, the PC appears to the Application Systems to be like any other terminal with no special capabilities. The user can then interact with the Application Systems just as with any other terminal discussed so far. Further, a printer attached to the PC can be used both as a printer for PC application programs and as a system printer for the AS/400 application programs. Hitting a simple keystroke combination temporarily suspends terminal emulation, and the PC is changed back into a normal PC able to run the many PC programs available today.

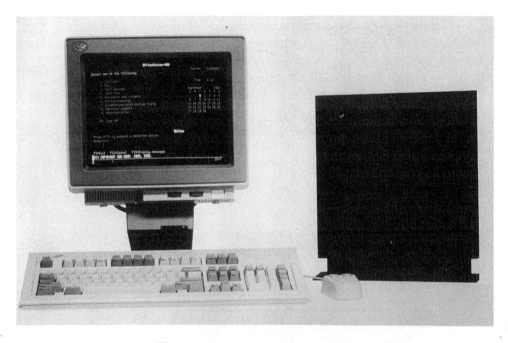

Display type: Personal computer display
                  (user selected)

Features: Separate Display Logic Module

Figure 2.2. Info Window II 3488 Modular Display Station. Separate display logic module can be seen on the right.

Because the PC is a computer, not just a terminal, it has its own **intelligence.** It is therefore called an **intelligent workstation.** This intelligence can be used to run PC programs independent of the Application Systems, or it can be used to work with the Application Systems, and it provides for the direct interaction between PC programs and those running on Application Systems. This type of interaction can be done without user intervention to perform functions ranging from simply transferring a file between the PC and the Application Systems to more complex program-to-program communications (e.g., cooperative processing). You can also concurrently interact with multiple Application Systems with a single PC or sign on to a single system as more than one terminal. Chapter 6 further discusses interaction between PCs and Ap-

Type:	Color/text and graphics
Features:	Local intelligence, advanced graphics
Options:	Various models, connection type

Figure 2.3. Properly configured personal computers can be used as work-stations for Application Systems.

plication Systems in the context of the Internet and of intranets. For more information about PCs, refer to *Exploring IBM Personal Computers, 9th Edition* (IBM document G325-0400, Maximum Press).

To simplify the ordering process for PC systems that will attach properly to the AS/400 systems, IBM has added the **ValuePoint/400** to its product line of orderable systems. The ValuePoint/400 systems come with all the necessary hardware and are preloaded with Client Access Family. If you have an existing PC system that you desire to attach to an AS/400 system with an appropriate twinaxial, ASCII, or LAN interface, but not including the proper level of software, the AS/400 will detect this and automatically download the current level of Client Access Family, providing you with the selection of either the Windows 95/NT support or Windows 3.1/OS/2/DOS support.

Retail Workstations

Retail workstations are basically PCs with a cash drawer and with some unique characteristics added to interface with customers and sales items.

Those characteristics include the ability to print receipts on a rolling tape and acknowledge receipt of checks, the ability to present to the customer and the operator the price of what is being checked out, and an interface to at least one and sometimes several forms of UPC (Universal Product Code) barcode reader. With the advent of token-ring and Ethernet local area networks (LANs) on both the PC and the AS/400e series, a method for direct connection of those workstations now exists. An illustration of a retail workstation is shown in Figure 2.4. Of course, in some situations the retail workstation is connected via wireless methods. The AS/400e series in the retail environment will be discussed in greater detail in Chapter 5.

IBM Network Station 8361

The IBM Network Station 8361 is a cross between a personal computer and a traditional non-intelligent terminal (Figure 2.5). It provides the

Figure 2.4.   A typical retail workstation.

Figure 2.5. The IBM Network Station.

flexibility of a personal computer and cost approaching that of a non-intelligent terminal while connecting to a local area network (LAN), and eventually to either coaxial cable or twinaxial networks. The Network Station cannot function on its own because it receives its programming from a server over a LAN.

In early publications the IBM Network Station was referred to as the Thin Client. The IBM Network Station is used with a personal computer display (VGA or higher), a mouse, and a keyboard. There is a parallel port (e.g., for connection of a printer), a serial port (e.g., for connection of a modem), and a built-in speaker. The LAN connection can be either Ethernet (8361 Model 100) or token ring (8361 Model 200) or either (8361 Model 1000).

Network Stations use a PowerPC microprocessor (the 8361 Model 1000 uses a 200 MHz version of the PowerPC microprocessor). The IBM Network Station comes standard with 8 MB of memory (expandable to 64 MB) and 1 MB of video memory expandable to 2 MB. No disk or diskette drive (or any other auxiliary storage) is used with the Network Station. All programming and data is provided to the Network Station by an AS/400 server. The IBM Network Station can be used with all existing AS/400 application programs (about 25,000 or so) and provides a new graphical Windows-like user interface (Figure 2.6). Other functions that may be downloaded include 3270 emulation, UNIX, AIX, X-terminal software, remote windows applications, Web-based applications, a Web browser, and a Java virtual machine. This allows the execution of Java applets (application programs written in the Java programming language and downloaded on demand).

The network station boots up (gets started) from any AS/400 equipped with the supporting software (program 5733-A06 for V3R2 or 5733-A07 for V3R7, or, for V4R1, Navio NC Navigator or IBM Network Station Browser). It can also boot up from other types of servers provided they have the necessary supporting software. An additional

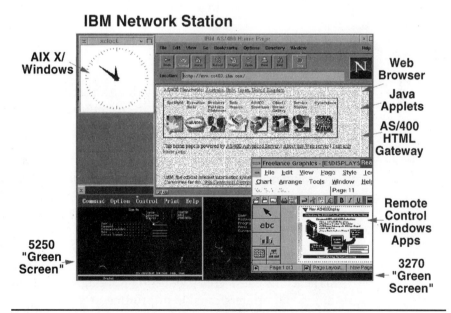

Figure 2.6. AS/400 ACXT Sample Screen, including Web Browser, Java Applets, AS/400 HTML Gateway, Remote Control Windows Apps, AIX X/Windows, 5250 Green Screen, and 3270 Green Screen.

piece of software that supports the Network Station is Network Station Manager for AS/400, which provides central client management for the Network Stations connected to the AS/400.

Printing Technology

Printing technologies have exploded, providing dramatically expanded choices in speed, resolution, connectivity, color, and paper handling function. The technology is important, but printing applications still drive printer decisions. Some of the key considerations are these:

- **Document Characteristics:** Electronic output documents, where the application composes the entire output page (as opposed to only variable data with preprinted forms), has greatly increased the use of electronic forms, bar coding, image and graphics, typographic fonts, and color. Preprinted forms remain a major requirement in many environments, particularly where carbon copies must be produced.

- **Printing Applications:** Where does the application reside, what output data stream is created, and where will it be printed.

- **Printer Location:** Where the printer will be located in the AS/400 computing environment, how will it communicate, and what systems and applications will be supported.

- **Relative Importance:** Where is the printing application on a scale from convenience or personal up to mission-critical. The characteristics and management required for mission-critical printing are normally significantly different from printing to a convenience printer.

- **Printing Volumes:** Printing at speed of 60 pages per minute and higher is generally considered production printing. The AS/400 supports individual printers capable of printing at greater than 1000 pages per minute. (InfoPrint 4000 Advanced Printing System)

- **Print Window:** Usually related to print volumes, the print window refers to the time duration available for a given print application. For example, a month-end statement run may need to be done within a three-day print window.

- **Printing Costs:** Includes both costs of acquisition and operational costs.

- **Other Factors:** Such as special forms, environmental considerations, etc.

AS/400 printing has traditionally meant printing simple lines of text on twinaxially connected impact printers. Printer decisions were primarily based on speed. With electronic printing, anything can be printed anywhere on the page. This has transformed the role of printing with business processes. The printed document becomes part of the organizational workflow. For example,

- Barcoded labels are scanned during order picking to automatically update shipped quantities.

- Documents with zip codes encoded in PostNet bar code are automatically routed by scanning equipment, and result in significantly lower mailing costs.

- Checks printed with MICR encoding are automatically processed.

- Payment coupons with invoice number and invoice amount encoded in bar code can be scanned upon receipt instead of being rekeyed.

- Scanned documents, such as checks or freight bills, can become part of the customer statement.

Electronic printing also means the design and quality of documents can be transformed through the use of typographic fonts, image, graphics and color. This provides for

- The elimination of preprinted forms, replacing them with applications that print the entire document on blank paper.

- The customization of documents for each customer, tailoring both design and message.

- Printed documents that are more effective and more readable, and that project a more professional corporate image.

Generally, AS/400 printed output comes from three types of applications, each with different print data streams or print languages:

- Line-at-a-time mode printing in SCS (SNA Character Set) format

- Page-mode printing in AFP (Advanced Function Printing) format

- Page-mode printing in ASCII format.

Traditional AS/400 output is lines of text and/or data in SCS printed a line at a time.

AFP applications have sophisticated electronic output, printing full pages instead of lines and using external print resources (electronic forms, fonts, images, graphics, and bar codes) in that process. Generally, these applications are created in system- and printer-independent format (AFP), then converted into printer-specific format (IPDS, or Intelligent Printer Data Stream). IPDS is termed "intelligent" because it is a two-way printing process with error recovery by page. IPDS printing is, in essence, a client/server application between the AS/400 (specifically, Print Services Facility/400) and the printer.

Client or LAN applications can create either line-mode or page-mode output, although most now tend to be full pages using either HP-PCL or Adobe PostScript print data streams. The AS/400 natively supports only AFP, SCS, IPDS, and line data formats. ASCII print formats, such as HP-PCL and PostScript, are supported through print transforms. As the AS/400 is a multiuser computing system, the print applications tend to be line-of-business ones with significant page volumes. Client or LAN applications, on the other hand, tend to be personal and have lower volumes.

Given these different kinds of printing applications the location of the printer becomes important. To date, most AS/400 printers have been twinaxially connected directly to the system. More and more, printers are LAN-connected, and organizations would like LAN-attached printers to handle both AS/400 and LAN print jobs.

Printers

Printer technology breaks down into two categories, impact and nonimpact. Within each of those categories are many subclasses, and line and page printers are available in each category. Impact printers essentially are divided into wire-matrix technology and band-matrix technology. Nonimpact printers include thermal fusion, inkjet, and laser. The business decision about which technology to select, impact or nonimpact, should be driven by the types of output documents required. If the output documents must have many copies that are legally guaranteed duplications (carbon copies), then impact printers must be used. If the required output documents are predominantly letters, memos, and so on, and a diskette or copy electronically stored is sufficient to meet the legal requirements, then nonimpact printers can be used. For the majority of businesses, the documentation requirements are a mixture of the two requirements, and some combination of the two types of printers will be required.

The remainder of the discussion of printers will discuss the characteristics of the printer technology as it relates to a business environment for each major category of both the impact and nonimpact printers, and a table will be provided that identifies the characteristics of some widely used IBM printers, listing at least one printer in each of the technologies. In the table, differences in the quality of print, the available throughput, the suitability of the printer for graphics output, and the external interface to the printer will be identified.

Impact Printers

Impact printers fit into two broad categories: wire-matrix and band printers. Band printers consist of straight alphanumeric band printers and matrix band printers. As mentioned earlier, the decision to use an impact printer should be driven by the need to produce carbon copies (documents of this type are commonly referred to as continuous forms). Five carbon copies are normally considered a maximum, after which the quality of the print deteriorates so badly that it may not be readable. In general, impact printers are noisy and, because of the forces involved, have been found to require a greater frequency of repair than nonimpact printers. As a result of the noise, impact printers should be located where they will disturb the fewest people. (See Chapter 4 for a detailed positioning of printing and electronic documents in the AS/400 environment.) Impact printers normally use pin-fed continuous forms. Impact printers can handle also non-text print elements such as bar codes, electronic forms, fonts and image

Wire-Matrix Technology.   Wire-matrix printers come in 9-wire and 18-wire formats. They produce documents by selectively firing magnetic hammers against the wires, which impact a print ribbon interposed between the wires and the document as the print head is scanned across the page. In general, the 9-wire printers produce a near-letter-quality document, whereas an 18-wire printer produces a letter-quality document. The wire-matrix printers produce good graphics output in black and white, but because the number of colors available in a ribbon is limited, the production of color is generally limited to three colors: black, red, and green, and little shade of gray differentiation. The available throughput varies from 60 to 700 characters per second, which correlates to 1 to 14 pages per minute. Graphical resolution varies from about 144 pels vertical by 240 pels horizontal for the 9-wire printers to 360 pels vertical by 360 pels horizontal for the 18-wire printers. Multiple fonts may be printed with relative ease with the wire-matrix technology printers. A pel is the number of dots which can be placed within a dimension of one inch either vertical or horizontal.

A new printer technology is the multiform printer. The IBM 4247 Multiform Printer supports up to two continuous form inputs and up to four cut-sheet form inputs. This provides the capability to combine printing applications and printers. For example, an IBM 4247 Multiform Printer can be set up with preprinted invoice forms in one continuous input, label stock for barcode labels in the other continuous input, and plain paper (for customer letters) in a cut sheet input.

Band Printers.   As mentioned earlier, band printers fit into two categories: the strict alphanumeric and expanded character set type, and the band-matrix type. The strict alphanumeric band printers produce letter-quality documents, but can do no graphics printing. The printer has a band with the characters that can be printed impregnated on it, a print ribbon is between the band and the document to be printed, and a set of hammers is moved across the document's surface. The band is moved in one direction at a very high speed, the hammers are moved across the document, and when a character to be printed is aligned with a hammer, the hammer is fired and drives the band into the ribbon, impressing the character onto the document. A 48-character band has four copies of each character on the band and four hammers, which are moved across the 80 or 132 possible print positions. A 128-character band has two character sets on the band for the same printer.

The throughput of the printer depends upon how fast the band is moving, how many characters constitute the print set, how many hammers there are, and how fast the hammers move across the paper. Some printers move the hammers at a fixed rate after every possible character has been optioned to that print position, some move their hammers when all have fired at the character for that print position, and some have a hammer for every print position, in which case when the hammers have all fired the line is complete and the document is moved. Character band printers can output documents at from 365 to 2200 lines per minute, which correlates to 7 to 67 pages per minute.

Shuttle-matrix printers (e.g., the 6408 and 6412) can produce limited graphics and near-letter-quality documents. Rather than using a band with all characters impregnated on it, shuttle-matrix printers use a shuttle that contains all the components necessary to make up a complete character. Each hammer must fire several times for each character position to form a full character from the components resident on the band. As a result, shuttle-matrix printers are typically slower than strict alphanumeric band printers. Also, the quality of the characters produced by shuttle-matrix printers is not quite as good as those produced by strict alphanumeric band printers because of fly-time variations, variations in belt speed, and the stretching/shrinking of the belt due to hammer impact. Shuttle-matrix printers produce documents at a rate of 475 to 1200 lines per minute, which correlates to about 10 to 24 pages per minute. Both of the band impact printers have the same difficulty as the matrix printer in producing multiple colors, and for the same reason: ribbon colors are limited. To change fonts, the band/shuttle must be changed. To change pitch, the band/shuttle must be changed and the hammer movement distance must also be changed.

The shuttle-matrix printers can produce limited graphics and near-letter-quality documents. Instead of having the *characters* impregnated on it, the shuttle has the *components* that make up a character impregnated on it. Each hammer must fire several times for each character position to form a full character from the components. Shuttle-matrix printers produce documents at a rate of 500 to 1400 lines per minute, which correlates to 10 to 42 pages per minute. The 6400-series printers can print in multiple fonts, pitches and lines per inch spacing under program control. Figure 2.7 shows a comparison and summary of the characteristics of various impact printer workstations available for the AS/400 System.

	4230 Matrix Printer	4232/4247 Matrix Printer	6252/6262 Impact Writer	6408/6412 Line Matrix Printer
Type	Near letter quality	Near letter quality	Letter quality	Near letter quality
Technology	9-wire dot matrix	9/18-wire dot matrix	Character band	Band matrix
Throughput Pages/min.	375–600 cps 1–16 ppm	200–700 700 cps 4–14 ppm	800–2200 lpm 24-67 ppm	500–1400 lpm 15–42 ppm
Graphics Resolution	144 pels vert. × 240 pels horiz.	144 pels 144 pels 4–8 colors	N/A	144 × 144 pels
Paper Handling	Continuous forms to 13.2"	Continuous forms to 13.2" +/ cutsheet	Continuous forms	Continuous forms
Data Stream Support	IPDS/ASCII/ APA/SCS	IPDS/AFP/ APA/SCS	SCS/ASCII	IPDS/SCS/ ASCII
Interface	Parallel or Twinax Serial	Parallel or Serial, Twinax, token-ring, ethernet	Twinaxial/ Serial, Parallel	Twinaxial/ Parallel (PC)/ token-ring/ ethernet
Desktop/Floor	Desktop	Desktop	Floor	Floor/Desktop

Figure 2.7. AS/400 impact printer summary comparison (ppm, pages per minute; cps, characters per second; lpm, lines per minute).

Nonimpact Printers

As stated previously, there are three general categories of nonimpact printer technology: thermal fusion, inkjet, and laser. Within those basic technologies, there are several variations. It is not the intention of this section to exhaustively describe the technologies, but to provide adequate information to assist in the business decision as to which printer might fit a particular business environment. The nonimpact printers to be discussed are called cut-sheet printers because they use the same single-sheet feed process and paper as a typewriter. They can all handle multiple fonts, and changing fonts and pitch requires only calling the desired font and pitch size.

Thermal Printers: Thermal printers are small and can easily be made portable. However, they require special heat-sensitive paper, and the paper eventually reacts to light, losing the image impressed. If portability is a requirement, the documents produced will be transposed to other media in a relatively short period of time (within a year), and the cost of the special paper does not create a problem, a thermal printer can be a good choice. Documents produced are of letter quality. Black-and-white printing is all that is available, and no distinguishable shades of gray can be produced, but graphics with a resolution of 360 pels by 360 pels is achievable. Throughput is slow—about 53 characters per second, which correlates to about a page per minute.

Inkjet Printers: Inkjet printers work by moving a set of nozzles from which ink can be sprayed across the surface of the document to be produced while that document is moved perpendicular to the nozzle scanning direction. Documents produced are of letter quality. Multiple colors of ink can be used, and the ink can be mixed to produce essentially any shade of color. Graphics can be produced with a resolution of 600 pels by 600 pels or greater. Throughput is from 83 to 400 characters per second, which correlates to 1 to 8 pages per minute.

Laser Printers: Although there are a number of different laser printing technologies, the basic concept is the same. The printer uses a laser to charge the surface of a drum in the image of the desired page. Ink or toner particles attach to the drum and are deposited on the paper as it is passed against the drum. Resolution, a fair determinant of print quality, is measured by the number of ink dots per inch deposited to compose the page. Laser resolutions are much higher than impact resolutions, and thus print quality is higher. This technology is also called EP, for ElectroPhotographic.

Laser printers are offered across a very broad spectrum, supporting applications from desktop to production printing and all points in between. As applications increase in print volumes, it becomes more critical to evaluate how the AS/400 interacts with and manages printing. For example, AS/400 AFP (Advanced Function Printing) applications can yield performance advantages because of an efficient data stream and efficient management of print resources (such as electronic forms and images). AFP applications also provide full page–level error recovery. This is less important if printing a 2-page spreadsheet, but critical when printing invoices at 30 pages per minute.

A new laser printer technology is the shared network printer. These printers can connect simultaneously to multiple servers (i.e., AS/400 and LAN) and can automatically handle print jobs in any "language" (such as SCS, IPDS, PostScript, and HP-PCL). (These "languages" are described in Chapter 4 under "Advanced Function Printing.") The IBM 3130 Advanced Function Printer and the IBM Network Printer family (Network 12, Network 17, and Network 24) are examples of shared network printers.

Laser printers provide throughput of from 5 to over 1000 pages per minute with the best print quality of any of the technologies discussed and also are quieter than any of the other printers in this section. See Figure 2.8 for a comparison and summary of nonimpact printers available for the AS/400.

Workstation Controllers

To attach any local workstation to an Application System computer system, the proper **workstation controller** must be installed in the computer's system unit or an expansion unit. (*Note:* Remote workstations are attached through communications lines, not through a workstation controller.) The workstation controller is a microprocessor-controlled intermediary between the workstation and the Application System processor. The workstation controller receives keystrokes

	4076 ExecJet II Printers	Network 12 Network 17 Network 24	Network Color	Infocol or 70	3160/3900 Infoprint Printers
Type	Letter quality	Letter quality	Letter quality	Letter quality	Letter quality
Technology	Inkjet	Laser/EP	ColorLaser	ColorLaser	Laser/EP
Throughput Pages/min. (ppm)	3	12-24	3 color, 12 mono	70	700
Graphics Resolution	600 pels × 300 pels	600 dots/ inch (dpi)	600 dpi	600 dpi	240 IPDS, 600 ASCII
Paper Handling	Cut sheet	Cut sheet	Cut sheet	Cut sheet	3160 cut sheet, 3900 fan fold paper
Data Stream Support	PPDS/APA	IPDS/ PostScript/ PCL	PostScript	IPDS, PostScript	IPDS, PostScript, PCL
Interface	Serial	Twinax serial, parallel, token-ring, ethernet	Serial, parallel, ethernet or token-ring	Token-ring, ethernet	Token-ring, ethernet, channel
Desktop/ Floor	Desktop	Desktop/ floor	Floor	Floor	Floor

Figure 2.8. AS/400 nonimpact printer comparison and summary.

from the workstation and sends back formatted views of screens for display on the terminal of the workstation. Managing the workstation traffic (e.g., keystrokes) leaves the system processor in the Application System computer free to run user application programs. The result of this multiprocessor architecture, as was discussed in Chapter 1, is that the AS/400 system is able to do more work in a given amount of time. Two types of workstation controllers can be used with AS/400 computers: twinaxial workstation controllers and ASCII workstation controllers.

Twinaxial Workstation Controllers

Twinaxial workstation controllers are the most commonly used type of controller. They allow the attachment of the most popular workstations (including all terminals and printers discussed in this book). The controller itself is cabled to a box that provides twinaxial connectors. One end of a twinaxial cable is attached to one of the connectors, called a port, on the box. The other end of the cable can be attached to from one to seven local workstations in a daisy-chain fashion over a distance of up to 5000 feet (see Figure 1.51). This daisy-chain feature is called **cable-thru** and greatly simplifies the wiring needed to connect workstations to an AS/400 system. Information moves through the twinaxial cable at over a million bits per second (bps), allowing for fast information flow.

The Entry Model 150 can support 7 twinaxial terminals in the entry version and 28 twinaxial terminals in the growth version. The LAN versions can support a maximum of 28 twinaxial terminals. The AS/400e system 600 and AS/400e system 620 come standard with base twinaxial support (feature code 9720). Base twinaxial support provides for up to 28 local workstations (any mix of terminals and printers) daisy-chained over 4 ports (up to 7 workstations per port). Feature 2722 provides 8 twinaxial ports with up to 40 active workstations. By adding multiple 2722 Twinaxial Workstation Controllers, up to 188 workstations can be attached to a Model 600, and, by using the Portable Computer Interface (PCI) adapters, the SPD bus-attached 6050 Twinaxial Workstation Controller, and the 6180 Twinaxial Workstation Adapter connecting 40 workstations for each instance of usage, up to 2392 workstations can be attached to a Model 620. A 9176 or 9177 Client Access Console can also be attached to base LAN machines. Because of their orientation to LAN operation, the S10 and S20 servers can support a maximum of 28 twinaxially connected workstations connected via 9720 base twinaxial support.

The AS/400e system 640 and the AS/400e system 650 come standard with a twinaxial workstation controller or an ASCII workstation controller. The twinaxial workstation controller for the 9406 provides 8 ports that can support a total of 40 workstations (no more than 7 on any one port). By adding optional 6050 Twinaxial Workstation Controllers, Model 640 and Model 650 can support up to 7000 twinaxially attached workstations over 175 workstation controllers, respectively.

The AS/400e server S30 and e server S40 can have 1 twinaxial workstation controller attached, providing for a maximum of 28 workstations.

For all AS/400e series twinaxial workstation connections, a 20-foot cable is attached between the controller and an external box that provides the 8 port connectors. This external box is designed to be mounted on the floor, wall, or tabletop. From 1 to 175 twinaxial workstation controllers can be installed in a single AS/400 9406 system for attaching those workstations.

ASCII Workstation Controllers

Although twinaxial workstations are preferred with AS/400 systems, the systems can also support low-cost American Standard Code for Information Interchange (ASCII) terminals and printers. ASCII workstations transfer information at a slower rate (maximum of 38,400 bits per second [bps]) than twinaxial workstations (1 million bps). However, an ASCII workstation controller is useful if you already have a significant investment in ASCII terminals and printers, because it allows you to use them with an AS/400 system. There is no ASCII workstation controller for either AS/400 Advanced Entry Model 150, or for the AS/400e Model 170 in either its general purpose computing system or server versions or Model 600s, or for the AS/400 e server S10. The AS/400e system 620 and AS/400e server 620 are only capable of attaching ASCII terminals if the SPD bus system unit expansion or optically connected expansion towers are present. The AS/400e system 640 and 650 and the AS/400e server S30 and S40 are capable of accepting ASCII workstation support in the base system unit. Base ASCII workstation support (feature code 9171) can be selected for inclusion in the standard configuration of any of the last identified systems. The 9171 ASCII workstation controller is able to support up to 12 workstations (6 terminals and 6 printers) over 6 ASCII ports. Actually, 1 terminal or 1 printer is cabled directly to each of the 6 ports—making for 6 devices.

To get to the base ASCII support's configuration maximum of 12 ASCII devices, you must directly cable 6 ASCII terminals to the 6 ASCII ports and then attach 1 printer to each terminal, totaling 12 devices. Adding the 6142 ASCII 12-Port Workstation Attachment adds 12 more ASCII ports for a total of 18. This allows 18 ASCII devices (any combination of terminals and printers) to be directly attached to the AS/400e system 6XX/SXX. Although this also allows up to 36 ASCII devices to be attached (18 terminals and 18 printers cabled to the terminals), 18 simultaneously active ASCII devices are the maximum number supported on a base ASCII attachment. The server systems identified earlier are capable of supporting only the base ASCII attachment. No expansion of ASCII terminals beyond the base is allowed.

To attach more ASCII workstations to e-systems that are not server systems, you can install one or more optional 6141 ASCII Workstation Controllers, each of which will add 6 ASCII ports to the system. For further expansion and more flexibility, you can add a 6142 ASCII 12-Port Workstation Attachment to each 6141 ASCII Workstation Controller. By adding a 6142 ASCII 12-Port Workstation Attachment to a 6141 ASCII Workstation Controller, you go from 6 ports capable of supporting 6 ASCII terminals and 6 ASCII printers to 18 ports capable of supporting 18 ASCII workstations (any combination of terminals and printers). The Model 620 can have up to 58 ASCII workstation controllers, each equipped with an ASCII 12-port workstation attachment, which provides for up to 1044 ASCII workstations.

As with the Model 620, Model 640 and Model 650 include support for twinaxial or ASCII workstations in their standard configuration. For those who choose ASCII support, a 6141 ASCII Workstation Controller is included in the standard configuration. In this standard ASCII workstation configuration, you can have up to 12 workstations attached to a system (6 terminals and 6 printers) over 6 ports. Again, 1 terminal or 1 printer is cabled directly to each of the 6 ports, making for 6 devices. To get to the standard configuration's maximum of 18 ASCII devices, you must add the 6142 ASCII 12-Port Workstation Attachment. Since 18 is also the maximum number of workstations that an ASCII workstation controller can handle, you get 1 port for each device and thus the flexibility to attach any combination of terminals and printers. The Model 640 and Model 650 support up to 175 ASCII workstation controllers. If each ASCII workstation controller is equipped with an ASCII 12-port workstation attachment, you can have 3150 ASCII workstations attached to each of these systems. The AS/400e server S20, S30, and S40 will only support a single ASCII workstation controller because of its LAN orientation, and only 6 ASCII workstation devices may be connected to that workstation controller.

LAN-Connected Terminals

Additional workstations may be attached to the local area networks (LANs) supported by these systems. These terminals must be intelligent terminals, including personal computers, network stations, or retail terminals. Each LAN can support up to 256 terminal addresses. The Model 150 with 2 LANs can attach 512 intelligent terminals, either personal computers or network stations. The Model 170 with up to six LAN ports can attach 1536 intelligent terminals. The Model 600 and S10 with 3 LANs allowed can attach 768 terminals. The Model 620 and S20 can attach 4096 intelligent terminals through 16 LANs. The Model 640 and S30 can attach 8196 intelligent terminals through 32 LANs. The Model 650 and S40 can attach 12,288 terminals through 48 LAN connections. The Model S40-SB1 can attach 1280 intelligent terminals through 5 LANs. The S30 and S20 ISV models can support the same number of LANs as the servers they derive from the S20 and S30.

Protocol Converters

Whether a workstation is attached locally or remotely, it must speak the same "language" or **workstation protocol** as the computer system and its programs. You should be aware of (but not necessarily understand) three workstation protocols: 5250 protocol, 3270 protocol, and ASCII protocol.

The **5250 protocol** is the set of rules used by workstations designed specifically for use with Application System computers as well as earlier System/36 and System/38 computers. The 5250 protocol and twinaxial cable can be considered the "native tongue" of IBM's Application Systems. The protocol gets its name from the 5250 family of workstations designed for the System/3X family. The **3270 protocol** is the set of rules used by workstations designed specifically for use with IBM's larger System/390 family of mainframe computers. This protocol gets its name from the 3270 family of workstations designed for the System/390 computers. Finally, the **ASCII protocol** is the set of rules used by a wide variety of devices (including terminals and printers) made for the computers of many different computer manufacturers.

If the user wishes to attach a workstation using a workstation protocol different from that being used by the AS/400 computer system, a **protocol converter** is required. This is a stand-alone device that accepts information from a workstation using the workstation protocol and converts that information to the desired workstation protocol being used by the computer system. The protocol converter can be thought of as a "translator" that sits between the workstation and the computer. There are many situations in which a user might need a protocol converter (for example, the user has a workstation that uses the 3270 protocol attached to a S/390 Computer System. Alternatively, a user might be switching from a computer that primarily uses an ASCII workstation to Application Systems. With a protocol converter, the investment in ASCII terminals could be preserved by using them with the Application Systems. However, the ASCII workstation controller is the preferred way of attaching ASCII devices to AS/400 systems. With protocol conversion native to the AS/400 via the MultiProtocol Transporting Network Architecture, external protocol converters are no longer necessary to attach ASCII or 3270 workstations. Those who already possess protocol converters may still use them with the AS/400.

Main Storage Expansion Options

Nothing seems to grow faster than the computer user's appetite for main storage. Several different options allow the user to expand the main storage in AS/400 computers. However, because of technical differences inside the systems, main storage expansion options are not necessarily interchangeable between the different Application System models.

Model 150 Main Storage Capacities

The AS/400 Model 150 comes standard with 64 MB of main storage in the entry version and 128 MB in the growth version. That base main storage may be expanded by adding either one or two additional 64-MB DIMM modules (3110) or 32-MB DIMM modules (3182) until a maximum total main storage capacity of 192 MB is achieved. (The DIMM Module is an industry standard for packaging silicon storage devices.)

The range of main storage sizes for the 9401 Model 150 is shown in Figure 2.9. All main storage plugs into the processor card and uses no I/O slot capability.

436 Main Storage Capacities

The AS/400 Model 436, when using processors 2102 or 2104, starts at 32 MB of main storage, which can be increased in 32-or 64-MB increments a total of three times to reach a maximum capacity of 224 MB. When using the 2106 processor, the Advanced 36 Model 436 starts with a base main storage capacity of 64 MB and can also be expanded a total of three times using the same 32- or 64-MB SIMM modules to achieve a maximum storage capacity of 256 MB. Figure 2.10 illustrates the main storage capacities supported by each of the Advanced 36 processor options.

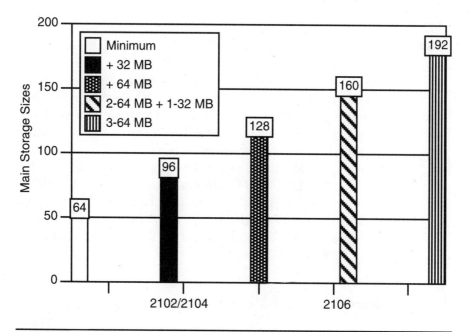

Figure 2.9. AS/400e system 150 main storage sizes.

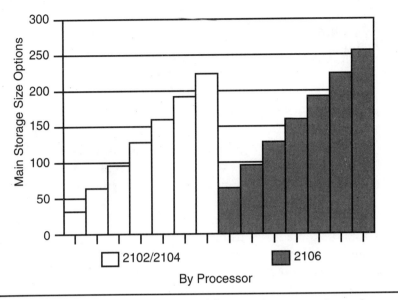

Figure 2.10. AS/400 Advanced 36 Model 436 main storage size options.

Model 170 Main Storage Expansion Options

The Model 170 supports the same main storage cards as the Model 600 and the S10, 64 MB, 128 MB, and 256 MB DIMM packages. The Model 170 systems with processors 2159 and 2160 start with the 64 MB DIMM and can grow to 832 MB by adding three 256 MB DIMM cards. The base 64 MB DIMM card continues to be used.

The AS/400 Model 170 systems with processors 2164, 2176, and 2183 start with a 128 MB DIMM card and can grow to 1024 MB by adding three 256 MB DIMM cards and replacing the base 128 MB DIMM card with a 256 MB DIMM card. Figure 2.11 illustrates the range of options available in main storage size defined by the processor present in the Model 170 systems.

Model 600 and S10 Main Storage Expansion Options

All Model 600 and S10 systems come standard with either 64 MB or 128 MB of main storage depending on the processor option selected.

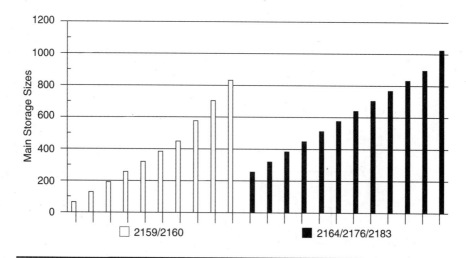

Figure 2.11. AS/400e system 170 main storage size options by processor.

Those Model 600 systems with a 2129, 2134, or 2135 Processor and Model S10 systems with the 2118 Processor start with 64 MB and can accommodate up to five additional 32-MB main storage (3182) or 64-MB main storage (3110) features, making for a maximum of 384 MB.

Model 600 systems with 2136 Processors and Model S10 systems with 2119 Processors start with 128 KB of main storage and can be expanded by installing three additional pairs of 32-MB main storage features (3182) or three pairs of 64-MB main storage features (3110). The maximum capacity for these models is 512 MB. Figure 2.12 illustrates the main storage capacities for these systems.

Model 620 and S20 Main Storage Expansion Options

All Model 620 and S20 systems come standard with a 256-MB base main storage plugged into a riser card, which plugs into the processor card.

- Model 620 systems with the 2179 Processor can accept either fourteen 32-MB DIMM main storage 3001 Expansion Cards plugged into the riser card or fourteen 128-MB DIMM main

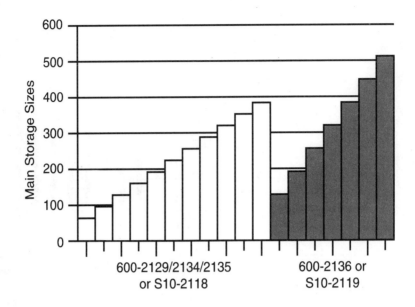

Figure 2.12. AS/400e system 600 and server S10 main storage size options by processor.

storage 3002 Expansion Cards plugged into the riser card, for a total capacity of 2048 MB of main storage.

- Model 620 systems with the 2180 Processor or Model S20 systems with the 2161 Processor can accept either fourteen 32-MB DIMM cards or fourteen 128-MB DIMM cards plugged into the riser card, for a total of 2048 MB of main storage.

- Model 620 systems with a 2181 Processor or S20 systems with a 2163 Processor can accept fourteen 32-MB DIMM cards or fourteen 128-MB DIMM cards plugged into the riser for a total capacity of 2048 MB of main storage.

- Model 620 systems with a 2182 Processor and Model S20 systems with a 2165 or 2166 Processor can accept up to thirty 32-MB or 128-MB DIMM cards to reach a total capacity of 4096 MB of main storage.

Figure 2.13 shows the possible main storage configurations available in Model 620 and S20 systems. (*Note:* In all cases, the DIMM cards regardless of their size must be installed in pairs of the same size.)

Model 640 and S30 Main Storage Expansion Options

Model 640 and S30 systems with processors 2257, 2258, 2259, and 2320 come standard with 512 MB of main storage and ten main storage expansion slots in the processor cage. To achieve the maximum main storage size of 12,288 MB, twelve 1024-MB main storage cards (3192) must be installed, including replacement of the two base 256-MB main storage cards. Other main storage sizes can be achieved by installing up to twelve 128-MB (3189), 256-MB (3190), or 512-MB (3191) main storage expansion cards in the available slots (installed in pairs of identical cards).

Model S30 with processors 2260, 2321, and 2322 comes standard with four base main storage cards and eight feature main storage slots. The base main storage is 1024 MB and can be expanded in groups of four identical mains storage cards to 12,288 MB. Figure 2.14 shows the main storage configurations available on Model 640 and S30 systems.

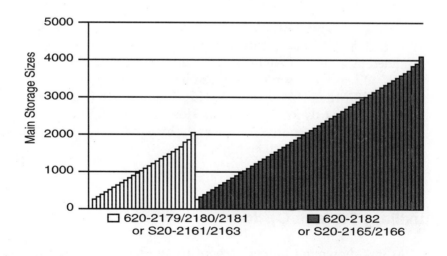

Figure 2.13. AS/400e system 620 and server S20 main storage size options by Processor.

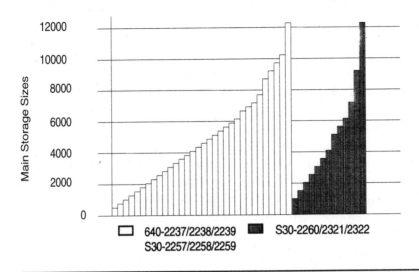

Figure 2.14. AS/400e system 640 and server S30 main storage size options by Processor.

Model 650 and S40 Main Storage Expansion Options

Model 650 and S40 systems come standard with 1024 MB of main storage and 16 main storage expansion slots. Main storage cards are added in groups of four identical cards for a total capacity of 20,480 MB. Other main storage sizes can be achieved by installing up to sixteen 128-MB (3189), 256-MB (3190), or 512-MB (3191) main storage expansion cards in the available slots (again installed in sets of four identical cards). Figure 2.15 shows the main storage capacities supported by Model 650 and S40 systems.

Auxiliary Storage Options

As was shown in Chapter 1, there are five basic types of auxiliary storage devices used with Application Systems:

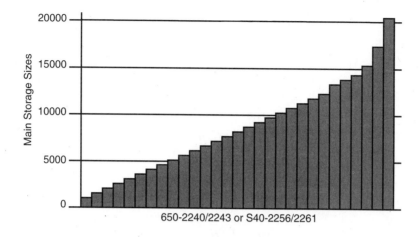

Figure 2.15. AS/400e system 650 and server S40 main storage size options by Processor.

1. Diskettes

2. Disk units

3. CD-ROM

4. Tape

5. Optical

Let us now look at the specific auxiliary storage options available for the Application Systems.

Diskette Storage

Diskette storage is commonly used by many different types of computer systems. It provides a convenient way to transfer small amounts of information between systems. Although diskettes can also be used for making backup copies of the information stored on disk units, they lack the storage capacity to be effective for this, particularly for larger disk units. AS/400 systems do not come standard with any diskette storage, but several options allow the user to have diskette storage on AS/400 systems.

Diskettes consist of a flexible circular magnetic medium enclosed in a square package. Diskettes are manually inserted into a diskette unit that spins them inside the jacket. The **read/write head** inside the diskette unit makes contact with the spinning disk much as a record player's needle contacts a record. As the disk spins, the head magnetically reads and writes information on the disk's surface. All AS/400e systems can be configured with diskette units that allow them to use diskettes either 5¼ inches or 8 inches in diameter (or both). Either type of diskette can hold up to 1.2 MB (million bytes) of information. (*Note:* The Entry system supports a 5¼-inch diskette drive option, but IBM does not offer an 8-inch diskette drive option for that system.)

9331 Model 11 and 9331 Model 12 Diskette Units

Either the 5¼-inch diskette unit 9331 Model 012 or the 8-inch diskette unit 9331 Model 011 can be externally attached to most AS/400 systems (except the Models 150, 170, 600, and S10) using a 6146 Diskette Adapter. This adapter attaches to the internal 2624 Tape Control Unit. Alternately, some (mostly older) AS/400 systems attach these diskette units via the 6112 Diskette Controller. The combination of adapter and diskette unit is useful for moving information between similarly equipped AS/400 systems, AS/Entry 9402 Y10 systems, or earlier System/36 and System/38 computers. However, this diskette unit is not compatible with the 5¼-inch diskettes used by IBM personal computers. Figure 2.16 shows the 9331 Model 12 5¼-inch diskette unit.

Disk Storage

All Application Systems need disk storage, also called a **Direct Access Storage Device (DASD)**, to be a complete computer system. We look at several options that allow the user to provide or expand the disk storage of Application Systems. Chapter 1 covered the standard and maximum disk storage configurations for all Application Systems. Figure

Figure 2.16.   The 9331 5.25-inch Diskette Unit for the AS/400 Advanced Series models.

2.17 summarizes the characteristics of the various disk units supported by the AS/400e systems. Here we look at the integrated disk storage options themselves and the new disk adapters as follows:

- AS/400 Advanced Entry Model 150 disk options

- AS/400 Advanced 36 Model 436 disk options

- AS/400e server 170 disk options

- AS/400e system 600 and S10 disk options

- AS/400e system 620 and S20 disk options

- AS/400e system 640 and S30 disk options

- AS/400e system 650 and S40 disk options

- AS/400 Disk Adapters

To be used in the 6XX or SXX systems, the disk units listed in Figure 2.17 may have to be packaged in either a tray or a carrier.

Feature Number	Disk Description	CEC	Storage Expansion Units and Tower					
			5052	5055	5057	5058	5082	5083
1602	Single Disk Unit Kit (1.03 GB)	X	X^1		X^1	X^1		
1603	Single Disk Unit Kit (1.96 GB)	X	X^1		X^1	X^1		
6605	1.03-GB Disk Unit /A	X	X	X	X	X	X	X
6606	1.96-GB Disk Unit /A	X	X	X	X	X	X	X
6607	4.19-GB Disk Unit /A	X	X	X	X	X	X	X
6650	Additional Disk Unit /A (1.96 GB)	X	X	X	X	X	X	X
6652	Additional Disk Unit /A (1.03 GB)	X	X	X	X	X	X	X
6713	8.58-GB Disk Unit	X^2	X^2	X^2	X^2	X^3	X^2	X^2
6906	8.58-GB Disk Unit	X^2	X^3	X^2	X^2	X^2	X^3	X^2
6907	1.96-GB Disk Unit	X^2	X^3	X^2	X^2	X^2	X^3	X^2
7607	Optional Disk (4.19 GB) Unit	X	X	X	X	X	X	X
7713	Optional Base 8.58-GB Disk Unit	X^2	X^3	X^2	X^2	X^2	X^3	X^2

Figure 2.17. Description of the disk units compatible with V4R2. *(continued on next page)*

Entry Model 150 Disk Options

The Model 150 system units come standard with 4.19 GB of disk storage mounted inside the system unit. The 4.194-GB of storage provided by the 3.5-inch disk unit (feature code 6907) can be expanded by adding up to three additional disk units, each with an additional capacity of either 4.19 GB or 8.58 GB, to achieve a total maximum capacity of 29.9 GB.

Feature Number	Disk Description	Storage Expansion Units and Tower						
		CEC	5052	5055	5057	5058	5082	5083
8713	Optional Base 8.58-GB Disk Unit	X^2	X^3	X^2	X^2	X^2	X^3	X^2
6714	Optional Feature 17.54-GB Disk Unit	X^6	X^3	X^2	X^2	X^2	X^3	X^2
8714	Optional Base 17.54-GB Disk Unit	X^5	X^3	X^2	X^2	X^2	X^3	X^2
6824	Optional Feature 17.54-GB Disk Unit	X^7	X^3	X^2	X^2	X^2	X^3	X^2
8824	Optional Base 17.54-GB Disk Unit	X^4	X^3	X^2	X^2	X^2	X^3	X^2
9606	Base Disk Unit (1.96-GB)	X	X	X	X	X	X	X
9907	Base 4.19-GB Disk Unit	X^2	X^3	X^2	X^2	X^2	X^3	X^2

[1] Single-byte disk units cannot be placed into slots K8 through K16,
[2] For best performance use with an Ultra-SCSI disk unit controller,
[3] No Ultra-SCSI when attached to this storage expansion unit,
[4] Optional base disk unit for Models 600/620/S10/S20/170,
[5] Optional base disk unit for Models 640/650/S30/S40/170,
[6] Optional feature disk unit for Models 500/510/530/620/640/650/S20/S30/S40/50S/170.
[7] Optional feature disk unit for Models 600/620/S10/S20/170.

Figure 2.17. Description of the disk units compatible with V4R2. *(continued from previous page)*

Advanced System 36 Model 436 Disk Options

Advanced System 36 Model 436 systems come standard with 1030 MB of disk storage in the base system. The standard disk storage is made up of one 1030-MB 3.5-inch disk unit (6605) that resides in the system unit. To expand disk storage in System 36 Model 436, three 1960-MB 3.5-inch disk units (6606) or three 1030-MB disk units (6605) can be added. All of these base system unit disk storage units must be 2-byte SCSI compatible. Adding any of the feature disk storage units beyond the second disk storage unit requires adding the 5135 Expansion Unit Power Supply. Disk storage can be expanded by a further eight disk storage units, to a total capacity of 23,600 MB, with the addition of the 7117 Storage Expansion Unit. The 7117 Storage Expansion Unit uses the same disk storage units as the base system unit to achieve the System 436 system's maximum capacity of 23,600 MB.

The first four disk units are attached to the 9751 MultiFunction I/O Processor (MFIOP) using a Fast and Wide SCSI interface that performs at 20 MB per second. Data protection may be invoked against a disk unit failure using data mirroring if all disk units are the same size. The eight disk units that can be added using the 7117 Storage Expansion Unit can be data protected using either data mirroring or RAID-5 parity protection. In either of these cases, all disk units must be the same size. Data mirroring may be accomplished with either the 6523 Storage Controller or the 6522 RAID-5 Controller.

Model 170 Disk Options

AS/400e system 170 comes standard with a 3½-inch 4,194-MB disk unit (6907) in the system unit. To expand disk storage in these systems, four more 4,194-MB disk units or five 3½-inch 8,580-MB disk units (6713) can be added, including replacing the base 4,194-MB disk unit.

To attain the maximum disk storage capacity for this model of 85.8 GB, a second disk cage can be added to accommodate five additional disk units (either of those mentioned above). To perform this addition, the bolt on expansion side-car must be added. Disk data protection can be invoked using either data mirroring or RAID 5. All disks are connected to the multi-function I/O processor (MFIOP) using an Ultra SCSI interface. All internal disk units listed for this model in Figure 2.17 are placed in a carrier tray to enable the drives to be concurrently maintained.

Model 600 and S10 Disk Options

AS/400e system 600 and server S10 come standard with a 3½-inch 4,194-MB disk unit (6907) in the system unit. To expand disk storage in these systems, four more 4,194-MB disk units or five 3½-inch 8,580-MB disk units (6713), or five 17.54-GB disk units (6714) can be added, including replacing the base 4,194-MB disk unit. To attain the maximum disk storage capacity for these models of 175.4 GB, a second disk cage can be added to accommodate five additional disk units (either of those mentioned here). Disk data protection can be invoked using either data mirroring or RAID 5. All disks are connected to the MultiFunction I/O Processor (MFIOP) using an Ultra-SCSI interface. All internal disk units listed for this model in Figure 2.17 are placed in a carrier tray to enable the drives to be concurrently maintained.

Model 620 and S20 Disk Options

AS/400e system 620 and server S20 come standard with a 3½-inch 4,194-MB disk unit that resides in one of the five spaces available for disk storage in the system unit. The standard 4,194-MB disk unit can be replaced with an optional 8,580-MB disk unit (7713) or an optional 17,540-MB disk unit (6714), and up to four additional disk units can be added in the base system unit without modification.

All system units regardless of processor type can accept a feature disk expansion cage (7128) into which five more disk units can be plugged. Model 620 systems with processors 2181 and 2182 and Model S20 systems with processors 2163, 2165, 2166, 2177, and 2178 can have a third disk expansion cage 7128 in the power compartment.

On Model 620 and S20 systems, up to 15 additional disk units may be added to these systems by means of the bolt-on 9364 System Expansion Unit. Further, the 5052 Storage Expansion Unit can be used to add another 16 disk units. Up to 15 additional disk units can be added to Model S20 systems through the 5064 System Expansion Unit. An additional 16 disk units can be added to either the Model 620 or S20 by adding the 5081 Storage Expansion Towers, to which may be added the 5068 Storage Expansion Units. Multiple storage expansion towers and storage expansion units may be added to Model 620 and S20 systems until a total disk storage capacity of 944.8 GB is reached.

Disk units used with Model 620 and S20 systems may be Ultra-SCSI or 1-byte Fast or Fast and Wide SCSI compatible. Figure 2.17 lists the compatible disk units that may be used with these systems. All internal disk units listed for this model in Figure 2.17 are placed in a carrier tray to enable the drives to be concurrently maintained.

All of the system unit disks are driven from the MultiFunction I/O Processor (MFIOP) with an Ultra-SCSI interface if the devices used can support the performance. These disk units may be concurrently maintained; that is, the units may be unplugged and replugged while the system continues to operate with no physical damage to either the disk units or the system (with no data loss if either data mirroring or RAID-5 has been enabled). AS/400e server S20-ISV supports the same disk unit capacity as the S20.

Model 640 and S30 Disk Options

AS/400e system 640 and server S30 come standard with 4,194 MB of disk storage provided by a 3½-inch disk unit (feature code 6907), which takes up one of the four spaces available for disk storage in the system unit. This disk unit may be replaced with the 8.580-GB 3½-inch disk unit (6713) or with the 17.54-GB 3½-inch disk unit (6714).

An additional eight disk storage units may be added by installing two 5055 Disk Cages inside the system unit. An additional eight storage units may be added by including a 5058 Storage Expansion Unit on the top of the system unit.

Additional disk units can be added to the system by connecting a 5082 Storage Expansion Tower and a corresponding 5058 Storage Expansion Unit. Each 5058 Storage Expansion Unit supports up to 16 additional disk units. Storage expansion towers and storage expansion units may continue to be added until a maximum disk unit capacity of 1340.0 GB is achieved. The Model S30-ISV supports the same capacity as the S30.

All disk storage in the Model 640 and Model S30 system units is Ultra-SCSI compatible and is attached to the MultiFunction I/O Processor (MFIOP). Supported disk storage units are listed in Figure 2.17. All internal disk units listed for this model in Figure 2.17 are placed in a carrier to enable the drives to be concurrently maintained.

The disk units in the system unit may be concurrently maintained if data mirroring or RAID-5 have been enabled. That is, these disk units may be unplugged and replugged while the system continues to operate with no physical damage to either the units or the system and no data loss.

Model 650 and S40 Disk Options

AS/400e system 650 and AS/400e server S40 come standard with 4,194 MB of disk storage. The standard disk storage is made up of one 4,194-

MB 3½-inch disk unit (feature code 6907) that takes one of the four spaces available for disk storage in the I/O tower of the system unit. The 4,194-MB disk unit may be replaced with the 8.580-GB 3½-inch disk unit (6713) or with the 17.54-GB 3½-inch disk unit (6714).

An additional 16 disk storage units may be added by including a 5058 Storage Expansion Unit on the top of the I/O tower of the system unit. More disk units can be added to the system by connecting a 5082 Storage Expansion Tower and a corresponding 5058 Storage Expansion Unit. Each 5058 Storage Expansion Unit supports up to 16 additional disk units. Storage expansion towers and storage expansion units may continue to be added until a maximum disk unit capacity of 1546.1 GB is achieved. The exception to this maximum disk storage capacity is the Model S40-SB1, which has a disk storage capacity range of 16.77 GB to 34.35 GB.

All disk storage on Model 650 and S40 systems is Ultra-SCSI compatible and is attached to the MultiFunction I/O Processor (MFIOP). Supported disk storage units are listed in Figure 2.17. All internal disk units listed for this model in Figure 2.17 are placed in a carrier tray to enable the drives to be concurrently maintained. The disk units in the system unit may be concurrently maintained if data mirroring or RAID-5 have been enabled. That is, these disk units may be unplugged and replugged while the system continues to operate with no physical damage to either the units or the system and no data loss.

AS/400 Disk Adapters

Disk adapters provide the circuitry necessary to transfer information between any attached disk units and the AS/400 main storage. These disk adapters (also called **Input/Output Processors** or **IOPs**) have their own computing power used to lessen the burden on the AS/400's main processor(s) when it comes to moving information to and from disk units.

A **MultiFunction I/O Processor** or **MFIOP** (9751) is provided with every AS/400 system and fills the role of disk adapter for the disk unit(s) that come as standard equipment (and for up to 19 additional disk units). The MFIOP supports two data protection algorithms called **data mirroring** and **RAID-5**. These data protection algorithms insure that in the case of a disk unit failure, no data is lost.

The 6502 Disk Unit Controller for RAID is an integrated disk storage controller with a 2-MB write cache to support internally attached disk units. Like the MFIOP, this disk adapter provides RAID-5 protection for internal disk units installed in the storage expansion units (5052, 5082, or 7117). Alternately, disk units attached through this adapter (and not in a RAID-5 array) can be mirrored.

The 6512 Disk Unit Controller for RAID is available for use as a disk storage controller. The 6512 provides an increased write-cache size (4 MB) and a faster microprocessor than the 6502.

The 2726 Disk Unit Controller is a PCI-bus-compatible disk adapter. The 2726 operates from the MFIOP as a controller for the disk devices. Both RAID-5 and data mirroring are supported. The 2726 can control up to 20 disk units of the types supported on a 40-MB Ultra-SCSI interface.

When fewer than five disk units are installed and RAID-5 is not desired, the 9728 Disk I/O Adapter can be used. This adapter is a PCI adapter that attaches to a MFIOP or to the MIKADO controller (the MFIOP for the PCI-bus-based systems).

Those needing to attach 9337 disk units to AS/400 9406 systems can use the 6500/6501 Disk Controller. This adapter consumes one I/O slot and uses the Small Computer System Interface (SCSI), which transfers information at an instantaneous rate of 5 Mbps.

The 6532 is the newest and fastest SPD bus disk controller. This disk adapter supports 20 disk storage units and supports both data mirroring and RAID-5 data protection. It uses an Ultra-SCSI interface to communicate with disk units.

The 6533 RAID Disk Unit Controller is a disk/tape controller that interfaces to internal disk and tape devices through Ultra-SCSI and provides RAID-5 protection and includes a 4-MB write cache. In addition to Ultra-SCSI, Fast and Wide, and Fast and Narrow SCSI devices may be controlled. The 6533 also can control disks protected by system mirroring or disks with no protection. The 6533 controller is disk compression enabled and can control a maximum of 16 drives. When placed in a system expansion unit (5064/9364), the 6533 can also support up to three internal tapes in addition to the 16 drives. The 6533 controls disk units installed in the 5058 Storage Expansion Units and 5083 Storage Expansion Towers, and can also control disk units installed in the 5052 Storage Expansion Unit and 5082 Storage Expansion Tower. When controlling disk units installed in the 5052 or 5082, the speed is limited to Fast and Wide or Fast and Narrow performance. For additional information on RAID-5 and System Mirroring see "Disk Failure Protection" in Chapter 4.

The 2740 PCI RAID Disk Unit Controller is an Ultra-SCSI disk and tape/CD-ROM controller including a 4-MB write cache that provides RAID-5 protection for internal disk units. The 2740 PCI RAID Disk Unit Controller works with Ultra, Fast and Wide, and Fast and Narrow SCSI disk and tape units installed in the base system unit. In addition to providing RAID-5 protection, the 2740 also works with disks protected by system mirroring or disks with no protection. The 2740 controller supports a maximum of 10 drives, plus one tape and one CD-ROM when installed in the system unit.

The 2741 PCI RAID Disk Unit Controller is a disk/tape controller that interfaces through Ultra-SCSI to drives, provides RAID-5 protection, and includes a 4-MB write cache. In addition to Ultra-SCSI, Fast and Wide and Fast and Narrow SCSI devices may be controlled. The 2741 also can control disks protected by system mirroring or disks with no protection. The 2741 controller is disk compression enabled and can control a maximum of 15 drives. The controller can also support one tape unit and one CD-ROM when placed in a system unit. When placed in a system expansion unit (5064/9364), the 2741 can also support up to three internal tapes in addition to the 15 drives. One high-speed PCI card slot is required in any unit where the 2741 is to be placed. For additional detail on RAID and System mirroring see "Disk Failure" in Chapter 4. Figure 2.18 shows the number of disk controllers supported by AS/400e system models.

Tape Storage

Computer systems are woven deeply into today's businesses and usually become the core of day-to-day operations. The information stored on the computer is itself a valuable asset and therefore must be protected like any other asset. Magnetic tape storage provides a cost-effective and efficient means of backing up the information on the disk units of computer systems.

A **tape unit** reads and writes information on the tape much as a cassette recorder records and plays music on audio cassette tapes, but the recording quality is much higher and the format employed is very different. In either case, the tape unit runs the tape across the read/write

Usage	Features	170	600	S10	620	S20	640	S30	650	S40	S40/SB1
External	6500 + 6501		0	0	20	20	36	36	36	36	0
Internal SPD	6502 + 6530 +6512 +6532 +6533		0	0	9	9	37	37	37	37	1
Total SPD Internal/ External			0	0	20	20	37	37	37	37	1
Internal PCI	2726 + 9728 +2740 + 2741	1	1	1	2	2					

Figure 2.18. Maximum combinations of disk unit controllers by system model.

head, which is in contact with the tape surface. Electrical impulses in the read/write head are used to transfer information to and from the tape surface. Tape storage units are able to store very large amounts of data in a relatively small area. Data stored on a tape storage unit is somewhat immune from damage by external effects, but because the writing and reading methodology involves small magnetic fields, large magnetic fields in the vicinity of the tape storage will destroy the data. Tape storage is the slowest performing of the auxiliary storage methods but with compression techniques holds the most data at the lowest cost.

The following paragraphs provide a summary of both the internal and external tape units used with AS/400 systems. The tape units are connected to AS/400 systems through control circuitry located on tape I/O processors.

Internal Tape Units

Here we take a look at some of the internal tape units commonly used with AS/400 systems.

4-GB ¼-Inch Cartridge Tape Unit (6382)

The 6382 4-GB ¼-Inch Cartridge Tape Unit reads and writes a ¼-inch tape cartridge capable of holding up to 4 GB of uncompressed information (up to 8 GB if compressed). This tape unit supports transmission speeds of up to 56,000 bps over digital data service networks (based on standards published in the Bell Systems technical reference PUB 62310) and is an option for all AS/400 systems. It supports sustained data transfers at a rate of up to 400 KBps when connected across a SCSI-2 interface. The 6382 4.0-GB ¼-Inch Cartridge Tape Unit can read and write the 120-MB, 525-MB, 1.2-GB, and 2.5-GB tape cartridges used by the 120-MB, 525-MB, 1.2-GB, and 2.5-GB ¼-inch cartridge tape units, thus facilitating the transfer of programs and data between different AS/400 systems. It attaches to the MultiFunction I/O Processor (MFIOP) provided as standard in AS/400 system units.

13.0-GB ¼-Inch Cartridge Tape Unit (6485)

The 6485 13-GB ¼-Inch Cartridge Tape Unit increases the performance and capacity of the ¼-Inch Cartridge (QIC) technology when the new QIC-5010 format is used to read or write data cartridges. The result is that the unattended save capacity for one QIC cartridge is increased while the save time required is reduced. Maximum direct capacity is 13 GB; compacted capacity is 26 GB. The effective data rate is 1.5 MBps direct, and 3 MBps compacted. The tape drive can be mounted in either the system unit or the expansion unit. Read/write compatibility is provided for all supported AS/400 (QIC) tape formats. Attachment is via the 6513 Internal Tape Controller using a 2-byte-wide Fast SCSI interface.

7-GB 8-mm Cartridge Tape Unit (6490)

The 6490 7-GB 8-mm Cartridge Tape Unit is a helical scan, high-capacity, streaming internal tape drive that is an option on all AS/400 system models. (*Note:* The external version of this tape drive is the 7208.) The sustained data transfer rate is 500 KBps. The tape unit includes data compression hardware using an adaptation of IBM's **Improved Data**

Recording Capability (IDRC) algorithm, which provides an effective capacity of 14 GB per cartridge and an effective transfer rate of 1 MBps, depending on the type of data transferred. Hardware Data Compression (HDC) is also supported. This unit uses the same medium as the 7208 Models 2 and 12. Full interchange of data is supported with the 7208 Models 2 and 12 and the associated systems.

External Tape Units

Here we will look at some external tape drives commonly used with AS/400 systems. External tape units are stand-alone devices that attach to AS/400 systems through a tape I/O processor using either a differential SCSI interface or a 370 Channel interface. Figure 2.19 lists some external tape units commonly used with AS/400 systems and provides some basic information about each. The table of contents offers links to more detailed descriptions of the devices listed in the table.

OS/400 V4R2 supports 3490E-FXX tape drives in F-mode. F-mode is a configuration option of the tape drive that provides the following new functions:

- 18-track write allows interchange and software distribution with previous-generation 3480 tape drives.

- The USEOPTBLK parameter is enabled for save/restore commands to increase the performance of the tape drive.

- Random mode for random selection of tape cartridges from the auto cartridge loader is supported.

Tape Libraries

The IBM Magstar MP 3575 Tape library Dataserver can connect to a single or to multiple hosts using homogeneous or heterogeneous systems. It can be configured to control up to six different control paths with simultaneous support for a maximum of 3 virtual libraries. The Tape Library uses the 3570 Model C1A tape unit identified in Figure 2.19. The typical drive load to ready time is 6.7 seconds, with an

Tape Unit Type	Interface	Number Models	System Models	Capacity GB w/o Compression	Autoloader Size Tape Cartridge	Interface Speed Burst Sustained	Compression/ Type
6365 Tape Unit	Differential SCSI	1	P03	0.840	NA	3.0 MB /300 KBps	HDC
7208 Tape Unit	Differential SCSI	5	600, S10,620, S20, 640, S30, 650, S40, 436	2.3-14	NA	500 KBps	IOP-IDRC 2× Compaction
3570 Tape Unit	Differential SCSI	2 w-w/o split mode	600, S10, 620, S20, 640, S30, 650, S40, 436	5	10/20	3.5 MBps	3× Compaction
9427 Tape Library	Differential SCSI	1	600, S10, 620, S20, 640, S30, 650, S40, 436	14	20	500 KBps	2× Compaction
9348 Tape Unit	Differential SCSI	2	600, S10, 620, S20, 640, S30, 650, S40, 436		NA	781 KBps	HDC
3490E	Differential SCSI	3	600, S10, 620, S20, 640, S30, 650, S40, 436	0.8	7	20 MBps/ 3.0 MBps	IDRC -3×
3494 Tape Library	Differential SCSI	5	600, S10, 620, S20 640, S30, 650, S40 436	0.8	210-3040	20 MBps/ 3.0 MBps	IDRC-3×

Figure 2.19. External tape units commonly used with AS/400 systems (includes tape unit/library device type, interface used, supported tape unit models, supporting AS/400 models, capacity of base media, autoloader support and capacity, interface performance, and compression.)

average search time of 8 seconds, and a cartridge move time of less than 4 seconds when a new cartridge is needed. The tape library is available in native data capacities of 300 GB, 600 GB, 900 GB, 1.2 TB, and 1.6 TB. Using 3:1 compression results in tripling the native capacities. Five different models are available, with the largest model supporting six of the 3570 tape units, and 324 tape cartridges arranged in 6 different loaders. The 3570 C1A tape unit is IBM's most reliable tape unit.

AS/400 Optical Storage Overview

For large volumes of information that is not needed frequently but must be immediately available when it is needed, **optical disk storage** should be considered. Unlike magnetic disks, which record information with magnetic fields, optical disks use plastic disks coated with a thin reflective alloy material and housed in a cartridge case. Information is stored on the plastic disk by actually burning holes into the reflective surface with a laser beam. This type of storage provides for extremely high data recording densities, which makes for relatively inexpensive storage. However, today's optical disk technology is slower than magnetic disk storage.

CD-ROM is an abbreviation for **Compact Disk–Read Only Memory**. CD-ROM drives read information permanently stored on **compact disks (CDs)**. AS/400 systems come standard with a CD-ROM drive.

WORM is an abbreviation for **Write Once, Read Many**. This technology stores information by using a laser to burn microscopic holes in the reflective surface of a CD. The information can then be read back by the same laser beam (at a lower power). Once the surface is burned, it can be read as often as needed. However, because this surface cannot be "unburned," no other information can be written to that particular portion of the optical disk.

WMRM, sometimes referred to as erasable optical disk technology, is an abbreviation for **Write Many, Read Many. With** this technology, information can be written, erased, and rewritten.

Optical libraries are devices that consist of arrays of optical disks associated with one or more optical disk read/write units. In some cases, the optical disk read/write units also have one or more conventional magnetic disk storage units associated with them to improve the write performance of the library system. The optical disks used may employ CD-ROM, WORM, or WMRM technologies.

CD-ROM

CD-ROM is an abbreviation for **Compact Disk–Read Only Memory**. CD-ROM drives are auxiliary storage devices that store and read information on the surface of an optical disk using laser light. This technique allows a large amount of data to be stored in a small physical space. Performance of the CD-ROM devices is faster than tape storage but slower than disk storage. In addition, the data is less subject to damage due to outside influences such as magnetic fields and temperature extremes.

A 650-MB 12/20× format WMRM CD-ROM drive is included in all AS/400 models. The 12X refers to the write performance of the CD-ROM and the 20X refers to the read performance of the CD-ROM. The CD-ROM drive is used for distribution of OS/400 and other licensed program products. It can also be used as an alternate **IPL** (Initial Program Load) device. It attaches to the MultiFunction I/O Processor (MFIOP) provided with every AS/400 system and supports transfer rates of up to 600 KBps. The CD-ROM is also used for the distribution of software by many independent software vendors and for use by application programs directly through the HFS API, which is a common application programming interface.

3995 Optical Library

The 3995 Optical Library family of products can be used to store large volumes of information using optical storage technology. These devices are self-contained boxes that rest on the floor near the computer system. There are five models of the 3995 that can be directly attached to an AS/400 system to provide storage capacity ranging from 52 GB to 671 GB (unformatted capacity). There are also models of the 3995 that attach directly to LANs and so can be used with AS/400 systems in a LAN environment.

Each optical disk cartridge used in a 3995 library can hold from 650 million to 2600 million bytes of information depending on the cartridge type. WMRM and WORM technologies are supported. The 3995 attaches to an AS/400 system through the 2621 Removable Media Device Attachment. Also needed is the Optical Library DataServer Support/400 program (PRPQ 5799-XBK). This program provides a programming interface for application programs to use when accessing information stored in the 3995. That is, the application program must be specially written to take advantage of the 3995 or else the information stored in 3995 will be unavailable to the application program.

Auxiliary Storage Controllers

Tape adapters provide the circuitry necessary to transfer information between any attached tape units and the AS/400 main storage. These tape adapters (also called **input/output processors** or **IOPs**) have their own computing power used to lessen the burden on the AS/400's main processor(s) when it comes to moving information to and from tape units.

A **MultiFunction I/O Processor** or **MFIOP** (9751) on AS/400e system 640, 650, S30, and S40 fills the role of tape adapter with the help of the attached tape/disk controller. This tape adapter allows you to have up to four internal tape units in the system unit or three internal tape unit and a CD-ROM drive (in addition to disk units). Figure 2.20 lists some tape I/O processors and their characteristics.

Communications Options

With the emergence of the Internet and the intranets driven by local area networks (LANs), businesses are placing increasing emphasis on computer communications. The full range of communications options is supported by AS/400 Application Systems. Connections to the Internet are established using Wide Area Network (WAN) protocols and controllers/adapters with modem connections to the pervasive telephone network and finally to an Internet Service Provider. Wide area networks are also used to connect computers together for different branches of the same business corporate entity. (One example is that IBM, like many other companies, has divisions located in many states that are connected

I/O Processor Number	I/O Adapter PCI/SPD	System Models	Device Interface	Internal/ External Tapes Supported	Device Set Supported
9751 (MFIOP)	2726 PCI	600, S10, 620, S20	Ultra-SCSI	Internal	6481, 6485, 6490
	9728 PCI	600, S10, 620, S20	Ultra-SCSI	Internal	6481, 6485, 6490
6501	SPD	620, 640, 650, S20, S30, S40,	Differential SCSI 436	External	9337-XXX, 3490E-XXX, 3570-BXX 3590-B1X
2621	SPD	620, S20 (w/9331 exp) 5032 (not on S20)	Fast SCSI	Internal	2440, 5032, 3995-XX, 7208-XXX, 9348-00X, 9427-21X
2644	SPD	620, S20, (w/9331 exp) 640, S30, 650, S40	S370 Channel	External	3422-XXX 3430-XXX, 3480-XXX, 3490-XXX, 3490E-XXX
2729	PCI	600, S10, 620, S20	Differential SCSI	External	3490E-XXX, 3570-BXX, 3590-B1X 7208-XXX, 9348-00X, 9427-21X,
2624	SPD	620, 640, 650, S20, S30, S40, 436	Fast SCSI	Internal	1379, 1380, 6380, 6390
6513	SPD	620, S20 (w/9331 exp)	Fast-Wide SCSI	Internal	1379, 1380, 6380, 6390, 6481, 6485, 6490
6534	SPD	620, 640, 650, S20, S30, S40	Ultra SCSI	External	3490E-XXX, 3570-BXX 3590-B1X 7208-XXX 9348-00X 9427-21X

Figure 2.20. Listing of disk and tape I/O processors, the supporting systems, the interface provided, and the device types that may be attached.

together by wide area networks.) Wide area network controllers also serve the function of connecting remote workstations, and the adapters connect the system console in some user-defined system configurations.

Intranet connections are established using local area network protocols and controllers/adapters to an appropriately wired network of personal computers or network computers and specially adapted network stations such as shared network printers. An intranet is a name for a local area network–connected system grouping that has in addition an external connection to the Internet. Not all LANs are intranets. The number of communications lines and local area networks supported by the Application System Series is identified in the system specifics for each particular model.

The following paragraphs constitute a communications tutorial and then an overview of some communications feature cards available for IBM's Application Systems. These feature cards may be complete communications subsystems, providing the communications controller and the necessary adapter on a single card, or the controller circuitry may be on a separate card designed to accommodate one of several different communications adapter cards, depending on the requirements. Chapters 4 and 5 provide an overview of the communications software structures supported on the AS/400 family. This chapter does not provide a comprehensive list of all communications options that are available for the Application Systems, but it does discuss representative options that fit the most common business needs. As there are configuration limitations governing which and how communications options can be used together in a single computer system, the assistance of IBM or an authorized dealer should be sought when configuring systems.

The AS/400 and Local Area Networks

A local area network (LAN) consists of a group of computers connected to a high-speed communications system that spans a confined region (i.e., a single building or campus). Computers of all sizes (e.g., personal computers to mainframes) can participate in a single local area network. The computers participating in a LAN can exchange information (e.g., programs and data) and share resources (e.g., disk storage and printers). AS/400 systems can fully participate in several types of LANs including Ethernet, token ring, FDDI, and wireless. In fact, a single

AS/400 system can participate in several different LANs at the same time (see Figure 2.21 for system maximums). The AS/400 server models have been optimized to offer or "serve" resources to other computers in a LAN environment. There is also an integrated PC server that makes the AS/400 an efficient server in a PC LAN environment.

Ethernet

Probably the most popular local area network is the Ethernet LAN (IEEE 802.3). With Ethernet, each computer is attached as a tap off a common cable or bus. For this reason, Ethernet is called a **bus-wired network**. Thus, an Ethernet LAN is a party line on which all computers can transmit a message for all other computers to hear. Every computer has equal access to the cable and can send a message at any time without warning. To ensure that only one computer transmits at a time, there is a protocol, called **Carrier Sense Multiple Access/Collision Detect (CSMA/CD)**, that each connection or node follows to transmit a message. This is the same protocol used in telephone conversations; that is, only one person can speak at a time or neither is clearly understood. One party waits for the other to finish before beginning to speak. Thus, the phone line only carries one party's voice at a time and the message is clear. This is the "CSMA" part of CSMA/CD.

The "CD" part of the protocol handles the times when two nodes start transmission simultaneously. To understand this part of the protocol, think of what happens during a telephone conversation, when two

150	436	170	600	S10	620	S20	640	S30	650	S40	S20-SB1	S30-SB1	S40-SB1
Maximum number of local area networks (other than wireless) allowed:													
3	4	5	3	3	16	16	32	32	48	48	5	5	5
Maximum number of wireless LANs allowed:													
0	0	5	0	0	3	3	3	3	3	3	2	2	3
Maximum number of integrated PC server IOPs allowed:													
1	0	2	1	1	16	16	16	16	16	16	2	2	2

Figure 2.21. System limits on various local area network types for AS/400e series models.

people begin talking at the same time. Typically, both stop talking and begin again a few moments later, hoping that this time one begins sooner than the other. This is equivalent to what CSMA/CD does. If two (or more) nodes begin transmitting at the same time, the messages "collide" on the network. The nodes monitor for such a collision, and when one is detected, all nodes stop transmitting and begin again after a pause of random length. Usually, one node will begin its retransmission before the other, thus gaining control of the network.

Ethernet adapters are available with either an SPD bus interface or a PCI bus interface. SPD bus Ethernet adapters consume one of the AS/400 SPD bus slots, or one of the card slots on the MFIOP or 2810 LAN/WAN IOP, or one of the card slots on the Integrated PC Server. PCI bus Ethernet adapters consume one of the PCI slots allocated to the MFIOP or the 2809 PCI LAN/WAN/Workstation IOP. PCI Ethernet adapters take one of three PCI slots assigned to a PCI controller, and if the 2838 PCI 100/10-Mbps Ethernet IOA is identified for system usage, the specific slot is defined to be a high-speed slot, only one of which exists on each PCI controller. Figure 2.22 summarizes the Ethernet controllers and adapters, the performance of each adapter, and whether it attaches to an SPD or a PCI bus.

Token-Ring Local Area Networks

The token ring is an IBM-developed local area network able to move information at speeds of either 4 or 16 Mbps, depending on the version. The participating computers (called **nodes**) are connected through a ring-shaped wiring scheme depicted in Figure 2.23. In addition to the token-ring methodology described, a faster, more flexible technology called ATM (Asynchronous Transfer Mode) of token-ring-based LAN communications will be described.

The protocol used by the token-ring local area network is called the **token passing protocol**. With this protocol, "packets" of information are passed around the ring from node to node in a continuous circle. These packets are called **message frames** (see Figure 2.24). A unique frame called a **token frame** controls access to the ring. When a node receives a frame, the node checks to see if it is a message or a token frame. If it is a message frame, the node examines the destination ad-

Controller/Adapter	Performance	SD/PCI Bus or Attaches to
2629 LAN/WAN/ Workstation IOP		SPD
9751 Multi-Function IOP		SPD
2810 LAN/WAN/ Workstation IOP		SPD
6616 Integrated PC Server		SPD
2851 PCI Integrated PC Server		PCI
2809 LAN/WAN/ Workstation IOP		PCI
6181 Ethernet IEEE 802.3 IOA	1 Mbps/10 Mbps	2629, 6616, or 9715 controllers
2838 PCI 100/10-Mbps Ethernet IOA	10 Mbps/100 Mbps	PCI
2723 PCI Ethernet IOA	1 Mbps/10 Mbps	PCI, 2851, 2809, MFIOP

Figure 2.22. Summary of Ethernet controllers and adapters.

dress to see if the message is intended for that node. If the message is not intended for that node, the message frame is passed on unchanged to the next node in the ring. If the frame received by a node is a token frame, the node knows that the network is idle and that it may send a message frame if it has information to transfer. After it sends a message frame, the node then sends a token frame to indicate that the ring is again inactive and ready to carry information.

All AS/400 systems can participate in a token-ring network if an appropriate token-ring network adapter is added. One such adapter is the 6149 Token-Ring Adapter, which attaches to the 2629 LAN/WAN/Workstation IOP.

The 2724 PCI 16/4-Mbps Token-Ring IOA performs a function identical to that of the 6149 Token-Ring Adapter except that instead of attaching to a 2629 IOP, it attaches to the 2809 PCI LAN/WAN/Workstation IOP. The SPD bus and the PCI bus are explained in "Hardware Architecture Overview" in Chapter 1.

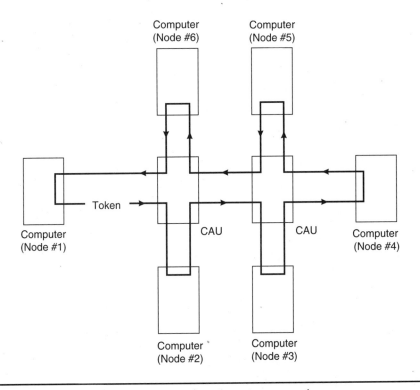

Figure 2.23. The basic structure of a token-ring network.

FDDI LANs

Fiber Distributed Data Interface (FDDI) networks are high-speed (100-Mbps) local area networks. These networks use fiber optic or twisted-pair cable to move information at a rate of 100 Mbps between the participating computer systems (nodes). Using light signals transmitted through the fiber optic cable, FDDI networks can move information more quickly and with greater immunity from electrical interference than can electrical LANs. The protocol used on FDDI networks is an enhanced version of the token-passing protocol used by the IBM token-ring network.

All AS/400 systems with the appropriate adapter can participate in FDDI networks. For FDDI networks using fiber optic cable, the AS/400 must be equipped with a 2618 Fiber Distributed Data Interface Adapter. For FDDI networks constructed from shielded twisted pair, the AS/400

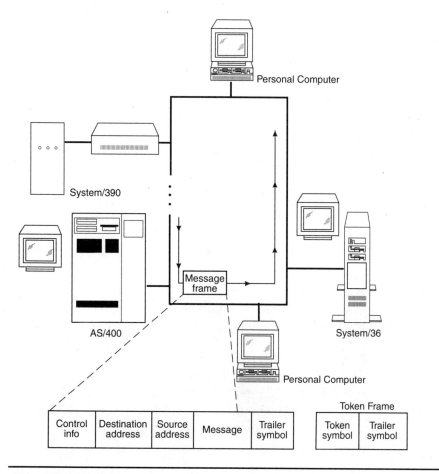

Figure 2.24. Token-passing protocol used on IBM token-ring networks.

must be equipped with the 2665 Shielded Twisted-Pair Distributed Data Interface. The 2665 Shielded Twisted-Pair Distributed Data Interface is often referred to as SDDI.

Asynchronous Transfer Mode (ATM)

ATM brings 155-Mbps performance to your local area networks. In addition, ATM can run over fiber, coax pairs, twisted-pair, and token-ring wiring. ATM can carry voice, audio, and multimedia over the same network, as well as provide video service. Functions such as remote save/restore work with the streaming functions of ATM, even in the presence of burst-mode network traffic. ATM allows remote clustering, remote journaling, and hot backup sites to become faster and more effective, providing for new kinds of data-intensive applications such as storing medical imaging, online real estate viewings, and just-in-time education. With ATM, the low latency of point-to-point (PPP), cell-based communication enables more effective OnLine Transaction Processing (OLTP), resulting in more effective file serving. The selection of which ATM adapter to use depends upon the pre-existing wiring of your facility. Six different ATM connection adapters are offered for AS/400 systems.

1. *PCI 25-Mbps UTP ATM (2811).* The PCI 25-Mbps UTP (Unshielded Twisted-Pair) ATM adapter allows the AS/400 to be attached using unshielded twisted-pair category 3 cabling. The 2811 should be considered when speeds of 25 Mbps are adequate and distances are less than 100 meters.

2. *PCI 34-Mbps Coax E3 ATM (2819).* The PCI 34-Mbps Coax E3 ATM card should be considered to allow the AS/400 to connect into an ATM network using coax cabling and the E3 interface. The 2819 should be considered when coax cabling and a 34-Mbps data transfer rate are adequate, and distances are less than 1000 meters.

3. *PCI 45-Mbps Coax T3/DS3 ATM (2812).* The PCI 45-Mbps Coax PCI card allows the AS/400 to be attached into an ATM network using coax cabling and the T3/DS3 interface. The 2812 should be considered when 45 Mbps is adequate for data transfer and distances are less than 1000 meters.

4. *PCI 155-Mbps UTP OC3 ATM (2815).* The PCI 155-Mbps UTP OC3 ATM card (2815) attaches into an ATM network using the UTP-5 interface and will be used where 155-Mbps speeds are required over distances of less than 100 meters. This interface can connect both to local area switches and directly to service provider equipment.

5. *PCI 155-Mbps MMF ATM (2816)*. The PCI 155-Mbps MMF ATM (2816) card attaches the AS/400 into an ATM network using the MultiMode Fiber (MMF) 62.5-micron interface. This interface can connect both to local area switches and directly to service provider equipment. The 2815 will be used where speeds of 155 Mbps are needed over distances of less than 2 km.

6. *PCI 155-Mbps SMF OC3 ATM (2818)*. The PCI 155-Mbps SMF OC3 ATM card (2818) attaches the AS/400 into an ATM network using the Single-Mode Fiber (SMF) 9-micron interface. This interface is primarily intended for direct connection to service provider equipment but can be used for local area switches. The 2818 will be used where 155-Mbps speeds are required over distances of from 16 km to 40 km.

Wireless Local Area Networks

The wireless network is a type of local area network that allows participating computer systems to communicate over radio waves. This can be useful in situations where users roam the building or campus with portable computing devices or where wiring is expensive or impossible. Where the computing resource and device layouts change periodically, the AS/400 Wireless LAN Adapter can provide a solution. Figure 2.25 illustrates a wireless LAN network with two wireless repeaters connecting a simple network of three computers.

AS/400 wireless LAN is enabled in one of two ways. For Version 4 systems, IBM Wireless Connection (5798-TBW) provides the system support to enable wireless repeater devices (access points) to be attached to an existing AS/400 token-ring or Ethernet LAN connection. Intelligent LAN-based devices (i.e., PCs) and portable transaction computers are supported in this environment. For Version 3 systems, an AS/400 wireless LAN adapter I/O attachment processor (feature codes 2663 and 2668) is necessary to provide the workstation controller support for portable transaction computers. Access points can be attached to an existing AS/400 token-ring or Ethernet LAN, or to an RS-485 port on the wireless LAN adapter.

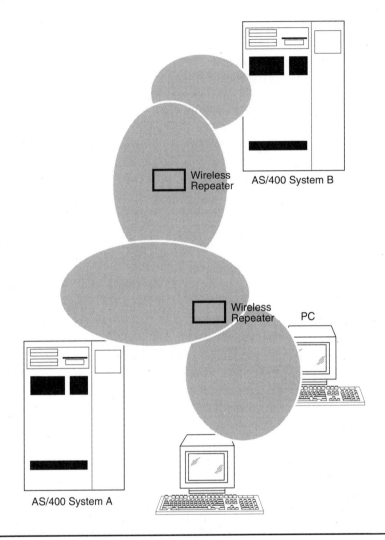

Figure 2.25. AS/400 wireless LAN with wireless repeaters.

The 2668 Wireless LAN Adapter uses direct-sequence, spread-spectrum radio, operating in the 2.4- to 2.4835-GHz band. Operation in the United States does not require a license from the **Federal Communications Commission (FCC)**. The 2668 Wireless LAN Adapter comes with an antenna and a cable for connecting the antenna to the adapter.

The area of coverage may be extended beyond the coverage provided by the antenna attached to the adapter by adding AS/400 wireless LAN **access points** to the network via either an Ethernet or token-ring LAN backbone, or an RS-485 (unshielded, twisted-pair-wired) backbone. In addition, access points may be connected without wires, acting as wireless repeaters. Each adapter or access point generates one cell of coverage area. Networks are designed by creating overlapping cells to ensure consistent coverage of the area desired.

The AS/400 2668 Wireless LAN Adapter allows transparent seamless movement of data and messages from cell to cell while maintaining a continuous host session. It operates with existing application software interfaces. Existing 5250 and LAN-oriented applications can use the AS/400 2668 Wireless LAN Adapter without change, and it supports the AS/400 family of wireless LAN and data collection devices. The AS/400 2668 Wireless LAN Adapter also operates with the **DATASPAN** 2.4-GHz family of products from the Telxon Corporation.

The raw bit rate for the AS/400 2668 Wireless LAN Adapter is configurable to 1 or 2 Mbps, shared by all active devices in the network. The range covered by one cell in most office environments is from 100 to 300 feet in all directions, depending on the building structure, antenna type, and antenna placement. Outdoors, with a clear line of sight between specialized antennas, a range of up to 3 miles may be achieved.

With Version 4 Release 1, it no longer is necessary to purchase either of these adapters because software is now able to use any local area network (Ethernet or token ring) to which an antenna attachment has been attached to communicate with your wireless devices. This is discussed in greater detail in Chapter 4. Figures 2.26 and 2.27 illustrate some of the devices that may be used with the AS/400 when operating in a wireless environment.

Integrated PC Server

The 6617 Integrated PC Server (IPCS), also called the **File Server Input/Output Processor** (FSIOP) is basically a personal computer built on an adapter that can be installed inside an AS/400 system unit. It includes a microprocessor (e.g., a Pentium Pro running at 200 MHz),

Figure 2.26. Wireless computers and access points.

Figure 2.27. Pen-based computer example.

two main memory slots (affording up to 512 MB of memory), and two communications adapter slots into which can be plugged either Ethernet or token-ring adapters. The 6617 Integrated PC Server can accept one of each type or two of either LAN type adapter. With the increased performance processor, the Integrated PC Server can now perform as a Windows NT Server using a combination of Microsoft Hydra and Citrix WinFrame to allow personal productivity applications such as SmartSuite. Database integration is accomplished through the Client Access ODBC driver. IBM is working with Microsoft for full BackOffice certification.

The 6617 also supplies Native AS/400 support for Windows Network Neighborhood (sometimes referred to as SMB Server), providing a fully integrated file serving environment with only one system to manage, and along with supporting AS/400 software, provides a high-performance file server for a local area network. That is, personal computers (running Windows, OS/2, or DOS) can freely and efficiently access AS/400 disk storage. The same file system can also be accessed by AS/400 host application programs and can provide LAN communications to AS/400 application programs using TCP/IP and APPN.

File access is also provided to the Lotus Notes/Domino application development environment, including facilities to support and enable workflow applications, electronic mail, document data storage and replication, and an integrated address book. Administration support—allowing users to share, track, store, access, and view data of any type in Notes databases—is included.

Also available to run on the Integrated PC Server is Novell NetWare 4.10. This integration allows the AS/400 disk to be used for NetWare file serving, enabling consolidation of AS/400 and NetWare servers into a single hardware platform. In Chapter 6 the Integrated PC Server is also discussed when serving as a firewall for your intranet connected systems.

The Integrated PC Server (IPCS) features require the support of OS/400 Version 3 Release 1.0 or later. Each IPCS feature may also require one or more of the following licensed programs:

- OS/2 Warp Server for AS/400 (5769-XZ1)

- Integration of Lotus Notes option for V3R2 (5763-SS1)

- Integration of Lotus Notes option for V3R7 (5716-SS1)

- Integration for Netware option for V3R2 (5763-SS1)

- Integration for Netware option for V3R7 (5716-SS1)

The 6617 supports the same IOAs as the 2854 PCI Integrated PC Server, and if running the NT operating system, requires the same cable, keyboard/mouse, and display support as the 2854.

Figure 2.28 illustrates the use of a 6616 Integrated PC Server (IPCS) LAN-connected network on an AS/400. The LAN network consists of two LANs in which the AS/400 is not only the server, but the 6616 Integrated PC Server (IPCS) in the AS/400 is performing a bridge function between the two LANs. The maximum number of 6616 Integrated PC Server (IPCS) features that may be installed on the AS/400 is 16 on a Model 650 system, but if the system maximum number of LANs is less than 4, the maximum number of IPCS features is that lesser number. The maximum is the aggregate number of all LANs. A two-port Integrated PC Server (IPCS) is counted as 2 LANs against the system maximum. Two card slots are required for the 6616 Integrated PC Server (IPCS) feature. Figure 2.21 shows the maximum number of LANs of all types allowed per AS/400 system. The 6616 Integrated PC Server (IPCS) now supports Novell's NetWare 4.10, including file serving, print serving, and data sharing with NetWare Loadable Modules (NLMs), and preserves NetWare's commands to manage the environment. It may also now be used as a Lotus Notes server, which expands the database structures available on the LAN network.

The 6616 Integrated PC Server also has the ability to act as the firewall processor for an AS/400, isolating the AS/400 and any intranet users from the Internet. The isolation hides the users and AS/400 addressing from the Internet while allowing Internet addressing to be visible to the users and AS/400 and e-mail and other Internet functions to pass through. The possible configurations in which the 6616 Integrated PC Server may be ordered are:

- 6516—16-MB One-Port FSIOP

- 6517—32-MB One-Port FSIOP

- 6518—48-MB One-Port FSIOP

- 6519—64-MB One-Port FSIOP

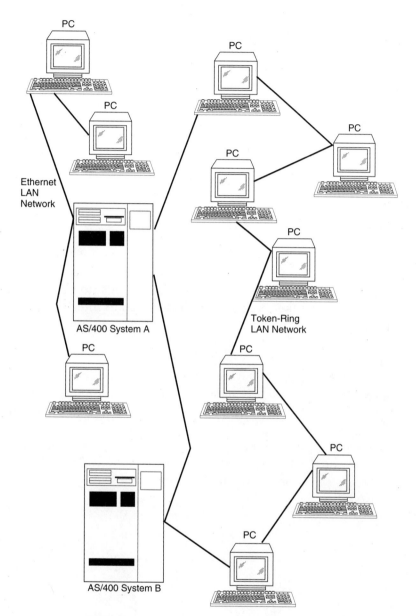

Figure 2.28. FSIOP LAN with AS/400 servers.

NOTES:
System A is a 9406 Model 310 with a dual-port FSIOP.
System B is a 9402 Model 200 with a single-port FSIOP.

- 6526—16-MB Two-Port FSIOP

- 6527—32-MB Two-Port FSIOP

- 6528—48-MB Two-Port FSIOP

- 6529—64-MB Two-Port FSIOP

Figure 2.29 identifies the configurations that may be specified for the local area network ports.

PCI Integrated PC Server (2854)

The 2854 PCI Integrated PC Server includes a 200-MHz Pentium Pro processor, four main storage card slots, and two LAN IOA positions. The adapter requires two reserved PCI card positions, one for the processor card and the second for a bridge card to interface the processor to the system. There is a special cable that converts the connector on the card to industry-standard keyboard, mouse, serial, and parallel connectors.

The memory card slots can be populated with either 32-MB memory cards (2861) or 128-MB memory cards (2862) to achieve a main storage range of 32 MB to 512 MB. At least one of the memory cards must be present.

Each LAN IOA slot can contain a PCI token-ring IOA, a PCI Ethernet IOA, or the 100/10-Mbps Ethernet IOA. The 2854 PCI Integrated PC Server can support two IOAs in any combination, with a maximum

Protocol	Connector	Medium
4/16-Mbps token-ring	9-pin D-shell	STP
4/16-Mbps token-ring	RJ45	UTP
10-Mbps Ethernet	15-pin D-shell	10Base5/AUI
10-Mbps Ethernet	15-pin D-shell	10Base2/External transceiver
10-Mbps Ethernet	RJ45	10BaseT

Figure 2.29. Possible port configurations for LANs.

of one 100/10-Mbps Ethernet IOA. The features for the LAN IOAs are from the following list:

- PCI Ethernet IOA (2723)

- PCI 16/4-Mbps Token-Ring IOA (2724)

- PCI 100/10-Mbps Ethernet IOA (2838)

- Base PCI Ethernet IOA (9723)

- Base PCI 16/4-Mbps Token-Ring IOA (9724)

- Base PCI 100/10-Mbps Ethernet IOA (9838)

If the Windows NT operating system is to be run on the 2854 PCI Integrated PC Server, then the 3025 IPCS Extension Cable for NT is required. The 1700 IPCS Keyboard/Mouse for NT is the default in the United States, and display Model 6546-00Z is recommended in the United States. IBM's Web site at *http://www.as400.ibm.com* contains a list of supported displays, keyboards, and mice. For additional details of Windows NT support see Chapter 5. If the OS/2 operating system is to be run on the 2854 PCI Integrated PC Server, then the 3025, 1700, and display features are not recommended.

MultiFunction I/O Processor (MFIOP)

The MultiFunction I/O Processor (MFIOP) is a specialized computer built on an adapter card. It is provided as standard equipment on all AS/400 models. The MFIOP does many jobs. First, it provides the control circuitry necessary to support the standard disk storage unit (and up to 19 additional disk units) with full data mirroring and RAID-5 capabilities. The MFIOP also controls the standard CD-ROM drive and the base tape storage unit, and provides additional I/O adapter slots.

There are two types of MFIOPs: one that attaches to the SPD bus and provides a private bus interface and one with PCI adapter slots. The SPD MFIOP provides three private bus interface adapter slots. One of these slots comes with a Multiprotocol Communications I/O Adapter

(2699) already installed. This adapter provides the electrical interface necessary to attach the AS/400 system to a communications line. Although this communications line can be used for any purpose, it is provided as standard with the intent that it be used with IBM's Electronic Customer Support (ECS) communications network. A second communications interface or twinaxial workstation controller can be installed in the second MFIOP slot. A third communications adapter or a local area network interface can be installed the third MFIOP slot. The communications adapters can be one-line or two-line adapters. The local area network adapters must be one-line adapters.

The PCI-based MFIOP is provided in some AS/400 systems (e.g., Models 150, 170, 600, 620, S10, and S20). This MFIOP performs the same functions as the SPD MFIOP but provides a slot for the required 2726 PCI Disk Unit Controller and three PCI slots for optional adapters. The first of those slots can accept either a 2720 PCI WAN/Twinaxial IOA or a 2721 PCI Two-Line Wan IOA. This is intended for use with the ECS function just mentioned. The other two slots can accept either of the following I/O adapters:

- 2720 PCI WAN/Twinaxial IOA (servers only)

- 2721 PCI Two-Line WAN IOA

- 2722 Twinaxial Workstation IOA

- 2733 PCI Ethernet IOA

- 2724 PCI 16/4 Mbps Token-Ring IOA

- 9723 PCI Ethernet IOA

- 9724 PCI 16/4 Mbps Token-Ring IOA

Wide Area Networks (WANs)

A **wide area network** (WAN) is a group of computers connected to a communications system. It is called a "wide area" network to indicate that the computers participating in the network need not be geographically confined to a particular building or campus (as is the case with a LAN). WANs can provide a connection between two computers located across town from one another or between hundreds of computers across global distances.

To participate in a WAN, the AS/400 system must have the proper programming (which is included in the OS/400 operating system) and be equipped with the proper electrical **interface**. The term "interface" refers collectively to the connector, electrical voltage levels, connector pin functions, and so on, that are provided for the physical attachment to a communications line.

Just as there are different rules of grammar and punctuation in English, French, and other languages, there are different rules for various types of computer communications. In computer communications, a set of rules is called a **communications protocol**. The protocols of most interest for our purposes are async, bisync, SDLC, X.25, and IDLC. Each of these different protocols is supported by OS/400 and has the same basic goal of moving information from one place to another efficiently and reliably, and each has advantages and disadvantages. The one you use will depend on your requirements in the areas of transmission speed, cost, and compatibility with the other device(s) in the network. At all times, however, each device using a given communications line must be using the same protocol.

Some popular electrical interfaces used with WANs are **232/V.24**, **V.35**, **V.36**, **X.21**, and **ISDN** interfaces. While it is not necessary to understand exactly what these cryptic names mean, it is important to understand that there are different types of interfaces necessary to support different types of WANs. The interface may be provided by a separate adapter card working with a communications controller card, or it may be built onto the same card with the communications controller circuitry. Now let's look at some specific communications adapters for the AS/400 family.

Six-Line Communications Controller (2629)

The 2629 Six-Line Communications Controller is a specialized computer on a card (I/O processor) that can handle the traffic of up to six independent communications lines. It requires a separately purchased interface adapter for each line. The adapters that can be used with the 2629 Six-Line Communications Controller include the following:

- The 2699 Two-Line WAN IOA is a multiprotocol I/O adapter. The adapter is programmed by the cables which are attached to a particular line protocol. The 2699 Two-Line WAN IOA can interface to communications lines using Async, BSC, SDLC, X.25, PPP, or Frame Relay. Several physical interfaces (EIA 232, V.35, V.36, and X.21) are also supported based upon the cable used. The cables that configure the line protocol are listed in Figure 2.30.

- A 6149 or 9249 16/4-Mbps/Token-Ring IOA (for token-ring LANs)

- An Ethernet IEEE 802.3 IOA (for Ethernet LANs; feature codes 6181 or 9381)

- A 6180 or 9280 Twinaxial Workstation IOA (for the attachment of workstations)

The AS/400 Advanced 36 comes standard with one communications line and can support up to eight communications lines. To add lines to the Advanced 36, you can have up to two adapters on the MFIOP or you can install the 2629 Six-Line Communications Controller, which can contain up to three communications adapters each containing up to two lines.

ISDN Basic Rate Interface Adapter

The 2065 Integrated Services Digital Network (ISDN) Basic Rate Interface Adapter provides an interface to the communications line compatible with the ISDN standards. ISDN is becoming prevalent in Europe and Japan and beginning to become more available in the United States. Like X.21, ISDN uses a digital interface to transfer information, improving the overall efficiency of the information transfer and eliminating the need for a conversion to traditional analog communications. Each ISDN basic rate interface adapter supports two 64,000-bps "streams of information" over an ISDN communications link (full du-

Adapter Feature Code	Cable Feature Code	Description
2699 Two-Line WAN IOA	0330	V.24/EIA232 20-ft cable
	0331	V.24/EIA232 50-ft cable
	0332	V.24/EIA232 20-ft Enhanced cable
	0333	V.24/EIA232 50-ft Enhanced cable
	0334	V.24/EIA232 80-ft Enhanced cable
	0335	V.36/EIA449 20-ft cable
	0336	V.36/EIA449 50-ft cable
	0337	V.36/EIA449 150-ft cable
	0338	V.35 20-ft cable
	0339	V.35 50-ft cable
	0340	V.35 80-ft cable
	0341	X.21 20-ft cable
	0342	X.21 50-ft cable
2720 PCI/WAN/Twinaxial IOA and 2721 PCI/WAN IOA	0348	V.24/EIA232 20-ft PCI cable
	0349	V.24/EIA232 50-ft PCI cable
	0350	V.24/EIA232 20-ft Enhanced PCI cable
	0351	V.24/EIA232 50-ft Enhanced PCI cable
	0352	V.24/EIA232 80-ft Enhanced PCI cable
	0353	V.36/EIA449 20-ft PCI cable
	0354	V.36/EIA449 50-ft PCI cable
	0355	V.36/EIA449 150-ft PCI cable
	0356	V.35 20-ft PCI cable
	0357	V.35 50-ft PCI cable
	0358	V.35 80-ft PCI cable
	0359	X.21 20-ft PCI cable
	0360	X.21 50-ft PCI cable
9720 BASE /PCI/WAN/ TWINAXIAL IOA	0348	V.24/EIA232 20-ft PCI cable
	0349	V.24/EIA232 50-ft PCI cable
	0351	V.24/EIA232 50-ft Enhanced PCI cable
	0352	V.24/EIA232 80-ft Enhanced PCI cable
9721 Base/Two-Line/ WAN IOA	0348	V.24/EIA232 20-ft PCI cable
	0349	V.24/EIA232 50-ft PCI cable
	0350	V.24/EIA232 20-ft Enhanced PCI cable
	0351	V.24/EIA232 50-ft Enhanced PCI cable
	0352	V.24/EIA232 80-ft Enhanced PCI cable

Figure 2.30. Configuration cables for various adapters to support various protocols.

plex). Each of these streams of information is called a B Channel. In addition, each ISDN basic rate interface adapter supports one 16,000-bps stream of information, called a **D Channel**, over that same ISDN communications link. Up to two ISDN Basic Rate Interface Adapters can be used with every 2629 Six-Line Communications Controller, but no other adapters may be used with that 2623 Six-Line Communications Controller. The ISDN adapter supports the ISDN Data Link Control (IDLC) protocol for communications over ISDN lines. A maximum of two ISDN adapters are supported per 2629 Six-Line Communications Controller.

The Async Protocol

The **Async** (short for asynchronous) protocol is a low-speed, low-cost communications method commonly used by many devices. With Async, individual bytes of information are transmitted (one byte at a time) with no fixed relationship between bytes. Figure 2.31 shows one way a byte might be packaged before it is sent over an Async communications line. The start bit tells the receiving end that information is coming down the line. The user's data follows the start bit. The parity bit is used by the receiving end to check for transmission errors in the user's data. Finally, the stop bit signifies the end of the transmission of the character. This is just one example of how information might be transmitted over an Async line. The user can select other organizations—including eight user data bits, no parity bits, and two stop bits. These different organizations exist primarily because of the many types of equip-

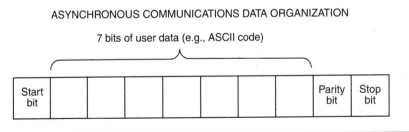

Figure 2.31. Example Async protocol data organization.

ment that have used this protocol over the years. The specific organization used must be established at both ends of the communications link before communications can begin.

The Bisync Protocol

The **Bisync** protocol (short for *bi*nary *sync*hronous communications, or BSC) is a byte synchronous protocol. The "synchronous" in "Bisync" means that a special character preceding the information synchronizes the receiver with the incoming information. This synchronization allows many bytes of information to be sent as a single block, in contrast to the asynchronous protocol, in which a single byte is sent at a time. The ability to send blocks of characters makes Bisync more efficient than the asynchronous protocol. Bisync is an older communications protocol used by terminals and other equipment to exchange information with many different types of computers, including IBM's System/360, System/370, and System/390 mainframes. As a result of its past popularity, many of today's computer systems still use this protocol.

The SDLC Protocol

The **Synchronous Data Link Control (SDLC)** is a bit synchronous protocol. The use of SDLC allows the sending of any data without the use of transparency. As with Bisync, SDLC is a synchronous communications protocol. However, SDLC is a more flexible protocol that is part of IBM's Systems Network Architecture (SNA). SNA is a set of communications standards published by IBM and used as a road map to ensure that compatible communications are provided for current and future computer systems and software. SNA is discussed further in Chapter 6.

The X.25 Protocol

The **X.25 protocol** is an industry standard used in packet-switched networks available to the public today. Although more traditional communications networks are based on **analog** or voice-type communications signals, packet-switched networks use **digital** or computer-like communications signals. Each packet is then sent to its destination elsewhere in the network through the most economical and available route. Because each packet is routed in the most efficient way, overall information flow is improved over conventional techniques. The X.25 protocol is fully supported in IBM's Systems Network Architecture and also supports TCP/IP and other protocols.

The IDLC Protocol

The IDLC protocol is similar to SDLC, except that with IDLC the other computer need not wait to be **polled** by the computer in charge of the network, as it is with the SDLC protocol. Instead, both computers have an equal ability to transmit messages to and receive messages from each other. The IDLC protocol is used by the AS/400 to communicate over an **Integrated Services Digital Network (ISDN)**, a type of digital network that fits more naturally with computer communications than do the traditional analog communications used with telephone networks. Currently more popular in Europe and Japan, ISDN communications services are starting to become more common in the United States. Computers attach to an ISDN with a digital connection, eliminating the need for the conversion to analog signals. There are different levels of ISDN service, which correspond to different transmission speeds. AS/400 systems can currently participate in the slower or **basic rate** of ISDN service. Even though this is the slowest ISDN service level, information is transferred at up to 64,000 bps per B channel with two B channels per adapter.

Frame Relay

A frame-relay network is a high-performance version of an X.25 network. Connections through the network are "permanent" and are labeled by a DLCI (Data Link Connection Identifier). The AS/400 uses LAN protocols over the frame-relay network. Essentially, frame relay provides a way to transport LAN traffic over a WAN. Frame relay is supported on the AS/400 via the SPD bus–attached 2666 High-Speed Communications IOP, the SPD bus–attached 2629 LAN/WAN/Workstation IOP with a 2699 Two-Line WAN IOA, and the PCI-attached

2809 PCI LAN/WAN/Workstation IOP with a 2721 PCI Two-Line WAN IOA installed.

Integrated FAX Adapter (2664)

In some previous releases of the AS/400 systems, when a fax connection was required, the user had to connect to a PS/2 or some other personal computer system to obtain a fax connection for receiving or sending data to remote fax locations over the telephone network. The 2664 Integrated FAX Adapter plugs directly into the AS/400 Models 620 and S20 (with SPD bus features or other expansion towers), 640, 650, S30, and S40. The 2664 Integrated FAX Adapter significantly reduces the cost and overhead of using fax on the AS/400. The 2664 Integrated FAX Adapter consists of a single-card-width book that plugs into the AS/400 logic card assembly and to a telephone line. Additional detail about the use of the 2664 FAX Adapter is provided in "Facsimile Support/400" in Chapter 3. Two ports are provided capable of transmission and receipt of facsimile data to or from a group 3–capable fax machine, an AS/400, or a PC with appropriately programmed fax adapters.

Modems

A **modem** converts computer information into communications signals and transmits them over telephone lines (i.e., it *modu*lates the computer information). A modem at the receiving end then converts the telephone line signals back into computer information (i.e., it *dem*odulates the telephone line signal). The term "modem" then derives from the terms "*modu*late" and "*dem*odulate." Computers need modems because telephone lines were originally designed to carry electronically encoded voice messages from one point to another. The telephone converts the speaker's voice into electronic signals suitable for phone line transmission. Although the information in a computer is already electronically encoded, it is not in a form that can be transmitted over standard phone lines. For this reason, a device is needed to convert the electronically encoded computer information into electronic signals suitable for telephone line transmission. A modem can be thought of as a telephone for a computer. Just as both parties need their own telephones to hold a conversation, both computers must have their own modems to transfer information over the phone lines. Modems are often used in the construction of wide area networks (WANs). Figure 2.32 lists some representative mo-

Modem Type Number	Interface Line	Data Rate -bps	Line Type	Full/Half Duplex	Auto-Call Support	Features
5853	V.24/EIA232	2,400	Switched	Full	Yes	Self-Test/ Data Rate Tuning
786X	V.24/EIA232	4,800/ 19,200	Leased,	Full	No	SNBU, Self-Test, LPDA, Data Multiplex/ Data Rate Tune
7855	V.24/EIA232	9,600	Leased Switched	Full	Yes, Switched	SNBU, Data Compression, Data Rate Tune
7852	V.24/EIA232 Data/Fax	33,600/ 14,400	Leased, Switched	Half	Yes,	SNBU, Password Protect/ Synch/Async Switching
5822 DSU/ CSU	V.24/EIA232 or V.35	56000	Leased, Switched	Half	NA	Complies with Bell Pub 62310/ DigitalData or Service Networks, Point to Point or Multi-Drop

Notes: Switched line typically means a standard voice-grade telephone line. Necessary connections are made when the user dials a phone number and terminated when the user hangs up.

Leased line means a telephone line maintains a predefined communications link (no phone number need be dialed).

Switched Network Backup Unit (SNBU) denotes the capability of a modem to automatically fall back to a switched phone line connection if the leased line normally used deteriorates to an unusable quality.

Figure 2.32. Characteristics of some representative modems commonly used with AS/400 systems.

dems commonly used with AS/400 systems. Figure 2.33 shows the 7855 Modem and Figure 2.34 shows the 5822 Digital Service Unit/Channel Service Unit.

Remote Workstation Controllers and Lines

An earlier section, "Wide Area Networks (WANs)," discussed attaching Application Systems to communications lines. This section discusses

Figure 2.33. The 7855 modem.

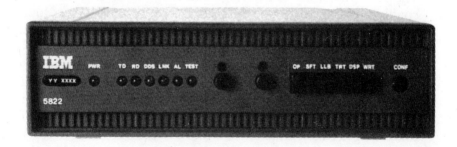

Figure 2.34. The 5822 Digital Service Unit/Channel Service Unit (DSU/CSU.

remote workstation controllers, the devices needed at the remote workstation end of the communications link. These devices perform basically the same function as the local workstation controllers. Remote workstation controllers are cabled directly to workstations and manage the workstation traffic for the computer system. The difference is that remote workstation controllers attach to the computer via a communications line and modems, as opposed to a local workstation controller, which is a card installed directly in the computer. Remote workstation controllers allow terminals and printers to be located at remote locations, giving distant users access to the Application Systems. Figure 2.35 illustrates a 5394 Remote Workstation Controller and Figure 2.36 illustrates workstations attached to an AS/400 using a remote workstation controller. Two models of remote workstation controllers are used with the AS/400, the 5394 Remote Workstation Controller, and the 5494 Remote Workstation Controller.

5394 Remote Workstation Controller

Figure 2.35 shows a 5394 Remote Workstation Controller. Functions supported include local screen printing, enhanced keyboard, reversed video, and file transfer through the Client Access Family for AS/400. The 5394 can support up to 16 workstations using twinax cable and cable-thru technology. The communications interface is either EIA 232/V.24 at up to 19,200 bps, or X.21 with SDLC at up to 64,000 bps.

5494 Remote Workstation Controller

The 5494 Remote Workstation Controller can do everything the 5394 could do plus it can attach 56 twinaxial workstations over four ports. In addition to standard twinaxial connections to workstations, the 5494 can connect directly to an Ethernet, token-ring, or wireless LAN at the remote site. This allows, for example, a token-ring network of PCs to access a remote AS/400 system. Alternately, the 5494 Model 002 could be attached to from one to five AS/400 systems over a token-ring network and twinaxially attached to the users' workstations. Only one token-ring network attachment is allowed per 5494, and the total number of workstations supported cannot exceed 80 (up to 56 twinaxially attached and the rest token-ring network–attached devices). The 5494

Figure 2.35. The 5394 Remote Workstation Controller.

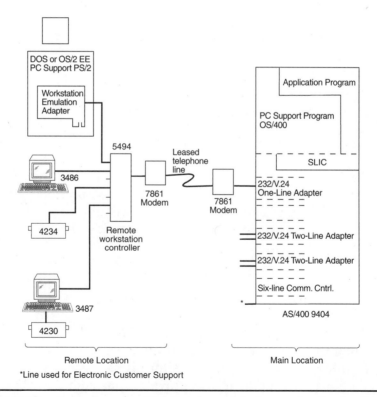

Figure 2.36. Remote workstations can be attached to an Application System through remote workstation controllers.

also supports the 5250 data stream extensions, which enable interaction with some application programs (specially written or used in conjunction with the IBM WindowTool/400 product [5798-RYF]) using a mouse and special graphical items (e.g., pop-up windows, scroll bars, radio buttons, pushbuttons, check boxes, and continuous window frames).

Power and Packaging Options

Figure 2.37 lists the power and packaging features for the various AS/400e systems and identifies which of the systems accept the particular feature and the function performed by the feature on that particular system.

Advanced System 36 Packaging Expansion Features

The following sections discuss the expansion features available for the Advanced System 36.

Card Expansion for Model 436

The 7108 Card Expansion option is used only with AS/400 Advanced System 36 Model 436 system. It provides two card slots that can accommodate various adapters including workstation controllers, communications adapters, tape drive adapters, optical library adapters, LAN adapters, and so on.

Storage Expansion Unit for Model 436 (7117)

The 7117 Storage Expansion Unit is used only with the AS/400 Model 436. It is used to provide for more auxiliary storage and I/O expansion slots. It has eight compartments for disk storage that can each house additional disk units. It also provides four additional I/O expansion slots and two additional tape unit slots. A maximum of one 7117 Storage Expansion Unit is allowed per system.

Feature Code	600/S10	620/S20	640/S30	650/S40
9364/5064		System Unit Expansion		
9331 SPD Cage		SPD Card Cage		
9329 PCI Cage		PCI Card Cage		
7128 DASD Cage	DASD Expansion Unit	DASD Expansion Unit		
External Battery Back-up Unit			Increase Battery Back-Up Time To 48-Hours	Increase Battery Back-Up Time To 48-Hours
7130 Cage		Tape Expansion CAGE		
5143 Power Supply		Prerequisite for 5052 Storage Expansion Unit	Prerequisite for 5052 Storage Expansion Unit	Prerequisite for 5052 Storage Expansion Unit
5153 Power Supply		Redundant Power Supply Storage Expansion Unit	Redundant Power Supply Storage Expansion Unit	Redundant Power Supply Storage Expansion Unit
5052 Storage Expansion		Storage Expansion Unit	Storage Expansion Unit	Storage Expansion Unit
5055 Storage Expansion			Storage Expansion Cage (4 disk units)	Storage Expansion Cage (4 disk units)
5058 Storage Expansion		Storage Expansion Unit	Storage Expansion Unit	Storage Expansion Unit
5073/5072 I/O Card Expansion		1063-Mbps System Expansion Tower	1063-Mbps System Expansion Tower	1063-Mbps System Expansion Tower
5083/5082 Disk Expansion		1063-Mbps DASD Expansion Tower	1063-Mbps DASD Expansion Tower	1063-Mbps DASD Expansion Tower
2686 Optical link Processor		266-Mbps Optical Link Card (not recommended)	266-Mbps Optical Link Card (not recommended)	266-Mbps Optical Link Card (not recommended)
2688 Optical Link Processor		1063-Mbps Optical Link Card	1063-Mbps Optical Link Card	1063-Mbps Optical Link Card
2695/2696 Optical Processor			System Unit Feature	System Unit Feature

Figure 2.37 Power and packaging feature matrix for Advanced Series 6XX/SXX systems.

UPS for Models 150, 170, and 436

An **Uninterruptible Power Supply (UPS)** significantly improves system uptime by minimizing the impact from power fluctuations and outages. The Models 150, 170, and 436 support an external UPS (9910). UPSs are available in two capacities: 660 VA and 1.3 KVA. The UPS offers continuous no-break power, a keypad and digital display with 15 programmable operation functions and alarm set points, and brownout boost to save battery run time.

In the case of the Model 170, two special CPM/UPS devices are offered, one at 800 VA and the other at 1000–1400 VA. The higher rated unit output VA capability depends upon the input voltage range. Contact IBM sales personnel if interested in this particular unit.

AS/400e series Packaging Expansion Features

The following sections discuss the expansion features available for the AS/400e series models 6XX/SXX.

System Unit Expansion (5065/9364)

The 5064/9364 System Unit Expansion is a bolt-on expansion unit that can expand the I/O function of the Model 620 or S20 system unit. The basic expansion unit contains a five-slot 3½-inch disk unit cage, a 650-watt power supply with space for redundant power supplies for both the expansion unit and the system unit, and either a 6-card 9331 SPD bus card cage, or a 14-slot 9329 PCI card cage. The function can be expanded by the addition of two 3½-Inch Disk Unit Cages (7128) and a 3-slot 5¼-Inch Tape Unit Cage (7130).

SPD Bus Card Cage (9331)

The 9331 SPD Bus Card Cage allows six SPD bus I/O cards to be plugged into the 5064 System Expansion Unit. The remaining card cage slot is reserved for an 2688 Optical Link Card used to attach up to four additional 5073 System Expansion Units or 5082 Storage Expansion Units to the system unit.

PCI Card Cage (9329)

The 9329 PCI Card Cage allows 14 PCI adapters plus two Optical Link Cards. The remainder of the PCI cage card slots are used by logical controllers, which manage the activity of the PCI cards inserted in the other slots. Some of these 14 slots are for high-performance PCI adapters, and some are restricted to slow performance adapters.

3½-Inch Disk Unit Cage (7128)

The 3½-Inch Disk Unit Cage can accept any five of the disk units listed under "Disk Storage." The interface within the disk unit cage is Ultra-SCSI, but may drive Fast and Wide SCSI or Fast and Narrow SCSI devices.

5¼-Inch Tape Unit Cage (7130)

The 5¼-Inch Tape Unit Cage can accept any three of the tape units listed under "Internal Tape Storage." The interface within the tape unit cage is Ultra-SCSI, but may drive Fast and Wide SCSI or Fast and Narrow SCSI devices.

Storage Expansion Unit (5058)

The 5058 Storage Expansion Unit mounts on the top of the 5073/5083 Bus Expansion Towers for all Advanced Series 6XX/SXX models except the Models 600 and S10. The 5058 Storage Expansion Unit provides the capability to mount up to sixteen 3½-inch disk storage units.

System Expansion Tower (5073)

The 5073 System Expansion Tower has four compartments for additional tape storage. In addition to tape storage, the 5073 System Expansion Tower provides 13 additional I/O expansion slots and can feature a 5058 Storage Expansion Unit on the top. The 5073 provides base power and redundant power for the tape units and the I/O expansion slots, and, when featured with the 5058 Storage Expansion Unit, both cooling and power for up to sixteen 3½-inch disk units. The 5073 uses a 1063-Mbps optical interface to connect to the system unit.

Storage Expansion Tower (5083)

The 5083 Storage Expansion Tower provides for up to 16 internal disk units. An additional 16 disk units may be added with the 5058 Storage Expansion Unit for a total of 32 disk units. The 5083 Storage Expansion Tower uses a 1063-Mbps interface. The 5083 Storage Expansion Tower and the 5073 System Expansion Tower have the same appearance and are illustrated in Figure 2.38.

Advanced Series Base Optical Bus Adapter (2696)

The 2696 Base Optical Bus Adapter is required on any Advanced Series Model 640/650/S30/S40. The 2696 Base Optical Bus Adapter generates both the copper bus internal to the system and up to six optical busses for attachment of bus or storage expansion towers. The 2696 can accept a maximum of three 2686 and/or 2688 Optical Link Processors.

Advanced Series 2686 Optical Link Processor (266 Mbps)

Each 2686 Optical Link Processor can attach two busses and up to two bus or storage expansion towers. Three cables are required to attach two towers; two cables are required to attach one tower. The towers are connected in a ring with the system unit. The 2686 Optical Link Processor executes at 266 Mbps. Any mixture of 2686 and 2688 Optical Link Processors may exist on an optical bus adapter as long as the total is not greater than three.

Advanced Series Optical Link Processor (2688)

Each 2688 Optical Link Processor can attach two busses and up to two bus or storage expansion towers. Three cables are required to attach

Figure 2.38. Disk Storage Expansion Unit for AS/400 Advanced Series 3XX/5XX mounted on a system unit.

two towers; two cables are required to attach one tower. The towers are connected in a ring with the system unit. The 2688 Optical Link Processor executes at 1063 Mbps. Any mixture of 2686 and 2688 Optical Link Processors may exist on an optical bus adapter as long as the total is not greater than three. The 2688 Optical Link Processor may only attach to a 2695 or 2696 Optical Bus Adapter.

Other Adapter Options

This section contains a group of attachments, either cards or other system elements which do not group with any of the other categories of devices and adapters.

Cryptographic Processor

The 2620/2628 Cryptographic Processor helps improve the security of an AS/400 system by encoding information using cryptographic techniques (ANSI Data Encryption Standard [DES]). That is, AS/400-resident information can be scrambled via encryption keys, making it meaningless to anyone except those who have the key. This capability is particularly beneficial where valuable AS/400 information might be exposed to unauthorized access via a communications network like the Internet. The 4754 Security Interface Unit (SIU) is an optional device that attaches to the cryptographic processor and allows the user to enter cryptography keys by sliding a personal security card through a reader. The 2620 Cryptographic Processor is restricted to use in the United States and Canada. Outside the United States and Canada, the 2628 Cryptographic Processor must be used. The 2628 uses a lower-precision algorithm.

0059 Transition Data Link

The 0059 Transition Data Link is used to ease the transition from System/36 or System/38 to AS/400. The 0059 is a stand-alone device that allows a S/3X to be attached to an AS/400 through local workstation controllers, as shown in Figure 2.39. This physical connection along with the System/36 or System/38 migration aids and OS/400 allows the operator to efficiently transfer information from one system to the other at twinaxial cable speeds (with a raw data rate of over 1 million bps). This provides an alternative to using the time-consuming and error-prone diskette or tape method of transferring information between systems.

The 0059 may be the only alternative for information transfer if the two systems are not configured with compatible tape or diskette devices. Local workstations can also be attached to the 0059, allowing them to access either system from a single terminal. The users hit a simple keystroke sequence to switch from one system to the other. Printers attached to the 0059, however, must be dedicated to one system or the other. The 0059 attaches to one workstation controller port on each system, providing seven addresses from each system. These seven addresses can be dedicated to information transfer between systems, workstation support, or any combination of the two. Usually, the more addresses assigned to transferring information between the two systems, the higher the transfer rate.

Terminal Multiconnector and Telephone Twisted-Pair Adapter

The most common way to attach local workstations to Application Systems is through twinaxial cable. The 5299 Terminal Multiconnector and Telephone Twisted-Pair Adapter (TTPA) shown in Figure 2.40 provides a wiring alternative. With TTPA, unused telephone twisted-pair wiring is used. That may already be installed in the building, as long as it conforms to IBM Type 3 Media specifications. This reduces wiring costs at the expense of the maximum distance allowable from the computer or remote workstation controller to any workstation. With twinaxial cable this distance is 5000 feet, with the less expensive twisted-

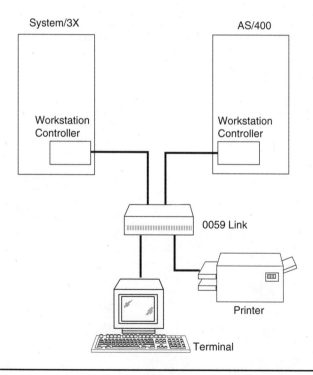

Figure 2.39.   Example of a 0059 transition data link configuration.

pair it is 1000 feet. The 5299 provides 10 telephone connectors that are used to attach up to seven workstations and one computer system (two connectors are used for problem determination procedures). The 5299/TTPA connections can coexist with twinaxially attached workstations on other ports of the computer system. The 5299 and TTPA do not require power to operate.

Figure 2.40. The 5299 Terminal Multiconnector and Telephone Twisted-Pair Adapter.

3

AS/400 Software

The previous chapters closely examined the system units and optional equipment of the Application Systems. This chapter begins the discussion of how that hardware is put to work, namely, the all-important **software**. Software is a general term for the many programs that execute in computers. It is software that harnesses the Application Systems' computational power and allows you to perform many diverse and useful tasks. The chapter begins by introducing you to the software structure used by the AS/400 and continues with a discussion of the kinds of software used to actually perform useful work with Application Systems. The three general categories of software along with the job each performs are discussed. Then, AS/400's compatibility with software written for System/3X computers is discussed, followed by a group of programs that fit into the applications category, but are useful across a wide spectrum of businesses.

AS/400 Software Architecture Overview

A computer system is divided into two functional categories, software and hardware. Hardware is the part of the computer system that provides some form of tactile feedback like hardness when you touch it and is recognizable as rectangular or oblong in shape when you look at it. Software is the part of the computing system that executes the work on the system. Software is programs. The model of software that constitutes the programs that execute on the AS/400 systems is divided into three segments, application programs, operating system programs, and SLIC programs. Figure 3.1 illustrates the layered structure relationship of the three segments. The user's view of application systems is illustrated by the arrows at the top of the figure, i.e., the user sees mostly the application programs which are being executed, with barely a glimpse at the operating system function, perceived primarily by the presentation methodology provided by the operating system.

Application programs (the shaded area in Figure 3.2) constitute the work that is desired to be performed on the computer. Those application programs range from a relatively straightforward function such as payroll (an individual's hours worked are multiplied by a pay rate, appropriate taxes are subtracted and retained, and finally a check is printed out for the individual) to data mining, which looks for subtle relationships in information accumulated indirectly, to the application programs signified by the arrows in Figure 3.1.

The operating systems layer in our model is shown shaded in Figure 3.3 directly below the application programming layer. The operating

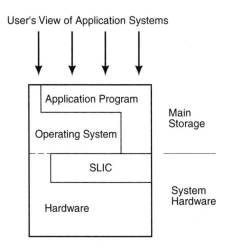

Figure 3.1. Conceptual software model of Application Systems basic software structure. The three layers of the software model work together, and with the hardware, to perform useful work for the user.

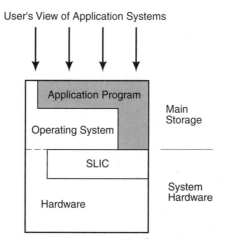

Figure 3.2. The application program software layer of the model. The application program defines the particular tasks the computer is performing for the user.

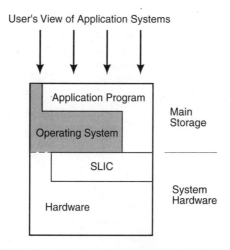

Figure 3.3. The operating system software layer of the model. The operating system provides the environment in which the application program(s) run.

systems layer interfaces directly to the application programs and performs tasks for the application under control of the application. Application programs rely on the operating system to perform many of the detailed housekeeping tasks associated with the internal workings of the computer. The operating system provides the environment in which applications execute. Operating systems accept commands directly from the user to do such things as copying files and changing passwords. The operating system must also manage the system variables used for tailoring the major types of objects supported by the system, such as programs, files, and communication protocols, and provide national language support. The details of operating systems are discussed in greater detail in Chapter 4, which is devoted to AS/400 operating systems. The integrated nature and the rich set of functions of the AS/400 operating system (OS/400) is among the things that make the AS/400 different from other midrange computers.

The third and final layer of software in the software model (the shaded area in Figure 3.4) is called the System Licensed Internal Code (SLIC) layer. SLIC in many ways is considered as part of the hardware

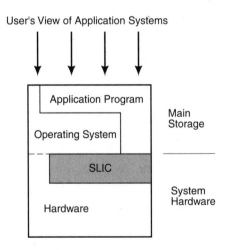

Figure 3.4. The SLIC software layer of the model. SLIC directly controls the hardware elements of the application systems and shields application programs and the operating system from hardware details.

because it instructs the hardware directly what to do for the software. Unlike application programs or operating systems, SLIC is used only by other programs. SLIC never interacts directly with the user or programmer and exists only to help application programs and the operating system perform their tasks. SLIC instructions help hide the hardware specifics from the application programs, making application program compatibility possible across a wide range of processing hardware implementations.

System Licensed Internal Code and some of its interfaces to the hardware and operating system are part of the Technology Independent Machine Interface which has enabled the AS/400 to continuously improve the hardware and operating system while maintaining compatibility to the applications set.

In the following paragraphs the usage of SLIC in the AS/400 is explained in more detail, and then the factors that differentiate the AS/400 and other computer software layers are described in "How the AS/400's Software Layers are Different." How the layers interact with each other is described in "How the Layers Work Together." AS/400 software compatibility with System S/3X programs is then identified in "AS/400 Software Compatibility—Will S/3X Programs Work?" AS/400 software compatibility through CISC and RISC hardware evolutions is discussed in "Inside AS/400 Compatibility." Finally, "Applications Architecture" addresses the areas of program portability, program interaction, and standard user interface. After the introduction to application program architecture, the remainder of the chapter is devoted to describing the characteristics and attributes of selected prewritten applications and positioning those applications versus custom applications.

System Licensed Internal Code (SLIC)

System Licensed Internal Code (SLIC) is the third layer of the software model. The set of SLIC instructions in AS/400 computers is embedded deeply within the computer system and is considered to be part of the computing machine itself rather than part of a program running on the machine. Unlike application programs or operating systems, SLIC is used only by other programs. It is the particularly rich SLIC layer in AS/400 that helps set its architecture apart from those of more conventional computers. The built-in database, single-level storage, object-oriented architecture, and other AS/400 features described in "Hardware Architecture Overview" in Chapter 1 are all designed into the SLIC layer of AS/400, making them part of the machine itself. This results in highly efficient, consistent, and easy-to-use implementations of these functions.

SLIC is a set of extremely simple instructions (never seen by the computer programmer or user) that are directly performed by the electronic circuits within the system processor. All user program instructions are automatically converted into a series of these SLIC instructions, which are then executed by the system processor. The portion of the instruction cache used for SLIC is dynamic and movable within the instruction cache space. In any case, because there are more SLIC instructions than can fit in the Instruction cache (I-cache), some must reside in the slower main storage area. All SLIC instructions in the I-cache will execute in one I-cache cycle time, or the time it takes the I-cache to respond to the system processor's request for the SLIC instruction. Because all actions of the system processor are dictated by SLIC instructions, the system processor runs in lockstep with the I-cache cycles. When needed SLIC instructions are in the slower main storage, the system processor is delayed, reducing the overall system performance. The larger I-cache area provided in the AS/400 computers holds more of the SLIC instructions, thus contributing to higher system performance.

How the AS/400's Software Layers Are Different

One of the basic differences between AS/400 and traditional computer systems can be seen by examining the software layers. Figure 3.5 shows the three software layers of our model (application, operating system, and SLIC) in a little more detail. The figure shows the traditional software layers side by side with those of the AS/400. The first thing to notice is the difference between where the various software functions reside in the layers. In the traditional system, functions such as security, database, and communications reside in the operating system layer, which is usually made up of a collection of separately purchased operating system products. With this traditional approach, each operating system product must be installed and maintained separately. This is why a highly skilled individual called a **systems programmer** is needed to support this kind of system.

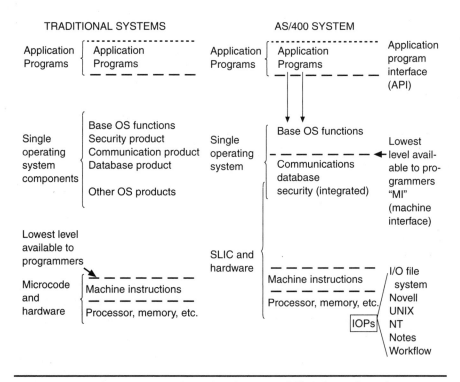

Figure 3.5. The AS/400's software architecture differs from that of more traditional systems. Implementing more function in the SLIC layer and providing a one-piece operating system results in improved efficiency, consistency, and simplicity.

With the AS/400 approach, much of the basic database, security, and other functions are built into the SLIC layer. Because SLIC implementations are in general more efficient by nature of their "closeness" to the hardware, overall system performance is improved. The operating system for the AS/400 (OS/400) provides all its functions in a single product. This eliminates the need for the operator to install, tailor, and manage the multiple operating system components in traditional operating systems and make sure that each works with the others as new versions are shipped at different times. The price you pay for this simplicity is that you get all OS/400 functions whether you need them or not, whereas the user of traditional systems can select only the traditional operating system components needed at a given time (of course the user is now responsible for ensuring that these selected components work properly together.)

Another basic difference lies in the way a programmer properly "sees" the systems. With the traditional system, system functions such as database management or security reside in the operating system and therefore can be modified by a systems programmer. This gives the systems programmer more flexibility in customizing the computer system at the expense of more complexity. With the AS/400, ease of use and efficiency are gained at the price of some flexibility. For example, because the database functions are built into the SLIC instructions, they cannot be modified. If programmers want to change how the database is managed, there are some things they simply cannot do. In a traditional system environment, the database functions are not part of the operating system but are purchased as a separate component, such as Oracle, Sybase, or Informix. Thus, there's a choice with other systems that is not available in OS/400. Now that there is an understanding of how the layers of the AS/400 software architecture make it different, perhaps a closer look at how the layers work together is appropriate.

How the Layers Work Together

To appreciate how the three software layers work together in performing tasks for the user, let us trace a typical series of events that might occur when you strike keys during a computer session. In our example depicted in Figure 3.6, a salesperson is using a word processing application program to type a memo to a prospective customer.

Let us set the stage and then see what the various software layers do. The word processing application program has finished processing the most recent set of keystrokes and instructs the operating system to provide the next set of keystrokes when they are available. To comply with the request, the operating system asks the SLIC instructions to provide the next set of keystrokes when available.

Now that the stage is set, let us see what happens as the salesperson types the next line in the letter. When the salesperson holds down the Shift key and presses the T key on the keyboard to start the next sentence, the terminal sends the **scan code** corresponding to each key over the twinaxial cable to the workstation controller in the AS/400. The workstation controller receives the scan code and translates it into its

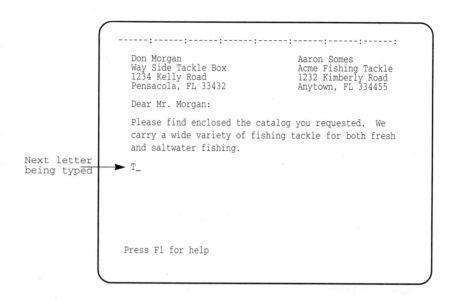

Figure 3.6. A salesperson is typing a memo using a word processing application program. The salesperson has just pressed the T key on the keyboard while also depressing the Shift key.

intended meaning. Because the workstation controller knows that the Shift key has been pressed and not released, the scan code associated with the T is translated into the letter T. Next, the workstation controller stores the T in a buffer area and echoes the T to the workstation, where it appears on the display. Notice that the workstation controller manages this entire transaction independent of the main processor or any of the software layers. This is typical of the multiprocessor architecture, which allows the main processor to concentrate on the user's application program rather than managing workstation traffic. In fact, the workstation controller will continue to manage all interaction with the salesperson's terminal until the salesperson presses the Enter key at the end of the line. The scan code associated with the Enter key signals the workstation controller to interrupt the main processor and notify it that new information is ready for use.

Here is where the software layers of our model come into play. First the SLIC verifies that all went well in receiving the information; then it notifies the operating system that the information is correct, ready, and waiting for use. The operating system makes the information available to the application program and then reactivates the application program, which was dormant, waiting for the next keystroke. The application program processes the information as necessary, instructs the operating system to wait for the next keystroke, and the whole thing starts all over again. For simplicity, we have glossed over many of the detailed steps that the computer must perform simply to process a series of keystrokes. As complicated as this process may be, computers easily perform these steps in small fractions of a second. Similar but more complicated cooperation among the three software layers occurs for most functions performed by the computer, such as reading or writing a file on a disk and communicating with other computers.

AS/400 Software Compatibility—
Will S/3X Programs Work?

Before the introduction of the AS/400, the System/3X computer family was the most widely used business computing system in the world. As a result, a wide variety of application programs had been developed for those computers. The flexibility afforded by virtue of this large and diverse software base allowed System/3X computers to fill many different needs. Of course, this plethora of available programs did not exist when the original System/3X computers were first announced. It took the independent efforts of a great many people over many years to develop the large software base that exists today for System/3X. To capitalize on that software base, software compatibility was a primary objective in the design of AS/400 computers. That is, most programs written for the System/3X family will either run directly on or can be easily migrated to AS/400 computers.

It is important to understand that of the three software layers in our software model, compatibility with programs in the application program layer is the most important. Why? First, application programs typically represent the primary share of a user's software investment. Being forced to abandon an application program because of incompatibilities may also make the user throw away whatever data and training/experience have accumulated with the application program—both of which can be substantial. Some users have developed custom application programs at considerable cost in development time and money.

Incompatibility at the application program level would render these programs virtually useless. Last, and perhaps most important, application layer compatibility allows AS/400 Application Systems users access to the thousands of application programs that have been developed for System/3X computers.

What about the operating system and SLIC layers? Maintaining compatibility with earlier System/3X operating systems software is not as important for several reasons. Operating systems typically represent only a small fraction of the user's software investment. The AS/400 maintained the S/38 machine interface (also referred to as the technology-independent machine interface) layer through the development of the AS/400, CISC, and RISC transitions, even though the microcode under that layer was allowed to change to accommodate the new hardware. Further, a new operating system is usually necessary to allow the users to have access to the new features of the computer system not considered by the programmers of the old operating system. In 1996, the AS/400 announced the capability for concurrent execution of System/36 SSP–compatible applications with OS/400 on all models of the AS/400. In 1994, AS/400 Advanced System 36 Model 236 was announced, offering direct execution of System/36 application programs. In 1995, coexistence and concurrent execution of OS/400 and SSP application programs on the Advanced 36 Model 436 was announced. Of course the user is automatically supplied with a new SLIC layer that fully supports the hardware with every AS/400 system.

Inside AS/400 Compatibility

To understand AS/400 compatibility you must understand something about how software is typically written. First, a programmer writes a program's instructions or **code** using a **programming language** (e.g., COBOL or RPG), which is basically a library of computer instructions from which a programmer may choose to write programs. The list of programming language instructions is called **source code**. To run the program on a computer, the source code instructions must be converted into instructions a computer can understand. This conversion process is called **compiling** the program. When source code is compiled, the result, called **object code**, can be directly executed by the computer hardware. In addition to programming languages, the programmer can use predefined lists of operating system commands to do things like start programs and present menus. These predefined lists are called **procedures**. With this background, let us look at how AS/400 provides compatibility with System/3X programs.

Programs written for System/38 computers, in general, are *object-code-compatible* with AS/400 systems. That is, you can take the object code for a program written for a System/38, load it on an AS/400, and run the program. This is possible because of AS/400's **System/38 environment**, which makes the AS/400 system look like a System/38 to the application program. Furthermore, most of the operating system commands used on the System/38 are the same as those used on AS/400. For this reason, System/38 procedures will also run with little or no change.

Programs written for the System/36 are supported on AS/400 through the **SSP operating system**. SLIC has an emulation that looks at every instruction from the S/36—operating system, utilities, compilers, and applications—and executes the correct sequence of AS/400 instructions. Regardless of basic differences between the architectures of the AS/400 Systems and the System/36, AS/400 systems are now object code compatible with System/36 application programs. There is no longer any need for a programmer to make any changes in the application program source code. Simply load the System/36 object code on an AS/400 without recompiling. The program can then be run under AS/400's SSP operating system. On all RISC-based systems, SSP programs, even with Assembler code embedded, will execute with the performance improvements provided by the RISC environment. OS/400 Version 4 Release 2 is provided with every AS/400 system unit purchased. SSP can only be obtained with a separate license for its usage.

Applications Architecture

In the early 1990s IBM had a project called SAA (Systems Application Architecture). The project's goals were to accomplish portability, interoperability, and user interface compatibility. All of IBM's system development locations were involved, and the rules to be followed to achieve those three objectives for the systems developed at the participating locations were established. The SAA project is no longer in existence, but the AS/400 system developers continue to follow the rules. As a result, the AS/400 is a leader in providing programs that meet the requirements in the emerging computing environments that support object-oriented programming, multimedia, client/server, and intranet/Internet computing.

Program Portability

Portability means that an application program can easily be migrated across family boundaries (e.g., from an AS/400 to a System/390 mainframe) with only minor changes. This allows the user to migrate any application programs to larger (or smaller) computers as business needs change. Further, the same application program can be used on multiple types of computers that may be found in a single business, bringing common function to all users. Another advantage of program portability is that programmers who follow the conventions established by SAA can offer their programs to users of computers in all three families. This gives users a wider variety of programs from which to choose.

Program Interaction

By following the communications conventions, one program can communicate directly with another program running on a different computer system. The programs in different families of computers in a network can cooperate directly with one another with little or no user assistance. This relieves the user of having to control the interaction between various computer systems and provides for a sophisticated computer environment.

Standard User Interface

It takes time for a user to learn to use a given application program. Not only must the basic function provided be understood (e.g., spreadsheet and database), the user must also learn the details of interacting with the user interface of a specific program. This includes function key definitions, how to select a menu item or call up help information, where commands appear on the screen, and so on. The Systems Application Architecture defined standards for these items, called Common User Access (CUA), and many other user interface details. The goal of these user interface standards is to allow for transfer of learning, ease of learning, and ease of use across programs for all major computer families.

Application Programs

The software architecture overview described how three basic software layers in Application Systems cooperate to perform useful work for the user. A layered model was used to illustrate the software architecture. This section concentrates on the top layer of the model—application programs. It is the application programs that "apply" the Application Systems' computational power to a particular business task.

IBM has created some naming conventions for AS/400 applications to distinguish those that execute on the preceding CISC-based systems from those that execute on RISC-based systems. The intention is that the CISC-based applications will always execute on the RISC-based systems, but eventually some programs will be written for the RISC-based systems that will not execute on the CISC-based systems. Therefore, when you see an application with "/400" with the name (e.g., Ultimedia/400), it will execute on both RISC- and CISC-based systems. However, when you see an application with "for OS/400" in the name (e.g., Ultimedia for OS/400), it will only be guaranteed to execute on the RISC-based systems.

Some businesses use application programs designed, written, and sold by other companies. These are called **prewritten** application programs. There are three groupings of prewritten application programs, those written by IBM, those written by IBM Business Partners, IBM AS/400 Client Series, and those written by general software vendors. The programs written by software vendors are supported on the AS/400 under Client Access/400 and execute on AS/400 client systems, not originally on AS/400. Examples of Client Access/400–supported programs will be discussed in Chapter 4. Other companies choose to design and write their own **custom** application programs or use a combination of prewritten and custom application programs. The remainder of this chapter looks at both application program alternatives. Some prewritten application programs for AS/400 are discussed, but by no means does this chapter provide a complete consumers' guide to all prewritten application software for AS/400. Comprehensive coverage of the many business application program products available today would fill many books, each of which would be obsolete by the time it was published.

This chapter helps the reader to make more informed purchasing decisions and gives examples of the kinds of things available from prewritten application programs. In the last part of the chapter, we briefly look at the custom software alternative.

Can Prewritten Programs Fit the Bill?

Today's prewritten application programs range from simple programs that concentrate on a very specific task to powerful and very complex groups of programs designed to work together. They perform a myriad of functions as diverse as the environments in which computers are found today. Many prewritten application programs are useful in most business environments (for example, word processing and accounting). These are known as **cross-industry** application programs because they are not specific to any particular industry segment. Other prewritten applications address the specialized needs of a particular industry (e.g., manufacturing or utilities). These are called **industry-specific** application programs. As a rule, the application programs written by IBM fit into a cross-industry category as opposed to an industry-specific category. The applications programs in the IBM AS/400 Client Series written by IBM business partners tend as a group to fit more readily into an industry-specific grouping set. In both cases, there are exceptions.

Cross-Industry Application Programs

Examples of popular available application programs written by IBM, which help fill the needs of many different types of businesses, include the following AS/400 programs:

- OfficeVision/400

- AFP PrintSuite for AS/400

- AnyMail/400

- Query/400

- AS/400 Business Graphics Utility

- ImagePlus/400

- Facsimile Support/400

- CallPath/400

- Multimedia

  - Ultimedia System Facilities

  - Ultimedia Business Conferencing/400

- Job Scheduler/400

- Lotus Notes/Domino

- Data Warehousing

- Data Mining

Brief descriptions of the functions of the listed application programs are now provided.

OfficeVision for AS/400

There are many time-consuming and labor-intensive activities involved in simply conducting business in a typical office environment—for example, generating/distributing documents, sending/reading notes, and scheduling/attending meetings. The **Office Vision for AS/400** (5763-WP1 for Version 3 Release 1 [CISC], and 5769-WP1 for Version 4 Release 1 [RISC]) application program for AS/400 systems is designed to streamline these types of activities, improving the overall operation of the office and thus of the business in general. Figure 3.7 shows an example of a simple OfficeVision for AS/400 environment. The AS/400 system is running OfficeVision for AS/400, and display stations, printers, and personal computers (PCs) are attached. Any user of any display station or PC can access the functions offered by OfficeVision for AS/400. OfficeVision for AS/400 also supports Lotus Notes 4.5 clients access to the mail, directory, and calendar services of the AS/400.

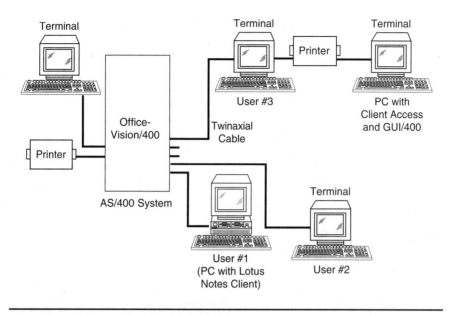

Figure 3.7. Example OfficeVision/400 environment.

The various functions provided by OfficeVision for AS/400 can all be accessed by selecting the appropriate series of icon options. This icon-driven approach makes OfficeVision for AS/400 easier to use. More experienced OfficeVision for AS/400 word processing users can bypass the icons by entering commands at the bottom of the screen. This allows the more experienced user to go more quickly to the desired function within OfficeVision for AS/400. Figure 3.8 illustrates the command interfaces to the OfficeVision for AS/400 main menu. Although OfficeVision for AS/400 will not run on an Advanced 36 system with only SSP support, many similar functions are provided by the DisplayWrite/36 (5716-DWT) and DW/36 Language Dictionaries (5716-DCN) products.

Now let us look at the types of functions provided by OfficeVision for AS/400. The new client/server versions of the AS/400 extend the OfficeVision for AS/400 functions beyond the boundaries of a single AS/400; that is, most of the calendar functions can be performed on a remote calendar as though it were local, including printing a remote calendar on a local printer, support for the industry standards on electronic mail (TCP/IP SMTP/MIME), providing extended application in-

```
                    OfficeVision/400
                                          System:    REBCO6
Select one of the following:
    1. Calendars                              Time:      2:16
    2. Mail
    3. Send message                       April          1992
    4. Send note                          S  M  T  W  T  F  S
    5. Documents and folders                          1  2  3  4
    6. Word processing                    5  6  7  8  9 10 11
    7. Directories/distribution lists    12 13 14 15 16 17 18
    8. Decision support                  19 20 21 22 23 24 25
    9. Administration                    26 27 28 29 30

   90. Sign off                          New Mail

                                  Bottom
Press ATTN to suspend a selected option.
Selection



F3=Exit    F12=Cancel     F19=Display messages
© COPYRIGHT IBM CORP. 1985, 1991.
```

Figure 3.8.   OfficeVision/400 main menu. Office Vision/400 functions can be accessed through menus or commands.

terface capability such as exits to call an alternate program (e.g., a fax application), and providing an alternate administration program for any setup that may be needed related to the integrated program with OfficeVision for AS/400.

OfficeVision for AS/400 has a graphical user interface and is designed for business professionals who manage a variety of appointments, projects, and people on a daily basis. This easily customizable software program combines the desktop personal productivity tools of a Windows-based Personal Information Manager (PIM) with the features and flexibility of IBM OfficeVision for AS/400. Through an intuitive graphical user interface, you can access host OfficeVision for AS/400 functions (e.g., electronic mail, document processing and management, calendar services, and information storage) from your PC. The following listing provides a thumbnail sketch of OfficeVision/400 functions:

- *Calendar Management.* An electronic version of a personal appointment book with group scheduling capability does for time management what word processing and electronic mail do for business correspondence. Calendars on the Notes client hard drive and AS/400 are synchronized. Figure 3.9 illustrates the OfficeVision calendar function.

- *Electronic Mail.* Electronic versions of written communications range from a hand-delivered note to a colleague down the hall to complex documents express-mailed across global distances. When electronic mail is received, the user can store, print, reply to, or forward the mail with a few keystrokes. Mail is sent to AS/400 user IDs and downloaded to the Notes client. Figure 3.10 illustrates the OfficeVision screen for sending an electronic message.

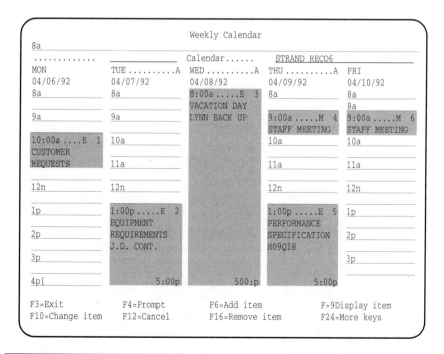

Figure 3.9. Screen from OfficeVision/400's calendar function.

```
                             Send Message

Type message.
    Todd, I need your report today on the sales results for the last quarter.
Debbie



Type distribution list and/or addressees, press F10 to send.
    Distribution list ........  _____  _____   F4 for list


-----Addresses-----
User ID   Address    Description
TJS       RCHTOWN
ADMIN     LOCAL
_____    _____
_____    _____
_____    _____
_____    _____
_____    _____

                                                         More. . .
F3=Exit    F4=Prompt   F5=Refresh   F9=Attach memo slip    F10=Send
F12=Cancel F13=Change defaults   F18=Sort by user id   F19=Display messages
```

Figure 3.10.   Screen used to send an electronic message to another user.

- *Document Management.* A document library function allows management of the large number of documents typically associated with the office environment. Documents in the document library are stored in folders with other related documents. The AS/400 security system limits document access to those authorized by the document author. Figure 3.11 shows the OfficeVision folder management screen

- *Word Processing.* Documents can be created and edited, including changing, inserting, moving, copying, and deleting text. Text can be underlined, highlighted, and centered on a page. With the Language Dictionaries/400 program (5738-DCT), various proofreading capabilities can automatically check for spelling errors against multiple dictionaries and make corrections. Figure 3.12 shows the screen used in OfficeVision to search for particular words or phrases in a word processing environment, and Figure 3.13 shows the screen used to create documents in that environment.

```
                    Work with Documents in Folders

  Folder ....  STRAND
  POSITION TO .......  _____     Starting characters

  Type Options (and Document), press enter.
     1=Create      2=Revise      3=Copy        4=Delete      5=View
     6=Print       7=Rename      8=Details     9=Print options  10=Send
     11=Spell     12=File remote 13=Paginate  14=Authority

  Opt Document      Document Description        Revised     Type

  __  _____
  __  LETTER        Practice Letter            04/08/92    RFTAS400




                                                              Bottom
  F3=Exit      F4=Prompt    F5=Refresh    F10=Search for document
  F11=Display names only   F12=Cancel    F13=End search      F24=More keys
```

Figure 3.11. OfficeVision/400 documents are organized into folders conceptually like those in filing cabinets.

```
                    Specify Document Text Criteria

  Document list description ............:  SAMPLE

  Language ...........................:  ENU   US English

  Type seach criteria, press F10 to start search.
     AND: +    OR:  |


                                            AND/
  Phrases                                    OR    Exact    Synonym
  Monthly * report _____  ±      N        N
  1992 _____  -      N        N
  _____  -      N        N
  _____  -      N        N
  _____  -      N        N
  _____  -      N        N
  _____  -      N        N
  _____  -      N        N
                                                           More. . .

  F3=Exit      F10=Start search    F11=Specify document details criteria
  F12=Cancel   F16=AND all phrases F17=OR all phrases  F24=More keys
```

Figure 3.12. Screen used to search for a document by specifying words to look for within the text of the documents.

```
LETTER P:12                    Edit                    pg:1    Ln:7
<2...T:...T3...T:...T4...T:...T5...Tv...T6...T:...T7...T:...T8...T:.
..T9
Today's office activities can be divided into four major categories-
business communications, administrative services, decision support
and business applications. IBM recognizes this reality, and IBM
office software is designed accordingly.

IBM office software programs are designed to work with each other.
This enables you to access information from an application in one
program, such as a spreadsheet, incorporate it into another applica-
tion, then distribute the document electronically to all branch
office locations.




────────────────────────────────────────────────────────────────
F1=Copy        F7=Window        F14=Get option      F20=Change formats
F2=Move        F8=Reset         F15=Table/Columns   F21=Nondisplay keys
F3=Exit/Save   F9=Instructions  F16=Adjust/Paginate F22=Spell functions
F4=Find char   F11=Hyphenate    F17=Function        F23=Word spell aid
```

Figure 3.13. Screen used to create documents in OfficeVision/400's word.

- *Contextual Help.* This is provided by pressing the Help key. **Hypertext links** are also provided in the word processing help text. It is also possible to completely replace the OfficeVision word processing function with WordPerfect for the AS/400. Images, graphics, tables, charts, may all be imported and embedded in documents created in OfficeVision for AS/400 word processing.

- *Directory Management.* Personal directories, distribution lists, and the system directory may all be managed with OfficeVision for AS/400. In a network of AS/400 systems running OfficeVision for AS/400, the system directory of one AS/400 can be **shadowed** on all other AS/400 systems. Nicknames and distribution lists can be downloaded to the Notes client. Figure 3.14 shows an example of a personal phone directory in OfficeVision.

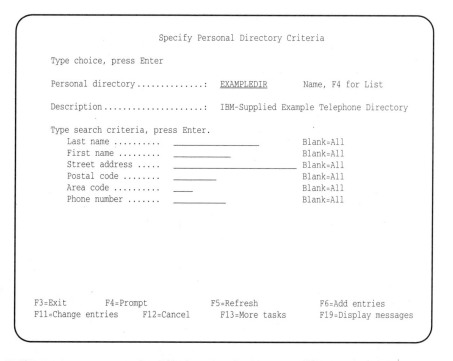

```
                        Specify Personal Directory Criteria

        Type choice, press Enter

        Personal directory ..............:   EXAMPLEDIR       Name, F4 for List

        Description .....................:   IBM-Supplied Example Telephone Directory

        Type search criteria, press Enter.
             Last name .........   _____    Blank=All
             First name ........   _____           Blank=All
             Street address .....  _____  Blank=All
             Postal code ........  _____             Blank=All
             Area code .........   ____                 Blank=All
             Phone number .......  _____           Blank=All




        F3=Exit        F4=Prompt           F5=Refresh          F6=Add entries
        F11=Change entries    F12=Cancel    F13=More tasks      F19=Display messages
```

Figure 3.14.   Example of a personal phone directory using the
OfficeVision/400 directory function.

- *Internet Addressing.* This function is provided by an alternate
  mail addressing panel into which either an Internet address or a
  regular OfficeVision for AS/400 address can be entered. The
  addressing panel will accept any Internet address. Distribution
  lists may also be entered using this panel. Figure 3.15 illustrates
  the appearance of this panel. PostNet Bar Code is also supported,
  enabling the business to take advantage of the Post Office discounts offered when zip codes are printed in the PostNet Bar
  Code on mailing envelopes.

  In addition to the functions that are built into OfficeVision for
AS/400, the capability to bring in additional functions is included. Up
to ten user options are allowed on the main menu. The OfficeVision for
AS/400 offers a decision support that provides a path to some sepa-

```
                                Send Note
        Type mailing information, press F6 to type note.


        Subject .............. _____
                              _____

        Reference ........... _____
                              _____

        Type distribution list and/or adresses, press F10 to send.
          Distribution list .......... _____  _____ F4 for list

        ----------------------Addresses----------------------
        Type nickname, user ID address, or internet address. One per line.
        BertM wlkas33 _____
        masie@vnet.IBM.com_____
        Langes@WLKAS33.DFW.IBM.COM _____
        MYRONA WLKAS19_____
        Bill_____
                              _____
                              _____
                                                              More....

        F3=Exit    F6=Type Note    F9=Attach memo slip    F10=Send    F11=Change details
        F12=Cancel    F13=Change send instructions    F14=Specify list    F24=More
```

Figure 3.15. Internet addressing mixed with local intranet addressing.

rately purchased program products such as Query/400, JustMail for AS/400, and the AS/400 Business Graphics Utility. Another OfficeVision for AS/400 capability is to provide a path to functions defined by programmers employed by the business owning the computer system. Finally, OfficeVision for AS/400 provides an application programming interface that allows other programs to interact directly with OfficeVision for AS/400. This type of program-to-program interaction allows a programmer to add custom programs that cooperate with OfficeVision for AS/400 while shielding the user from the complexities of the interaction.

OfficeVision JustMail for AS/400 (5798-TBT)

OfficeVision JustMail for AS/400 (5798-TBT) can help provide the critical information a business needs when and where the business needs it. Like OfficeVision for AS/400, JustMail for AS/400 supports Lotus Notes

4.5 clients. JustMail for AS/400 is an entry-level mail system that allows business professionals to create, address, and transmit electronic mail worldwide. JustMail for AS/400 allows the AS/400 users to share and communicate messages, notes, documents, and PC files through a network. If the business needs to create and revise documents, customers can activate their favorite word processing editor and call it from the JustMail for AS/400 application enabler. JustMail for AS/400 uses the wide variety of communications protocols available on the AS/400 for mail exchange between IBM and non-IBM systems, public networks, and PC LANs.

JustMail for AS/400 supports Internet addressing through a mail addressing panel into which an Internet address or an OfficeVision for AS/400 address may be entered. Any Internet address can be used without having a corresponding address in the system. Distribution lists may also be entered using this panel.

JustMail for AS/400 supports PostNet Bar Codes, allowing a business to take advantage of the Post Office discounts offered when those bar-coded zip codes are printed on mail envelopes.

AFP PrintSuite for AS/400 AFP

PrintSuite is a family of print enabling applications for transforming traditional line-mode printing to effective full-page documents and reports—output that blends application data with a variety of fonts, electronic forms, images, text, graphics, and bar coding. Although AFP printing is already supported by the Data Description Specifications (DDSs) and printer file functions, these techniques do not serve every business requirement. For example, not every business wants to change their invoicing program in order to implement an electronic invoice. Many would like this new print formatting to be independent of the invoicing program.

With a family of solutions that includes Advanced Print Utility, Page Printer Formatting Aid, AFP Toolbox, and SAP R/3 AFP Print, AFP PrintSuite for AS/400 provides new choices. Moving output to electronic printing is important because it achieves a number of business benefits:

- *Reduces the cost of printing.* Paper costs, document revision and control costs, and operator costs are lower.

- *Facilitates the reengineering of workflow.* Documents encoded with bar codes, OCR (optical character recognition), MICR (magnetic character reader), and images become part of the business process.

- *Documents and reports are more effective, more readable, and more responsive.* The use of fonts, images, electronic forms, and documents customized to application data can communicate more than lines of print on fixed, preprinted forms.

AFP PrintSuite enables Advanced Function Printing (AFP) and is both a document architecture and a print management system. AFP includes a structured, high-performance print data stream that is system and printer independent, integrated print management that is interactive with the printer, and flexibility, with options to view, to fax, and to print on either Intelligent Printer Data Stream (IPDS) or ASCII printers. The following paragraphs describe the capabilities available from each of these AFP PrintSuite elements. AFP PrintSuite is composed of the following four separately orderable document formatting applications.

Advanced Print Utility (APU) is an interactive end-user system that transforms existing application output into advanced electronic documents. No application changes are required because APU works from the output spool file created by the application. Through a standard AS/400 user interface, a new document is designed. The new document can incorporate electronic forms, images, fonts, bar codes, text, and other elements. The existing output data is brought up visually, so placement of each element on the page can be changed and the existing application data can conditionally determine page layout and the types of copies produced.Once the document design is complete, the new application can be put into production using the APU monitor.

Page Printer Formatting Aid (PPFA) provides the capability to create AFP page and form definitions. These two definitions provide electronic print formatting by controlling how line-mode application output is mapped to a page. Once these definitions are created and specified in the printer file, existing application output is dynamically changed. When the application is next run, it creates full pages of AFP output, not lines of SNA character sets. PPFA is the compiler that converts page and form definition source code into AS/400 objects.

AFP Toolbox allows full control over the AFP print data stream, using an object programming interface. The AFP Toolbox consists of a set of C and C++ objects, functions, and callable APIs that can be used to format complex printed electronic output. Two application areas in which AFP Toolbox is particularly useful are (1) when each page is tailored to the data contained on that page and (2) when applications have a standard interface to output, allowing the addition of enhanced output characteristics in one place. With AFP Toolbox it is possible to:

- Combine variable data with electronic forms, signatures, and images.

- Define variable-length paragraphs and precisely control alignment and formatting while using multiple fonts.

- Have precise control of each page, including the capability to dynamically draw lines and boxes, and dynamically place text, images, and overlays.

- Include indexing tags for use in efficient viewing and archiving/retrieval.

- Distribute runtime Data Link Library (DLL) components of AFPToolbox with applications.

SAP R/3 AFP Print provides AFP print support for SAP R/3 applications. Basic support enables R/3 reports to be printed on IPDS printers. Extended support enables enhancement of existing R/3 output (for example, an invoice) with electronic forms, typographic fonts, and image. SAP R/3 AFP Print is built into R/3 print processing for maximum efficiency.

AnyMail/400 and POP3

The AnyMail framework for mail in OS/400 embeds open network access, OfficeVision/400 directory, store-and-forward service, and customization options, giving the user a complete mail service offering. Through the directory users can keep track of the location of the people with whom they wish to exchange mail. The directory information can automatically connect one user's system to any of the open networks that cannot connect to the Internet—ARPA, Internet, CompuServe,

America Online, Prodigy, and so on. In addition to the open network connection capability, AnyMail can also bridge between local area networks and can be customized to match the security and multimedia functions that are desired. If the Fax for AS/400 product is installed and fax connections have been set up correctly, it is possible to send any document directly from your print spooler out on fax.

Multimedia content can be included in e-mail, which previously only included text. This means that images, video clips, and binary attachments such as spreadsheets and word processor documents can accompany e-mail. This support is compatible with the Internet mail protocol (MIME), and with the OfficeVision/400. These functions only work from an intelligent workstation such as a PC, not from non-programmable terminals such as the 5250 workstation.

Post Office Protocol, Version 3 (POP3) is the Internet client/server protocol that allows e-mail to be delivered temporarily to a post office server when the final destination client is not available or logged onto the post office server. POP3 mail is the SMTP/MIME format. The POP3 server is built as an extension on the AnyMail framework described earlier. POP3 allows a server to behave as if the destination for e-mail isn't a client but a server that receives mail on behalf of the client. The POP3 protocol then defines how a client will interact with its POP3 post office server. POP3 protocols allow a client to identify its POP3 post office on a server. The client can then ask about the mail stored there, request that the server deliver the mail, and allow the deletion of any unwanted mail. When a POP3 mail client logs onto a POP3 server, the user doesn't actually see the POP3 protocol being used. Usually POP3 retrieves all the e-mail received since the last time the client logged on. User clients supported by POP3 and AnyMail/400 include Windows 95 CC:Mail Release 7, Lotus cc:Mail, all versions of Eudora, OS/2 Warp's UltiMail Lite, all versions of Netscape 2.0, Windows 95 Microsoft Exchange, and Macintosh Claris Em@iler.

Query/400

To manage a business is to make many decisions based on the information available. Since computer systems manage the information of the business, it makes sense that the computer system should provide the management information necessary to make good business decisions.

AS/400 database files organize vast amounts of business information. Since too much information can be as bad as not enough, the business problem is to find what information is necessary. **Query/400** (5769-QU1) is designed to help summarize and sift through the information in AS/400 databases. Query/400 can be started either from an OfficeVision for AS/400 menu, with appropriate function keys, or by issuing a command on any AS/400 command line.

To get the information wanted from an AS/400 database in the form desired, a **query must be used**. A query provides the *blueprint* specifying which information will be retrieved from the database and how it will be presented. Figure 3.16 shows the main menu for a query to a telephone directory database, and Figure 3.17 shows the report resulting from a query. Users can create their own queries by answering a series of questions presented on the screen. Since no programming experience is required for this, users' dependence on programmers is reduced, al-

```
QUERY                           Query

Select one of the following:

      1. Work with queries
      2. Run an existing query
      3. Delete a query

     20. Files
     21. Office tasks




Selection or command
===> _____
     _____
     _____
F3=Exit         F4=Prompt      F12=Previous
     _____
[ ]
```

Figure 3.16. Main menu of the Query/400 application program.

```
NAME              STREETADDR        CITY            STATE   ZIPCODE
───────────────────────────────────────────────────────────────────
Susan P Ganters   987 Abbey Hwy     Mushroom Manor  OR      67891

Perry C Swenson   19821 Metro Hwy   St. Paul        OR      67891

Matt F Thomas     961 S 19th Ave    Piney Island    OR      67898
```

Figure 3.17. Report resulting from a user query to a telephone directory database.

lowing the computer system to become a more flexible tool. However, users do need to learn some simple steps to create a query.

Depending on motivation and sophistication, users may or may not wish to create their own queries. If need be, a programmer can create a library of commonly used queries for users. Once the query is defined, it can be saved in the system, allowing any authorized user to generate the query report at any time by issuing a single command. The results of a query can be displayed on a terminal's display, printed on a printer, or saved in a new database file. The information can be merged into documents using OfficeVision/400 or the DisplayWrite word processing program used on Personal System/2 computers. Query/400 can be used on any AS/400 database defined using the Interactive Data Definition Utility (IDDU), Data Description Specification (DDS), or Structured Query Language (SQL), all discussed in the section on OS/400. A version of Query/400 called **Query/36** is available for Advanced 36 SSP–based systems.

AS/400 Business Graphics Utility

Humans have always drawn images to present and interpret information. Images are native to humans and thus are both enjoyable and powerful communication devices. The greater the amount of information to be conveyed, the greater the need for graphic representations. It is therefore not surprising that business relies heavily on images to convey information to customers, employees, management, and so on. With the increased use of computers, it is also not surprising that computer-generated images (called computer graphics) are common in today's business environment. The **AS/400 Business Graphics Utility (BGU)** (5716-DS1) provides Application System users with a tool to construct a computer image. The BGU provides straightforward menus and contextual online help text. This, along with the exercises and tutorials provided in the "BGU User's Guide," allows nonprogrammers to create and use computer graphics.

This is how you create graphics with BGU. First, through a series of menus (or commands for more experienced users), the appearance and format of the desired image are defined and the type of image (pie graph, bar graph, line graph, surface graph, histogram, Venn diagram, or text chart) desired is selected. Font style, size, color, and position are also selected. Once the format and appearance of the graphic image are defined, the data is input to the graph. The data can be provided by specifying a database file containing the data or by keying in the data from a keyboard. After the data have been placed into the graph format by either means, BGU can display the image in black and white or color on a graphic workstation such as a PS/2. Because data are input separately from designing the graph format, the same BGU graph format can be used over and over again with different versions of the data. The chart management facility of BGU allows you to manage (copy, rename, etc.) your BGU graphics library. The data can be modified and then immediately regraphed to perform a "what-if" type of analysis. Images can also be printed on a plotter or graphics printer (e.g., a 4076 ExecJet II printer) or stored on the system using the **Graphics Data Format (GDF)**. As a GDF file, the image can be integrated into OfficeVision for AS/400 documents and business application programs, and be used by other GDF-compatible computer systems (e.g., System/390).

Although there were BGU versions for the System/36 and System/38 computers, AS/400 BGU has been enhanced in the areas of GDF support, database input, number of chart types and fonts, and so forth.

Most of the graphic images created with BGU/36 (5716-BGU) can be migrated to AS/400 BGU through available migration aids. System/38 BGU graphics easily migrate to AS/400 BGU through available migration aids.

ImagePlus/400

Even though computers have become the preferred way of collecting, managing, and distributing information in business, a lot of paper is still circulating in today's offices, because a lot of the information needed to support daily business operations does not lend itself to being encoded in traditional computer systems. Examples of such information are signed documents, photographs, and documents that contain both text and drawings. Because of this hard-to-manage information, many highly computerized businesses still have to resort to the manual methods of doing business that have been with us since before the advent of computers. They must still deal with rows of filing cabinets, overflowing in-baskets, envelopes, stamps, mail delays, wastebaskets, couriers, and folders. Often, handling this hard-to-manage information creates bottlenecks in an office's productivity and can significantly delay the entire business cycle. Advances in computer performance and optical storage technology have resulted in products, such as IBM's ImagePlus systems, to handle this hard-to-manage information.

ImagePlus/400 is a family of hardware and software products designed to capture, store, and manipulate images. An **image** is an electronic photograph of a document that is stored inside a computer. Any type of document can be captured inside a computer system as an image. ImagePlus facilitates the office changeover from a paper system to an electronic image system. That is, ImagePlus does for hard-to-manage documents what word processing did for standard letters and reports. To understand the concepts, let's trace some hard-to-manage documents through a hypothetical insurance company using ImagePlus. The ImagePlus example that follows relates to Mr. Lowrey's claim as a result of hurricane damage to his home. For this example, a claim made by Mr. Lowrey (a customer) for the repair of damage caused by a recent hurricane will be processed.

Figure 3.18 shows the ImagePlus system used by our insurance company to process claims. First, the insurance company receives three estimates from various contractors for the repair of Mr. Lowrey's home.

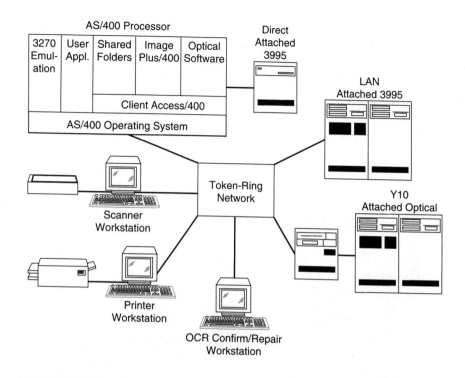

Figure 3.18.　An example ImagePlus system.

Since these are signed estimates with handwritten notes and include photographs of the damage, they fall into the category of hard-to-manage documents. The documents are first sent to the operator of the **scanning** workstation to prepare an image of each estimate document in the computer. The scanning workstation consists of a Personal System/2 running the PS/2 ImagePlus workstation program and an image scanner plus a printer. The scanner is similar to a copy machine, but rather than producing a duplicate image on another sheet of paper, the scanner electronically produces a duplicate image in the PS/2's memory. The extra-wide 8508 monochrome display allows the user to view an image on one side of the screen and enter textual information (e.g., name, address, phone number, account number, and date the case was opened) on the other.

Once the image is in the PS/2, it is compressed to conserve disk space. The images are sent to the AS/400 via Client Access/400 over the interconnecting LAN, using the communications capabilities of Client Access/400, and are stored in a shared folder on an AS/400 disk unit. Then the ImagePlus/400 Workfolder Application Facility/400 (5733-055), which is specially written to use the facilities of the ImagePlus system, takes over. The Workfolder Application Facility uses the AS/400's built-in database functions to index the stored images. This indexing associates the images with Mr. Lowrey's account number and other pertinent information to facilitate the quick retrieval of the images; that is, all information related to Mr. Lowrey's claim is linked together inside the computer system, in an electronic workfolder called a **case**.

Another thing the Workfolder Application Facility does is to place a copy of the images on the 3995 Optical Library DataServer, which is described in Chapter 2. In our example, the Workfolder Application Facility allows the claims supervisor to prioritize Mr. Lowrey's case with the other active cases and assign the case to a claims processor who is using a **viewing** workstation. There is no need for a scanner or a printer at the viewing workstation. The claims processor using the viewing workstation can now view all of the information associated with Mr. Lowrey's case. During the processing of Mr. Lowrey's claim, the claims processor can take actions such as suspending the case while waiting for additional information, suspending the case for a specified number of days, or completing the processing and closing the case.

Since the information about Mr. Lowrey's case is all in order, the claims processor completes the necessary processing and closes the case. Selected information about Mr. Lowrey's case is sent to the computer located at corporate headquarters. For now, the images pertaining to Mr. Lowrey's case are removed from the AS/400's fixed disk, freeing space for other active cases, but the 3995 Optical Library DataServer keeps a permanent record on optical disk for audit purposes. Later, if some of Mr. Lowrey's case images are needed, they can be recalled from the 3995 Optical Library DataServer. They can be displayed on a viewing workstation as before, or they can be sent to a printing workstation if hard copies are required—for external correspondence. This is one example of an ImagePlus environment.

A very important point about the whole ImagePlus system architecture is that it is designed to accommodate other application programs. That is, any programmer can write an application program that uses image capture, manipulation, storage, indexing, and printing functions provided by the Application Programming Interfaces (APIs), found in the Workfolder Application Facility/400 (5733-055), to accommodate many different business environments. For example, a real estate office can capture photographs of the exterior and interior of the houses that are for sale and store them in an ImagePlus system. Then, via computer images, a real estate agent can essentially "walk" prospective buyers through the house before they ever leave the real estate office, saving everyone a lot of time. This is just the beginning. Image processing is in its infancy; it will clearly play a role of increasing importance in businesses of the 1990s and beyond.

Facsimile Support/400

Facsimile Support/400 (5798-TBY), is a program for AS/400 systems that may either use the 2664 Integrated FAX Adapter, described in Chapter 2, or operate in conjunction with PCs and other programs and provides basic support for sending and receiving facsimiles (faxing). Support is present for sending or receiving single- and double-byte character set fonts, compressed image objects, uncompressed image objects, and barcode objects. Figure 3.19 shows a simple setup that can be used to send and receive faxes at a company named Atole Enterprises. In our example setup, a 2664 Integrated FAX Adapter is attached to a standard telephone line (or more than one). The 2664 Integrated FAX Adapter is used to control the communications between the AS/400 and any of the millions of fax machines in the world that conform to the industry-standard Group 3 Facsimile Service. A complete menu interface is available to support the fax environment. That menu interface is called Enhanced Services.

Facsimile Support/400 can also be used without the 2664 Integrated FAX adapter. A PC with an IBM fax concentrator or GammaLink fax adapter could also be used to send and receive faxes if attached to the AS/400 via a token-ring network, an Ethernet network, or a 2699 Two-Line WAN IOA using a twinax cable. The other PCs and terminals are general-purpose personal computer workstations used as AS/400 workstations attached to the AS/400. With either of these setups, all of the other fax machines in the world appear to the AS/400 system to be printers, so anything that an Atole user could print, that user can now send to any fax machine, together with a cover sheet generated by Facsimile Support/400. Alternately, the Atole user could request that the

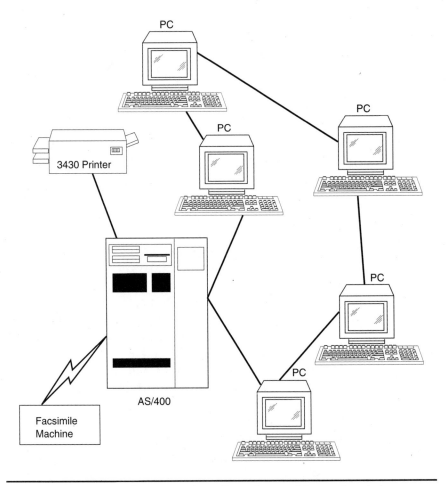

Figure 3.19. Facsimile Support/400 allows fax machines to be used as remote printers and scanners for the AS/400 system.

AS/400 system automatically send the fax after business hours, when the phone charges are less expensive. When someone sends Atole a fax, it is received over the phone lines by the 2664 Integrated FAX Adapter. The fax is then transferred to the AS/400, where it can be stored in a document folder, displayed on a graphics-capable workstation or 3489 InfoWindow II Display, or printed on any printer supporting the compressed image function of Advanced Function Printing (e.g., a 3816 Printer). In addition to providing this basic fax support, Command Language (CL) commands can be embedded in programs to allow programmers to incorporate fax functions in their application programs.

Facsimile Support (5798-TBY) also provides support for Windows NT clients for AnyMail integration of facsimile activity and inbound routing of faxes to clients on an intranet. It is possible to print to fax through the Client Access AFP print driver in Windows NT using Client Access for Windows 95/NT for AS/400, as well as to browse the Facsimile Support/400 phonebook databases. It is possible to customize cover pages and attach level-one PostScript, GIF, TIFF, and BMP mail attachments.

CallPath/400

CallPath/400 (5716-CP3) is a programmers' tool for the AS/400 that allows programmers to write applications that coordinate a business's telephone system with application programs. For example, application programs can be written to automatically sequence through and dial a list of potential customers, making the telemarketing staff more productive. In another example, a CallPath/400 application program could be written to identify a caller by phone number (using the calling line identification service offered by the phone company) and automatically pull up that customer's information to the operator's display. If the call needs to be transferred to another extension, the user can simultaneously transfer the telephone call along with the screen of customer information to the telephone and workstation of the other employee with a few keystrokes.

It is important to understand that CallPath/400 by itself cannot perform these functions. CallPath/400 is a program that is basically an extension to the OS/400 operating system, to make it easier to write application programs that interact with telephone equipment. For this reason, CallPath/400 is really an enabler rather than an application program. An **enabler** is a program that provides services to application programs to make the programmer's life easier and to provide an insulation layer to help maintain application program compatibility as hardware and software evolve. That is, CallPath/400 is a tool for the programmer who wishes to write an application program that conforms to IBM's CallPath services architecture. This architecture is IBM's stated long-term direction for coordinating application programs and telephone equipment.

Multimedia

In the discussion of the Workfolder Application Facility/400 (5733-055) in ImagePlus/400, the ability to embed photographs into an insurance industry report using the capabilities of ImagePlus/400 was described. In this section, the ability to combine visual images with audible commentary and video feedback (including, in the insurance example, customer or client testimonials and videos of wind damage, etc.) in presentations and other business activities will be described. This can all be done over the Internet between branches and the home office of the insurance company. No other multimedia system uses PC multimedia, in which the PC is the client and the AS/400 is the server, each platform doing what it does best. The AS/400 runs the applications, database, and communications, and the PC delivers the multimedia. All of the processing impacts are on the PC.

A sample multimedia configuration is shown in Figure 3.20. Among the characteristics that make this a multimedia configuration are the mixture of media, analog/digital communications, optical/DASD storage devices, local and remote connections, and networking of the workstations. It is of further significance to the multimedia characteristic that the connection capabilities provide nearly equivalent performance for both the locally connected devices and the remotely connected devices. The AS/400 in this environment provides security, system management (SystemView System Manager for AS/400 [5769-SM1]), ease of use, networking, and object/database management, including shared repositories.

Client Access Ultimedia Tools for AS/400

Client Access Ultimedia Tools for AS/400 (5716-US1) is an enabler product that allows users to enable their applications with multimedia. It requires Client Access/400 and supports both OS/2 (2.11 or higher) and Windows (3.1 or higher) clients. The workstations in a multimedia environment are at the minimum PS/2s or equivalent with a minimum of 8 MB of main storage and one or more of the following: audio adapter, motion video adapter, audio speakers, CD-ROM drive. Figure 3.21 shows the software interface between the AS/400 function and the in-

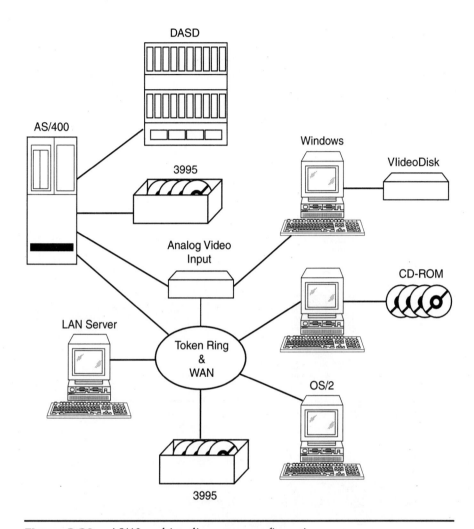

Figure 3.20.   AS/40 multimedia system configuration.

telligent workstation (PC) function. Effectively the workstation handles the capture and presentation of the objects of the multimedia session while the AS/400 performs the manipulation of the objects and manages the network and takes care of the security and storage of the objects.

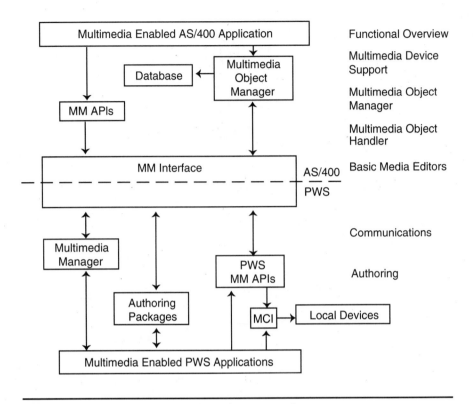

Figure 3.21. AS/400 multimedia software interface.

Ultimedia Business Conferencing/400

To assist in illustrating the functions of the Ultimedia Business Conferencing for AS/400 (5716-UB1), functions will be discussed from the viewpoint of a medical clinic with an associated hospital networked into the configuration as shown in Figure 3.22. The doctors in the clinic are concerned about a heart patient who has completed an ultrasound test. The ultrasound test was videotaped, and the sound of the blood movement was superimposed upon the videotape. The videotape is played back through the Picturetel to combine the video, audio, and blood-pressure/heart-rate data on a single path. The AS/400 captures all of this information, ties it into the patient's record (a shared folder),

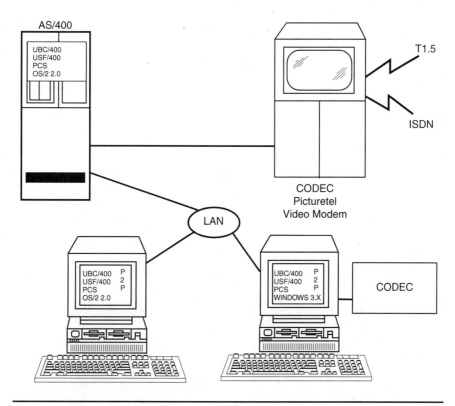

Figure 3.22.   AS/400 configuration support for Business Conferencing/400.

stores the information on the optical storage library for future retrieval, and networks the information to the connected PCs.

The information is presented simultaneously on both PCs, one at the clinic and one at the hospital. The doctors confer about the images seen and the sounds recorded during the test by talking to their PCs, essentially as they would over a telephone. The conversations are captured by the AS/400 and made a permanent part of the patient records. With Ultimedia Business Conferencing/400, the conference was scheduled by the AS/400 for each doctor and the Picturetel, the needed patient information was identified to make the conference useful, and a set of minutes was produced about the conference. The minutes were then dispatched to each doctor's PC, where they became part of the doctor's records.

IBM Job Scheduler/400

IBM Job Scheduler for AS/400 (5716-JS1) facilitates unattended operations, which can result in improved efficiency and accuracy in managing batch applications, by providing a multisystem full-function job scheduler and control of the report distribution system. Scheduling functions include

- Automation

- Batch job stream management

- Forward planning and production forecasting

- Full calendaring of operations

- Dependency scheduling

Any batch-capable function can now be scheduled. The job scheduling can occur on a single system or across a network consisting of multiple systems. Job Scheduler/400 includes a set of additional functions, consisting of

- Job reporting

- Repetitive distribution

- Capturing job streams as they are submitted

- Passing job parameters via Local Data Areas (LDAs)

- Operator notification via paging support

Jobs can be scheduled either via calendar functions or by dependency functions. The calendar scheduling functions include

- Multiple processing schedules per day or multiple holiday calendars

- Individual calendars

- A hierarchy of calendars

- Fiscal calendars

- Full audit trails of processing activity

Examples of control methods for how jobs can be run include daily, by a calendar, by date, by day, once, at the end of the month, by minute, based on a number of days, by sequence, the first week of the month, the last week of the month, and based on job dependencies. These provide **batch job stream management.**

Jobs can be sequenced to run based on three types of dependencies:

1. *Completion of previous jobs.* Jobs or groups of jobs that depend on each other can be set up (e.g., a payroll job can be set up to run only after preceding dependent payroll jobs have been processed). The jobs can be run in parallel or serially based on user definitions.

2. *Other job activity or lack of activity.* A list of jobs that cannot be active when the specified job is to be submitted can be defined; the job will be delayed until all the jobs in the list are inactive.

3. *General object dependencies.* A list of object dependencies used to control jobs can be defined (e.g., a central site receiving payroll information from a remote site). The condition that an object must not exist before a job will run can also be defined.

Job Scheduler/400 can also track the completion history of jobs and complete a log of the activities that went into processing the job. The completion history is a job-by-job log of when Job Scheduler/400 last ran, how long it took, and what the results were. It presents a detailed history of Job Scheduler/400 activities including changes to the job schedule, job processing, and the starting and ending times for the Scheduler.

Job Scheduler/400 also provides reports of applications, calendars, command lists, dependencies, distribution recipients, job histories, job lists, library lists, logs, parameters, and schedules, and can automatically distribute reports and their associated spool files to users wherever they are located, thereby providing the functions of **job reporting, repetitive distribution, and the capture of existing job streams as they are submitted.**

Automation means that Job Scheduler/400 can assist by adding to the list of managed jobs those jobs normally submitted through other application software packages. With proper placement of a special command, Job Scheduler/400 will capture the parameters and values associated with those jobs and automatically add them to the job list. Administration by function and specific job scheduling authority is allowed using the flexible security support of the OS/400. The combination of being able to control the job sequencing and the reports to be received as a result provides for **forward planning and production forecasting**. The ability to schedule jobs by the calendar functions provided and the logs that result from the execution of those jobs yields **full calendaring of batch operations**. As the job parameters are captured into a local data area of the database files, they can be passed between networked systems acting as peers using Distributed Data Management (DDM). This is what is meant by **passing job parameters via Local Data Areas (LDAs)**. Finally, Job Scheduler/400 allows a pager message to be sent to a user upon completion of a job, which results in **operator notification via paging support**. Multiple pager messages can exist on the system to be sent to different users based on normal or abnormal completion of jobs.

IBM Job Scheduler can schedule a dependent job and can copy jobs to another AS/400 system. A calendar can be used with most schedule codes to schedule a job, and there is also member-level object dependency. A formula can be used to perform date manipulation, such as setting a value to be "today's date plus 57 days". Commands can be run from a job in restricted state using a console monitor, including a view to show the different types of dependencies that exist for a job, and a status value can inform you when a job is waiting on a dependency. If you are submitting a job, parameters are present to allow you to override checking dependencies and to update dependency flags when the job is completed. The days of the week can be used for report distributing to determine when a recipient receives a report, and the spooled file can be removed when reports have been distributed.

Data Warehousing

Data warehousing is an emerging concept of applying information technology to solve business problems. Estimates are that over 90% of the

Fortune 2000 businesses had in place some form of data warehouse before the end of 1996. Data warehousing consists of a set of hardware and software components that analyze the massive amounts of data that companies are storing to improve business decisions. That data used to operate the business includes a wealth of knowledge and may be a partially wasted asset. Data warehousing applied properly can make it possible to

- Understand business trends.

- Improve forecasting decisions.

- Bring better/more timely products to market.

- Analyze daily sales information.

- Speed decisions that can affect a company's performance.

Data warehousing concepts define *operational data* and *informational data*. **Operational data** is the data that runs a business. This data is typically stored, retrieved, and updated by the Online Transactional Processing (OLTP) system. An OLTP system may be a reservations system, an accounting application, or an order entry application. Operational data is typically stored in a relational database, but it can be stored in legacy hierarchical or flat file formats. Characteristics of operational data include the following:

- Updated often and through online transactions

- Not historical data (not more than 3 to 6 months old)

- Optimized for transaction processing

- Normalized in the relational database for easy update, maintenance, and integrity.

Informational data is stored in formats that make analysis easiest. Analysis can be

- Decision support (queries).

- Report generation.

- Executive information systems.

- In-depth statistical analysis.

Informational data is created from the operational data within a business. Informational data makes up a data warehouse. Informational data is summarized operational data, denormalized and replicated, infrequently updated from operational systems, optimized for decision support applications, possibly "read only" (no updates allowed), and stored on separate systems, reducing the impact on operational systems.

Creating the data warehouse, the informational data, from the operational systems, is a requirement for the data warehousing solution. Transformation or propagation tools are used to build the informational database, during which, data may be moved from multiple operational systems and manipulated into a format appropriate for the warehouse. This may:

1. create new fields derived from existing operational data,

2. summarize data to the most appropriate level needed for analysis,

3. denormalize the data for performance purposes, and

4. cleanse the data to ensure that integrity is preserved. (To **cleanse the data** means to ensure the integrity of data when it is loaded into the warehouse. For example, if data were pulled from two operational systems that use different field names for the same data, cleansing techniques would ensure that the data fields conform to the warehouse definition upon loading.) Two examples of why a transformation is needed follow.

A retail outlet's database contains every detail about every purchase in the form of operational data. That database contains the answers to the following questions:

- What items were purchased?

- At which store did the transaction take place?

- How was it paid for?

- Who was the consumer?

Because the data is stored in a format appropriate for recording of these transactions, querying this data to analyze it can be a time-consuming effort and can adversely affect the performance of the transactional system.

In the second example, a business analyst tracking sales may want to review data collected from every store by product to forecast inventories, determine profit margins, or track revenues compared with the previous year. The ability to generate summary-level informational data from the operational data provides the performance benefits the analyst can take advantage of to quickly view the trends and problem areas affecting the business.

Relational databases store data in a two-dimensional format: tables of data represented by rows and columns. Multidimensional data structures provide additional dimensions. Multidimensional data structures provide a way to analyze data stored in the warehouse, resulting in fast response times when dealing with different levels of data common in a decision support environment. Answers to business questions can be determined by slicing and dicing through the data, or by drilling down or rolling up to different hierarchical levels. The structure of the data can be changed as the business changes. In a relational database system, multidimensional analysis can be achieved through specific database designs, (e.g., a series of indexed summary tables, or through hypercubes or multicubes). Cube approaches can be described as an extension of the spreadsheet model, that is, storing aggregate values in cells of a multidimensional spreadsheet.

On-Line Analytical Processing (OLAP) products are multidimensional analysis tools that store data using these data structures. **Data marts** contain informational data that is departmentalized, tailored to the needs of specific departmental work groups, and characterized by small size, generally less than 10 GB. **Metadata** is information about the data warehouse and the data contained in that data warehouse, and is composed of two parts, *technical data* and *business data*. **Technical data** contains descriptions of the operational database and the data warehouse. The warehouse administrator uses technical data to maintain the warehouse so as to know where all of the data is coming from. **Business data** helps locate information in the data warehouse without knowing the base implementation of the database. Business data information is presented in business terms instead of the terms the programmer used when the database was built and provides information about how recent the data is, which operational database the information came from, and how reliable the data is.

Business intelligence software refers to the tools used to analyze data, and consists of Decision Support Systems (DSS), Executive Information Systems (EIS), and data mining tools. DSS tools allow the building of ad hoc queries and generate reports. EIS combine decision support with extended analysis capabilities and access to outside resources. Data mining tools allow automation of the analysis of data to find patterns or rules used to tailor business operations. The tools are easy to use and graphically oriented, with point and click functionality.

Data Mining

Data mining is the search for relationships and segmentations in the data in the data warehouse. Discovery-driven data mining is the finding of new relationships and segmentations that are totally unexpected. IBM's new product in this area, Intelligent Miner, provides a framework for using all of IBM's current and emerging data mining techniques. Intelligent Miner is scalable, flexible, and open, integrating components and extracting data from many environments, including all DB2 for AS/400 relational database family products. It provides client support for Windows, Windows NT, and AIX. Intelligent Miner is designed for business users, not data analysts, offering the derivation of new, comprehensible information through predictive modeling, database segmentation, link analysis, and deviation detection using data mining techniques. Figure 3.23 illustrates the functions and layers of the construct for data mining.

A question needing answering is, What makes the AS/400 with its OS/400 operating system a good server on which to perform data warehousing and data mining? The five requirements of a data warehouse server are performance, capacity, scalability, open interfaces, and multiple data structures.

Among the better-known examples of data mining was when data mining found an unsuspected relationship between young men with small children who enjoyed football, beer, Thursday nights, and diapers. If

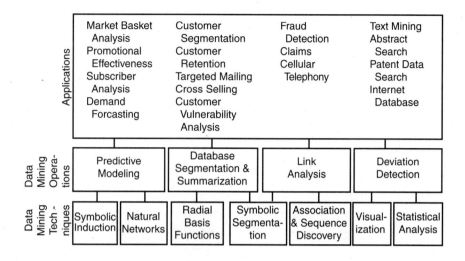

Figure 3.23. Data mining constructs.

these young men went to the store on Thursday night during football season to buy diapers for their young children, they also would stop at the beer display and pick up some beer to drink during that weekend's games. If a brand of diapers was located on the same aisle, the young men would pick up whatever brand of diapers it was, regardless of price. Needless to say, the retailers located the most profitable brand of diapers on the same aisle as the beer.

Performance

The performance of the database server must be capable of supporting the user's performance expectations during analysis. Many warehouses are found containing over 100 GB of data, with very complex analysis tasks being executed against the database. Parallel computing technologies become quite important when dealing with this large size. The AS/400 at the single e-system level supports parallel computing, using its DASD I/O processors on the DB2 for AS/400 database, and Symmetrical MultiProcessing (SMP), which can apply the resources of up to 12 processors cooperatively for a single job/query. In addition, with

Opticonnect (described in Chapter 1) up to 32 systems can be connected in a loosely coupled relationship. The power of all thirty-two 12-way SMP systems can be brought to bear both in containing the warehouse size and in performing the analysis required. DB2 Multisystem must be installed to support the loosely coupled technology.

Capacity

The capacity of the server and hardware must be enough to store your entire data warehouse. Data warehouses may be partitioned or split across multiple systems, but the server must support a data view that hides the data's physical location. Again the Opticonnect capability comes into play, providing 32 times the maximum disk storage on a single server (1,546 GB), or about 48,000 GB along with DDM (Distributed Data Management) and DB2 Multisystem, which are discussed in greater detail in OS/400.

Scalability

The typical data warehouse starts out at the data mart level serving a department and grows over time to an enterprise-wide warehouse. The AS/400 is scalable from a minimum of 4.196 GB of DASD space on the Advanced Entry to up to 1,546 GB on a Model S40, to the previously described 32 processing systems cooperatively interconnected with Opticonnect.

Open Interfaces

Open interfaces are needed to support the analysis tools required to extract the information a business needs. Locking itself into proprietary interfaces could cause a business to incur major expenses to support new analysis tools as the business changes. AS/400 supports both IBM-supplied solutions such as DataPropagator Relational Capture and Apply for OS/400, which moves data from DB2 regardless of what type of system it resides upon, and products from vendors such as Information Builders Inc., Oracle, ExecuSoft, Sybase, Praxis, DataMirror, and so on.

Multiple Data Structures

Multiple data structures, both relational and multidimensional, must be supported. Multidimensional data structures are supported by database designs such as star-schema using the DB2 for OS/400 architecture or by products from IBM business partners such as AMIS/400 from CAP Gemini, MIT/400 from SAMAC, Data Tracker from Silvon Software Inc., Infomanager from Infomanager OY, and the suite of data access products, including ESSBASE/400 from ShowCase Corp.

Collaborative Computing

Collaborative computing is an environment in which many users require the coordination of multiple actions toward the accomplishment of a common goal. Programs that enable the achievement of that coordination are known collectively as **groupware**. Groupware applications help organizations communicate, collaborate, and coordinate strategic business processes both within and beyond the boundaries of the business to achieve improved business results. Examples of groupware are Lotus Notes and Domino. Lotus Notes 4.5 supports the client functions, and Domino 4.5 supports server functions. Lotus Notes 4.5 client functions support

- Advanced client/server e-mail.

- Direct Web browsing, Web agents, and off-line access to Web pages.

- Calendaring and scheduling for personal calendaring, task management, and group scheduling.

- Support for mobile workers.

- Bundling and integration with Netscape Navigator and Microsoft Internet Explorer.

- Optional, high-performance Lotus components.

Domino 4.5 Server Powered by Notes provides

- HTTP Web Server accessed using a standard Web browser.

- Calendaring and scheduling with freetime search and interoperability.

- SMTP-MTA (Simple Mail Transfer Protocol–Message Transfer Agent) providing mail coexistence between Notes Mail and OfficeVision mail (OfficeVision for AS/400).

- Support for Internet standards, including SMTP/MIME, X.400, JAVA, Netscape plug-ins, ActiveX, POP3, HTTP, HTML, MAPI, SNMP, SSL, and CGI.

- Integration with corporate data, including AS/400 data via DataPropagator/400 (5716-DP1).

Lotus Notes provides a work environment centered on people as individuals, teams, and organizations. It is the leading client/server platform for developing and deploying groupware applications. In communications, Lotus Notes Rich Text E-Mail includes images, video, audio, spreadsheets, and graphs, as well as a wide range of protocols. Remote employees can review and edit the same document, and each team member sees the others' comments highlighted in a different font and color, helping to enable effective collaboration. Coordination is achieved by the management of the workflow among a dynamic task force.

Notes 4.5 and Domino 4.5 are supported on the Pentium version of the AS/400 Integrated PC Server (6617). With the RISC models, a CD-ROM provides for installation of the Integrated PC Server. For the CISC-based models, the CD-ROM installation requires Client Access/400 to install Notes 4.5 Domino on the Pentium Integrated PC Server (IPCS). AS/400e server Model 150 with the Integrated PC Server does not receive a complementary copy of Lotus Notes client and Domino Server code. All other orders for Integrated PC Server include AS/400 Integration BasePak for Lotus Notes, which includes one copy of the Domino Server software and one copy of the Lotus Notes client software in addition to the installation software. Also available is AS/400 Integration Enhanced Pak for Lotus Notes, providing database integration support between DB2 for AS/400 and Lotus Notes and advanced backup and recovery options using Adstar Distributed Storage Manager for AS/400.

Lotus Notes

Lotus Notes uses a Rapid Application Development (RAD) environment to deliver its capabilities. The RAD environment employs a range of skills from user-created views to agents, formulas, macros, LotusScript, and C++ APIs for the professional developer. Lotus Notes also uses a *document-centric database management system,* in which each database can include the full range of text combined with Notes Access Control Lists to ensure appropriate security (Notes includes RSA encryption for high-sensitivity information); and an *integrated messaging system,* in which anything you can see or hear in Notes can be mailed over a wide range of supported protocols. Lotus Notes replication functionality sets it apart from other groupware products by providing the following features:

- Notes Database Management System (DBMS) allows for on-demand or automatic scheduled synchronization of geographically separate copies of a database. Efficiency is achieved by only updating new and changed documents or fields, and updating is accomplished in the background.

- Notes DBMS distributes information via the Internet, thus having no concern for geography. TCP/IP, LAN connections, SLIPs, and PPP aid in this effort, and Notes manages data authentication and encryption. (TCP/IP, SLIP, and PPP are Internet protocols.)

- Notes DBMS allows a user located remotely to use the same data as an office co-worker.

- Each *Integrated PC Server* (IPCS) can support up to 200 concurrent users. Up to 8 Notes servers can be consolidated in AS/400 CISC-based systems, and up to 16 Notes servers can be consolidated on AS/400 RISC-based systems.

IBM offers two AS/400 integration packs for Lotus Notes: The AS/400 Integration BasePak for Lotus Notes allows the Integrated PC Server to act as a LAN adapter, provides software to install Notes on the Integrated PC Server, and includes one copy each of Lotus Notes R4 server and a full application development client license. The AS/400

Integration BasePak for Lotus Notes also includes server administration, adding Notes users via the AS/400, the ability to exchange mail between OfficeVision for AS/400 and Notes Mail, and shadowing of the AS/400 SDD (System Distribution Directory) to the Notes Name and Address book.

With the availability within Notes of SMTP-MTA (Message Transfer Agent) and POP3, AS/400 notes users can communicate with a wide variety of other mail clients. Even non-programmable terminals have interoperability, as they will receive the text and attachments as storable, forwardable PC files.

The Integrated PC Server supports existing Notes database functions, including replication and compression. DB2/400 data can be imported to Notes databases. Options are available for shadowing DB2/400 data into Notes as either a full or an incremental refresh. An optional user exit program allows Notes updates to DB2/400. Web Navigator allows Notes clients to simply click wherever they want to go. Web Publisher, a separate Lotus product, allows for batch conversions of Notes-created documents to HTML.

Native Domino

The Domino for AS/400 program is the Domino 4.6 release combining the AS/400 systems's features of strength of integration, ease of use, and scalability with Lotus's leading groupware offering. Domino for AS/400 is a full-function Domino server incorporating the Domino architecture. The AS/400 system implementation of Domino includes full integration with the OS/400 operating system. Domino software runs as an application on the AS/400 systems using PowerPC technology, provides the Notes client and Notes applications with direct access to the DB2/400 program database, and can coexist with the aforementioned Integrated PC Server including Domino software. The Domino software supports two-way directory synchronization, can exist with other AS/400 mail services, and leverages the reliability of the AS/400 system. The AS/400 Kernel Threads model is leveraged by Domino Software to save time by avoiding job initiation and allow it to scale to thousands of mail users on the AS/400 system.

Lotus Notes clients both with and without an ODBC driver can access the DB2/400 program database to import DB2/400 data directly into Notes rich-text fields. Notes C and C++ interfaces are provided, enabling AS/400 versions of standalone applications, server add-ins, database hook drivers, extension manager hook libraries, and external database drivers.

Two-way directory synchronization between the AS/400 System Distribution Directory and the Domino Name and Address Book is provided in real time, and any change in either location is automatically reflected in the other location to minimize administration activity related to both locations.

The AnyMail framework incorporates the Lotus Simple Mail Transport Protocol-Mail Transport Agent (SMTP-MTA), enabling the Domino for AS/400 program to interact with other mail systems on the AS/400 system including OfficeVision/400.

The Domino for AS/400 program has been tested for greater than 3000 concurrent users and projected to more than 10,500 users on the 12-way server Model S40. The high availability and reliability of the AS/400 result from the combination of the overall reliability of the AS/400 system and the incorporation of data mirroring and RAID-5 capabilities. This combined with the capability to support up to 16 Integrated PC Servers, each of which may also perform as a Domino server, plus the capability to support Multiple Instances via Partition Server Support for an additional 16 partition servers provides additional scalability. This partitioning of the Domino servers on a single system enables the workload to be split up for various applications. In addition to the Domino program's real-time Web serving capability with its HTTP server, the Domino.Action and Domino.Merchant programs enhance the AS/400 system's position as a Web server. Domino.Action provides easy building of home pages for the Web, and Domino.Merchant (discussed in greater detail in Chapter 5) provides the functions needed to conduct Internet commerce, from registering site visitors and delivering information on demand to maintaining a catalog, accepting orders, and processing payments securely via credit card or purchase order.

NotesPump (Domino.Connect)

NotesPump is a Lotus product that allows data transfer automation between heterogeneous data sources including Notes, DB2, Oracle, Sybase, and many 32-bit ODBC-compliant databases. The NotesPump for AS/400 program includes all applicable functions supported in the NotesPump 2.5 release. A variety of data transfer requests are allowed by NotesPump, including query and transfer of a results set to a different target data source; replication of data between two dissimilar (or similar) data sources; propagation of data from the DB2 program to a NotesPump program target using the IBM DataPropagator program activity; polling for a condition and a scheduled transfer when the condition is met; archiving data based on condition or timestamp; or accessing data in real time using a Domino application and a NotesPump program-support back-end (relational) database. The initiation of these transfer activities can be scheduled, event driven, or executed ad hoc, and administration is performed from the NotesPump Administration Notes database. Synchronization of data authorizations between DB2/400 and Notes databases is an additional activity between the AS/400 system and the NotesPump program.

Customized data transfer requests can be written in addition to the NotesPump predetermined activities to provide additional data transfer control or manipulation. These customizations use the NotesPump program extensions to LotusScript and the NotesPump C APIs. The NotesPump Administrator database can be used to select data source views and fields, and Web clients can be enabled to submit NotesPump program activities from any browser.

Additional information can be found at *http://www2.lotus.com/ services/notesua.nsf* and *http://www.edge.lotus.com.*

Client Series and Application Development Programs

In September 1992, IBM initiated the IBM AS/400 Application Development Program to facilitate the selection of a full array of high-level languages, CASE, and object-oriented development tools offered by a variety of third-party vendors. This business partners program was later expanded to include products developed for the client/server environment.

The AS/400 Application Development Program identifies independent software vendors providing advanced application development tools to the AS/400 marketplace. The AD Program provides a means to select vendors with quality tools and identify those tools through the use of a unique "AS/400 Application Development" emblem (shown in Figure 3.24).

The AS/400 Client Series is an exclusive set of applications recommended for use in the AS/400 client/server environments. The applica-

Figure 3.24. AS/400 Application Development emblem.

tions can come from either IBM or independent software vendors. After qualifying for the series, applications can be identified by the "AS/400 Client Series" emblem (shown in Figure 3.25). Additional detail on Client Series products can be found on the Internet at *http://www. softmall.ibm.com/as400*. IBM also supplies a CD-ROM including this information.

Industry-Specific Application Programs

The cross-industry application programs discussed up to this point are of a highly general nature, able to fill the common needs found in even the most diverse business environments. They were designed to be as general as possible to cover the largest market possible—sort of the "all things to all people" approach. For example, the OfficeVision for AS/400 office application program might be used to fill the needs of a department store in one instance and a legal office in the next. In most cases, a business also has some needs that are more specialized to its particular industry. Therefore, another type of prewritten application program, called an **industry-specific** application program, may be desirable. As the term "industry-specific" implies, this type of application program is specially designed to address the needs of a well-defined business category. A real estate office has application program needs that differ

Figure 3.25. AS/400 Client Series emblem.

from those of a dental practice. Each would benefit by an appropriate prewritten yet highly specialized industry-specific application program.

Many software companies have put a great deal of effort into developing industry-specific programs for the System/3X computers. Since AS/400 systems can run many of these programs as well as those specially written for the AS/400, highly specific business/professional environments can be addressed. There are industry-specific applications designed for manufacturing companies, insurance companies, real estate offices, medical practices, construction companies, law practices, churches, and so on. These programs are often **modular**, meaning that they are really several different programs designed to work closely together. Each program or module can be used individually or share information with the others. Modular programs allow you to select only the modules you need, reducing costs for those not needing "the works."

An example of a modular, industry-specific application program is IBM's **Manufacturing Accounting and Production Information Control System/DataBase (MAPICS/DB)**. MAPICS/DB is designed to meet a wide variety of needs for manufacturing (e.g., a furniture manufacturer) and process companies (e.g., a gasoline refiner). It consists of 17 separate programs or modules, each providing specific functions. They can be broken down into three areas:

1. Order processing and accounting

2. Advanced manufacturing

3. Process

The order processing and accounting modules of MAPICS/DB meet basic business needs in the areas of general ledger, accounts payable, accounts receivable, order entry, purchasing, and so on. Many of these modules are really very general in nature, allowing them to fit very well in manufacturing or nonmanufacturing companies. The advanced manufacturing MAPICS/DB modules focus on the manufacturing flow through the plant. They help manage the bills of materials of products, monitor in-process inventory, balance work center loads, track labor, cost jobs, and schedule production. These modules are designed specifically for manufacturers and would be of little use to a legal office, for example. Finally, the process MAPICS/DB modules fill the very specialized needs of the process companies. This includes dealing with recipes, batch quantities, yield calculations, and batch/lot tracking.

In addition to the basic MAPICS/DB modules, other companies have produced companion programs that work with MAPICS/DB to provide additional functions. These types of "add-on" program offerings are very common when dealing with the more popular industry-specific application programs. MAPICS/DB is just one example of an industry-specific application program. Hundreds of software companies have written thousands of industry-specific application programs for Application Systems, and new application programs are appearing almost daily. Before custom software, discussed next, is purchased, industry-specific software should be carefully considered.

Custom Application Programs

Prewritten application programs fit many needs. They are comparably inexpensive, flexible, and convenient tools. In some cases, however, users may find that the fit of their application program to the way the business operates needs to be that of a tight glove. This is especially true in environments in which the Application Systems are needed to perform highly unusual and specific tasks or there is a need to conform to existing company procedures. In these cases, it's better to develop custom application programs written to the user's exact specifications.

Custom application programs are designed and written by programmers employed by the company or by consultants contracted just for that purpose. In either case, the basic development steps are the same.

First, a software specification is developed that describes the actions of each program, and the specific interface is projected for the input and output of the program. Then a preliminary version of the program is written that demonstrates the function that will eventually be in the final program. This preliminary version is evaluated by the user, and the specification is altered to reflect any needed changes. Last, the final program and user manuals are written and put in place at the user's location. Typically, user training will be provided by the developer and any problems will be ironed out.

Once the user accepts the program, the software has to be supported: Users will need a place to go when they have questions not addressed by the manuals. Support also includes making necessary changes to the application program, as the changing business environment will often require. This kind of ongoing support is critical to the success of any computer automation project.

Most of the time, custom application program development is more expensive and time-consuming than the prewritten application program approach. In many environments, however, this additional expense and time can be recovered by the increased productivity that can result from custom applications that precisely fit the needs of the environment. An additional benefit of custom application programs is their ability to change as a company changes. Getting major modifications to prewritten application programs may be difficult or impossible.

The AS/400 functions and programming tools including the basic architecture of AS/400 systems makes for a very productive program development environment. The built-in database and single-level storage provide high-level structures and consistency. According to IBM, this, along with the programming tools available for AS/400, can increase programmer productivity by about 3 to 1 over that of the System/36. Custom application programs used with System/36 and System/38 computers can be run on the AS/400 through the use of appropriate migration tools. In Chapter 4, the following are considered:

- "Application Development Facilities" discusses some of the AS/400 tools and Integrated Language Environment (ILE) which assists in the development of custom application programs.

- "Emerging Application Development Environments" describes C++ object-oriented programming.

- "Emerging Applications Environments" describes Frameworks, Java, and Open Doc application environments.

Before leaving custom application programs, it is appropriate to discuss the use of existing applications for the new system purchaser or migrating system purchaser. Most system purchasers have a set of programs that were fine for the centralized system they are moving from. They now must choose to maintain that environment or move into a client/server computing environment. This is particularly true if the business has invested in some PC systems that need to be networked with a host system as a server. In addition to Frameworks, Java, and Open Doc, "Emerging Applications Environments" in Chapter 4 identifies the choices the system purchaser has, related to older programs migrating to a client/server environment.

4

Operating Systems

Few areas in information processing create more confusion and apprehension than the operating system. This chapter is designed to help remove some of the mystery associated with the operating systems used with Application Systems and make you familiar with operating system topics such as interactive processing and multiuser capabilities and how these concepts apply to the business environment. You will also be introduced to the concepts of client/server environment, network computing, including the client/server variations called Internet computing and intranet computing, and how this type of computing differs from interactive processing, as well as the special characteristics imposed upon the client and the server to support these emerging types of computing. The two AS/400 operating systems, SSP and OS/400, will be discussed, including when each should be used and when both might be used. The object technology languages C++ and Java are discussed, and the San Francisco frameworks objectives and Open Doc standards are positioned. The Application Development Facilities supported by the AS/400 operating system are functionally outlined, and the programming language environments for that development are described. A perspective is provided on SystemView tools for managing the AS/400 resources and the resources of other connected computers and peripheral equipment.

Operating System Products

Application Systems use one of two operating systems. The Advanced 36 computers use the IBM **System Support Program (SSP)** originally developed for System/36 computers. All models of the AS/400 systems exclusively use the IBM **Operating System/400 (OS/400)**. This section provides an overview of both operating systems and then looks more closely at OS/400.

Introduction to Operating System Concepts

The operating system provides the necessary interface that allows the user and application programs to interact with computers. The user interacts directly with the operating system's user interface to manage files on a disk, start application programs, print files, and so on. The operating system performs those tasks that all applications must perform, providing a uniform, consistent method for accomplishing those tasks. The operating system also performs tasks directly under the control of application programs without any user assistance. The application program initiates tasks by directly interacting with the operating system through the **Application Program Interface (API)**. This is simply a set of operating system commands that can be issued directly by the application program. The API simplifies the job of the application programmer because it is not necessary to become involved with the details of hardware interaction. Further, when an application uses the API, it is shielded from changes in the computer hardware as new computers are developed. The operating system can be changed to support new computer hardware while preserving the API unchanged, allowing application programs to run on the new computer. To understand the job of the operating system, it is necessary to understand two basic concepts:

1. Batch vs. interactive processing

2. Multiuser and multiapplication

The AS/400 uses an integrated operating system, either SSP or OS/400 or both SSP and OS/400. Unlike a personal computer (PC), in which the operating system comes in pieces—Windows, Paradox, Internet support, Communications support, etc.—the OS/400 operating system comes with all essential pieces and the user need not be concerned with whether the interfaces will operate properly together. IBM has done extensive testing on the system to ensure that those interfaces operate properly. The disadvantages of the integrated approach are that the user must take OS/400 as an entity, and it is not possible to tune the operating system to suit the user's desires.

Batch vs Interactive Processing

To understand the concepts of **batch** and **interactive processing**, consider an analogy between the postal service and the telephone. If you wish to ask a distant friend some questions, you can either write a letter or phone. With the first option you gather all your thoughts, put them on paper, and put the letter in a mailbox. A few days later (assuming your friend is responsive) you go to your mailbox and get the responses to your questions in the form of a document. This is analogous to batch processing with a computer: You request the computer to answer some question(s) or perform some task(s). Some time later (from minutes to days) you go to the printer and get the computer's responses in the form of a report. In the early days of computing, batch processing was the only alternative for computer interaction. Batch processing continues today, and many jobs are still handled this way. As an example, a remote branch of a company quite often has the hours worked by the employees keyed in during the day, stores the information (accumulates it in a database) until the lower telephone rate evening hours, and then sends the data to the computer system located at the company central office. The data is then processed, and the checks are printed and mailed to the remote location for distribution to the employees.

Moving back to our analogy, at times you cannot simply write down your list of questions in a letter because some of the questions will depend on answers to one or more initial questions. In this case, you must either send several letters back and forth or call your friend to discuss the questions. Calling is preferable if you need an answer to your question in a hurry. Having a dialogue with your friend over the phone would be analogous to interactive processing on a computer. With interactive processing, you have a dialogue with the computer system from a terminal: You type in questions or requests and the computer immediately responds. The primary advantage of interactive processing is that the user gets an immediate response, which is required in many business applications (e.g., airline reservations and a retail checkout lane). Interactive processing was developed after batch processing and is now widely used in most business environments.

Some business applications of computers use a combination of batch and interactive processing. For example, a payroll clerk might type information from time cards into a computer terminal in a dialogue style (interactive processing). Once all time cards are entered and verified to be correct, the clerk may issue a command to the terminal that tells the computer to print all checks (a batch job). The clerk would later get the checks from the printer. The operating systems of Application Systems support both batch and interactive processing.

What Are Multiuser and Multiapplication Computer Systems?

A **multiuser** computer system exists when the hardware and software of a single computer system can be shared by two or more users simultaneously. For contrast, personal computers (PCs) contain hardware and software that are designed to interact with one user at a time and thus are called **single-user** computer systems. There are two categories of multiuser systems, multiuser–single task, and multiuser-multitask. The multiuser–single task systems have not been seen since the early days of computers, and as the name implies, many users performing exactly the same application used the system at the same time. Airline scheduling systems are examples of this type system. It was not required that the users operate in synchronization. In a multiuser multitasking system, each of the users can be using a different application. Regardless of the definition, in a multiuser computer system, from two to many hundreds of computer terminals are attached to a single computer. Each terminal used in this manner is referred to as a **Non-Programmable Terminal (NPT)**. Personal computers emulating 5250 data streams when attached to AS/400 systems are in reality being used as non-programmable terminals because their internal intelligence is not being exploited to perform any part of the computing task other than serving as a repository for data. Each terminal provides its user with a "window" into the computer system and allows the user to perform tasks independent of all other users. Although the single computer system is being used simultaneously by many users, users are usually unaware of the activities of other users and seem to have their own computer system. However, a user may see the computer "slow down" (increase response time) as more and more users sign on to the computer and start doing work.

There are advantages in a multiuser computer system versus a single-user computer system. Because the computer system hardware and programs are simultaneously shared by many users, no one is standing in line waiting for a turn on the computer. Everyone (assuming enough terminals are attached) has access to the computer whenever it is needed to do a job. Other advantages offered by a multiuser system are in the areas of security, accounting, backup/recovery, and the like. "Personal Computer Local Area Networks" (Chapter 6) discusses the pros and cons of multiuser systems versus single-user systems and local area networks. As seen in the OS/400 executive overview, the operating systems used with Application Systems support a full multiuser environment.

Multiapplication (also called **multitasking**) means the ability, provided by some operating systems, to switch between two or more independent application programs from a single workstation. The opposite of multiapplication is **single-application**, which means that the computer user must finish using one program before another can be started. The operating systems for all Application Systems support a multiapplication environment, just like an office environment in which workers are often interrupted in the middle of one task to perform another. This multiapplication capability of operating systems is particularly useful in that it allows the user to easily switch back and forth between several simultaneously resident application programs as interruptions occur. This means that the many users connected via terminals do not all have to be executing the same application, yet all appear to be receiving the same service simultaneously.

OS/400 in the Client/Server Environment?

The client/server environment is described in "Client/Server Computing Model" later in this chapter. Here, the changes to the operating system of the AS/400 system are identified. Those changes are dealt with in greater detail in the discussion of the operating system and of the various elements of the operating system that evolved to support the changes. The changes involved supporting the data structures of the personal computer systems that were to be attached. ODBC was added to achieve that support, new communications structures were added, and the relational database structure was modified to what became called an integrated file system, supporting data streaming, triggers, stored procedures, declarative referential integrity, two-phase commit, and long field names. These functions were added as basic to the integrated file system and as a result apply to all of the file systems supported on the AS/400 system, not only those that apply to client/server and open systems environments.

The new communications methodologies that were added support local area networks and packet-switched networks. These new methodologies evolved because the communications structures that were in place to support the small data content (typically less than 2000 characters at a time) of the **Non-Programmable Terminal (NPT)** type of device were inadequate to support the larger information transfers (typically in the range of 10,000 to several million characters at a time) needed for the transfer of applications and full computing data needed by the intelligent clients.

The **server** started out having the single function of providing files to the clients, but, over time, the functions of the server have expanded to include security control of the data, database control and management, networking, application frameworks, and systems management. In the sections dealing with OS/400, database control and management, application frameworks, network file systems, remote file systems, and systems management are discussed. Internet and intranet are discussed in Chapter 5 under the headings "intranet" and "AS/400 and the Internet." Security is discussed from the aspect of Internet and intranet security requirements, and from a total systems management perspective under "Security" in Chapter 6.

Network computing using Internet and intranet connections changes the view of client/server computing. The specific view perceived depends upon if you are resident on the Internet, on an intranet, or on the connection system between the two networks. The Internet is a series of interconnected servers between which the users (clients) bounce as they perform computing activities. Clients may be connected to an intranet and sharing an Internet server connection.

The intranet user is a Internet client when connected to the Internet through an Internet Connection Server. Two intranet users whose only logical and physical connection is through the Internet may ping-pong from client status to server status if allowed to share resources directly.

SSP—An Executive Overview

The **System Support Program** (5716-SSP), commonly called **SSP**, was the operating system originally offered for IBM System/36 computers. Because of the popularity of that computer family, SSP has become widely used in the business community. As a result, many application programs were developed for SSP and the System/36 by many different software companies. As the System/36 computers evolved, SSP was revised to support the enhancements in the computer hardware. Although each new version of SSP provided additional functions, compatibility with earlier application programs was maintained. SSP is the operating system used on the Advanced 36 systems and provides full compatibility with earlier System/36 computers. It consists of a set of programs designed to perform many diverse hardware "housekeeping" tasks under the control of either the computer user or an application program. Tasks performed by SSP include managing multiple users, providing security, managing the flow of batch and interactive jobs through the system, sending information to a printer, and so forth.

After users sign on to an Advanced 36, they can see SSP's main help menu, shown in Figure 4.1. From this menu, the user has two methods of initiating SSP tasks. More experienced users will issue SSP commands (called Operation Control Language [OCL]) at the SSP command line. OCL allows quick access to all SSP functions. Groups of OCL statements can be stored as a **procedure** and thereby executed by a single command. Less experienced users can step through a series of menus to perform operating system tasks. Although this method is not as fast as using OCL commands, the user is prompted at every step, which is easier for novices. These menus, along with online (computer-based) help text, reduce the number of publications needed to operate the system. SSP contains over 2000 screens of online help text similar to that shown in Figure 4.2. If users get stuck while performing some operating

```
                              MAIN
                   Main System/36 help menu

Select one of the following:

        1. Display a user menu
        2. Perform general system activities
        3. Use and control printer, diskettes, or tape
        4. Work with files, libraries, or folders
        5. Use programming languages and utilities
        6. Communicate with another system or user
        7. Define the system and its users
        8. Use problem determination and service
        9. Use office products
       10. Sign off the system




Cmd3-Previous menu    Cmd7-End    Cmd12-How to use help    Home-Sign on menu
 Ready for option number of command
                                            COPR IBM Corp. 1985
```

Figure 4.1. The main help menu presented by the SSP operating system used on the AS/400 Advanced 36.

system task, they can press the Help key. SSP's help facility then presents users with textual information concerning the operation in question.

In addition to performing tasks under direct control of the user, SSP can perform tasks under direct control of an application program. A user can issue SSP commands through keyboard entries. Application programs issue SSP commands through the SSP Application Program Interface (API). This is a defined protocol for passing information and requests directly between the application program and SSP with no user interaction required. It is the job of the operating system to provide for communications. SSP comes standard with the basic communications facilities to support remote workstations. Separately ordered extensions to SSP, such as the SSP communications feature and the **3270 device**

```
How to Use Help                    Introduction

This tutorial describes how to use the help support provided with the system.
It is divided into the selections listed below. Select the option number for
the item you wish to display and press the Enter key.  From the first display
shown you can view the next display by pressing the Roll Up key.  To view a
previous page in this tutorial, press the Roll Down key.  To use the Roll
keys, you must press and hold down one of the shift keys, and then press one
of the Roll keys.

Select one of the following:

        1. The command and function keys you can use
        2. How to use help menus
        3. How to use help procedure and control command displays


Option:


Cmd3-Return to previous menu    Cmd7-End tutorial
                                                COPR IBM Corp. 1983
```

Figure 4.2. Examples of SSP's help text, presented in response to pressing the Help key.

emulation feature, add communications functions such as asynchronous communications support and communications with S/390 computers. Other optional SSP add-ons include the **tape support feature** and the System/36 Utilities. The tape support feature allows a tape backup device to be attached. The System/36 Utilities are a package of programs designed to aid the programmer in writing application programs.

The SSP can coexist with the OS/400 operating system in any Advanced Series model. The Advanced 36 Model 436 is the only model on which the SSP may exist by itself without OS/400. Up to three copies of the SSP operating system are capable of cooperative processing with the OS/400 operating system on systems with adequate memory and disk capacity. In those systems on which cooperative processing is implemented, the OS/400 operating system has overall control and the SSP operating system can make calls for OS/400 I/O resources to perform functions and execute across I/O interfaces that the SSP would not normally be capable of doing because the support code was never written within the SSP itself.

OS/400—An Executive Overview

Operating System/400 (5769-SS1), commonly called OS/400 Version 4, is a multiuser operating system exclusively used with all AS/400 computer systems. It works closely with the System Licensed Internal Code (SLIC) instructions in AS/400 systems to implement the database, security, single-level storage, and so on that are basic to AS/400 architecture. OS/400 represents a divergence from the more traditional operating systems used with the earlier System/36 computers. Like SSP, OS/400 is a set of programs that perform housekeeping tasks based on requests from both users and application programs. Any AS/400 user can load and switch between multiple batch or interactive tasks, each protected from disruption by other tasks or users. Unlike SSP, however, OS/400 participated in the Systems Application Architecture (SAA) activity described in "Applications Architecture" in Chapter 3. OS/400 provides a platform for the development of new application programs in that host-centric environment consistent with the Systems Application Architecture.

The environment for application development has changed from the host-centric focus prevalent at the time of the definition of SAA to an application-centric one. During the evolution from host-centric computing to client/server computing, the name SAA has been dropped by IBM even though the principles of SAA (interoperability and communication between IBM-produced systems independent of the intended marketplace for those systems or the location within IBM that produced the system) have been continued. For example, OS/400 along with the Client Access/400 extension to OS/400 provides the first step in supporting the distributed relational database.

Although OS/400 offers the user complex and sophisticated features, many things have been done to make OS/400 easier to use. One of the ease-of-use enhancements is the uniting of the AS/400 and the Windows 95/Windows NT 4.0 desktop to provide a new graphical interface for users who are familiar with the Windows interface. Other OS/400 items that directly address ease of use include automatic configuration of devices and table-driven customization.

Extensive help and online (computer-based) documentation is provided to reduce the need to go to reference manuals when the user needs more information. Online education using CD-ROMs is built into OS/400 (see "Education" in Chapter 6 for additional details on CD-ROM education programs), allowing users to learn how to use the system while sitting in front of their terminal.

In addition to performing tasks under the direct control of the user, OS/400 performs tasks under direct control of an application program, which issues OS/400 commands through the OS/400. There is a defined protocol for passing information directly between the application program and OS/400 with no user interaction required. Often, OS/400 subsequently calls on the routines of the SLIC instructions to effect the desired action. This interaction between the different software layers was discussed in "AS/400 Software Architecture Overview" in Chapter 3.

OS/400 provides multiple application programming interfaces to maintain compatibility with programs written for System/36, System/38, and of course AS/400. The AS/400 application programming interface provides some new capabilities not found in earlier operating systems, such as the structured query language method of dealing with databases. If a user gets stuck on some operating system screen, pressing the Help key causes some help text to appear on the screen. The particular help text shown depends on where the cursor was on the screen when the Help key was pressed; that is, the text will address the particular item at which the cursor was positioned. This is called **contextual** help.

Extensive database and communications support allows AS/400 to manage large amounts of information and participate in many communications configurations. Available application development tools improve the productivity of programmers for those writing their own custom application programs. For current users of System/36 or System/38 systems, the AS/400 uses SSP and will run System/38 object code.

A Closer Look at OS/400

The previous section provided an overview of OS/400. Even though OS/400 is fairly easy to use, it has many complex features and functions.

A complete description of these features would require a separate book. However, the remainder of this chapter looks briefly at some of the most important topics and the impact upon those topics as a result of the movement to the client/server, networking, and open environments:

- Integrated File System

- Database Support

- Communications Support

- Systems Management Features

- Application Development Facilities

- Integrated Language Environment (ILE)

- Open Standards–Based Interoperability

- System/3X Compatibility

- Emerging Object-Oriented Languages

- Emerging Application Development Environments

- Software Solution Packages

Integrated File System

An enhancement to the AS/400 database support is the addition of an **integrated file system**. The integrated file system supports **stream input/output** and **storage management** similar to PC and **UNIX** operating systems while providing an integrating structure over all information stored in the AS/400 system. The integrated file system provides support for the following:

- Storage of information in stream files that can contain long continuous strings of data (e.g., the text of a document or the picture elements in a picture). The stream file support is designed for use in client/server applications.

- A hierarchical directory structure that allows objects to be organized like fruit on the branches of a tree. An object is accessed by specifying the path through the directories to the object.

- A common interface that allows users and application programs to access not only the stream files but also database files, documents, and other objects stored in the AS/400 system. Figure 4.3 shows the relationship of the new integrated file system, directories, and stream files to the existing folders, libraries, database files, documents, and objects of the AS/400 system.

The integrated file system enhances the data management capabilities of OS/400 to better support emerging and future forms of information processing (e.g., client/server, open systems, and multimedia). The benefits provided by the integrated file system include the following:

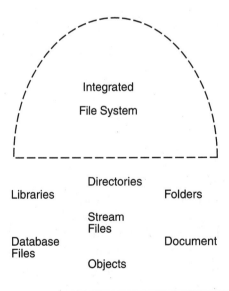

Figure 4.3. OS/400 integrated file system structure.

- Fast access to AS/400 data, especially for applications using the PC file server (shared folder) facilities.

- More efficient handling of the increasingly important types of stream data, such as images, audio, and video.

- A file system and directory base for supporting UNIX-based open system standards such as POSIX and XPG. This file and directory structure also provides a familiar environment for users of PC operating systems such as DOS and OS/2.

- File support with unique capabilities (such as record-oriented database files, UNIX-based stream files, and file serving) can be handled as separate file systems while being managed through a common interface.

- PC users can take better advantage of the graphical user interface. For example, OS/2 users can use the OS/2 graphical tools to operate on AS/400 stream files and other objects in the same way as they operate on files stored on their PCs.

- Continuity of object names and associated object information across national languages ensures that individual characters remain the same when switching from the code page of one language to the code page of another language.

The integrated file system provides support for stream files, file system structure, and CICS/400 files.

Stream Files

To better understand stream files, it is useful to compare them with AS/400 database files. A database file is record oriented: It has predefined subdivisions consisting of one or more fields that have specific characteristics, such as length and data type. A stream file is simply a file containing a continuous stream of data. Documents stored in AS/400 folders are stream files. Other examples of stream files are PC files and the files in UNIX systems. Figure 4.4 illustrates the difference between record-oriented database and stream files. The different structure of stream files and record-oriented files affects how an application is written to interact with them and where each type of file is best used in an application. A record-oriented file, for example, is well suited for storing customer statistics, such as name, address, and account balance, because these predefined fields can be individually accessed and manipulated using the extensive programming facilities of the AS/400. A stream file is better suited for storing information such as a customer's picture, which is composed of a continuous string of bits representing variations in color. Stream files are particularly well suited for storing strings of data such as the text of a document, images, audio, and video.

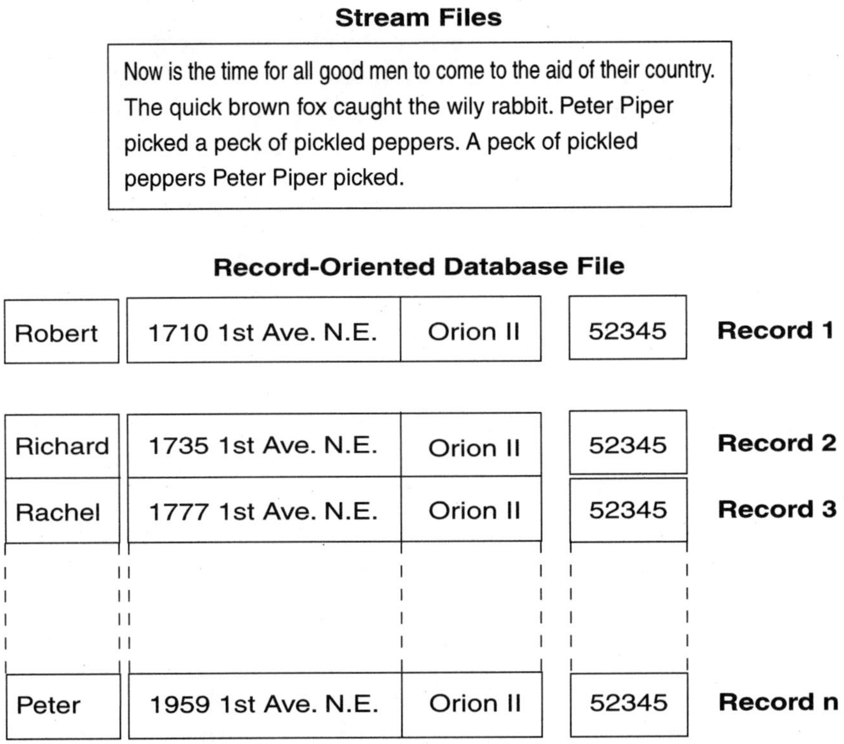

Stream Files

Now is the time for all good men to come to the aid of their country. The quick brown fox caught the wily rabbit. Peter Piper picked a peck of pickled peppers. A peck of pickled peppers Peter Piper picked.

Record-Oriented Database File

Robert	1710 1st Ave. N.E.	Orion II	52345	**Record 1**
Richard	1735 1st Ave. N.E.	Orion II	52345	**Record 2**
Rachel	1777 1st Ave. N.E.	Orion II	52345	**Record 3**
Peter	1959 1st Ave. N.E.	Orion II	52345	**Record n**

Figure 4.4. Stream file structure vs. record-oriented file structure.

Integrated File System Support

From the perspective of structures and rules, the OS/400 support for accessing database files and various other object types through libraries can be thought of as a file system and is called **QSYS.LIB**. Similarly, the OS/400 support for accessing stream files is a separate file system, called **QDLS**. Other file systems supported under the integrated file system include the following:

- **"root"**: the "root" file system is designed to take full advantage of the stream file support and hierarchical directory structure of the integrated file system, and it has the characteristics of the DOS and OS/2 file systems.

- **QOPENSYS**: the open systems file system is designed to be compatible with UNIX-based open system standards, such as POSIX and XPG. It is stream file oriented and supports case-sensitive object names.

- **QLANSrv**: the LAN server file system provides access to the same directories and files as are accessed through the OS/2 Warp Server licensed program. It allows users of the PC file server (shared folders) and AS/400 applications to use the same data as OS/2 Warp Server (5769-XZ1) clients. OS/2 Warp Server will run applications that do not require Graphical User Interface (GUI) interaction. OS/2 Warp Server increases save/restore performance and provides printer serving capability and TCP/IP support including NetBIOS over TCP/IP, and LAN to LAN print capability.

Users and application programs can interact with any of the file systems through a common integrated file system interface. This interface is optimized for input/output of stream data in contrast to the record input/output provided through the data management interfaces. A set of user facilities (commands, menus, and displays) and Application Program Interfaces (APIs) is provided for interacting with the file systems through this common interface. As stated earlier in this chapter, triggers, stored procedures, declarative referential integrity, two-phase commit, and long field names are supported under all file forms and therefore improve DB2 for AS/400 as well as CICS/400.

Structured Query Language (SQL)/400

Recent changes to SQL (SQL Version 2) have made several enhancements to the original SQL product for the AS/400 (called SQL/400 Version 1). First, the speed at which SQL statements are executed has been improved. For users (not necessarily programmers) who perform SQL queries to AS/400 databases, an improved user interface called the **SQL Query Manager** is included with SQL Version 2. The SQL language is supported on larger IBM System/390 computers as well as on Personal System/2s. This means that application programs can use SQL functions while maintaining the ability to more easily migrate among System/390, AS/400, and personal computers (PCs). For programmers, SQL/400 has the **Common Programming Interface (CPI)**, which is designed to make applications written for the AS/400 more portable to other systems (e.g., PCs with OS/2 or S/390 computers). This is a step

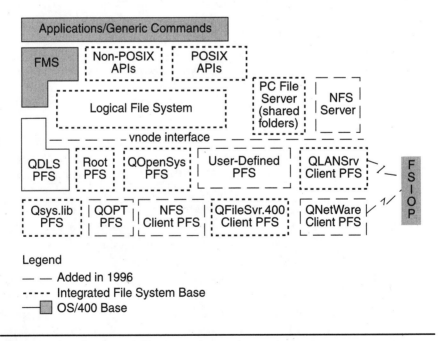

Figure 4.5. Integrated file system internal structure.

toward the goal of the application program compatibility across the major IBM product families. This new CPI also makes it easier to access databases on other systems over communications networks (i.e., better support for **distributed databases**).

Network File System (NFS)

The internal structure of the integrated file system is shown in Figure 4.5. There are five new components to that file system structure. The QOPT PFS (Physical File System) is there to support both CD-ROM and optical libraries. The user-defined physical file system supports long-named objects, as well as allows the user to identify specific groupings of hardware to belong to particular auxiliary storage pools. The NFS Server and NFS Client PFSs are UNIX specific and will be discussed further in the following paragraphs. QNetWare Client PFS is there to support the needs of an Internet set of clients, and is dealt with in greater detail in the section "AS/400 and the Internet".

The NFS Server and NFS Client communicate using Remote Program Calls (RPCs). The NFS Client is a physical file system that implements the AS/400 Virtual File System architecture. The NFS Client provides seamless access to remote files for local applications. The remote files could be on a remote UNIX machine, the AIX IOP, or any machine that is running an NFS Server. The Network File System contains both a lock manager and a system monitor. The design of the system between the server and the client is a stateless design (one in which after completion of the current activity it is impossible to go back to a previous activity, because there is no coherent tracking of separate activities), so changes made at the client cannot be acquired at the server until the data stream is received at the server. Therefore, the server *locks* all data that has been sent to the client until received back from the client. The server monitor keeps track of the state of the systems in the network.

Remote File System

The AS/400 Remote File System allows users to share access to devices such as optical libraries or Integrated PC Controllers (FSIOPs) among

AS/400s, manage a network from a single AS/400, share data in a homogeneous AS/400 network, and get data from multiple AS/400 systems with one connection from a PC. The Remote File System allows an AS/400 to act as a client to other AS/400s to allow access, using the Integrated File System commands, to any object on those AS/400 systems. It can only talk to other AS/400 systems, and Client Access can use this connection to access data on those other AS/400 systems. It is possible to chain system connections this way, but you must pay a propagation delay penalty. The connections can be across TCP/IP, APPC, or both. Functions not supported across these connections include multiple entities like authorization lists and group profiles, extended attributes and byte locking, and save/restore functions. Also, all users share the same connection to the remote system, and symbolic links can be traversed but not created.

Database Support

To deal with large amounts of information efficiently, it is necessary to organize the information in a uniform manner. For example, the information in a telephone book is organized into an alphabetical list of names, addresses, and telephone numbers. If you have ever lifted a Manhattan telephone book, you know that phone books can contain a fair amount of information. Computers also require that information be organized in some fashion. A collection of information stored inside a computer system is called a **database**. There are various ways to organize the information in a database, and the best way depends on how you intend to use the information. There are two basic database structures, hierarchical and relational. In hierarchical database structures, files are ordered in a hierarchical manner similar to the organization of royalty in the European countries of the seventeenth century: There are files, subfiles, sub-subfiles, and so on. In two-dimensional relational database structures, the organization is the same as that in a table, rows and columns. The rows are called records, and the columns are called fields. All fields in a single relational database are related, however vaguely. A complete database may contain multiple relational databases just as a hierarchical database may contain multiple hierarchies of files. The primary database structure in the AS/400 is a relational database called DB2 for AS/400. In addition to the primary database, the AS/400 also supports the CICS/400 database originally designed for the System 390 as well as others identified in the discussion on the integrated file system earlier in this chapter.

A database provides a tool used to organize large quantities of similarly structured information in a computer system. Databases contain information about a department store's inventory, a library's books, personnel records, medical records, and virtually any other type of information. Organizations such as banks, airlines, and insurance companies use extremely large databases shared by many users. Examples of information commonly found in databases are telephone directories, inventories, application programs, and personnel records. OS/400 works together with the SLIC instructions in AS/400 computers to provide a "built-in" relational database. The fact that the AS/400 database is designed into the basic functions of AS/400 computers sets them apart from more conventional computers. In this section, we look at some features of OS/400 that allow you to use AS/400's database functions.

The first step in creating a database of information is to define the **database structure** you desire. In defining the structure, variables such as the length, name, and type of data (for example, numbers or textual characters) of each field are specified. In our example structure (shown in Figure 4.6), a database organized like a telephone book, the first field, which is the name field, is 30 characters long and holds alphanu-

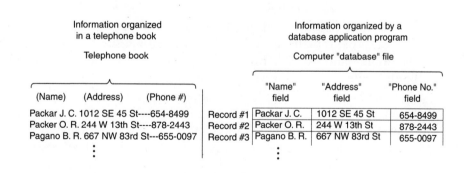

Figure 4.6. Information in a database is organized much like the information in a telephone book.

meric characters. With AS/400, this structure information is defined within the built-in database itself rather than within a program (Figure 4.6). The database structure can be defined through the Data Description Specifications (DDSs) or the Interactive Data Definition Utility (IDDU) functions provided as standard with OS/400. Either of these approaches provides a central repository of structure-related information containing information such as field names, field lengths, and data types.

After the database structure is defined, data is typically input through application programs designed for that purpose. Products such as the Data File Utility (DFU) programs provide the programmer with a tool to help develop simple application programs necessary to load a database structure with information. After the database is loaded with information, the user can manipulate the data with SQL, DFU, Query/400, or application programs written for that purpose.

Built-In Database

Deeply embedded in the architecture and operating system of AS/400 computers lies the support for the development and manipulation of a **relational** database structure. In a relational database, each piece of information is "related" to the others using a simple tabular structure. This provides great flexibility when defining the database and using the information it contains. Inside the AS/400's database, information is stored as **records** and **fields**. Do not be intimidated by the words. This is exactly how the information in a phone book is structured. Figure 4.6 shows an example of a telephone book listing and the corresponding relational database structure found in an AS/400 computer. The phone book itself is analogous to a set of information or a database.

The telephone example is explained in greater detail in "Relational Database—Telephone Book," which follows this section. The database example defines externally described data, and the independent structure of the database. The second example, "Relational Database—Physical and Logical Files," about a business called Atole Enterprises, explains the difference between physical and logical files. The example then explains how logical files in relational databases can eliminate redundancy in data records by providing different views of the same physical file.

The third example, "Relational Database—Concurrency and Lock Management," explains the problems that can arise when logical files are replaced by multiple physical files with redundant fields.

There are ways to keep multiple copies of information up to date on computer systems without logical files, but if the examples are extended to a real business environment with many different clerks, many different programs undergoing changes, and many different types of databases, managing the problem of multiple physical files becomes time-consuming and difficult. With the logical file approach, there is no data redundancy problem to manage. These three examples illustrate how logical database files can be used to provide the user with the information needed in the way that it is needed. Other logical database file structures are possible with the AS/400 computer, which can, for example, pull together selected information from multiple (up to 32) physical database files into a single logical file. This further expands the ability to deliver the right information to the various users without duplicating information in different databases. Through the AS/400 "built-in" database, users have access to information, the security and integrity of the data is protected, and programmer productivity is improved.

Telephone Book

The telephone book provides us with a method of illustrating what a relational database is, allows us to describe how such a database works with a different view for different users, enables us to define how logical files relate to the different users views, provides a capability to present a perspective on data security and data integrity, and then demonstrates one problem set associated with multiple physical databases. The information about one person in the phone book would be analogous to a record. The record contains the information for a given entry, and all other records contain similar information about their respective entries. (An employee's record contains all of the pertinent information about that employee regardless of the number of fields needed.) In this case, a record contains the name, address, and phone number of the person. Each one of these three items is analogous to a field. For example, in a relational data base, the address part of a phone book entry is called the "address field."

Manually looking up information in a phone book is time-consuming and quickly becomes fatiguing. The same is true for manually manipulating any large body of information. Once information is entered into a database, its retrieval by the computer is quick and easy. What does the built-in database capability of the AS/400 have to offer? In AS/400 computers the database structure is defined independently from user programs, the data in the database is available to all user programs for analysis, report generation, update, and so on, but the database definition does not reside in a user's programs. The data is therefore said to be **externally described**, meaning no single user's program on the system describes the structure or content of the database. Instead, the definition "lives" inside the AS/400's built-in database system and in that respect is independent from any one program. This is an important point, because it improves the consistency and thus the maintainability of application programs. Now the programmer has one source for all information pertaining to the database structure and how application programs use the database. Externally described data contribute to improved programmer productivity because the database will fit itself to the application program rather than the application program fitting itself to the database.

The examples in "Relational Database—Physical and Logical Files" and "Relational Database—Concurrency and Lock Management" use simple database structures. In the sections on data warehousing and data mining in Chapter 3, multidimensional database structures are mentioned. Those more complex logical database file structures are possible with the AS/400 computer, which can, for example, pull together selected information from multiple (up to 32) physical database files into a single logical file. This further expands the ability to deliver the right information to the various users without duplicating information in different databases.

Physical and Logical Files

Another important feature of AS/400 database support is the support for **logical files**. The telephone book example deals with real, or **physical**, database files, which are groupings of information inside a computer. The concept of logical files allows a system administrator to change the appearance of the physical database to better suit individual needs. For example, suppose there is a personnel database on an AS/400 computer for a fictitious company named Atole Enterprises. The organization of the personnel information is shown in Figure 4.7. This physical database file contains all personnel information and was described externally to any user programs. A clerk (Jim) has the job of keeping an up-to-date mailing list of all employees for the company magazine, but to protect employees' privacy, Jim must not have access to the wage information that is part of the physical database file. To meet these needs, a logical database file is defined that contains no information but only a "view" of the physical database that meets Jim's needs. The logical database file restricts Jim's view of the physical database file to only the information he needs. Furthermore, since Jim looks up employees by name, this is the **key** field defined in his logical database file. He is able to access the information by alphabetical order of employee name (his key field) rather than by the order in which the names actually appear in the physical database file. Jim's logical database file structure is shown in Figure 4.8.

Another logical database file for a different clerk (Nancy) exists using the same physical data. Nancy tracks employee service anniversaries. Her logical database file structure is shown in Figure 4.9. Nancy

	Name	Address	Phone	Wages	SS#	Date of Hire	Marital Status
Record 1							
Record 2							
Record 3							
Record 4							
Record 5							
Record 6							
Record 7							
Record 8							
⋮							
Record X							

Figure 4.7. Physical database containing personnel information.

Jim's Logical Database
(Key)

	Name	Address	Phone	Wages	SS#	Hire date	Marital status
Record 1							
Record 2							
Record 3							
Record 4							
Record 5							
Record 6							
Record 7							
Record 8							
⋮							
Record X							

Figure 4.8. Jim's logical database provides a "view" of the physical database needed to perform his job.

looks up employees by their date of hire, so this is the key field in her logical database file. Only the fields needed to do her job are made available to Nancy. As the needs of Atole change, many logical database files can be defined to meet the different employees' needs without affecting any other user or the physical database file. The restrictions provided by unique views for different users/user groups inherently guarantees data security and data integrity. Also, within any particular view, fields may be further identified as read only for additional data integrity. Users are allowed to view and change data contained in the fields to which they have authorization to make changes.

This example illustrates how multiple users can use a single copy of a physical database to do completely different jobs. Without logical files, multiple physical databases would have to be kept in the computer system, wasting space. The Atole Enterprises example is extended in Relational Databases—Concurrency and Lock Management to illustrate the problems of data concurrency and lock management across multiple physical databases containing redundant data.

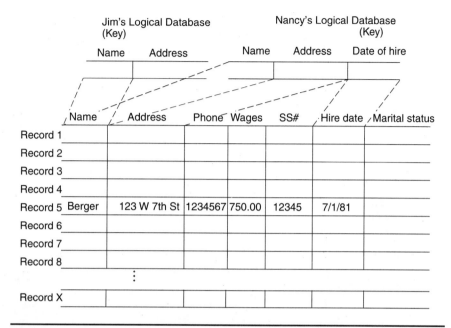

Figure 4.9. Multiple logical databases can be constructed, providing different views of the same physical database.

Concurrency and Lock Management

Figure 4.10 illustrates a situation at fictitious Atole Enterprises that can occur when multiple databases contain redundant information. The figure shows three different databases (one for Jim, one for Nancy, and one for payroll), each of which contains name and address fields for Atole Enterprises employees. In addition to wasting space because of the redundancy, other problems are associated with having multiple physical databases. For example, one morning Jim receives notice that an employee (Mr. Berger) has a new mailing address and Jim promptly updates the database. Later that same morning, Nancy searches for that month's service anniversaries and finds that the month is Mr. Berger's seventh anniversary with the company. She checks his address and sends him an anniversary card. Without the logical file approach, in which Jim and Nancy share one physical copy of the data, Mr. Berger's card would be sent to the old address. With the logical database of the AS/400

Jim's Database		Nancy's Database			Payroll Database					
Name	Address	Name	Address	Hire Date	Name	Address	Phone	Wages	SS	Hire Date
Berger	333 E 7th St	Berger	333 E 7th St	7/1/81	Berger	333 E 7th St	1234567	750.00	23422	7/1/81
⋮		⋮			⋮					

Physical Database #1   Physical Database #2   Physical Database #3

Figure 4.10. Without logical database views, multiple physical databases would be necessary, wasting space, compromising data integrity, and complicating processing.

computers, as soon as Jim updates Mr. Berger's address it is available to Nancy, and Mr. Berger gets his card on time. The problem solved by the single physical file with multiple logical views is one of concurrency (synchronization); that is, when multiple physical files exist with redundant data defined across those physical files, an update to a redundant field in one of those files makes it different from the identical field in the other physical files. One alternative solution is to maintain a cross-reference file that identifies all of the redundant fields of each of the physical files and an application program that updates the redundant fields of the other physical files when any of the fields receives a change.

A second problem that arises from the concurrency problem is lock management. Lock management becomes a problem because once the computer knows that a redundant field has received a change, the computer must prohibit processing with those fields of the physical files containing old data because either this will cause erroneous results or, as in our example, the information will be sent to the wrong location. To prevent that processing, the computer system locks those fields until update processing has completed. If a program has started that uses a locked field, it must be backed out of the computing system or put into a suspended state. The illustration selected is a simple one because the data that changed was entered by an individual, but consider the problem when the redundant field is changed under control of an application program, with other application programs referencing that field for processing information. With multiple physical files with redundant fields, situations have arisen in which the entire computing system became deadlocked because the total resources of the computer were tied up and the update program could not gain access to the resources to execute to resolve the lock situations. Lock management programs are very complex programs. Lock management is also a problem when redundancy occurs over distributed databases on distributed systems.

There are ways to keep multiple copies of information up to date on computer systems without logical files, but if our example is extended to a real business environment with many different clerks, many different programs undergoing changes, and many different types of databases, managing the problem becomes time-consuming and difficult. With the logical file approach, there is no data redundancy problem to manage. This example illustrates one method of using logical database files to provide the user with the information needed in the way that it is needed.

Distributed Data Management

In a networked system environment, the **Distributed Data Management (DDM)** function of OS/400 allows an AS/400 user to access data on a remote AS/400 as if the data were located on the local AS/400 system. With distributed data management, the user need not know which computer system has the needed data. If the needed database resides on a different AS/400 located elsewhere in the communications network, DDM will automatically get the information for the user.

Distributed Data Management has always allowed distributed database activity with remote AS/400 systems, but there was no support for interacting with any compatible databases on other computer systems (e.g., IBM's ES/9000 line of computers). Enhancements in the Distributed Data Management function of OS/400 include full support of the **Distributed Relational Database Algorithm (DRDA)**. One element of Distributed Data Management's support for DRDA is called the re-

mote unit of work. This allows an AS/400 application program to include compatible System Query Language (SQL) statements that interact with data residing on another compatible database on a distant computer system. That is, the user now has access to the data stored on other computer systems (e.g., an IBM ES/9000 computer system with an SQL/DS database). The user can interact with multiple remote databases during a single database transaction

DB2 for OS/400—An Overview

DB2 for AS/400 (DB2/400) is a relational database supporting large physical file structures, built on a records/fields structure, supporting multiple views, logical views, and read-only fields, and incorporating access-level security and data integrity.

Among the more popular databases supported by OS/400 is DB2. Triggers, stored procedures, declarative referential integrity, two-phase commit, and long field names are supported under all file forms and therefore improve **DB2/400** as well as CICS/400. The **DB2/400** capability provides support for

- ANSI X3.135.1992, ISO 9075-1992, and FIPS 127-2

- Structured Query Language (SQL)

- IBM's Distributed Relational Database Architecture (DRDA)

- Distributed Unit of Work—Application Directed

- Microsoft's Open Database Connection (ODBC)

- Java DataBase Connection (JDBC)

- Apple's Data Access Language

Parallel index building capability is added to DB2 Symmetric MultiProcessing (SMP) for AS/400, extending the SMP capabilities to utilize multiple processors during the creation or rebuilding of indices.

DB2 for OS/400

Over 25,000 commercially available AS/400 application solutions take advantage of the power, flexibility, and ease of use of the DB2 for AS/400 database manager. These applications are written for a wide range of industries and users, ranging from small businesses with basic accounting needs to large corporations with complex computing environments.

DB2 for AS/400 performs all the functions described in the examples used to introduce relational database concepts: multiple physical databases within a single database structure each of which contains records, fields, and some relationship; and multiple views for each physical database within the structure. Since there is no redundancy, there is no reason for concerns about concurrency and lock management. Both Open DataBase Connection (ODBC) and System Query Language (SQL) are supported for accessing the database.

DB2 for AS/400 has been enabled to become a partitioned database with its tables spread across the multiple system nodes, using either user-defined ranges or hash partitioning, but still presenting a single table view to the application, which operates in support of the potential interconnection of 32 loosely coupled systems using Opticonnect/400. **DB2 Multisystem for AS/400** is a separately priced option for OS/400. The data partitioning does not allow ranges, although the user can specify where the hash result of individual values should reside. The main benefits of multisystem are high-end growth and greater processing power. A query issued against a distributed file will be submitted in parallel to all applicable systems in the node group, resulting in all the systems working on the query in parallel, and inside each system the query is also running in parallel. A database monitor tracks events inside the database and provides the information about those events to the administrator.

Queries executed against the DB2 for AS/400 database items see improved performance when executed on a system with more than one processor because the query workload is evenly distributed across the processors within the system, a process called **symmetric multiprocessing**.

DB2/400 has been enabled for Internet application serving, which allows immediate use of existing data on the Internet to or from a terminal no matter where in the world the terminal is located, provided the usage meets the security requirements to use the Web server and has an appropriate Web browser. The results of a query are returned to your Web browser as an HTML document. Figure 4.11 illustrates how the Internet connection to DB2 for AS/400 parallels the AS/400's generalized support for client/server computing.

The Data Propagator Relational Capture and Apply product enables easy management of DB2-family distributed databases containing local copies of master databases by providing automatic update support for the shadow copies and the capability to replicate entire copies of a file. It takes advantage of the remote journaling function to run the capture process at the remote journal location, which off-loads the capture process overhead from the production system. The apply process no longer needs to connect to the production system for differential refresh, as the staging tables will reside locally instead of on the production system. A new exit program lets you automatically delete source file journal receivers that are no longer needed by the capture process.

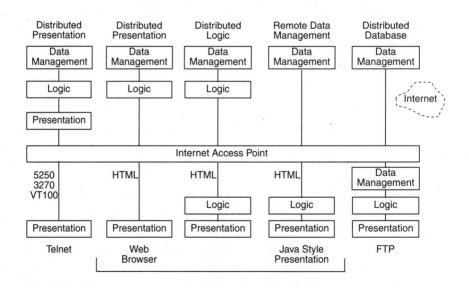

Figure 4.11. DB2 for AS/400 Internet-style application development environment.

Open DataBase Connection (ODBC)

Open DataBase Connection is a Microsoft-provided Application Program Interface specification for database access, the objective of which is to provide interoperability between applications and databases without writing database-specific code in the application. This definition sounds very similar to the program independence objective identified for the relational database in "Relational Database—Telephone Book." DB2 for AS/400 supports Open DataBase Connection. As a result, applications such as Net.Connection that use DB2 may exchange data with other applications that use ODBC. The SQL Call Level Interface is compatible with ODBC, allowing an application to be written on a PC using ODBC and then be ported to run on the AS/400 directly. ODBC is also supported by Client Access Family for Windows and Client Access Family.

Java DataBase Connection (JDBC)

The Java DataBase Connection provides the same capabilities for Net.Data as ODBC provides, including the capability for applications written in Java to access applications that use ODBC and as a result to access DB2 applications.

Data Striping

IBM improved the performance and capacity of DB2 for AS/400 by automatically **striping** all writes to the data files upon which the data will be stored. (A database file consists of many blocks of information. These blocks are randomly spread/striped across multiple devices. A single DASD device can store multiple blocks from a single file—most likely the multiple blocks for a file on a device are *not* logically contiguous.) This spreading across multiple DASD devices allows the data to be accessed in parallel. The result is a significant performance improvement because the data can be brought into main storage in parallel, instead of serially. This is made possible because the multiple I/O Processors (IOPs), supporting disk units on the AS/400 system, preprocess the data on writes and reads to improve access time.

Partitioned Database

To better serve users who have implemented or are considering implementing the loosely coupled structure of systems allowed by the Opticonnect/400 capability of interconnecting up to 32 systems optically, DB2 for AS/400 has been enabled to become a partitioned database with its tables spread across the multiple system nodes, using either user-defined ranges or hash partitioning but still presenting a single table view to the application. This can apply the power of 384 processors (if all of the processors are 12-way symmetric multiprocessors, all working in parallel) to a query. This massively parallel database supports parallel insert, update, and delete while allowing the DB2 for AS/400 database size to grow from a previous single system maximum of 1,546 GB up to a maximum loosely coupled parallel database limit of 49.47 TB. Symmetric MultiProcessing (SMP) is supported with the optional DB2 for Symmetric MultiProcessing for AS/400, which provides parallelism in index builds and queries. SMP uses parallel table scan, parallel index scan, parallel hash join, parallel hash group by, and parallel index build algorithms.

The response time of queries executed in a symmetric multiprocessor environment resolve themselves more quickly because the power of all of the distributed processors is applied in parallel against the distributed database. This is particularly applicable when performing data mining against a data warehouse.

Database Monitor

A database monitor has been added to DB2 for AS/400. The database monitor provides information about what the database is doing, such as how many temporary indexes have been created, which information people are using the most, how many queries have exceeded a specified time limit, and which queries are using the most system resources. The data from the monitor is collected at the job or system level. The monitor provides all information from either a debug or print sequence plus the following:

- System and job name

- SQL statement and subselect number

- Start and end time stamp

- Estimated processing time

- Total rows in file queried

- Number of rows selected

- Estimated number of rows selected

- Estimated number of joined rows

- Key fields for advised index

- Total optimization time

- Join method

- Join type and others

Database Management

A single program can use any combination of old (System/3X) functions and new AS/400 functions. This allows maximum flexibility for new database application programs and added capabilities when modifying System/3X application programs that have been migrated to AS/400. Furthermore, different application programs can simultaneously use different methods to access the same database files without interfering with one another. Although OS/400 provides the programmer/user with many ways to "get at" database information, other functions are necessary to make a complete database management system. In a typical database environment, many different users are constantly making changes to the information in the database. These changes are called database **transactions**. To maintain the accuracy or **data integrity** of the information in the database at all times, OS/400 plays the role of a traffic director.

First, OS/400 prevents two people from simultaneously updating the same information. Without this protection, the integrity of the database is at risk. For example, two travel agents making a reservation for their respective customers simultaneously call up the same seat in an airliner. Both reservationists see the seat as available. The first reservationist reserves the seat for Mr. Jones and posts that change to the database. The second reservationist, who still sees the seat as available, reserves the seat for Ms. Smith and posts this change to the database, overwriting Mr. Jones's reservation. Neither reservationist knows that an error has been introduced! That is a data integrity problem. Although this may seem to be an unlikely series of events, if it can happen it will, particularly in very active database environments in which many thousands of transactions are generated every hour. OS/400 prevents two people from updating the same database information. This is called **record level locking**.

Other improvements have been made. As an example, deleted database records are automatically reused, eliminating the need to execute the physical file command to recover unused disk storage space, and support is provided for **variable-length fields**—a new data type for the AS/400.

CICS/400

Using application programs (prewritten or custom) to access and manipulate information in an AS/400 database, businesses can combine all of the methods of accessing information to provide an environment that is tailored to their particular needs. These application programs may, unknown to the users, employ one or more of the previously discussed database access methods, depending on the specific need. Using the CICS/400 (5738-DFH) extension to OS/400, programmers can run CICS application programs (COBOL) on an AS/400 and access data on the AS/400 or some other computer (e.g., an S/390 or OS/2 computer) running CICS. Application programs that use CICS are very common in the IBM S/390 user community. CICS/400 allows programmers to migrate S/390-based CICS application programs to the AS/400 or use their CICS experience to write new CICS application programs specifically for the AS/400. The communications functions provided by the CICS environment provide another way for AS/400 programmers to write/migrate application programs that give users access to information stored in the AS/400 and other computer systems. The CICS/400 functions have been extended to include client/server support, two-phase commit, and C application language support.

Many of these different methods and tools for creating, loading, and accessing AS/400 files and databases were carried over from the System/36 and System/38 product lines. Some of these different methods and tools provide functions that are highly redundant with others. This was done intentionally to provide application program compatibility with the System/36 and System/38. Providing all these different methods for managing AS/400 databases makes it easier to migrate System/3X application programs to AS/400. This helps preserve the significant investment made by businesses in application programs, user training, data accumulation, and so on. At the same time, improved database tools (e.g., SQL/400 and CICS/400) not available with System/3X computers are provided for the AS/400.

Communications Support

Communications facilities included in OS/400 allow a properly equipped AS/400 computer to communicate with different computing equipment in a variety of ways. First, OS/400 provides support for remote workstations, allowing terminals and printers to be located far away (e.g., across the country) from the AS/400 computer system itself. This allows remote offices to perform all the functions available to those users located in the same building as the AS/400. Further, OS/400 provides the programming support for communications with other computer systems (both IBM and non-IBM) such as System/390, personal computers, System/3X, Macintosh, and other AS/400s. In any case, there are different communications protocols that can be used, as discussed in "Wide Area Networks (WANs)" and in "The AS/400 and Local Area Networks" in Chapter 2. OS/400 includes support for the following protocols, the first five of which are used in wide area networks, the last four of which are used in local area networks:

- Async

- Bisync

- SDLC

- X.25

- IDLC (ISDN networks)

- IEEE 802.5 (IBM token-ring networks)

- IEEE 802.3 (Ethernet networks)

- ISO 9314 (FDDI networks)

- Wireless Local Area Networks

Communications configurations provide some hardware and software configurations for various communications networks. For now, it is only necessary to understand that OS/400 comes with the programming required to support these different types of communications environments.

Additional information about additional subjects supported by OS/400 communications can be obtained by referring to the following sections:

- TCP/IP

- Systems Network Management

- Systems Network Architecture (SNA)

- Display Station/Printer Pass-Thru

- S/390 Communications Support

TCP/IP

Another extension to OS/400, called AS/400 TCP/IP Communications Utilities (5738-TC1), allows AS/400 systems to participate in communications networks that use the Transmission Control Protocol/Internet Protocol (TCP/IP). TCP/IP is commonly used over a Local Area Network (LAN) in which computer systems of different brands communicate with one another. The IBM TCP/IP Server Support/400 product (5798-RWY) gives clients access to AS/400 database files and folder files via Sun Microsystems' Network File System (NFS), which is commonly used in TCP/IP environments. The TCP/IP protocol has become increasingly significant as the client/server environment has moved into a networked environment including both intranets and the Internet. Standards supported by AS/400 TCP/IP include Dynamic Host Configuration Protocol (DHCP) and Domain Name Server. Dynamic Host Configuration Protocol support allows the AS/400 to dynamically assign IP (Internet Protocol) addresses when new hosts are added to the network, such as when a network station or PC is turned on in an intranet. Domain Name Server converts the text names as used in URLs to the 32-bit codes used for network routing. As an example it converts *www.as400.ibm.com* to *205.217.130.11*. Other functions supported are TCP/IP dial-in via PPP and ISDN as well as full TCP/IP routing. Operations Navigator provides a Windows-like graphical interface to the TCP/IP configuration function.

Systems Network Management

Having AS/400 systems participate in a communications network is one thing, but managing that communications network is something else. Systems network management tasks include such things as problem determination, problem tracking, making network configuration changes, and distributing necessary changes. In addition to this list of management tasks, the AS/400 can provide operations monitoring, automated operations, problem management, software distribution, change management, backup and recovery, media management, security, performance management, and capacity planning not only for the AS/400 systems in your network, but also for the attached clients. Rather than discuss each of these functions individually, we shall discuss the benefits that arise for the business as a result of the management function.

Among the benefits is that the user is not involved in the following activities because the system performs them automatically: problem data collection and logging; hardware problem prediction and logging; automated configuration and resource data logging; performance data capture and logging; alert generation, logging, and reporting; and Electronic Customer Support (ECS), which provides automated problem reporting, electronic PTF selection/distribution, automated service dispatching, and an electronic interface to the IBM information/database. This automation allows a reduction in staff. The AS/400 will do the distribution automatically, take care of the security related to the software, detect the problems that occur on the clients whether those clients are from IBM or other vendors, and provide backup and recovery for those clients as required. The distribution of the functions that accomplish these tasks within the AS/400 is accomplished under a set of programs named Systems Manager/400 and Managed System Services/400 within OS/400. The next section shows how this might work between an AS/400 system and a System/390 computer. See the Systems Network Management example.

Systems Network Management Example

The systems network management functions needed vary depending on the type of communications network involved. For example, in a simple token-ring network, OS/400 can automatically notify the network operator of any problems that develop in the token-ring adapter or cable and record the error to help in problem determination. In more complex communications environments, OS/400 has other functions that help manage the enterprise. Suppose an AS/400 in Pittsburgh, Pennsylvania, is part of a network managed from a central System/390 computer located in San Francisco. The network operator in San Francisco uses a System/390 program called **NetView** to manage the entire network. Now a problem develops in the communications link between the AS/400 in Pittsburgh and the System/390 in San Francisco. OS/400 automatically notifies the network operator in San Francisco that a network problem has been detected. This is done through an **alert** message that is automatically sent by OS/400 to the computer in San Francisco.

Once an alert notifies the network operator of the problem, several OS/400 functions help identify and correct the problem. First, the **Network Remote Facilities (NRF)** program allows the network operator to interact with the AS/400 as if the System/390 terminal in San Francisco were actually a remote AS/400 workstation in Pittsburgh. Using another OS/400 network management feature called the **NetView Remote**

Manager (NV/RM), the network operator can also issue network commands to test the health of network elements (e.g., modems). Once the cause of the problem is determined, the necessary fix can be put in place. If a change to some AS/400 programming is necessary, OS/400's **SystemView Managed System Services (MSS)** program provides a way to distribute and install new programs or changes directly from San Francisco. Alternately, to exchange files between the S/390 host (running MVS/ESA) in San Francisco and the AS/400 in Pittsburgh, the **NetView File Transfer program** (5730-082) can be used. Thus, the San Francisco–based network operator can use his or her expertise to analyze and fix the problem without having to travel to Pittsburgh. This kind of network management environment makes for speedy problem determination and correction, resulting in less system downtime.

Systems Network Architecture (SNA)

OS/400 supports IBM's Systems Network Architecture (SNA). This is a published set of rules governing various aspects of computer communications from protocols (e.g., SDLC) to document formats (e.g., Document Content Architecture [DCA]) and electronic mail (e.g., SNA Distribution Services [SNADS]). It is SNA that provides the common ground on which different types of computer equipment can efficiently exchange information. OS/400's **Advanced Peer-to-Peer Network (APPN)** architecture, originally developed on the earlier IBM S/36 computers, has now been adopted as part of SNA. Further, APPN support has been expanded (APPN end-node support) to allow more direct interaction with traditional SNA networks.

Wireless Local Area Network

The IBM Wireless Connection for AS/400 (5798-TBW) is a networking software program for the OS/400 operating system at Version 4 Release 1 that connects AS/400 Wireless Portable Transaction Computers (PTCs) to RISC-based AS/400 systems by means of a wireless Local Area Network (LAN). The system administrator can name PTC device sessions, change the PTC configuration without first ending Wireless Connection for AS/400, remap the PTC keyboard, and reformat the PTC screen to display existing applications. This networking software product uses Internet Protocol (IP) and TCP/IP sockets to support wireless networks through locally attached Ethernet and token-ring LANs and at remote locations through routers, allowing easy integration between wireless networks and installed LANs. An existing LAN wiring infrastructure can be used for this connection by dropping a 2480 Ethernet or token-ring access point from the existing wiring.

This networking software product is particularly applicable to the Model 150, Model 170, Model 600, and Model S10 because the 2668 Wireless LAN Adapter can only be attached to an SPD bus, and no equivalent is available for the only bus supported by these system models, a PCI bus. This software networking product does not work on the CISC-based Version 3 Release 2 systems, for which the 2668 Wireless LAN Adapter was designed.

Display Station/Printer Pass-Thru

Other communications functions provided with OS/400 include **Display Station Pass-Thru (DSPT)** and **object distribution**. DSPT allows a user of one system to sign on to some other computer in the communications network as if the two systems were directly attached. This allows one workstation to access any computer system in the network. The object distribution facility of OS/400 makes sending information or programs to remote locations much simpler. A common use for this facility is to distribute application programs developed at a central site to remote computers.

A recent addition to the pass-thru functions is **printer pass-thru**. This allows a print spool function to be performed on any computer in the systems network and later be printed either on the printer that is most local to the display station that originated the print spool function or at a printer located anywhere in the system network that the user selects. Figure 4.12 illustrates the connection for display or printer pass-thru.

S/390 Communications Support

The AS/400 Communications Utilities (5738-CM1) software product complements the communications function of OS/400 for interacting with System/390 computers. This set of programs augments OS/400

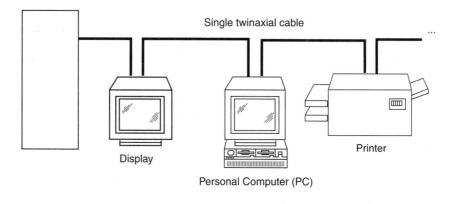

Single twinaxial cable

Display

Personal Computer (PC)

Printer

Figure 4.12.   All Application Systems use the cable-thru approach to attaching local workstations.

communications functions in the area of interchanging electronic mail and files with various System/390 computer environments over a SNA communications network. For example, AS/400 Communications Utilities allows AS/400 Office users to exchange information with users of the **OfficeVision/VM** and **OfficeVision/MVS**. These programs run on the System/390, providing those users with functions like those of OfficeVision/400 (e.g., electronic mail and calendaring). The other basic function provided by AS/400 Communications Utilities is called the **Remote Job Entry Facility (RJE)**. RJE allows an AS/400 system to emulate an RJE workstation used to submit batch jobs to or receive output from System/390 computers. Figure 4.13 illustrates one methodology for connecting an AS/400 system to a System/390 computer.

Client Access

Client Access/400 has been divided into two separate components, AS/400 Client Access Family for Windows (5769-XW1) and AS/400 Client Access Family (5769-XY1). AS/400 Client Access Family for Windows includes Client Access for Windows 95/NT and Client Access Enhanced for Windows 3.1, and supports those customer environments, which concentrate on Windows as a client platform. Client Access Enhanced for Windows 3.1 includes communications and management

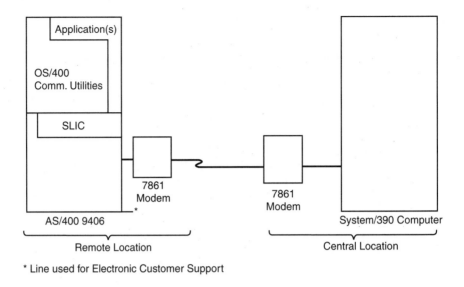

Figure 4.13. Example of a communications configuration used to attach an AS/400 to an S/390 computer.

enhancements. Client Access Family for Windows supports Windows NT 4.0 and Windows 95, and includes Lotus Mail 4.5. Both Client Access/400 products provide fully graphical viewing of AS/400 output files, faxes and image files. Full-page documents (such as AFP spooled files) are completely rendered on both Windows and OS/2 clients. A functional extension (AFP Workbench for Client Access/400) provides for printing, faxing, and annotating the viewed document. The Client Access/400 Viewer means business processes can be easily extended beyond printed output, to archival, indexing, retrieval, customer service viewing, reprint and fax.

AS/400 Client Access Family includes Client Access for Windows 3.1, Client Access Optimized for OS/2, Client Access for OS/2, Client Access for DOS with Extended Memory, and Client Access for DOS, and is intended to be used in environments that are not predominantly using Windows as a client platform. Client Access product positioning information can be obtained at *http://www.as400.ibm.com/clientaccess*.

Client Access Family for Windows

Client Access Family for Windows provides AS/400-to-Windows desktop connectivity and function. Connectivity includes TCP/IP, IPX, and SNA for token-ring and Ethernet LANs (IPX is only supplied with Client Access for Windows 95/NT). SNA supports SDLC, asynchronous, X.25, and twinax communications. AnyNet protocol independence provides the ability to run APPC over TCP/IP. Display and print emulators that can access AS/400 facilities are PC5250, Graphical Access, Systems Object Access, and Operations Navigator with the Client Access for Windows 95/NT. AS/400 resources are extended to the desktop using End User Tools (e.g., graphical data transfer, network print, network drives, and file serving). APIs (ODBC, Data Queues, Remote Commands, and Remote SQL) further extend the services and resources of the AS/400.

Client Access for Windows 95/NT provides e-mail support through Lotus Mail 4.5 on TCP/IP, IPX, and SNA/APPC networks to send and receive mail anywhere in the world. The support includes a single log-on and directory function like the AS/400 System Directory.

TCP/IP Enhancements

TCP/IP enhancements include many functions that previously were only available for the SNA/APPC environment. Those functions include the ability to define and run a PC5250 printer emulation session, enabling users to send AS/400 printed output to a PC-attached printer. PC Printer output placed on the AS/400 spool file can also be redirected to a PC-attached printer. Increased printing flexibility is provided by allowing the use of standard Windows 95/NT print drivers or a customized PC5250 print menu. TCP/IP also now has the ability to designate a specific 5250 Workstation device ID for display and printer emulation sessions and the ability to bypass AS/400 screens.

Data Serving

It is now possible to access AS/400 data from a Windows 95/NT workstation by viewing AS/400 data from the integrated file system, analyzing data with PC applications through ODBC or transferring data through the interactive and batch data transfer interfaces. Data serving enhancements include both AS/400 Data Transfer and ODBC support improvements. Data Transfer improvements include the following:

- PC5250 emulation tool bar ability to launch data transfers.

- Downloading AS/400 data to an HTML file.

- Acceptance of Native SQL commands.

- Server and Workstation code performance tuning.

- ODBC support that now includes multiuser support of the Client Access ODBC driver for the Windows NT server environment, allowing users connected to the NT server to access AS/400 database information without installing Client Access on every desktop. The NT server can be the Integrated PC Server or it can be another NT server in the network, and SQL package caching improves the performance of ODBC, accelerating the presentation of data to the end user.

- Installation and usability enhancements, which include the presentation of a welcome wizard with two paths (describing new functions for the experienced user, suggestions about getting started for the novice user), and cascading menus, which allow quicker access to Client Access from the Windows programs menu.

- Improved SNA and twinaxial support by NetSoft router wizard integration with step-by-step instructions during configuration, and by allowing more than one router instance to use a shared service access point. In the case of 100% IBM-compatible twinax cards, an integrated installation of a twinax virtual device driver is supported as well as support for 5250 Express Data Stream twinax cards and other twinax adapter cards that use unique device drivers.

- Providing Windows NT with the same fax support functions as Windows 95 currently has.

- A new release of PC5250 that incorporates common PC keyboard defaults like the Enter and Print Screen keys with improved diagnostics and hot-spot activation of URL addresses, which launches a Web browser and connects you to the Internet by clicking on the hot-spot.

- Gateway support for the Netware SAA 32-bit client and IBM communications server for NT.

- Operations Navigator's extension of the range of graphical OS/400 tasks available to the network administrator by allowing the launch of the Network station manager and configuration of the Internet connection server and firewall, providing a single view of TCP/IP information such as sockets and host table–started servers through a properties panel, as well as support for PPP and Windows Network Neighborhood. Ultimedia Systems Facilities managing multimedia applications and objects are now available on Windows 95/NT clients.

AS/400 Client Access Family

The AS/400 Client Access Family offers client/server capabilities for connecting personal computers (PCs) to AS/400 systems. Graphical interfaces are provided for accessing AS/400 databases and PC files stored on the AS/400 system, using network printers and faxes, running AS/400 and PC applications, and administration.

Industry-standard frameworks supported include Open Database Connectivity (ODBC), Messaging Application Programming Interface (MAPI) for mail enabling applications, Desktop Management Interface (DMI) for centralized inventory of client hardware and software, and the Simple Network Management Protocol (SNMP). Support is also provided for multimedia. The Internet can be used as a connection mechanism, using TCP/IP.

Popular PC desktop environments supported by Client Access Family include OS/2, Windows 3.1, OS/2 Warp, DOS, and DOS Extended. As can be seen, this list includes 16-bit versions of Windows and 16- and 32-bit versions of OS/2, as well as both popular versions of DOS.

Client Access Family provides for the exchange of information between the PC and the AS/400 system. For example, information in AS/400 databases can be manipulated on the PC using a spreadsheet program, and a document created on the PC can be manipulated on the AS/400 by OfficeVision/400 text processing or sent through OfficeVision/400's electronic mail system. Shared folders allow the usage of the AS/400's disk storage to share information among a network of PCs and AS/400s.

Client Access Family provides full graphical viewing of AS/400 output files, faxes, and image files. Full-page documents are completely rendered on OS/2 clients. Print and display emulation is provided using Rumba/400, PC5250, and Workstation Function. The Client Access Viewer means business processes can extend beyond printed output, to archival, indexing, retrieval, customer service viewing, reprinting, and faxing.

Printers and communication links can also be shared through Client Access's **virtual printer** functions. Through the use of **Advanced Program-to-Program Communications (APPC)**, the functions available to PC users are the same regardless of the communications method being used. The users get the same benefits from Client Access/400 whether they are twinax-attached local workstations, remote workstations, or workstations attached via a local area network.

The administration functions of Client Access Family perform systems management tasks (e.g., update the software on a group of PCs) on any PC in the network from the AS/400 system and provide a call-level interface for PC-based application programs that allows a PC program to send SQL statements, which are then executed on the AS/400 system. Client Access can now coexist with Novell NetWare LAN client functions in the same workstation. This means that a single workstation can concurrently access information on both an AS/400 (OS/2 Warp Server/400) and on Novell servers (with Novell NetWare software).

SystemView

To bring more order to systems management tools, IBM defined a framework called **SystemView** to improve the efficiency and reduce the cost associated with systems management activities. The SystemView strategy is to publish a framework (blueprint) to guide the development of a family of integrated systems management tools. By publishing the SystemView framework, IBM has encouraged the many companies developing systems management software products to modify their systems management tools or to create new systems management tools that follow the SystemView framework. The user gets SystemView-compliant systems management tools. The SystemView framework is depicted in Figure 4.14. There are three elements in the SystemView framework: the *end-use dimension*, the *data dimension*, and the *application dimension*.

The **end-use dimension** addresses a consistent user interface for all systems management tools. All SystemView tools should present a common appearance and behavior to the user. Having a consistent user interface reduces the training requirements for the users because concepts and techniques learned on the first SystemView tool are transferable to other SystemView tools. The user interface specified by the SystemView end-use dimension complies with the Common User Access (CUA) interface.

The **data dimension** of SystemView defines the information types and formats shared by all SystemView-compliant tools and provides facilities for accessing data consistently. Re-entering the same data for independent data structures of systems management tools wastes time and provides opportunity for data inconsistency. By providing a set of shared

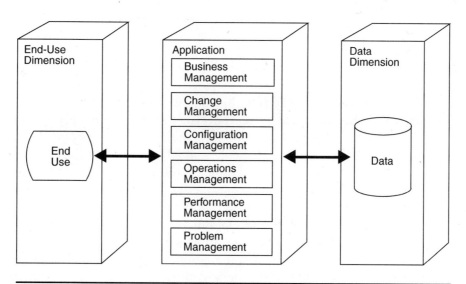

Figure 4.14. The SystemView framework.

data, SystemView allows for data to be entered one time and then be used by as many different systems management tools as necessary.

The **application dimension** of SystemView defines six types of systems management tools or **disciplines:**

1. **Business management** allows users to track physical assets and manage the finance and accounting associated with a computer system(s).

2. **Change management** allows systems management personnel to plan, implement, and track changes made to the computer system(s).

3. **Configuration management** helps in documenting, planning, and modifying the configuration (physical and logical relationships between components) of the elements comprising the computer system(s).

4. **Operations management** helps devise/maintain the policies and procedures used to efficiently process a business's workload with the computer system(s).

5. **Performance management** helps define, monitor, and plan the level of performance users should expect from the computer system.

6. **Problem management** helps plan how computer-related problems are prevented, detected, tracked, and resolved.

These functions have been combined under SystemView's **Systems Manager/400** and **Managed Systems Services/400** and have been extended to contain equivalent functions for remote AS/400 systems. The user can run remote programs and can remotely perform an IPL (Initial Program Load) on systems. All results are returned to the central site system for monitoring and tracking. Network-wide job schedules can be implemented by specifying when functions are to be run on the systems.

Figure 4.15 shows where OS/400 and some example extensions to OS/400 fit into the application dimension of the SystemView framework. As shown in the figure, many functions provided as standard in OS/400 can be mapped into the SystemView framework. For example, as users begin to use the AS/400 system, the disk storage begins to accu-

Business	Change	Configuration	Operations	Performance	Problem
APIs	COMMAND LANGUAGE INTERFACE			OUTPUT FILES FOR DATA	
• ECS - IBM Link Access - Hardware Upgrade - Order Processing • Job Accounting	• ECS - Service Request - PTF Ordering - PTF Management • DSNX • Object Distribution • PC Support	• Resource Manager • Auto Configuration • Vital Product Data • Inventory - Hardware - Software • Client Inventory - Hardware - Software • Retrieve Configuration Source	• Remote Power Control • Remote IPL • Store Management • Backup/ Recovery - Save While Active • Security Management • Workstation Pass-Thru • SNMP • SNA/MS Transport • Remote PC Command Execution • DSNX Job Initiation • Network Routing Facility • Operational Assistant	• Performance Monitor - Performance Measurement - Data Collection - Scheduling	• Problem Analysis • Alert Log and Manager - Alert Filter/ Router • Problem Log and Manager • Problem Log Filter/Router • ECS - Service Request - Question and Answer Facility • Remote Commands - Copy Screen Image - Pass Through • APPN Session PD

Figure 4.15. How OS/400 and other AS/400 system programs fit into the SystemView framework.

mulate business information that is often vital to the day-to-day operations of the business. This information becomes an asset to the business and should be protected as such. OS/400 provides several functions that protect against loss of information from user errors, hardware failures, intentional corruptions, and so forth. These include backup/recovery (BRMS/400), ADSM/400, commitment control and journaling, EDMSuite OnDemand for AS/400 Operations Navigator, disk failure recovery, utility failure recovery, and SMAPP.

Commitment Control and Journaling

Two other functions of OS/400 are commitment control and journaling. **Commitment control** allows an application program to be designed so that a user must complete all changes related to a database transaction before the transaction is permanently reflected in the database. This helps ensure the data integrity of the database in the event of a system failure in the middle of a transaction. It also allows a transaction to be canceled in process if the user feels the transaction is erroneous.

Journaling is a task performed by OS/400 in which every database transaction, in addition to changing the database, is stored in a separate file of transactions. This journaling works in conjunction with normal backup procedures to allow for recovery of database information in the event of information loss—for example, if the information in an AS/400 database becomes corrupted through a user error or hardware failure. The recovery process would involve loading a previously made backup tape and restoring the database through a simple restore command. However, none of the database transactions made since the backup tape was made would be reflected in the newly restored database. Thus, the database has been recovered only to the point at which the last backup copy was made. Thousands of transactions may have been made since the last backup, and these will have to be reapplied to the restored database. This is where journaling comes in. Because all transactions performed since the last backup are stored in the separate journal area, these transactions can be automatically applied to the newly restored database to bring it to the point immediately before it was corrupted. Without journaling, every transaction performed since the last backup would have to be manually reentered, which can be a very time-consuming process. Remote journaling allows database changes to be sent immediately to another system for high-availability applications to help off-load Central Processing Unit consumption from the source machine so that it can achieve more throughput by capturing and transmitting journal images between source and target systems. This can significantly reduce the time and effort required to reconcile source and target databases following a system failure, because database changes are transported immediately to the remote system assuring no loss of transactions.

Backup/Recovery

For example, as users begin to use the AS/400 system, the disk storage will accumulate business information that is vital to the day-to-day operations of the business. This information becomes an asset to the business and should be protected as such. OS/400 provides functions that protect against loss of information from user errors, hardware failures, intentional corruptions, environmental disasters, and so forth.

First, the system's operator can make backup copies of the information on disk storage to magnetic tape. With OS/400 these backup copies can be made while users are actively using the systems. This feature is called **save while active**. Save commands have been improved to remove many of the inhibitors that prevented many users from using the save while active feature by allowing generic library names and objects to be saved and by making it easier to use multiple tape drives during the save activity. It is also possible to use multiple tape drives during a restore to concurrently restore objects to a single library or restore document library objects into a single ASP.

Before the save while active function was provided, the systems operator had to regularly reserve a block of time and dedicate the AS/400 system to backup operations, making it unavailable to the users. Now the backup operations occur while users are still performing useful work. If the information on the AS/400 disk storage is lost, the backup tapes can be used to **restore** the AS/400 disk storage to the state at which the last backup was made. With the additional journaling functions and the BRMS/400 and ADSM/400 functions of OS/400, not only can all transactions subsequent to the backup but prior to the failure be posted to the restored information, the recovery of the lost data can be done without the user being aware of its occurrence. This typically completes the recovery procedure, and the information on the AS/400 system is restored to the point just before the failure occurred.

The backup/restore/journaling, archiving, battery backup/UPS, and checksum/RAID-5/data mirroring methods of protecting and recovering information reside in the "operations" discipline of the SystemView framework.

Another area of concern is the recovery of the business in the case of environmental disaster. Hurricanes, tornados, fires, and floods are examples of environmental disasters, which unfortunately happen too frequently. IBM Business Recovery Services is a group of consultants who will help the business design, setup, and manage a recovery strategy.

Two other areas of concern that haven't been addressed are user error and intentional corruptions. The greatest defense against intentional corruption is to install and follow the security functions provided by the system. The AS/400 has attempted to provide the widest range of security methods available on any system, from passwords to firewalls.

It is possible to isolate the system data from outside corruption in this time frame of networked systems. User error cannot be eliminated, because all users are only human, but if the users are restricted to the smallest logical view of the system functions needed to perform their function, the impact of user error can be minimized.

Operations Navigator

The AS/400 is designed for office environments in which technical skills are usually limited, so systems management tasks (such as collecting information about system problems, backing up user libraries, enrolling users, and automatically cleaning up the system messages/job logs) can be accomplished through the Operations Navigator Graphical User Interface (GUI). The Operations Navigator simplifies the interaction between the system's operator and OS/400 through the use of familiar Windows concepts to make it easier for users unfamiliar with AS/400 systems to perform OS/400 tasks.

Operations Navigator supplies many AS/400 functions used by system administrators and users on a daily basis. These functions include: job manipulation, message handling, printer management, printer output handling, user and group administration, database administration, file systems, security functions, authorization lists, security and auditing policies, backup support, and hardware and software inventory. In addition to the previous support for Client Access, Operations Navigator has been extended to provide Windows-like interfaces to functions that include journals, journal receivers, network setup for point-to-point communications, protocols, server environments, interprocess communications interfaces, and the interfaces for users and group-type activities such as Lotus Mail, and remote server entries. These functions may be accessed for a particular system from either a local or a remote system workstation. For example, a large company may have one AS/400 system at the headquarters location and multiple AS/400 systems distributed to other locations throughout the country or around the world. Rather than provide AS/400 and OS/400 personnel at each of the locations, it is often desirable to have a centralized staff of experts that can support all of the AS/400 systems throughout the company—a central help desk. That help desk can then coordinate all outside resources (e.g., IBM's customer support structure or an application software company's support system) as the single point of contact for the whole company.

EDMSuite OnDemand for AS/400 (5769-RD1)

The **EDMSuite OnDemand for AS/400** formerly referred to as **Report/Data Archive and Retrieval System (R/DARS)** consists of a set of four archive program features that allow the storage of large volumes of data and the retrieval of selected data. That data may be stored on disk, optical, or tape storage media. OnDemand helps maintain accessible and secure archives and can improve the cost and usability of long-term data storage. The OnDemand features can be ordered separately or in any combination of the following:

- Spool File Archive can store large volumes of spooled print data from current applications on magnetic, tape, or optical storage media. Users can retrieve selected pages or documents on demand. The management features include automated capture, auto indexing, immediate compression, and unattended storage migration.

- Record Archive can use IBM's 3995 Optical Libraries to store and retrieve aged data records, such as historical sales or customer data. Users can continue to use existing applications with the added capability of retrieving historical data from optical files and current data from magnetic disk. For quicker access, only pointers to the data are stored on magnetic disk; the actual data is stored on optical disk.

- Object Archive can compress and archive a variety of AS/400 objects such as program source files, database files, or entire application libraries on tape or optical media. Multiple generations of archived objects such as monthly or annual detail files can be managed.

- AnyStore, which requires the Spool File Archive, allows the storage and retrieval of binary large objects (BLOBS) such as PC files (spreadsheets, X-rays, MRI's) and small scanned images (remittance slips, insurance cards). AnyStore is a toolkit of API's intended for programmers to use to create archive/retrieval applications or to enhance existing applications with archive functions. The enhanced application passes the index data and BLOB to OnDemand Spool File Archive to manage the data. The application does the segmentation and extraction of the indices while OnDemand provides storage, migration, and retrieval capabilities to and from media, whether disk, optical or tape.

Backup Recovery and Media Services (BRMS)

Backup Recovery and Media Services/400 (BRMS/400) is an integrated comprehensive tool for managing backup, archiving, and recovery environments for single or multiple AS/400 systems in a single site or across a network in which the principal data exchange is by tape. BRMS/400 is designed to perform complex backups easily. The definitions of a backup and changes to those definitions are easy. Full error checking is performed, and messages are provided to the operators to ensure that errors do not go unnoticed. BRMS includes "EXITs" to allow processing of user commands or programs during the backup procedures. BRMS performs full, incremental, or noncumulative incremental saves, saves to save files, and save while active.

BRMS/400 offers a step-by-step recovery in the form of a report printed after the nightly backups are complete. Recovery includes full and detailed feedback during the recovery process by means of an auto-refresh screen, updated as each library is restored.

BRMS/400 archives data from DASD to tape and tracks information about objects that have been archived. Locating data in the archives is easy: The restore can be triggered from a work-with screen. Dynamic retrieval for database files is possible, and archived files can be restored upon access with the user application. No changes are required to the user application to initiate the restore.

BRMS/400 provides a comprehensive inventory management system for all tapes, cataloging and managing an entire tape library, as well as output reports as instructions to operators about required actions.

BRMS/400 provides for policy-driven backup, recovery, tape media management, and archive services for tape devices. This means there is an automatic recall of archived database files from tape devices to Direct Access Storage Devices (DASDs) when required, which relieves the user from having to become involved. BRMS/400 is intended for the system environment with over 50 tapes and therefore may introduce excess complexity in the operation of a smaller system. Operations Navigator is intended to provide the backup/restore functions for this less complex environment.

Adstar Distributed Storage Manager (ADSM)

The **Adstar Distributed Storage Manager** (**ADSM**) (5763-SV2) for AS/400 is a client/server product that provides administrator-controlled, highly automated, centrally scheduled, network-based backup and archive functions for the following listed workstations and LAN file servers. Enhancements included in Version 2.1 of this product include

- off-site backup and recovery for the server database and storage pools,

- enhanced Administrative Graphical User Interface (GUI), and

- Hierarchical Storage Management (HSM) for the AIX client.

ADSM/400 protects data on workstations and LAN file servers by automatically backing up critical LAN and workstation data and archiving files that are used infrequently. A disaster recovery solution is provided for LANs and workstations. ADSM is administered from a client workstation attached to an AS/400, and with BRMS/400 can be used to back up an entire AS/400 client/server environment.

ADSM also now includes an AS/400 API to allow users to develop their own applications, enabling the AS/400 system to function as an ADSM backup-archive client, an Oracle Backup Agent to allow ADSM to back up the Oracle database by providing an API into Oracle's Enterprise Backup Utility, and HSM for Solaris 2.5. ADSM backs up data from clients running on

- AIX

- Apple Macintosh

- Auspex (supported by SunOS client)

- Bull DPX/2

- Bull DPX/20 (Bull AIX, supported by AIX client)

- Digital ULTRIX (formally referred to as DEC ULTRIX)

- Digital UNIX

- DOS

- Hewlett-Packard HP-UX

- Microsoft Windows and 32-bit Windows

- NCR UNIX SVR-4 (formerly AT&T GIS)

- NEC EWS-UX/V

- Novell NetWare

- OpenEdition MVS

- OS/2

- Pyramid Nile (supported by SINIX RISC client)

- SCO UNIX 386 and SCO Open Desktop

- Sequent PTX

- Siemens Nexdorf SINIX 386/486 and SINIX RISC

- Silicon Graphics IRIX

- Sun Microsystems SunOS and Solaris

ADSM also provides a backup agent for Lotus Notes database backup and recovery.

System Managed Access Path Protection (SMAPP)

A function called **System Managed Access Path Protection (SMAPP)**, which automatically records the access path information according to a mathematical algorithm set by the user, has been added to the systems management function. Users tell the system manager how long they are willing to wait for recovery to take place after a long utility outage, and the system manager ensures that the access paths will be journaled frequently enough to achieve that recovery period. The recovery period may be identified to be either systemwide or by **Application Storage Pool (ASP)**. An application storage pool is a grouping of files related to a common set of applications. The file grouping is generally both logically and physically related. In the case of a utility outage on a system with internal battery backup or a UPS power system, when the main storage data has been dumped to disk and the system then powered down, the access paths to the data dumped to disk have been lost if SMAPP has not been enabled. Before the main storage contents can be reloaded and processing resumed, the access paths to the data resident in main storage must be rebuilt. This can take many hours of interaction with the systems administrator or SMAPP can journal the access path information and recovery time can be reduced to the identified time interval in SMAPP.

Utility Failure Recovery

So far, the backup and recovery methodologies discussed have related to data protection from hardware failure of a disk storage unit. A failure mechanism that occurs about thirty times more frequently is a utility failure. A utility failure will not as a rule cause any permanent damage to an AS/400 system, but it can severely damage the efficiency of your business operation. As discussed in "Packaging Technology" in Chapter 1, the AS/400 provides either an internal battery backup system or an interface for a Universal Power Supply (UPS). The primary purpose of these items is to protect the information resident in the main storage of the system that is related to the applications currently running on the system. In most situations, the internal battery backup system or the UPS can supply enough capability for the system to ride through the outage, even though the lights went out and your local screens went blank. However, everyone has experienced the 15-minute or longer outage. Statistics on utility systems indicate that the frequency of the longer outage is increasing and that on the average seven outages of longer than 5 minutes per year will occur no matter where you are located in the United States. The AS/400 has been programmed to allow a certain period (changeable by the user) to pass after the first occurrence of an outage and then to dump the contents of main storage to disk storage. This process will prevent the loss of data from the current applications but will not achieve minimum recovery time for the user. The user will still experience significant recovery time because the access paths to the data have not been saved. To assist in the recovery of those access paths, the user has the option to turn on System Managed Access Path Protection (SMAPP).

Disk Failure Recovery

Another recovery function in OS/400 used to guard against disk unit failures is known as **checksum**. With the checksum approach, a mathematical formula is used to store redundant information on disk storage in addition to the business information. If one of the disk units fails, the redundant information on the remaining disk units can be used to automatically regenerate the lost information on the replacement fixed disk. Checksum provides a way, at the cost of increased disk storage requirements and an additional load on the computer, to avoid having to do a restore from backups in the event of a disk unit failure. The RAID-5 controller hardware relieves the load on the central system computer for calculating the mathematical formula. (RAID-5 is a hardware methodology for performing the checksum function.)

The RAID-5 disk controllers on the AS/400 systems require a minimum of four drives of identical capacity to create a valid RAID-5 configuration. A maximum of three arrays are allowed per RAID-5 controller, and a maximum of ten drives per array. All drives in an array must be the same capacity. When an array consists of from four to seven drives, parity is spread across four drives. When an array contains from eight to ten drives, parity may be spread across either four drives or eight drives. If a system is started with from eight to ten drives in an array, parity will be spread across eight drives. If a system is started with less than eight drives and later upgraded to include from eight to ten drives in that array, the parity function must be stopped and then restarted before the parity function can be spread across eight drives. The AS/400 no longer uses the software checksum approach because of the impact on system performance.

Another data loss protection methodology available on the AS/400 is called **data mirroring**. In data mirroring, a second copy of the data is written to a second disk storage unit, which in the ultimate implementation is located on a separate disk unit controller located on a separate system bus. Data mirroring is the most expensive of the protection methodologies because it requires a total duplication of the data, which requires a doubling of the data storage space. When ranked in the order of highest reliability and minimum impact upon performance, data mirroring would be followed by RAID-5 and software checksum as data protection methods. Data mirroring also offers some performance improvements in a read-intensive database environment because the second copy of the data is available while the first copy may be busy being read by another application.

Systems Manager/400

With any computer system, various tasks must be performed in support of the computer system itself by someone trained to be the system's **operator**. These tasks include such things as authorizing new users, making backup copies of the information kept on disk storage, documenting and resolving system problems, installing software upgrades, identifying and resolving communications network problems, and more. These tasks necessary to support the day-to-day operation of a computer system are collectively called **systems management** tasks.

Both simple and complex environments benefit from automated tools (i.e., more computer programs) to help with systems management. Today's System Manager/400 provides the capability to extend the management complexity to include a heterogeneous environment, which means that the systems do not have to be IBM only, but may include systems from other vendors such as Apple, Sun, or Hewlett-Packard. The level of the management function reflects the degree to which those systems support the emerging standards related to the distributed management environment as it is being defined by the Open Systems Foundation (OSF).

SystemView System Manager/400 (5738-SM1) allows a central AS/400 system to manage a network of AS/400 systems and their associated personal computers. An AS/400 user can access a remote System/390 from an AS/400 workstation. This is possible because OS/400 can make an AS/400 workstation act like or **emulate** a 3270-type display used with the larger System/390 computers. This **3270 emulation** capability allows the local user of an AS/400 computer attached to a System/390 to interact with the System/390 as if his or her computer were a 3270-type device. Conversely, OS/400 allows remote 3270 terminals to access programs and data on the AS/400 system as if they were AS/400 workstations.

The **SystemView System Manager/400** (5769-SM1) provides facilities to support centralized systems management. System Manager/400 allows a central AS/400 system/site/staff to perform systems management tasks for a network of remote AS/400 systems. System Manager/400 addresses the following disciplines of systems management: problem management, change management, Client Access/400 client inventory, problem tracking for those clients, and PC software management. Interfacing with the System Manager/400 function is easier because of its Graphical User Interface (GUI), session management support, and support for a roving user. (A roving user is one who needs to use multiple workstations, but only one at a time.) The user can move from one workstation to another and maintain the same capabilities and interface characteristics as those used on the prior workstation.

In the area of problem management, System Manager/400 provides a way to maintain an electronic problem log. That problem log is managed automatically and includes the clients attached via Client Access/400. As users or the AS/400 system itself report a problem, that problem is automatically noted in the electronic problem log. The problems are prioritized, and notes are kept on the activities associated with each problem. If IBM's customer service needs to get involved, the problem, with all of its notes, is sent electronically to IBM's support network. If the central support site has a S/390 computer system, System Manager/400 cooperates with the S/390, allowing all support activity to be performed from that system. In the area of hardware/software inventory and software management, System Manager/400 automatically detects what hardware is connected on the LAN networks, and then downloads the operating system required (Windows, DOS, etc.). Corequisite PTF installation is simplified by System Manager for AS/400 and Managed System Services enhancements for automated tracking and management within a product. System Manager for AS/400 allows distribution and remote application and removal of corequisite PTFs as a group reducing the complexity and risks of managing these relationships.

AS/400 Performance Tools (5716-PT1)

The IBM **AS/400 Performance Tools** (5716-PT1) feature accesses system load information automatically logged by the system. With these tools, the performance of the system can be "tuned" and future performance requirements projected. The tools provide performance reports that can be as high-level or as detailed as needed. System use, response time, and number of transactions are statistically treated. The expert systems–based "advisor" function assists the system manager in interpreting performance analysis and often recommends specific actions. AS/400 Performance Tools help the system manager determine where the system is and where it is going in terms of capacity and performance. For smaller systems or those not requiring the function of AS/400 Performance Tools, the Performance Tools/400 (5763-PT1) provides basic performance planning tools. Also, the Performance Investigator/400 (PRPQ #5799-PRG) runs on a PC under DOS/Windows and graphs in real time (15-second samples) items such as CPU use, response time, and so on. One PC can monitor up to 16 AS/400 systems.

Managed System Services for AS/400

SystemView Managed System Services for AS/400 (5769-MG1) makes it easier to distribute software and manage software changes for clients attached to AS/400 systems by adding a change control server function. The change control server enables unattended software distribution and installation for NetFinity clients. Software distributions to clients can be scheduled and tracked from the AS/400 system managing the network. Distribution and change requests can be sent to the clients over SNA and TCP/IP networks. Additional client management function is also provided for sending files, programs, and data to a client; retrieving files, programs, and data from a client; deleting files, programs, and data on a client; running a command or calling a program on a client; performing a remote IPL or reboot on a client; or applying or removing a software fix on a client. These changes might be Program Temporary Fixes (PTFs) that correct known problems or might involve installing a whole new version of OS/400. The updates can be sent electronically to the remote AS/400 systems over existing APPN or traditional SNA networks or over TCP/IP and the Internet.

NetFinity for AS/400

NetFinity for AS/400 (5716-SVA) enables the movement of systems management tasks from end users to more experienced system administrators. NetFinity contains an inventory server that collects hardware and software inventory information from the clients being managed and stores it in DB2/400 databases on the AS/400 server. This information is used to perform management tasks such as software distribution, distributed monitoring, and remote control. NetFinity enables the system administrator to perform remote control of the PC clients, allowing the identification and correction of potential problems before they impact business. NetFinity also provides a graphical interface to software distribution by defining custom reports for querying the hardware and software database, runs the reports and displays results, generates a node list for distributing software, and distributes the PC software. Other NetFinity capabilities include critical file monitoring, workstation discovery, performance monitoring, activity scheduling, enhanced security, user profile data collection, alert management and processing, and problem analysis and correction.

NetFinity for AS/400 has two components: **NetFinity Server for AS/400** (5716-SVA) is the server component, installed on the AS/400 servers and the central site system. **NetFinity AS/400 Manager** (5716-SVD) is a manager component installed on a PC connected to an AS/400 server in its workgroup. NetFinity Services for AS/400 (5716-SVE) contains the PC client code supporting NetFinity for AS/400. All the PCs to be managed within the enterprise must include this code, which performs the responses directed by the NetFinity Manager and Netfinity for AS/400 software. NetFinity Server for AS/400 includes an easy-to-use GUI for setting up proactive resource monitors and alert conditions on the clients. Client alerts notify the manager GUI when conditions are met, such as changes to critical files, the start or end of a critical process, and performance and capacity statistics. Administrators can view a snapshot of the screen, start a command-line session, transfer files, browse information in the desktop management interface, and view current hardware and software configurations on remote clients.

In order to support remote control of Windows NT Server on the Integrated PC Server, NetFinity requires a local managing workstation for the remote server, control of the remote console/keyboard/mouse, the capability to inventory the software and hardware and to perform software distribution through the AS/400 using **Managed System Services (MSS)**. PC systems supported as clients are Windows 3.1, Windows 95, Windows NT, and OS/2.

Application Development Facilities

Many businesses find that writing their own custom application programs is the best method of solving business problems through computers. To this end, the basic architecture of AS/400 has been optimized to make writing and maintaining custom application programs as easy as possible. The database built into all AS/400s is one example of this. The ability to create databases that do not reside in any one program (externally described data) and to create different logical views of the same or related physical data is a major benefit to programmer productivity. This is particularly true when it becomes necessary to modify or add programs that use the database information in a different way. Single-level storage and the concept of objects help the programmer by automatically managing the complexities of main storage sizes, disk storage allocation and paging, and file sizes. Programmers can therefore spend their time making the application program more powerful or easier to use instead of managing internal computer logistics. Later in this chapter, we discuss the need to evolve (redevelop existing programs that executed in the host-centric environment so that they are usable in the client/server environment) and how object-oriented technology can be used to help solve that migration problem. The programmer has several **programming languages** from which to choose, including

- AS/400 PL/1

- IBM Pascal

- VRPG/400

- ILE RPG/400

- AS/400 BASIC

- ILE COBOL/400

- VisualAge C++ for OS/400

- ILE C/400

- RM/COBOL

- FORTRAN/400

These commonly used programming languages can be thought of as the library of instructions from which a programmer constructs a program. The language selected depends on the requirements of the application program and the skills of the programmer(s). The "ILE" languages conform to the AS/400's Integrated Language Environment.

Designed into OS/400 are functions that allow the application programmer to participate in the **Document Interchange Architecture (DIA)**. The Document Interchange Architecture consists of a set of rules published by IBM that allow the smooth flow of electronic documents through different types of computers and programs, and allow the user to file and search for those electronic documents. Other OS/400 features make it easier for the programmer to provide online help text and use graphics (i.e., GDDM support), making the application program easier to understand and use. To further augment tools available to the programmer, the separately purchased IBM AS/400 Application Development Tools (ADTS/400) package is available. This programmer tool kit is based on programmer tools available with earlier System/3X computers and consists of the following tools, designed for use on a non-programmable terminal.

The IBM AS/400 Application Development Tools package has been divided into six sections. The first section, Application Development Tool Set/400, contains the Data File Utility (DFU), Screen Design Aid (SDA), Source Entry Utility (SEU), and Program Development Manager. The second section, Application Development Tools—Printing, contains the Advanced Printer Functions (APF) (5727-AP6), Advanced Function Printing (AFP), and AFP Font Collection. The third section, Application Development Tools—Programs Group 1 includes Structured Query Language (SQL, 5763-WP1), Business Graphics Utility (BGU, 5716-DS1), and Query/400 (5769-QU1). The fourth section, Application Development Tools—Programs Group 2, contains the Application Program Driver (5649-PD1), Application Dictionary Services/400 (5738-

AD1), and WindowTool/400 (5798-RYF). The fifth section, Application Development Tools—Debug and Maintenance, includes the Interactive Source Level Debugger (ISLD), the Cooperative Debugger, and the File Compare and Merge Utility (FCMU). The last section contains other application development methodologies, CODE/400, VRPG Client, Computer-Aided Software Engineering (CASE), and KnowledgeTool/400 (5798-RYE). The Neural Network Utility/400 (5798-RYB) has been absorbed by Intelligent Miner (5733-IM1).

Application Development Tools Set/400

This set of application development program tools eases the programmer's task of writing new applications and maintaining existing applications. The tools include capabilities for managing the development project, specifically designing a database management program, designing the appearance of the interface to the application, and editing and checking the program code itself as the design progresses. Any and all of the programming languages listed in Application Development Facilities are supported by each of these tools.

Data File Utility (DFU).   This utility program is primarily intended to help a programmer write simple database management programs. Typical programs in this area include data entry (filling up a database with information), retrieving information (inquiry), and making necessary changes to a database (file maintenance). Although OS/400 itself provides a way to perform these tasks, DFU and user-written application programs make these tasks easier for the user.

Screen Design Aid (SDA).   This program allows the application programmer to interactively design, create, and maintain the user interface of a program—that is, the screens seen by the user of an application program can be generated through the SDA. This tool saves the programmer considerable time that would otherwise have to be spent programming all screen images from scratch. Since SDA is interactive, the programmer can easily change the screen being designed (e.g., different color, text, and fields) and immediately see the results of the change. Once a screen image is completed, it can be printed for use in program documentation.

Source Entry Utility (SEU). This tool can be thought of as a specialized **word processor** for programmers that is used to write applications programs. It provides a **full-screen** editor, which means that you can work on an entire page of text at a time. It provides the basic capabilities of copying, deleting, and moving text (programming statements) as well as language-sensitive dynamic prompting and automatic **syntax** checking. A search function allows you to automatically locate particular statements in a program. The split-screen function allows you to simultaneously view two different areas of a program or two separate programs for purposes of comparison, change, and copying. Many of the commands used with SEU are similar to those used in development support utilities and source entry utility programs of System/3X computers

Program Development Manager. This program provides all the elements of ADTS/400 assembled into one integrated programming environment. It allows the programmer to work with lists of items being developed. Rather than copying each item individually, the Program Development Manager allows you to perform the copy with one operation. It provides convenience that improves productivity and makes for a more pleasant programming environment. The Program Development Manager is similar to the **Programmer and Operator Productivity (POP)** environment on the System/36 with a few enhancements.

Application Development Tools—Printing

This set of tools address the needs of the programmer relative to setting up and managing the appearance of output documents, whether provided directly by a printer or indirectly by an electronic interchange methodology such as fax.

Advanced Printer Functions (APF). This tool provides a potpourri of special printing functions such as printing **Optical Character Recognition (OCR)** characters that can be read by machines and **barcode labels** read by scanners. APF also lets you generate bar graphs and define your own print styles and special symbols. APF can be used in the printer pass-thru mode described earlier.

Advanced Function Printing (AFP). AFP comprises a document architecture, a printer dialog and datastream, and a process for fully system-managed printing. As a document architecture, AFP is also known as MODCA-P, or Mixed Object Document Content Architecture—Presentation. As the name implies, AFP defines pages of output that mix all of the elements normally found in organizational documents-text in typographical fonts, electronic forms, graphics, image, lines, boxes and bar codes. The AFP datastream consists of a series of structured fields that implement all of these elements. AFP output can be created on an AS/400 using printer file keywords, DDS, Advanced Print Utility (APU), page and form definitions, AFP Utilities (AFP/U), the AFP Toolbox as well as many third party applications.

Once a print application is enabled using AFP, many complementary applications work with the electronic output that is produced. These include the Client Access/400 AFP Viewer which provides fully graphical document viewing as well as fax and printing services. Any AFP output can be faxed using Facsimile Support/400. AFP documents can be indexed, archived, retrieved, reprinted, and faxed using OnDemand for AS/400.

AFP is also an interactive printer datastream called IPDS (Intelligent Printer Data Stream). This datastream is similar to the AFP datastream, but is built (on the fly) specific to the destination printer in order to facilitate the interactive dialog between the AS/400 system (specifically Print Services Facility/400 or PSF/400) and the printer. AFP, SCS, line data, and ASCII files are transformed into IPDS prior to printing in order to support this dialog.

The two-way function of IPDS is a key component in AFP's system-managed printing process. This process includes document services, printer services, and print process management. Document services include identifying and automatically downloading externally referenced document resources such as overlays, images (page segments), and fonts to the IPDS printer. Printer services include monitoring printer resources and memory. Finally, the entire printing process is managed page by page to ensure each spooled file is printed completely and accurately. Error conditions at the printer are monitored and full error recovery is enabled at the AS/400.

The system-managed printing process with IPDS takes on added significance in a network TCP/IP environment. Placing printers within the network and attaching them with an IP connection provides great flexibility. However, TCP/IP print support is very limited-essentially a one-way send of the print file. The AFP printing process bi-directionality of IPDS provides a bridge across this type of connection. The result is the same application (i.e., document capabilities) function and print management supported with twinax-attached printers.

AFP Font Collection.   Good typography through the use of fonts is essential for effective business documents. The AFP Font Collection provides a comprehensive set of AFP fonts, with over 1000 fonts from the most popular type families, including Times New Roman, Helvetica, and Courier. A full range of sizes, resolutions (240 dots per inch [dpi], 300 dpi) and languages (over 48) are included. Outline formats are also supplied, enabling the creation of additional sizes or variations as well as supporting the full viewing of AFP output using the Client Access Viewer.

Print Services Facility/400 (PFS/400).   **Print Services Facility/400** is an integrated feature of OS/400 that provides full system-managed printing to IPDS printers. It is automatically invoked by OS/400 print management when its services are required. PSF/400 is the driver subsystem for Advanced Function Printing (AFP) on AS/400.

PSF/400 manages the printing of the following types of AS/400 spooled files to the IPDS printers:

- SCS files

- SCS with printer file options (i.e., front or back overlay)

- SCS with page or form definitions for print formatting

- AFP created from DDS printer file specifications

- AFP from the Client Access/400 AFP driver

- AFP from other systems or AFP Toolbox (a PrintSuite product)

- PostScript and image files converted by Host Print Transform (HPT)

- IPDS files

All of these files (except IPDS) are transformed into IPDS and managed to the printer. As the system-managed print driver, PSF/400 provides full document services, printer services, and print process management.

Application Development Tools—Program Group 1

These application development tools are also application programs that fit the definition of cross-industry applications. As such, they are used by a wide variety of other applications as well as for developing new custom applications.

Structured Query Language (SQL). SQL provides the programmer with additional commands that can be embedded in application programs to efficiently manipulate database information.

Business Graphics Utility (BGU). BGU is a programmer's tool for creating computer-generated graphics. Although users with no programming experience can use BGU interactively to create their own graphs, the programming interface provided by BGU gives the application programmer convenient access to graphics functions.

Query/400. Query/400 can be used by the programmer to define database reports that can be executed by the user. Once the query has been defined, the AS/400 system need not have the Query/400 program to simply execute the query. Again, although the user can often use Query/400 without the assistance of a programmer, a programmer can also take advantage of Query/400 when writing application programs.

Other Application Development Tools—Program Group 2

In addition to the Application Development Toolset/400, there are other separately purchased tools for the AS/400 programmer. Among these are the Application Program Driver (5730-095), Application Dictionary Services/400 (5733-080), WindowTool/400 (5798-RYF), and Lotus Notes.

Application Program Driver. The **Application Program Driver** (5738-PD1) is yet another tool for programmers that provides many of the services commonly needed by application programs (e.g., menu design, fast-path support around menus, and security). Further, the Application Program Driver can provide a single menu interface to all application programs. This makes for a consistent user interface for users who need access to more than one application program.

Application Dictionary Services/400. This tool builds a directory of data and programs residing on the AS/400 system. It is used by the programmer to keep an inventory of the data and program items stored on the system and can be used to evaluate the impact of a proposed change to an application program and to re-create impacted objects if desired.

Window Tool/400. This is a tool used to build a text-based Windows user interface for existing AS/400 application programs on non-intelligent terminals (Figure 4.16). With WindowTool/400 systems, operators and programmers can subdivide the screen into boxes (called windows) and provide user interface items such as pull-down windows, pop-up menus, action bars, and so on. Although no graphics is supported with

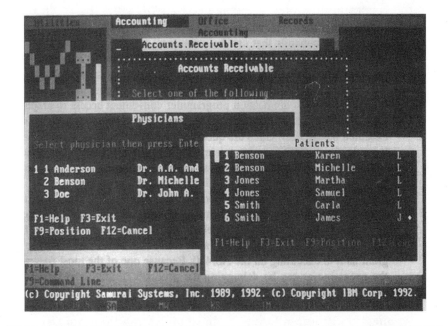

Figure 4.16. User interface created by Window Tool/400 on a text-only, nonintelligent workstation.

WindowTool/400, the user interface provided on non-intelligent text-only workstations with WindowTool/400 is a step toward the graphical user interface that has become so popular on intelligent workstations (e.g., Windows and OS/2 Presentation Manager on a PS/2).

Alternately, application programs can be written to some enhanced OS/400 application programming interfaces (**DDS Windows support**) to provide the best user interface available to the user. That is, a user with a personal computer or InfoWindow II workstation will automatically be presented an enhanced user interface with pop-up windows, scroll bars, and so on. A user of a workstation that doesn't support the enhanced user interface functions of OS/400 will be presented a standard user interface (e.g., a simple menu). The programmer writes the application programming using the DDS Windows application program interfaces. The OS/400 and associated hardware automatically tailor the user interface for each user's workstation based on its capabilities. RUMBA/400, mentioned earlier, recognizes and works with application programs that use the new DDS Windows application programming interfaces.

Application Development Tools—Debugging and Maintenance

Once the programs have been written using AS/400 programming tools, they must be tested for correctness and any problems must be diagnosed and fixed. OS/400 provides an **interactive debugging facility** for this purpose. This facility allows the programmer to closely control and monitor the new or modified application program as it is executing on the AS/400. Because one of the most frustrating tasks for the programmer is debugging the program (finding and fixing programming errors), this facility is very important. The only thing constant is change. Even when an application program is completely tested and put into productive use, there will be a need to make changes as the business environment changes and to fix newly discovered program errors that were not caught during testing. This activity is called **supporting** or **maintaining** the application program. In addition to AS/400's externally described database design, there are some tools that help with this maintenance. OS/400's **cross-reference facility** and **data dictionary** support provide the programmer with the means to determine which application programs use what database information. With this information, the programmers can assess the impact of a proposed change to an application program or database. The data dictionary support also provides a single place to go for information concerning database field names, data types, and the like.

Interactive Source Level Debugger (ISLD). This tool provides the program developer with a debugging facility with which the developer can interact as the code is being designed.

Cooperative Debugger. This tool provides the developer with a debugging facility with which the developer can debug code on OS/400 from an OS/2 client. The tool applies to C++ and other ILE languages, including CODE/400.

File Compare and Merge Utility (FCMU). The functions of this tool are apparent from the name. It will compare a new file against an existing file, and it will merge two existing files together, making a single larger file.

Application Development Tools—Other Methodologies

A couple of IBM workstation-based products are emerging in application development: CODE/400 and VRPG Client. CODE/400 is a tool for server- or host-based development, and VRPG Client is a visual programming tool to create RPG client/server applications. The built-in features of AS/400 and OS/400 along with additional tools (e.g., Application Development Tools, SQL, etc.) make for productive application program development and maintenance. However, there are other AS/400 programming tools for those wishing to implement the more structured **Computer-Aided Software Engineering (CASE)** methodology. CASE is a structure and methodology for managing and executing application development projects from inception of the project through ongoing software maintenance activities. Finally, **knowledge-based tools** support the development of a class of custom application programs that employ expert system techniques for solving problems. **Expert systems** are application programs that attempt to capture the knowledge of a human expert and then draw conclusions on any presented information based on that expert knowledge. Although expert systems are not the answer to all application program needs, they can be very effective in addressing many business needs.

Two examples of knowledge-based tools are the **IBM Knowledge Tool/400** (5798-RYE) and the **Intelligent Miner** (5733-IM1). KnowledgeTool/400 is a tool used by programmers to write application programs that use rule-based expert system technology. These application programs are designed to capture the expertise of humans in a set of rules later used by the application program to make decisions and recommendations on any new data provided. For example, a rule-based expert system application program for the medical profession might try to diagnose an illness based on a set of symptoms entered into a computer system.

Neural networks take a different approach. Rather than having the expert and programmer develop a set of rules, the neural network analyzes a set of existing information in order to identify and classify patterns in the information. For example, if a bank has a database containing information about loan applicants and their subsequent payment records, neural networks can be employed to look for patterns in the information and identify characteristics that tend to indicate that the party will pay off a loan on schedule. During this analysis phase, the neural network is said to be **training on the data**. Once the neural network is trained, it can then look at the information collected from new loan applicants and help management determine the risk associated with each applicant based on history. Neural networks for the AS/400 have been repackaged under the Intelligent Miner/400 (5733-IM1) product.

In the next phase of the application program development project, production and maintenance, the **test, maintenance,** and **redevelopment** tools are introduced. Building tools are used to "assemble" all the pieces of the application program(s) (e.g., object code modules, subroutine libraries, etc.) into a working system. Testing tools help the programmers simulate inputs to the application program and monitor outputs. Tests can be defined and then run during initial testing and rerun later to validate any changes made to the application program after it is in use. Maintenance tools include things to increase the productivity of the programmers when they correct errors or implement changes in the application program while it is in use. An example of a maintenance tool is an impact analysis tool, which allows programmers to assess the amount of effort needed to implement a requested change before the change is started. This allows the level of effort required for the change to be measured against the value of the change in order to help prioritize work.

AS/400 Kernel Threads

A **thread** is an independent unit of execution within a program. The amount of system resources used for a thread is far less than the resources used for a job. Threads share a common address space and have access to all job resources. Threads are used to run different parts of an application concurrently. Multithreading provides simplified algorithms and more responsive programs in that the functions of I/O, calculations, and user interface are each dealt with through separate threads, and threads use less resources than a multiprocess solution. Initial implementations of threads will be in Java, C, and C++. When using POSIX APIs, there are multithreading considerations including added complexity to manage shared resources and data, concerns with data synchronization and race conditions, a potential for deadlocks, and a non-threadsafe environment. The Java language eliminates many of the POSIX multithreading considerations. The AS/400 positioning relative to threads support is to provide kernel threads at a level sufficient to support porting of multithreaded applications and servers from other platforms, such as Domino, to provide a competitive platform for multiuser/multithreaded servers, to provide thread performance equal to or better than the best of AIX and Windows NT, to support integration of existing code with threads, and to stage **threadsafe** OS/400 functions over several releases, based on application requirements. Additional information on threads may be obtained by accessing the Internet at *http://www.rchland.ibm.com/projects/Threads*. A threadsafe function can be invoked simultaneously in multiple threads. A function is threadsafe if and only if all functions' it calls are threadsafe. OS/400 is not threadsafe. OS/400 will allow access to non-threadsafe functions with the following exceptions:

- Thread-unsafe file systems

- Thread creation in non-multithread-capable jobs

- File types other than database files or print files with SPOOL

- File overrides

- Reclaim resources

- Shared opens in secondary threads*

- Save/restore

- Change job attributes in secondary threads*

- Swapping user profiles from secondary threads*

- Swapping user profiles from initial threads when a job has secondary threads*

- Performance explorer from multithread-capable jobs*

The items with asterisks in this list should be threadsafe by V4R3 in the latter half of 1998, and the remaining items should be threadsafe by V4R4 in early 1999. The following listing identifies the limitations of AS/400 thread support:

- Batch jobs only.

- No CL commands are threadsafe in V4R2.

- If the Activation Group encounters conditions that will result in destruction of that group, the job will be terminated, and it is necessary to abort the job.

- Non-threadsafe AS/400 functions need to accessed in separate jobs.

- Integration of existing code into multithreaded applications requires separation of the job or synchronization to access the function.

Integrated Language Environment (ILE)

The **Integrated Language Environment (ILE)** provides a new set of tools and system support designed to enhance program development on the AS/400 System. ILE offers benefits over previous program models, including binding, modularity, reusable components, common runtime services, and coexistence. ILE also offers better control over resources, better control over language interactions, better code optimization, and a better environment for the supported languages. ILE produces a module object (MODULE) that can be combined (bound) with other modules to form a single executable unit, that is, a ProGraM (PGM) object. The module objects may be written in several languages, and the binding is performed by calls from each individual module. The development of the modules results in faster compiling time, simplified maintenance, simplified testing, better use of programming resources, and easier porting to other platforms. The presence of reusable components in ILE means that a segment of code that has been developed previously does not have to be rewritten to be used in a new application but can be picked up as a module and integrated with the new application. The ILE's common runtime services include a selection of off-the-shelf components (bindable APIs) that are supplied as part of the ILE, ready to be incorporated into your applications. These APIs provide services such as:

- Date and time manipulation

- Message handling

- Math routines

- Greater control over screen handling

- Dynamic memory allocation

ILE programs can coexist with existing programs, each being able to call the other. ILE program modules may be written in **C, C++, RPG, COBOL,** and **CL.** In addition to the traditional programming languages (C, RPG, and COBOL), OS/400 provides another language, called **Command Language (CL),** which can be used as a scripting language to control flow within an application, and for performing operating system tasks. CL can be used to issue a single operating system request or to create complex programs that present the user with menus and initiate other application programs.

Emerging Application Development Environments

Although the foregoing paragraphs provide a valid insight into the world of third- and fourth-generation language application development, they fall somewhat short of describing the emerging programming environment. The following paragraphs provide the reader with an overview of application development in the time frame of emerging programming languages and evolved computing paradigms that provide a new environment for the old host-centric programs, and the need to somehow migrate these old programs to a new computing paradigm that includes client/server and distributed computing as a base.

Like the evolution of hardware from the ability to mix and match parts from different vendors within the same system (personal computer systems, the IBM-compatible phenomenon) to the ability to mix and match computing systems from many different vendors (the Distributed Computing Environment [DCE] as defined by the Open Systems Foundation [OSF], X-Open, and other standards groups), emerging programming languages are defining interfaces that enable programs to be picked up in pieces that are developed by different groups and will be guaranteed to work together without the need for additional programming glue. What this means is that it is possible to take existing third-generation language applications (procedural languages such as RPG, COBOL, and Pascal), add an input interface and an output interface around them, add them to other programs that provide a distributed computing environment, and, after compiling, execute them in a distributed computing environment. The programming languages that provide this capability are the object-oriented programming languages, foremost among which are SmallTalk, C++, and Java. The characteristics of object-oriented programming languages will be discussed later, in "Object-Oriented Technology."

Five possible steps may be taken along the path to full client/server distributed computing as applications are moved from a host-centric environment. A business may elect to stop at any one of those steps, depending upon the investment needed to move along the path. Figure 4.17 illustrates the steps, and the text in "Client/Server Computing Model" describes how the client and server relate to the function of executing programs using the environment provided at each step. Over the last few years the definition of client/server computing has been clarified, and most vendors accept the set of models defined by the Gartner Group—the base for Figure 4.17, which focuses on three facets of computing:

1. The distribution of the presentation part of the application, whether or not it is graphic, and whether the software that manages the screen is on the server or on the workstation (called Presentation in Figure 4.17).

2. The distribution between client and server of function or "logic"—the processing or procedural part of the application (called Logic in Figure 4.17).

3. The distribution of data—where it resides, how it is accessed, and who accesses it (called Data Management in Figure 4.17).

Client/Server Computing Model

What Figure 4.17 shows is that there are many ways to view the client/server application approach. They cover a wide range of ways to distribute data, logic, and presentation, but they appear to the end user to all be client/server. The AS/400 supports all of the models just as it supports the original host-centric non-programmable terminal model. The next few paragraphs describe each of the models, describing the level of function that is executed on both the client and the server.

Host-Centric Model. All processing functions are performed in the central processing system for presentation, logic, and data management— no intelligence is required to exist in the terminal. The terminal may have intelligence, but the intelligence is not being used to support the programming function. Only the display and keyboard of the terminal are effectively functional. The greatest proportion of existing applications have been written for this model, and there is no additional cost to maintain that software.

Distributed Presentation Model. Presentation services in this model are provided by both the client and the server. The server completely formats the presentation, then a client-based application intercepts and interprets the display data stream generated by the server. For the AS/400,

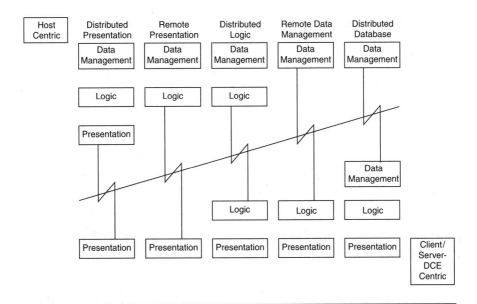

Figure 4.17. Client/server computing models.

the communication between client and server could be either the 5250 data stream or TCP/IP. The original applications remain unchanged. This technique is relatively simple to implement, and software costs can be minimal. The user benefits of this type of applications conversion should not be downgraded: the ease of use and integration advantages for the user's workspace can be significant.

Remote Presentation Model.   In this model, the remote client provides the presentation services via some form of dialogue manager. The application drives the remote display as in an application programming interface, typically a conversational interface such as Advanced Program-to-Program Communications (APPC). System services (at the server) provide the protocol and data streams to transport the application commands to the client. A dialogue manager in the client then provides the screen formatting and user interface, and sends the results to the server application, which is performing the data management and application logic functions. Using the AS/400 fourth-generation languages and application generators, it can be quite easy for a user to achieve client/server applications employing remote presentations. The code generator will optionally create a set of application interfaces, communications code, PC programs, and local PC data to accomplish screen display.

Distributed Logic Model. In this model the application logic is split between the client and the server, with pieces residing on both. Application components interact with each other using some form of remote access. The communications style can vary from conversational (APPC), to Remote Procedure Call (RPC), to queued messages (MQI or DAE), to the emerging distributed object-oriented messages (CORBA). The logic could be split, with the server executing a transaction processing subsystem to handle the business rules and procedures, interfacing to a rules-driven database, also on the server, while the client carries the application flow as directed through user-driven events.

Remote Data Model. Presentation services and application logic reside on the client while the server provides data services, usually through a SQL interface. Remote data management typically involves a PC-oriented application generator that accesses data on the server through SQL. These SQL-based tools are generally highly open to the server of choice. This type of development provides an inexpensive start because it only requires a PC development license, but additional costs come when data integrity and security become important. The AS/400's integrated relational database and systems management provide advantages both in data integrity and security not generally available with other server platforms.

Distributed Computing Model. Data is distributed across the clients and the servers by means of the networks and requires sophisticated data management. The data security, locking, and file structure may be on the client or distributed between client and multiple servers. When data is distributed, the interface is normally one of the database-to-database standards, such as IBM DRDA, Oracle Transparent Gateway for SQL/400, and Sybase Open Client–Open Server. The AS/400 provides support for all of these standards.

Object Technology

The following paragraphs answer these questions: Why object technology? What is object technology? How is object technology different from the other programming languages and development paradigms described here? A set of definitions are provided to identify the fundamental concepts of object technology, and three benefits of object technology are described. The AS/400's support for object technology and strategic direction are outlined, and application development tools currently on the AS/400 supporting object technology (such as frameworks and Java) are described.

Why Object Technology?   As was pointed out in the discussion of application development, a need exists to reduce the cost of software in every phase of the process called application development. That need is being driven by the fact that the business environment is changing at a faster and faster pace, and no two businesses operate in exactly the same way. Businesses need application packages tailored to their specific operation, or at the least application packages modifiable to their operations, and the testing and maintenance of those packages has to be made simpler. Software developers need new tools and methodologies to provide application packages faster and with less expense. Object technology offers significant promise of being able to deliver those capabilities.

What Is Object Technology?   Object technology is not a product, it is an enabling technology that provides an approach to software development supported by several products and system and network enablers. The approach models the business world and has properties that support the reuse of software components. The AS/400 currently supports C++ and SmallTalk (supported on client, not native) object-oriented application development and Java execution and services for the Internet. Modeling the business world and reusing software components leads to reducing development expense and providing software applications faster. These application packages can be built with existing methodologies (procedural, structured programming) or object technology. The transition to object technology is expected to take several years for software developers; as a result, coexistence with existing procedural applications is a critical requirement of object technology.

What Makes Object Technology Different from Procedural Programming Approaches?   Object technology holds out the promise of being able to build applications from parts of other applications. Procedural programming technologies had no capabilities for achieving this. It was difficult to separate the beginning of one procedure from another, and it was difficult to identify what a particular procedure was actually doing, which is what made maintenance so expensive. Data was easy to access and change, many times by accident. In object technology data is hidden from the rest of the program and action must be taken overtly to change data. Object technology allows the inheritance of properties from other objects and the ability for objects of a subclass of a particular class to respond to the same message with different results. These differences are clarified in the definitions of the fundamental concepts in object technology. Two subjects that result from the move to object-oriented technology are frameworks and Java. These two subjects have achieved sufficient importance in the AS/400 strategic direction that they deserve separate sections devoted uniquely to that specific subject.

Fundamental Concepts of Object Technology

Some fundamental concepts are defined in the following list.

- **Object.** A software entity that combines data elements and the operations that can be performed on the data. This combination of data and operators into a single entity differentiates object-oriented programming from procedural programming, in which data and operators are separate. An object is a specific individual entity. For example, a car with a particular serial number is an object. Its data elements might include the serial number, the make of the vehicle, the owner's name, the date purchased, the date sold, the purchase price, the interest rate, and the down payment. Its operators might include addition, subtraction, remainder, logical, assignment, and greater than.

- **Class.** The abstraction that describes all objects that share the same data elements and operations. For example, all vehicles constitute a class. Your particular car is an instance of the class.

- **Instance.** Same as object.

- **Inheritance.** The derivation of a new subclass from an existing base class by using the "kind of" hierarchy. For example, a truck and a car are kinds of vehicles, so they can be derived from the vehicle class. In addition to operation descriptions and data elements unique to the subclass, the derived subclass contains information from the original base class. That information enables the subclass to reuse the code and data in the base class without having to repeat them. Reuse is the main reason why object technology leads to increased programmer productivity. Inheritance allows programmers to derive subclasses to meet specific needs by customizing applications and extending designs.

- **Encapsulation.** The hiding of internal data structure and operations of an object from client programs. Client programs cannot see the implementation details inside the object. All they can see is the interface to the object.

- **Polymorphism (many forms).** The ability of subclasses of the same class to respond to the same message and produce different results. Polymorphism combines inheritance and dynamic binding.

- **Dynamic binding.** The ability of some languages (including C++, Java, and SmallTalk) to bind the names of variables and expressions to their types at run time instead of at compile time. Sometimes referred to as *late binding*.

- **Framework.** A set of classes that provide infrastructure and the flow of control in an application. Frameworks call your code; you do not call the frameworks. Well-designed frameworks provide the general design and implementation for a specific problem, allowing the developer to customize it to a particular situation.

- **Message.** The mechanism by which one object requests services of another. The message identifies the method that the object will use to perform the request. This term is used only in SmallTalk, not in C++ or Java.

- **Method.** Another name for an operation that an object performs. An object may have many methods.

- **Object Request Broker (ORB).** The mechanism that enables objects to communicate with each other across a network. The ORB handles services for security, registration, and object management. The Object Management Group (OMG) is an industry consortium that has defined the Common Object Request Broker Architecture (CORBA) to specify standards so that different ORB implementations in the industry can work together.

- **Part.** A preexisting software component that can be combined into an application by visual programming and construction.

Benefits of Object Technology

Software developers benefit from solving complex business problems by assembling or extending reusable software components. Since object applications model business problems more closely than procedural applications do, object applications are easier to develop, particularly once many frameworks exist. Object applications are easier to maintain, because if objects model real-life business processes, as processes change, corresponding object changes are both obvious and containable, with modularity and encapsulation data hiding. Maintenance is the greatest part of development expense. Programming effort can be used again and again. This reuse results in shorter development cycles, customizable delivery, and lower development expense. To be useful across systems, objects must reside in open, distributed environments. To allow movement of objects within the network, these objects must be portable. This portability enables dynamic re-engineering of the application to match the evolving flow in the business. Distributed objects that are CORBA compliant provide software developers with a simple method to develop open, distributed applications for the client/server market. The end user benefits because object technology can result in solutions that address many end-user requirements:

- More consistent accessibility to information and to the computer system resources with better integrity.

- Better integration of applications.

- Greater flexibility of applications. The end user can create or customize visual applications instantly.

- Investment protection. Object-oriented applications can be phased in gradually and can coexist with procedural applications.

The information technology industry benefits because adoption of object technology facilitates two significant changes in the marketplace: distributed computing and component software.

Distributed computing means that remote objects and information can be created and used across platforms in a network. Software reuse from component software will operate the way component hardware is reused today, facilitating both quality and productivity. Every major vendor in the computer industry has declared object technology key to its strategic business goals. Industry standards are emerging, led by the OMG and the open cross-platform CORBA specification for distributed objects. Object-oriented languages are moving to ANSI standards.

How Can the AS/400 Participate in Object Technology?

The AS/400 perceives the existence of object technology in an environment that is multiuser, business oriented, adaptable/customizable, reliable, integrated, simplified, and distributed. Not only is data to be distributed, so is the function. The distribution is across many vendor platforms connected by local networks (LANs, intranets) and remote networks (the Internet). Applications are perceived as distributed networking computer models that support task-centered client applications as well as server- and host-centered collaborative applications running the business.

This business environment has certain requirements for tools, base operating system support, and parts/frameworks. The tools need to support team development of projects that scale from small to large, that support legacy and object-oriented code development and run time, and that span low-level (system) to high-level (visual) development. The operating system must support multiuser, commercial business applications in a manageable way that hides complexity and provides low cost of ownership. The frameworks must span the industry segments and be shareable and portable across platforms and businesses.

AS/400 Object Technology Development Tools

Basic to the success of object-oriented applications is the availability of programming languages and tools integrated into a development environment. An integrated environment must be provided for the development, run time, and administration of distributed client/server applications. The AS/400 provides application development environments based on the three dominant object-oriented languages: C++, Java, and SmallTalk.

VisualAge C++. The C++ application development environment is provided by the VisualAge C++ family of products. The VisualAge C++ product family is a central technology for enabling cross-platform development using C++. VisualAge C++ for AS/400 (5716-CX4) and VisualAge for C++ for AS/400 (5716-CX5) combine the development environment of C++ for OS/2 with the capability to develop C++ code that is targeted for AS/400. This combination enables the development of powerful client/server applications written in C++ that take advantage of the advanced data and security features of OS/400. The AS/400 Access Class Library (ACL) provides object interfaces to OS/400 functions and data.

VisualAge/SmallTalk. VisualAge is an integrated application development environment designed for commercial client/server applications through visual programming and construction from components. VisualAge is the repackaging of ENVY/400 with its access class libraries. It is not just a Graphical User Interface (GUI) builder or prototyping tool, it is a power tool to build online transaction processing and decision-support applications. In visual programming, the user selects interface components and reviews the results as the interface is built. Applications can be built by selecting from a palette of categories of parts that are laid out and connected. The connected code is then automatically generated. A part may represent a database, a communications link, or an external source such as another program. Team programming, including version control, change management, and library functions, enables multiple developers to work on the same application simultaneously. More experienced programmers have the benefit of the underlying SmallTalk language, including an integrated suite of productivity tools (editors, browsers, debuggers, and inspectors). The AS/400 Access Class Library (ACL) provides object interfaces to OS/400 functions and data, and similar Access Class Libraries are in VisualAge/SmallTalk for AS/400.

Emerging Applications Environments

Three application environments are on the verge of being available, Frameworks, OpenDoc, and Java. Those environments are being developed by many vendors. OS/400 is putting in place the support structures to embed these environments as quickly as they are available. Frameworks is the nearest to reality. Since the frameworks environment is so near to reality, it is described here in some detail.

Frameworks

The frameworks environment is one in which a company such as IBM will develop the skeleton of an application, leaving to the final user the tuning of the application to the business's needs. Object-oriented technology provides for programming—the reuse of parts and components that have been a part of the hardware environment for the last 5 to 10 years. Frameworks group those components into compatible software sets. Frameworks capture the collective experience of a design team and provide a model for a common solution to particular problems, thereby automating much of the development effort. Examples of what frameworks can do include

- Automating tasks associated with distributed applications.

- Allowing applications to move easily between different operating systems, by disguising the differences in those operating systems.

- Automating graphical user interface development.

- Masking/dealing with the complexities within and between transactions and communications.

Two different types of frameworks will be developed. One type will deal with applications, the other with systems. The application frameworks provide a basic set of cross-industry and vertical functions/objects, which include basic financial management objects, distribution objects, and customer/supplier objects. Over time, application frameworks are expected to provide a rich base of application frameworks to enable the software parts business. IBM is developing a set of frameworks using the code name San Francisco, the first of which, General Ledger, is available now.

The San Francisco Framework. San Francisco focuses on business management software. The user can elect to build an application starting from any of the three layers of San Francisco. The layers of San Francisco are illustrated in Figure 4.18 together with its positioning relative to the Java Virtual Machine and the technology independent interface. The three layers are

1. *Base layer.* This provides the technical infrastructure needed before object technology can be used above it.

2. *Common Business Objects layer.* This consists of the building blocks application developers can use to create business applications.

3. *Core Business Processes layer.* This layer is built for one specific application containing the basic functions all applications of this type require.

The final layer of San Francisco is the Commercial Applications layer, which is created by the software developers who buy and extend the San Francisco frameworks. This layer is illustrated by the vertical rectangles in the figure and may extend to any of the IBM-supplied layers above the base layer, depending upon how much advantage is perceived in San Francisco for the developers' application. In most cases this final layer will be created using Java.

Within the second type of framework, the system framework, the system developer will provide the frameworks to support the traditional operating system functions in an object-oriented environment. These functions include graphical operations, data access, and network man-

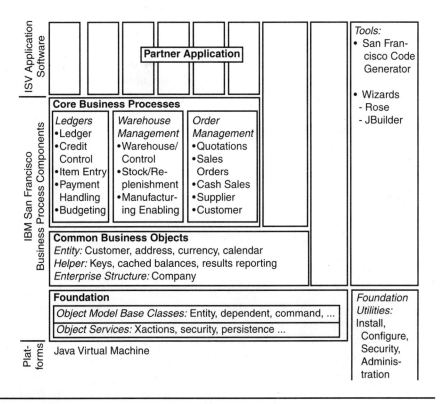

Figure 4.18. San Francisco block diagram.

agement. In addition, security, data integrity across multiple cooperating systems, save/restore, activation, and national language support need to be included as business objects. The concept of frameworks has been introduced here to set the stage for what to expect in the long run in system development.

OpenDoc

OpenDoc is a cross-platform compound-document architecture designed to simplify creation of documents, including the multimedia elements of text, spreadsheets, charts, tables, graphics, images, video, and sound. End users can combine the parts as desired.

Java

Java is a set of rules being set in place for defining an Internet object-oriented programming language. Those rules are being established by Sun Systems. The AS/400 representatives who have studied Java state that Java is a pure object-oriented language similar in syntax to C++ and similar in behavior to SmallTalk. Java is an interpretive language and is machine independent, meaning programs written to Java rules will execute on any system. Java includes a just-in-time compiler and a virtual machine. The virtual machine is a fictional processor that is emulated in software. The instructions for that fictional processor, called Java bytecodes, are identical no matter which hardware or OS platform the virtual machine is running on. As each bytecode arrives, the virtual machine reads it and executes the native instructions appropriate for that particular local environment. The just-in-time compiler is plugged into the Java Virtual Machine, and when the virtual machine is ready to execute a method in a class or object, it passes the bytecodes for that method to the just-in-time compiler, which then compiles the bytecodes on the fly to native code. Without a just-in-time compiler, the Java Virtual Machine must interpret and execute each bytecode in succession, a much slower process. Java applets will be downloadable to any system from the Internet. The Java Virtual Machine provides the AS/400 with a Java run-time environment.

AS/400 has a Java Virtual Machine residing below the technology-independent machine interface for fast interpretation and execution, and also has a direct-execution static compiler to generate RISC machine code as well as portable Java bytecodes. IBM is including the AS/400 Java Developers Kit for AS/400 (JDK 1.1) and the AS/400 Java Virtual Machine program with every OS/400 V4R2 system shipped in the AS/400 BonusPak.

The AS/400 Toolbox for Java includes a set of enablers that support an Internet programming model. Provided functions include a set of client/server programming interfaces for use by Java applets and applications plus a set of applets that can be integrated into HTML documents. Client support required is Java Virtual Machine and JDK. The Java environment on the AS/400 includes a standardized set of class libraries (packages) that support creating GUIs, controlling multimedia data, communicating over networks, and accessing data in stream files and relational databases. AS/400 Toolbox for Java intercepts GUI requests coming from a Java program and reroutes the requests to an attached workstation running its own JVM, which will interpret and display the JAVA.AWT graphical components. AS/400 toolbox for Java is a Sun-certified 100% pure Java application. AS/400 Toolbox for Java provides Java classes at the client to access AS/400 resources such as Client Access/400-lite. The Toolbox can access the AS/400 database, use the integrated file system, and print data queues, using AS/400 program calls and commands. Java objects on AS/400 will be full-fledged AS/400 objects, allowing them to be persistent, shared, secure, backed up, and restored, something not available in two-level-store operating systems.

Other support for Java includes the AS/400 Development Kit for Java (also referred to as VisualAge for Java), which is certified by Sun to be Java compatible with Sun's Release 1.1 (JDK 1.1). The AS/400 Development Kit for Java is a Java development tool to build Java applets and applications that includes help files and documentation. The AS/400 Development Kit is intended to be used by those who wish to develop Java applets and applications that must be portable. VisualAge for Java is integrated into OS/400 at V4R2.

Using Java at the Client

The AS/400 will also include a copy of Borland's J-Builder on a "try and buy" basis for those who do not like VisualAge for Java and who still need to develop Java applications.

Open Standards (UNIX)

In the early 1980s a movement started toward open standards computing, which eventually evolved to become known as UNIX. The objectives of open standards computing were to achieve interoperability and portability. UNIX is an operating system created by AT&T and adapted by everyone else. Today no two UNIX operating systems are identical, so the objectives of interoperability and portability touted for open standard computing have not been 100% achieved, but they are quite close (some say 90 percent, others say better). The Open Standards Foundation has its own UNIX version called AIX. OS/400 is compatible with most of the various UNIX operating systems in the world and addresses the two questions of interoperability and portability by compliance to the standards upon which the UNIX operating systems are based.

Open Standards–Based Interoperability

Support for the open standards environment (client/server) has been enhanced by incorporating the popular database standards and transmission protocols. There is significant overlap between the characteristics of this support and the needs of the UNIX environment, which will be addressed in the next section. The DB2/400 capability provides support for:

- ANSI X3.135.1992, ISO 9075-1992, and FIPS 127-2 Structured Query Language (SQL)

- IBM's Distributed Relational Database Architecture (DRDA)

- Distributed Unit of Work—Application Directed

- Remote Unit of Work

- Microsoft's Open Database Connection (ODBC)

- Apple's Data Access Language

The AS/400 supports the TCP/IP, APPC, and APPN transmission protocols. The combination of the database and transmission protocols supported allows the user to exploit the maturity and stability of the AS/400 database server with a wide range of client applications running on OS/2, DOS, Windows, AIX, and Apple Workstations. Over 25,000 commercially available AS/400 application solutions take advantage of the power, flexibility, and ease of use of the DB2/400 database manager. These applications are written for a wide range of industries and users, ranging from the small business with basic accounting needs to the large corporation with complex computing environments. The Data Propagator Relational (5716-DP1) product enables easy management of DB2-family distributed databases containing local copies of master databases by providing automatic update support for the shadow copies.

UNIX C Portability

The AS/400 supports over 80 percent of the POSIX 1003.1 APIs, and together with the BSD sockets, TCP/IP, and X-Open (often referred to as UNIX Spec 1170) support, the portability of UNIX Commercial APIs has nearly doubled. With the addition of the Integrated File System (IFS), the support of DCE Base Services/400 (5798-TBF), the improvements for sockets and Anynet/400 over TCP/IP, and the addition of Security Level 50, most UNIX/AIX applications are now portable to the AS/400 and execute with performance competitive with the industry.

System/3X Compatibility

To preserve most of the System/3X user's current investment in application programs, OS/400 provides a way to use most existing System/3X application programs on an AS/400. OS/400 and related products allow most programs written for a System/36 or System/38 to be migrated with little or no change to an AS/400. OS/400 supports this capability by providing multiple programming interfaces, as shown in Figure 4.19.

First is the **AS/400 native** programming interface. This provides support for functions such as the Structured Query Language. The System/38 programming interface provides a high level of compatibility with System/38 application programs. Because AS/400 was based on the same basic architecture as the System/38, the two are naturally very compatible and there is little system performance impact to operating in OS/400's System/38 environment. OS/400 is automatically switched into the System/38 environment when a System/38 program is executed. OS/400's System/38 environment can also be activated through CL.

The System/36 programming interface of OS/400 with the changes instituted in Version 2 is nearly as clean a fit as that for the System/38 and provides a migration path for most System/36 application programs. OS/400's System/36 environment interprets the OCL used with the System/36 and can execute RPG II and COBOL application programs after they are adapted to the AS/400 environment. Since applications originally written for the System/36 don't take advantage of the AS/400 architecture, the performance of the AS/400 is reduced when executing in the System/36 environment. With the System/36 and System/38 environments of the AS/400, programs for the S/36 and S/38 can be developed on an AS/400. However, they must be compiled on the S/36 or S/38 before they can be used on those systems. As discussed in ("SSP—An Executive Overview"), it is now possible to run up to three copies of the SSP operating system concurrently with a single copy of OS/400 on the same system. This guarantees S/36 code compatibility at both the

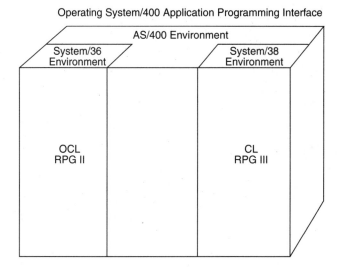

Operating System/400 Application Programming Interface

Figure 4.19. The three basic elements of the OS/400 application programming interface provide a high level of compatibility with application programs written for System/3X computers.

object-code and source-code levels. When S/36 programs are executed in an SSP environment on the AS/400 the performance improvements to be realized by that environment are achieved.

Two tools are available to help migrate System/3X application programs to AS/400: the **AS/400 System/38 Migration Aid** and the **OS/400 System/36 Migration Aid**. These tools run on their respective System/3X systems and provide the programmer with a way to analyze data, libraries, files, and programs that are to be migrated to AS/400. The sections "Migrating Programs and Data from a S/36" and "Migrating Programs and Data from a S/38" (in Chapter 6) provide more detail on performing these migrations.

Software Solution Packages

IBM is offering two software solution packages at a reduced price. One of those software solution packages is tailored for the entry client/server environment (Enhanced Advanced Entry BasePak for OS/400 [5649-

EP3]) and offers support for improved performance, Internet functions, and new versions of Client Access Family for Windows clients, including capability for wireless connection on the entry model and support for Windows 95 and NT. The second software package is for the business that has an overloaded IS/IT (Information Systems/Information Technology) staff and is finding it difficult to manage the scheduling of the necessary backup functions required to control the state of recovery in the case of a system emergency (device or system crash, or environmental disaster).

The first of these solution packages only functions on the Entry Model 150 System and includes

- OS/400 Version 4 Release 2

- AS/400 Client Access Family for Windows—Windows 95/NT Client

- Advanced Function Printing DBCS Fonts for AS/400 (5716-FN1)

- Query for AS/400 (5769-QU1)

- DB2 and SQL Development Kit for AS/400 (5769-ST1)

- Facsimile Support for AS/400 (5798-TAY)

- Performance Tools/400 (5716-PT1)

- Lotus Domino for AS/400 (Native Notes)

- Java support to enable Java application development

- AS/400 Integration for Windows NT Server, which provides the ability to attach NT clients for application serving

PSF/400 fax support, PSF/400 1 to 19 IBM print support, CPA toolkit, and TCP/IP Connectivity Utilities features for AS/400 are included. Integration services for FSIOP, Novell Netware, and Lotus Domino 4.5 are also part of BasePak. BasePak helps consolidate and manage PC applications on a LAN, access a central relational database from applications, share information among systems within a network, and integrate the Internet into a business with the Entry Model 150 as an Internet host.

The second of these software solution packages, AS/400 Operations Productivity Pak (5716-OPK), includes

- IBM Job Scheduler for AS/400 (5716JS1)

- Backup Recovery and Media Services (BRMS) for AS/400 (5716-BR1)

- ADSTAR Distributed Storage Manager (ADSM) for AS/400 Version 2.1 (5716-SV2)

Product Previews

Client Access Family for Windows 95/NT

- Visual Basic drop-ins wizard support

- Full-function AFP Workbench Viewer included

- Client management support with managed services system policies

- Windows desktop managed using policy templates from a managed services system policy editor

- Autosync support for Windows 95/NT

- Global sign-on support

Operations Navigator

- Performance monitoring

- LDAP (Lightweight Directory Access Protocol) interface

- DCE interface

- Security wizard

- Enhancements to existing Operations Navigator function

- Customization/administration of Operations Navigator

- Database enhancements

- Refreshes lists automatically

Threads

- Allows integration of existing AS/400 applications and solutions with multithread solutions

- Can develop general-purpose multithreaded solutions (e.g., improved AS/400 Query and Save/Restore performance)

- Provides additional threadsafe OS/400 APIs and commands

- Provides additional threadsafe ILE languages

- Improves AS/400 performance using threads

Cryptography

- Complies with U.S. export restrictions on encryption technology

- Requires only a single form for the number of programs to be released

- The LPP identifyies what encryption algorithm to use

Domino Go Webserver

The name and packaging have been changed to match the IBM Network Computing Framework and other IBM platform package branding. The package includes

- HTTP/HTTPs Webserver

- Enhanced Application Services

- Persistent CGI, enabling multiscreen transactions.

- Persistent connections so that the CGI program has complete control over browser response.

- Persistent connections to handle a rapid sequence of browser requests more quickly and with less network traffic.

- The ability on the server side to dynamically insert information, reuse common HTML text, include CGI output in the content.

- CGI Support for Java, REXX, and PERL, enabling additional program language options (PERL remains an unsupported language).

- Java servlets, which extend the function of a Java-enabled server with the server-side counterparts of applets.

- GWAPI (ICAPI rebranded), which provides server exit points that let an administrator extend the function of the server.

- Cookie support to provide for the use of browser cookies in CGI applications.

- Net.Question.

- Web Usage Miner.

- Complementing the encryption packaging change to reduce the number of products and release complexity.

- Digital ID Certificate options.

- User identification to a CGI program providing user tracking and preference customization.

- Application authentication for users in a validation list enabling a registration program to register "Internet users" and register their certificate for future access.

- Application authentication by UID/PW association to associate a certificate with an OS/400 user profile to run an application under that user's authority.

- Equivalent to OS/400 UID/PW providing full system access as if signed on with user ID and password. Most useful in intranet environment.

- Enhanced Administration

- Proxy/cache, which enables the server to request documents from other servers and cache them locally. (Supports HTTP, HTTPs, GOPHER, WAIS, FTP.)

- Enhanced GUI interface, which uses frames and Javascript for improved look and feel.

- Directory icon support, which uses default icons for directories viewed with a browser and can be customized.

- Symbolic links in server directives to make file administration easier.

Server Java

- Built-in Java Development Kit 1.2

- San Francisco

Persistent Net.Data provides a business application framework for multiscreen transactions with transaction commit and rollback controls in a browser environment that features the ability to:

- Designate multiple sections of a macro, or multiple macros to act as a single transaction.

- Designate the variables of a macro persistent.

- Open files and cursors for commitment control, providing commitment checkpoints and rollback.

- Commit and roll back groups of changes.

- Explicitly close files and cursors.

- Handle HTTP server interface for persistent CGI.

- Use no browser cookies.

Additional information on persistent Net.Data can be found at *www.as400.ibm.com/netdata*; also see Figure 4.20.

Net.Question administrator user interface translation to NLS (National Language Standards) is expanded as part of AS/400 release translation as a no-charge feature of Domino Go Webserver.

Digital Certificates Accepted for Authentication

- HTTP and LDAP servers support digital certificates.

- Use certificate for identification only.

- Associate a certificate with user profile.

- Associate a certificate with a user in a validation list.

- Accept certificate as system sign on.

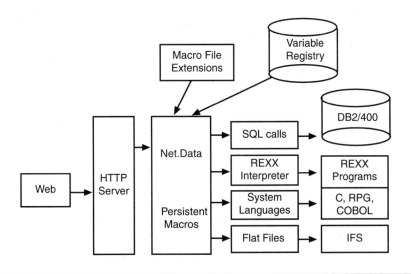

Figure 4.20. Persistent Net.Data block diagram.

Firewall Enhancements

- Ipsec transport encryption.

- Setup wizard.

Cryptolopes

An encrypted envelope around content that enables sale and online distribution of intellectual property that is only to be used by the buyer (e.g., music, news, software) and sends a file access control program along with the package.

San Francisco Frameworks

- PERPL OO Database

- Persistent Objects for Java

- No special Java bytecodes

- No special Java compiler

- Persistent objects for San Francisco

- Persistence for general Java users

- Persistent objects grouped into pool

- Integrated file system

- Sizes

  - Pools are huge (tens of gigabytes)

  - Small overhead per packed object

- Easy administration

- Authorize users to a pool

- Save/restore pool to save file or media

- Multiple classes/types per pool

5

AS/400 and Communications—
An Introduction

As/400's standard functions plus the many communications options and supporting software provide users with flexibility when configuring AS/400 for various communications environments. However, this flexibility can also cause confusion when trying to determine which options and programs are needed for a particular environment. This section provides a guide through the jungle of business communications available through Application Systems. "Communications Options" in Chapter 2 looked at some communications hardware for Application Systems, and "Communications Support" in Chapter 4 looked at communications software support in OS/400. In this section, some of the most popular communications environments are examined, and where appropriate example configurations are provided.

Computer Communications in the Office—
An Introduction

If one activity is most crucial to a business of any size, it is the act of communicating accurate, timely, and manageable information to the proper decision maker. Based on the information available important choices are made that can have far-reaching effects on the success of the business. Improve communications in a business and productivity and profitability are likely to improve. As a business grows, it becomes both more important and more difficult to maintain efficient, accurate communications—the very thing that facilitates business growth in the first place. Communications difficulties grow geometrically with the size of the business.

Today's businesses are quickly finding that computers are a communications tool unequaled in significance since Bell invented the telephone. Computers are already commonplace in the business environment, and now there is an increasing emphasis on computer communication. This communication can occur between two computers or among a group of computers in a communications network and allows business information to move at electronic speeds. Furthermore, communication allows users at remote locations access to vital business information on a distant computer. AS/400 computers represent a powerful communication tool. All provide a choice of standard communications features to facilitate getting computer support through IBM Electronic Customer Support (ECS). As was seen in "Communications Options," there is a full complement of communications options and peripherals, which, with the associated software, allow AS/400 to participate in many different communications environments.

This chapter discusses System Networks Architecture (SNA), Electronic Customer Support (ECS), remote workstation communications, distributed computer communications, AS/400 distributed networks, AS/400 system clustering, IBM's overall network blueprint, and network computing, including environments created by intranets, retail systems, electronic business (e-biz), and the Internet.

What Is SNA?

In the not too remote past, computers were like islands, each performing very specific tasks independent of any other computer. As computer systems became more popular, they grew in number and spread over wide geographic distances. Then, almost as an afterthought, it became desirable to attach remote users to computers as well as to link distant computer systems. This led to specialized communications hardware and programming that limited the flexibility of both the communications configurations and the communications functions available. Businesses were constantly faced with massive programming changes and incompatible hardware elements when trying to grow or adapt to new requirements. For this reason, in 1974 IBM introduced a set of communications conventions called the **Systems Network Architecture (SNA)**. This set of published communications standards provided a direction for the evolution of flexible, cost-effective communications.

SNA is the set of standards that IBM committed to support as a strategic direction for future products. It defined communications protocols, hardware specifications, and programming conventions that made for coherent growth of communications facilities. Since 1974, IBM and many other companies have provided computer hardware and programming products that conform to SNA, and SNA is now a widely accepted direction for computer communications in the business environment. Furthermore, SNA itself has been expanded and updated in an evolutionary way to meet the changing and growing needs of business environments. All Application Systems support SNA communications. Since SNA is still IBM's strategic direction for communications, investments in SNA hardware and software will be protected over time.

IBM Electronic Customer Support Communications

AS/400 systems come standard with the communications equipment necessary to participate in IBM Electronic Customer Support (ECS). This is a link to IBM or other support providers that allows you to obtain answers to technical questions, report problems, receive Program Temporary Fixes (PTFs), and the like. Although its not necessary to be a communications expert to use IBM Electronic Customer Support, understanding the basic communications link can remove the mystery.

Figure 5.1 shows the AS/400 communications link to IBM Electronic Customer Support. Every AS/400 system comes standard with a EIA 232/V.24 adapter used to communicate over a switched telephone line. The EIA 232/V.24 adapter provides the electrical interface and handles the communications protocol used with IBM Electronic Customer Support. A modem adapts the computer information into electrical signals suitable for telephone line transmission. OS/400 comes standard with the necessary functions to manage the telephone commu-

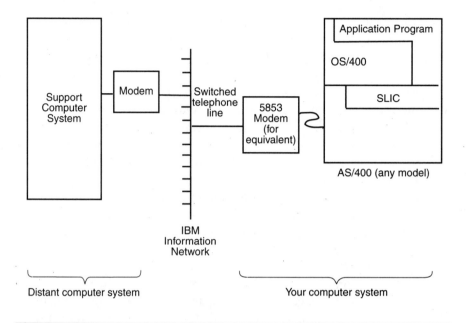

Figure 5.1. Communications configuration used for Electronic Customer Support.

nications link. When IBM Electronic Customer Support is desired, the user instructs OS/400 to place a toll-free call to the **IBM Information Network**. This is a nationwide communications network that provides many services, including connections to the appropriate Electronic Customer Support computer system. The user is then linked to IBM Electronic Customer Support and can perform the desired tasks. For simplicity, the rest of the communications configurations provided in this chapter do not show the IBM Electronic Customer Support communications link. You should understand that all communications configurations shown are in addition to the IBM Electronic Customer Support link that is provided with most AS/400 systems.

No matter what computer system a business chooses, the system and its users will require ongoing support. They will have questions that need answering, hardware problems that must be addressed, software updates that must be installed, and so forth. This support can be delivered in many different ways. Personnel from the computer manufacturer, the software company, or the business's own staff are generally involved in supporting the computer system and its users.

With AS/400 systems (as well as with other IBM systems) much of this support can be provided electronically over communications networks. This is called IBM **Electronic Customer Support (ECS)**. Just as electronic mail and online business information streamline a business's operation, the delivery of the various types of support needed can also be improved through IBM Electronic Customer Support. IBM provides five basic areas of IBM Electronic Customer Support:

- IBMLink

- RETAIN

- Question-and-answer database

- File transfer

- Copy screen

The communications hardware and software necessary to participate in IBM Electronic Customer Support are provided with every AS/400 system. Access to IBM Electronic Customer Support is provided through the **IBM Information Network (IIN)**. The kinds of things provided through IBMLink include electronic announcement letters, product catalogs, education catalogs, publication catalogs, pricing information, product configuration aids, and lists of local dealers. Users can exchange electronic notes with IBM marketing and support personnel. With proper authorization, you can also place orders, access a database of technical questions and answers, author new questions, report service hardware or software problems, and so on, all electronically over IBMLink.

IBM Electronic Customer Support also provides direct access to IBM's **RETAIN** network. Over RETAIN, you can electronically report a hardware problem and send accompanying information helpful in diagnosing the problem. IBM service personnel can then automatically be dispatched—all over the RETAIN network. Similarly, software problems can be reported, and any missing programming fixes (PTFs) that are indicated by the symptoms can often be automatically sent over RETAIN. With the addition of the SystemView System Management Utilities for the OS/400, the user's central AS/400 system can become a repository for PTFs and service any other AS/400 systems over a communications link, thus becoming centralized support for their own organization. Another element of IBM Electronic Customer Support is the technical question-and-answer database. Each AS/400 system is shipped with its own electronic copy of the most commonly asked questions and their answers. If the question is not contained in this local database, IBM Electronic Customer Support provides access to an IBM database with additional questions and answers. With proper authorization, the user can also author new questions that will be answered (electronically) by IBM support personnel.

The file transfer capability of IBM Electronic Customer Support allows you to exchange information (e.g., a file containing your system's configuration) with IBM marketing and support personnel as necessary. The copy screen facility of IBM Electronic Customer Support allows remote support personnel to see the same image you see on your display for the purpose of education or problem troubleshooting. With IBM Electronic Customer Support, help is delivered electronically, improving access to technical and product information and streamlining communications between IBM and the users. AS/400 online education and IBMLink tutorials are provided along with the online user's guide and help text to make the interaction with IBM Electronic Customer Support easier to use.

Remote Workstations

Often those who need access to Application Systems are not conveniently located at the same location as the computer system. In these cases, Application Systems' communications can be employed to provide access to distant or **remote** users. The way to provide computer access to remote users is to provide them with workstations (terminals and printers) attached to Application Systems over telephone lines. Figure 5.2 shows an example of how remote workstations can be attached to an AS/400 (9406). As with local users, the remote users are provided with workstations including terminals and printers. The remote workstations are attached to the 5494 Remote Workstation Controller. This device helps manage the traffic between the remote workstations and the AS/400. It provides the same services to remote workstations as the Twinaxial Workstation Controller provides for locally attached workstations.

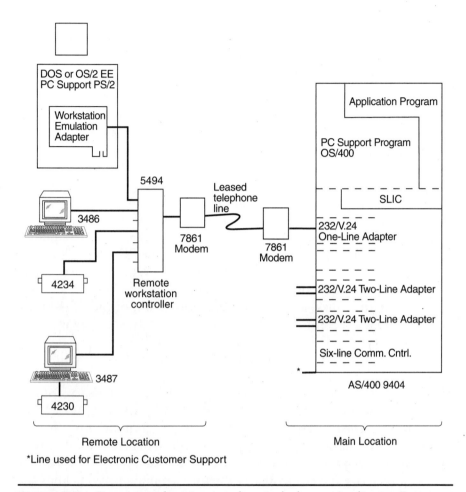

Figure 5.2. Remote workstations can be attached to an Application System through remote workstation controllers.

The telephone line in our example is a **leased line,** meaning that it provides a continuous connection between the remote site and the AS/400. The modems at each end handle the electronic details associated with sending and receiving information over the telephone line. The 7861 Modems were chosen because they allow for communications at up to 19,200 bps on leased telephone lines. Any of the workstations can be remotely attached in this fashion. In our example, we have

3486 and 3487 Terminals, a personal computer, and 4234 and 4230 Printers. Except for the 4230 Printer, all these workstations are attached directly to the 5494 Remote Workstation Controller with twinaxial cable. To illustrate how the printer port provided on the 3487 (and 3486) Display can be used, the 4230 Printer is cabled directly to the printer port on the 3487 Display. With this type of arrangement, the 4230 is still under direct control of the remote AS/400. It is simply another way of cabling the printer, one that may be more convenient, depending on the user's environment.

The personal computer (PC) workstation is equipped with the **System 36/38 workstation emulation adapter**. This provides the electrical interface necessary to attach the PC to the twinaxial cable used with Application Systems. AS/400's **Client Access Family for Windows** program provides the programming for both the PC (running DOS, Windows, or OS/2) and the AS/400 allowing the PC to act like an Application Systems workstation. In this configuration, the PC has access to the information, disk storage, printers, and so on, of the AS/400 (i.e., the AS/400 is a server for the PC client). Alternately, specially written application programs residing on the PC and AS/400 can directly interact (cooperative processing), allowing for a highly flexible computing environment.

On the AS/400 side, OS/400 provides the necessary communications functions to support the remote workstations as if they were locally attached—that is, the application program need not be specially written to support the remote workstations. In fact, the application program cannot tell the difference between local and remote users. In our example, we have provided 5 separate communications lines that can be used to attach remote workstations from 5 different locations. Larger AS/400 systems can support up to 250 lines. This allows a single AS/400 to serve the needs of users at many different remote locations. In the preceding example, we achieved the first line by installing a 2699 Two-Line WAN I/O Adapter and a 0330 EIA 232/V.24 Cable, which is supported by the MultiFunction I/O Processor provided as standard with all (on the Models 150, 170, 600, 620, S10, and S20 systems, the MFIOP functions are performed by a base system controller but are still there) AS/400 systems. The remaining four lines were provided by installing a 2623 Six-Line Communications Controller and two 2699 Two-Line I/O Adapters and two 0330 Cables (except on Model 600 or Model S10 where the 2721 Two-Line Adapters and the 0330 Cable plug directly to the PCI card cage).

Distributed Computer Communications

In some cases, the computing needs of a business can be met with a single computer system. This is particularly true for smaller businesses or businesses in which most computer needs are at a single location. In many cases, however, the needs of a business may be best satisfied by using multiple computer systems. Instead of providing remote users with remote workstations, as discussed earlier, remote users may be provided with their own small computer system. For example, a retail chain may want a computer system at each retail location as well as a computer system at headquarters as illustrated in Figure 5.3. As shown, all computer systems are joined through a communications network that allows them to easily move information (for example, daily cash register receipts) from place to place as necessary. This is called a **distributed computing network**.

When computer systems are placed or **distributed** at the site where they are needed, several nice things happen. First, because all users are

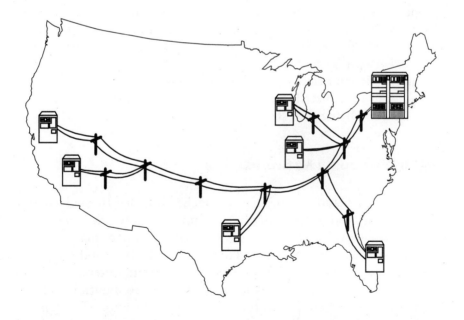

Figure 5.3. Example of a distributed network for a retail chain headquartered in New York City.

locally attached to their respective computer system, they often enjoy improved system performance (reduced response time) as compared with remotely attached workstations, which are slowed down by communications line limitations. Further, the distributed computer system can consolidate communications. This is particularly true at larger remote locations, which may need a large number of communications lines to support all the remote workstations. With a distributed computing approach, remote users would be locally attached to their distributed system, which could then communicate summary information to other computers through a single communications line.

In some cases, it may be an advantage to provide the remote location with some control over the distributed system. It may have unique requirements that can be met by an available prewritten application program. It could then acquire the program and get the support of the software firm in meeting its unique needs, all without becoming computer experts or blindly relying on the headquarters computer staff. This makes the remote location more productive while reducing the workload at headquarters. The disadvantage is that a large distributed computer network is often more difficult to manage than a single computer system. However, because Application Systems were designed for a distributed environment, there are system management and network management tools that ease this task. As discussed in OS/400, SystemView System Manager/400 provides some of these tools. An example communications environment in which Application Systems participate in a distributed computing environment is shown next, in "AS/400 Distributed Networks."

AS/400 Distributed Networks

Multiple AS/400 systems can be attached together through communications lines to create a distributed computer network. An example distributed network of this type might consist of five small AS/400s (e.g., Model 150s), each distributed to a remote location, and a larger AS/400 (e.g., a 9406 Model 640) at the business's headquarters. Figure 5.4 is an example of AS/400 hardware and software configurations for one of the remote locations and the headquarters location. The remote location configuration (Model 150) would be duplicated for every remote location. Furthermore, the AS/400 at each end would be equipped with the appropriate local workstations to support the users at the respective locations. These are not shown to avoid confusion with options needed to support the communications link. The hardware configurations needed to meet the communications requirements for this distributed network are listed in the following paragraph.

Distributed AS/400 Network Example

The 9401 Model 150 used at the remote location is equipped with a 2721 PCI Two-Line WAN Adapter and 0330 EIA 232/V.24 Cable that

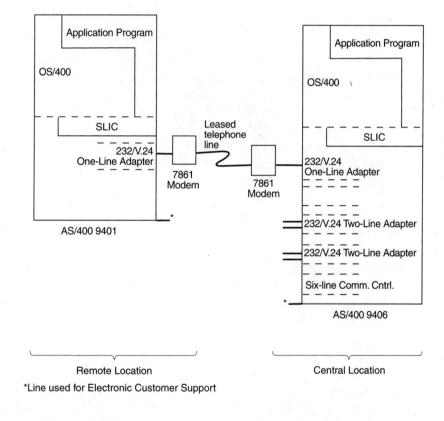

Figure 5.4. Configuration used for attaching distant AS/400 systems together.

provide one communications line (in addition to the standard communications line used for IBM Electronic Customer Support). This adapter is supported by the equivalent MultiFunction I/O Processor function provided as standard equipment with all 940X systems. Since the remote AS/400 system needs to communicate only with the central AS/400 system, this is the only adapter needed. The 7861 Modem allows for communications at 19,200 bps over leased telephone lines. OS/400 has the communications functions necessary to manage the communications link. At the central location, the larger AS/400 is in constant communication with all remote locations. It collects the summary information needed by headquarters to consolidate all remote location activity.

In our example, one communications line is used for each remote location. This means the central AS/400 must have at least five communications lines (in addition to that used for IBM Electronic Customer Support). To meet this need, an 2699 Two-Line WAN I/O Adapter and an EIA 232/V.24 cable is first added. This adapter works with the MultiFunction I/O Processor provided as standard with all AS/400 systems. Next, a 2623 Six-Line Communications Controller and two additional 2699 Two-Line WAN I/O Adapters and EIA 232/V.24 Cables are added. Thus, the AS/400 system now has five communications lines (in addition to the one used for IBM Electronic Customer Support). One 7861 Modem is required at the central site for each communications line, making a total of five (one is shown).

With our example communications configuration and appropriate application programs, there are several different ways in which the distributed AS/400 systems can work together. In the simplest form, the distributed computing environment could use OS/400's **Distributed Data Management (DDM)** support, which allows a user of a remote AS/400 to query a database on the central AS/400 or any other AS/400 in the network. The user need not even know that the database needed is located on another computer system. The DDM function of OS/400 will automatically locate, retrieve, and present the information to the user, reducing the complexity of the system from the user's viewpoint. Alternately, a user of one system may actually want to sign on and directly interact with one of the other systems in the network. Another OS/400 function, called **Display Station Pass- Thru (DSPT)**, supports this type of interaction by allowing a user to sign on and interact with any other AS/400 in the distributed network as if the user were directly attached to that system.

The preceding example is a network connected by Wide Area Network (WAN) communications, using non-intelligent workstations, an alternative would be to use the Internet to connect and communicate between the AS/400 systems. A configuration of this type will be discussed in the section of this chapter on the Internet.

Often, the central location provides technical support to all remote locations. This support includes troubleshooting network communications problems and distributing new software and software updates. Through IBM Electronic Customer Support, the central site can also provide its own technical question/answer database. This database can contain any type of company-related information from operating procedures to technical information about a custom application program. Thus, any user anywhere in the distributed network can look up questions and the corresponding answers without playing telephone tag or waiting for the headquarters staff to respond. If a question is not covered in the database, it can be submitted to the headquarters staff. Once the staff responds with an answer, it is added to the database so that it will be available the next time that question is asked. SystemView System Manager/400 provides functions that allow the central support site to manage changes to the AS/400 systems in the network and any problems that are reported.

APPC/APPN

Sophisticated cooperative processing between the central and remote AS/400 systems is becoming more prevalent. OS/400 functions such as Advanced Program-to-Program Communications (APPC) and Advanced Peer-to-Peer Networking (APPN), along with OS/400 extensions such as Client Access and Structured Query Language/400, let programmers write application programs that can efficiently delegate processing tasks and share information among the various AS/400 and personal computer systems in a network. APPC is a communications convention that allows a program on one AS/400 system to initiate actions on a remote computer system (e.g., start a program or perform a database query) without any assistance from the user. APPN is a networking scheme that manages the logistics necessary for one AS/400 in the network to know details (location, communications links, available application programs and data, etc.) about all of the other AS/400 and personal computer systems in that network. APPN also dynamically selects the most appropriate communications link (if more than one is available) based on variables such as cost, line speed, and security level.

IBM's Systems Network Architecture (SNA) has adopted APPN as a strategic networking scheme, making it important in other environments (e.g., personal computer and S/390 communications networks). Since OS/400 supports SNA, documents can be freely exchanged between nodes using SNA's Distribution Services (SNADS) conventions. This provides a coherent electronic mail environment in which users need not concern themselves about who is where in the network. Furthermore, any AS/400 file can be sent from any node to any other node on the network. This can be useful for distributing program or data updates from a single point in the network. Further discussion of these OS/400 communications functions can be found in "Communications Support."

APPN support includes two different types of filter lists, the session endpoint filter list and the directory endpoint filter list, that provide a firewall security operation for local networks as well as for the Internet.

Filter Lists

Filter Lists enable the invocation of security functions for either local network protection or Internet network isolation. Two filter lists are provided under Advanced Peer-to-Peer Networking (APPN). The **session** endpoint filter list controls access to and from local locations, and the **directory endpoint filter** list controls access to and from peripheral nodes.

The session endpoint filter list defines the remote locations that are allowed or rejected from communicating with local locations. As a rule, the session endpoint filter list should be used in conjunction with the **APPN remote location** list and password security. There is no need to duplicate location in the remote location list. The session endpoint filter list controls user and control-point sessions, and supports generic and wildcard naming.

The directory search filter list is used to restrict the locations with which peripheral nodes can establish sessions by using the network identifier and control-point name of the peripheral node. Locations on the peripheral node are called **filtered locations**. Locations that peripheral nodes want to access are called **partner locations**. The directory search firewall is only as strong as its weakest link. When both session endpoint filter and directory search filter lists have been identified for a single location, the session endpoint filter list will manage the security access function for that location.

AS/400 System Clustering

As described earlier, the networking function supports both local and wide area network capabilities on the AS/400. The local area networks provide one method for **horizontal growth** of the system. Horizontal growth implies the ability to increase the networked system from both a capacity and performance perspective by adding components to the existing system without having to exchange existing system components. The capacity increase occurs because the addition of a system implies the capability to add all functions of the system independent of the path by which the interconnection is achieved. The performance of a system cluster connected in a local area network is limited by the performance of the local area network itself.

The types of local area networks supported on the AS/400 are the token-ring and Ethernet networks. The instantaneous bandwidth of each of these local area networks is 16 and 100 Mbps, respectively (FDDI is a special case of a token-ring network with 100-Mbps instantaneous bandwidth). The instantaneous bandwidth identifies how fast data can be passed from one system in a cluster to a different system in that cluster once a connection has been established. More important than instantaneous bandwidth is the **utilization rate** of the network. The utilization rate is the proportion of the instantaneous bandwidth that is available for information exchange between systems after contention for network resources, the overhead of the network, and recovery from errors has been accounted for. The following ratios for utilization rate are approximate, but they illustrate that local area networks, although a vast improvement upon wide area networks, still leave a significant region for performance improvement.

Utilization starts to saturate for token-ring networks at 70 percent, for Ethernet at 40 percent, and for FDDI at 70 percent. A second methodology for adding system performance and growth via system clustering is offered by the AS/400 Optical Interconnect with Object Connect/400. The hardware necessary to perform the interconnect is described in "Opticonnect/400 Systems" and "Packaging Technology," both contained in Chapter 1. The hardware has the capability of inter-changing data between any two systems at an instantaneous data rate of 1063 Mbps, with a theoretical utilization rate of 70 percent. Further-more, if more than three systems are in the cluster, as many as $n/2$ si-multaneous conversations (where n is the total number of systems in the cluster) may be going on at the same time, as long as the data needed exists on at least one set of each pair of systems. Data Propagator Rela-tional/400 also works over this connection and may be used to ensure that the needed data replication exists. Opticonnect/400 with Distrib-uted Data Management (DDM) is the application support needed to exploit this capability.

In this environment, if an application needs greater performance than is available in the existing systems, an additional system is added to the clustered system network. Using the capability of parallel threads, that system will decrease the load on the other existing systems in the network, thereby providing the performance boost that previously re-quired the replacement of the existing processing system (**vertical growth**).

An additional capability, besides the system and performance growth, that occurs as a result of the ability to cluster systems levels as described is the capability to build redundancy into the processing, data files, and networking functions. The redundancy methodology may include a mixture of approaches—including N+1, mirroring, RAID-5, and checksums—at system and subsystem levels as needed to achieve the protection desired. All of the pass-thru functions for displays and print-ers continue to function in the clustered system environment. In fact the user of the application has no perception of which system in the cluster of systems is actually executing the application. LANs and WANs may coexist on each system in a system cluster. Opticonnect/400 is the loosely coupled connection referred to in Chapter 3, in "Data Warehousing" and "Data Mining."

ObjectConnect/400

ObjectConnect/400 is a PRPQ (Program Request Per Quote) that sim-ply and efficiently moves individual objects, entire libraries, or entire Integrated File System (IFS) directories from one AS/400 system to an-other over a standard communications connection or over a high-speed fiber optic bus.

IBM'S Overall Networking Blueprint

The **IBM Networking Blueprint** (Figure 5.5), is a guide to IBM's networking commitments. The Blueprint lays out the framework for integrating into a single network multiple separate networks and their applications that use different communications protocols, different hardware components, different bandwidths, and different network management techniques. The Blueprint incorporates existing and anticipated industry standards and open systems standards. It complements the Systems Network Architecture (SNA) communications standards as well as Open Software Foundation's **Distributed Computing Environment (DCE)** and ISO communications specifications, but it does not replace them.

The IBM Networking Blueprint framework provides the freedom to choose network elements to meet application and business needs, rather than force-fitting those requirements to inappropriate networking solutions. The Blueprint allows a mixture of international standards, industry standards, and architectures. As standards evolve, the Blueprint will

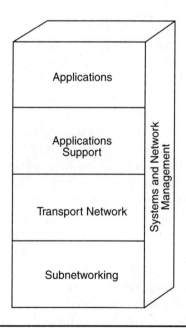

Figure 5.5. IBM's Networking Blueprint structure.

change to keep pace. The Blueprint is divided into four layers, representing the elements necessary to make up a network: the Applications layer, the Applications Support layer, the Transport Network layer, and the Subnetworking layer.

Applications Layer

The IBM Networking Blueprint provides all major interfaces for distributed computing. The first layer, starting from the top of the Blueprint, is the **Applications Layer** (see Figure 5.6), which represents the full range of applications and application enablers (e.g., high-level languages and program generators) that support an organization's business. The applications and enablers make use of the underlying capabilities of the network.

Application Support Layer

The second layer, the **Application Support layer**, represents multivendor application interfaces and services. There are three primary interfaces (see Figure 5.7): **Common Programming Interface for Communications (CPI-C)**, **Remote Procedure Call (RPC)**, and the **Messaging and Queuing Interface (MQI)**. Each of these interfaces is described in greater detail in "Multivendor Application Program Interfaces."

The Application Support layer also contains a set of distributed networking services for handling messages, security, directory, and transaction processing. Standard networking applications, such as file transfer programs, also fall within the Application Support layer. Although not shown on the IBM Networking Blueprint, CICS/ESA and CallPath could be considered to span both the Applications layer and the Application Support layer. Both products contain APIs and provide application support services, so they fit within the Application Support layer, but the APIs are application-enabling APIs, also making them part of the Applications layer. The CICS API may be thought of as an extension to many of the application development languages, allowing application development without the concern for the underlying network. CallPath provides an API that allows applications to combine voice functions of the telephone with the data processing capability of a computer.

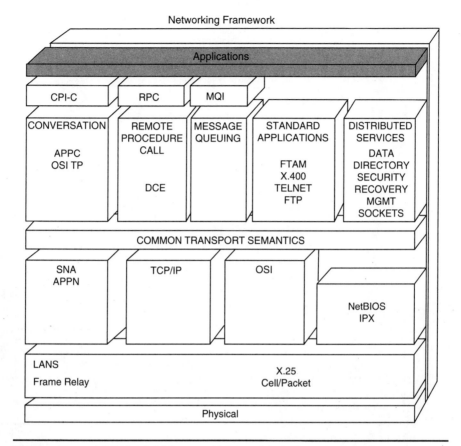

Figure 5.6. AS/400 Multi-Protocol Networking Blueprint Interface-applications layer.

Multivendor Application Program Interfaces

The CPI-C Interface

The CPI-C interface supports communication between application programs over private logical connections called conversations. Conversational communication is a sophisticated method of program-to-program communication requiring simultaneous execution of partner programs. It is designed primarily for a structured exchange of information be-

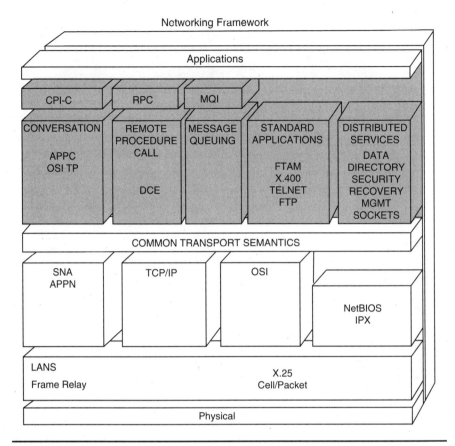

Figure 5.7. AS/400 Multi-Protocol Networking Blueprint Interface-applications support layer.

tween programs and requires that a network session be reserved exclusively for the communicating programs. CPI-C applications are generally client/server or peer-to-peer implementations. The operating systems implemented Advanced Program-to-Program Communication (APPC) services to assist in the implementation of conversational applications through CPI-C. In spite of the sophistication of conversational applications, they are surprisingly easy to implement. APPC/MVS in MVS/ESA, for example, offers built-in server functions that can be used in client/server conversations. APPC/MVS services are callable services, so they can be accessed from a high-level language application without the necessity of writing assembler language routines.

The Remote Procedure Call

The **Remote Procedure Call (RPC)** function provides communications between applications using a call/return mechanism, much like doing FORTRAN library subroutine calls. RPC applications are client/server implementations. The client program (the caller) is responsible for determining the server location (the called procedure) in the network, establishing the necessary communication, and passing the required parameters for the procedure execution. This is a synchronous operation. The caller waits until the procedure finishes execution, and the results are passed back. Again using MVS/ESA as the example, different vendor implementations of Remote Procedure Call are supported. Today, workstations with applications implementing RPC can operate as clients with MVS/ESA using the TCP/IP product. TCP/IP also supports Apollo Computers' Network Computing System RPC. The OSF/DCE RPC is supported using the POSIX-compliant application programming interface.

The Messaging and Queuing Interface

The Messaging and Queuing Interface (MQI) MQSeries (5716-MQ1) is an asynchronous program-to-program interface that supports message-driven, deferred processing. Communication is through queues, not through private connections. Programs that use MQI fill and empty message queues. The calling program places the request in a queue but does not wait for a response; instead, it continues with its processing, and when the response arrives, it is placed in a queue to await processing. MQI services route the messages to the appropriate destinations in the network for access by the programs servicing the queue. MQI applications can be client/server, peer-to-peer, or more complex implementations. MQI provides guaranteed message delivery, recoverability, and, where applicable, sync-point participation. (When messages are broken into multiple packets that are sent over separate routes, the packets do not necessarily arrive in the correct order, and the sync points allow the message to be reconstructed regardless of the order of the packet reception at the final destination.) MQSeries allows use of distribution lists to put a single message in multiple queues with a single call. Channel definitions can be automatically created for receiver and server channel connections. Large transactions can use message segmentation ordering and grouping to improve checking of transactional data. The ability to reference messages with chained exits allows large amounts of data to be transferred between nodes. The ability to use C++ for MQI applications and the ability to perform static bindings in ILE RPG programs make programming easier. Channel heartbeats provide faster recovery when the system stops or resets, and when data needs fast delivery, more programs can take advantage of fast nonpersistent messages.

Transport Network Layer: SNA-TCP/IP-MPTN-APPN

The **third** layer, the **transport network layer** (see Figure 5.8), is the layer for integrating multivendor network protocols into one efficient network. Networking protocols are used for sending and receiving information throughout the network. Typically, applications and application services are bound to a specific networking protocol. CPI-C applications use SNA networking; RPC applications use TCP/IP; X.400 applications use Open System Interconnection (OSI); other applications use NetBIOS, Internet Packet Exchange (IPX), DECnet, or other protocols, but within this layer, the **Common Transport Semantics framework** (see Figure 5.8) provides a structure for supporting multiprotocol networking capability.

Multiprotocol Transport Networking (MPTN)

The Multiprotocol Transport Networking (MPTN) architecture defines much of the Common Transport Semantics. MPTN architecture is open and general, eliminating the forced networking protocol bindings between the application support layer and the transport layer. In other words, the application support APIs and their services can communicate over a protocol other than the one for which they were originally implemented. The applications must be matched pairs, however—both designed to communicate using the same communication protocol. For example, two APPC programs originally designed to communicate over SNA could now communicate over TCP/IP, two socket programs originally designed to communicate over TCP/IP could now communicate over SNA, but an APPC program cannot communicate with a socket program over either SNA or TCP/IP.

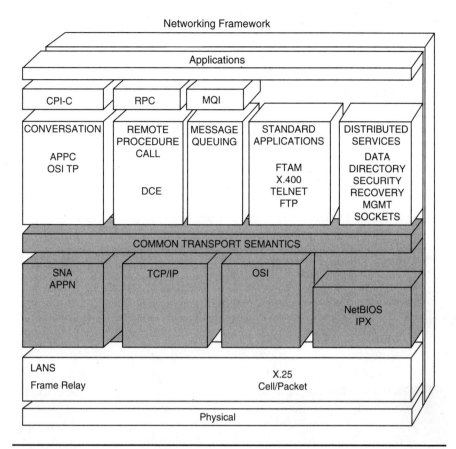

Figure 5.8. AS/400 Multi-Protocol Networking Blueprint Interface-Transport network layer.

Client Access offers a multiprotocol transport feature (called AnyNet/400), which allows the application to be separated from the network transport. This feature provides OS/2 functions. The OS/2 function is installed at the host and downloaded to the workstation. CICS/400, IMS/400, TM, DB2/400, DRDA, or any APPC application is able to communicate with an OS/2 workstation in a TCP/IP network that has the APPC API (e.g., OS/2). APPC over TCP/IP can be host to workstation, workstation to workstation, or host to host. AnyNet/400 also supports an interface for Berkeley Software Distribution (BSD) sockets over SNA for OS/2. The sockets interface uses APPC as the underlying network service. AnyNet/400 also supports Client Access for users who use Windows 3.1. Even before the introduction of the MPTN architecture, NetBIOS, IPX, and some other protocols' traffic could be transported over TCP/IP. NetBIOS and X.25 traffic could also be transported over SNA. Novell's Internetwork Packet Exchange (IPX) protocol is now available on AnyNet/400.

Advanced Peer-to-Peer Networking (APPN)

Advanced Peer-to-Peer Networking (APPN) provides value to existing SNA networks by reducing the complexity of maintaining network definitions. APPN minimizes the need for coordinated systems definition. Network resources are defined only at the node at which they are located, and APPN will distribute information about these resources through the network as it is needed. Switching to an APPN network can save considerable system programmer time because a high percentage of network definitions are eliminated by the dynamic nature of APPN routing. Device definitions, link definitions, and path definitions are all significantly reduced. The APPN end-node and network-node specifications are published as Common Communications Support protocols, facilitating implementation by others. Because APPN is based on LU 6.2 and T2.1 protocols, existing Original-Equipment Manufacturers' (OEMs') T2.1 LEN nodes and LU 6.2 applications can take advantage of APPN networking.

The APPN program has been enhanced to improve network reliability by automatically rerouting around failures, by automatically adjusting to network congestion to get data through without a timeout, and by automatically using high-speed links through increasing throughput on underutilized links.

Subnetworking Layer

The **fourth** layer, the **subnetworking layer** (see Figure 5.9), represents a piece of a larger network, a connection to Local Area Networks (LANs), Wide Area Networks (WANs), host channels, or other high-speed transmission services. The IBM Networking Blueprint provides a framework for integrating LAN and WAN networks, providing management services, efficient link utilization, and high availability, all with predictable response time. A key component of the Blueprint, systems and network management, applies to all four Blueprint layers. It encompasses all management disciplines and supports multiprotocol and multivendor environments through industry standards such as SNA management services, the TCP/IP Simple Network Management Protocol (SNMP), and the OSI Common Management Information Protocol (CMIP).

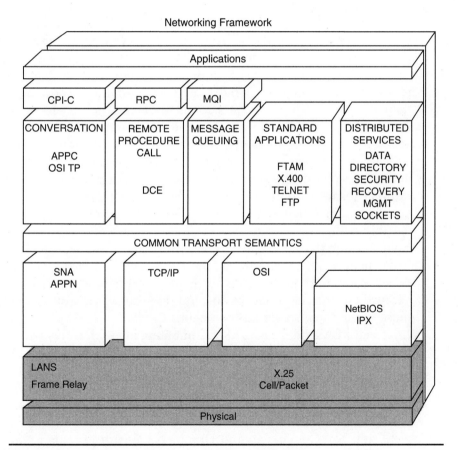

Figure 5.9. AS/400 Multi-Protocol Networking Blueprint Interface-Subnetworking layer.

SystemView is the framework for providing enterprise-wide systems and network management, planning, coordination, and operations. It enables both centralized management and distributed management. The proposed OSF Distributed Management Environment (OSF/DME) fits with the SystemView structure. Two SystemView-conforming products, NetView and NetView/400, help manage applications in an MPTN environment, where the applications use transport protocols different from the ones for which they were originally designed.

Network Computing

The Network Computing environment can be viewed as either a subset or a superset of client/server computing. One or more intranets may be connected within a network computing environment. Each of the intranets may share one or more servers. In addition to the intranets, there may be one or more connections to the Internet. Each connection to the Internet should contain both a firewall and Internet Connection Secure Server (ICSS) to isolate the intranet data and activity from the Internet. If a server connected to both an intranet and the Internet does not include a firewall, all intranets connected to that intranet via bridges or other forms of routers are exposed to Internet data access and contamination, in which case it may be necessary to isolate that particular intranet with a firewall to prevent the exposure of the other intranet environments that are secure. What distinguishes network computing from client/server computing is that thick servers are generally used in network computing. (In thick servers the server function is expanded because the Internet connection requires security capabilities beyond those of the client/server environment.)

The IBM AS/400 Networking Computing Internet site provides many details on the following subjects: Getting Started on the Internet, Workstation Gateway, Net.Data, CGI Programming, Network Station, Exit Programs, TCP/IP, HTTP, SLIP, Security, Java, Java Development Kit, Java Toolbox, Domino.Merchant, Domino/Notes, Net.Commerce, Net.Question, and I/NET Solutions. From this list of addressed areas, Net.Data, Net.Commerce, and Domino.Merchant are related to electronic business (e-biz), and will be covered in "Electronic Commerce."

Getting Started on the Internet will also be covered as part of "AS/400 and the Internet".

The AS/400 Workstation Gateway function of the Internet Connection for AS/400 allows the usage of existing development tools for creating World Wide Web (WWW) applications. Also, existing AS/400 applications will execute over the World Wide Web without code modification. This is possible because Internet Connection for AS/400 intercepts the 5250 data stream and converts it to HyperText Markup Language (HTML), which any WWW browser can display. This also means that any PC that has a WWW browser installed can run AS/400 applications. Business capabilities are expanded by using the WWW browser to connect to AS/400.

Common Gateway Interface (CGI) Programming refers to an HTTP standard for running programs requested by browsers on servers, usually with input data sent by the browser. An AS/400 CGI programming tools library is available using the "Snippets" link under "Resources" on the AS/400 Web Builders Workshop site.

Exit programs customize File Transfer Protocol (FTP) access to the AS/400. Exit programs allow anonymous FTP access to specific files and control access for specific users.

Intranet

An intranet is a local area network, or network of local area networks, which uses Internet tools such as a WWW browser, File Transfer Protocol (FTP), or TCP/IP to move data and programs between the server and the clients. As a rule, the security functions on an intranet are more relaxed than they are on the Internet because the users are trusted users. Some security policy still needs to be used, and this should include user authentication, resource protection, system integrity, data integrity, and a security audit. Being trusted users means that the users do not fit the definition of hackers, or crackers, at least as far as the enterprise using the intranet is concerned. The transport protocols for the local area network may still be token-ring or Ethernet, but the messaging protocols embedded within the token-ring or Ethernet delimiters is webcompliant. A hacker is any unauthorized person who tries to break into the system. A cracker is a hacker with malicious intent.

AS/400 and Retail Terminals

Figure 5.10 shows a typical retail system configuration. In many of those configurations, the AS/400 has been the in-store processor. The 4680/4690 Point of Sale Controller controlled the StoreLoop, which interfaced to the AS/400, and if the store was a member of a chain, the AS/400 received information from and sent information to a host processor at the chain's home site. Initially the 4680/4690 Point of Sale Controller talked directly to the host controller, which in many cases was an AS/400. The point of sale terminal is described in "Retail Workstations" in Chapter 2, but basically it is a personal computer with some specialized I/O functions and a cash drawer. As a result, it already has the capability of participating in a token-ring local area network, either connected with wire in one form or another or with the new wireless technology.

With wireless technology, several desirable capabilities become available: additional security and password control, elimination of the

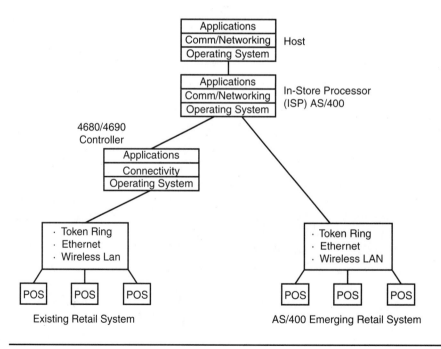

Figure 5.10. The AS/400 in a retail environment.

4680/4690 segment of the link, which increases the reliability of the network, portable terminal replacement of a potentially failing terminal, and redundancy in the network provided by the token-ring connection. To incorporate this connection a suite of applications has been developed by IBM and the AS/400 business partners and integrated with the AS/400. That suite of applications includes the following retail-based functions: price lookup, electronic funds transfer, credit authorization, time and attendance, labor scheduling/forecasting, shelf price audit, store accounting, store reports, sales analysis, merchandise replenishment, pharmacy, direct store delivery, e-mail, word processing, clienteling, and so on. Figure 5.11 contains a business functions chart for retail applications and Figure 5.12 contains a listing of IBM business partners and the area(s) of the retail industry in which they offer products.

AS/400 and the Internet

This section considers the system connection shown in Figure 5.13. In this connection there are several AS/400 systems and PCs linked via a local area network. One of the AS/400 systems is a server to the local network and acts as a firewall to the modem connection to the Internet systems. The Internet, which grew out of the ARPA net defined as a result of the Cold War and today consists of over 44,000 total networks, is composed of a worldwide network of networks connected to each other and a suite of cooperating applications that allow computers connected to this network of networks to communicate with each other.

The Internet provides browsable information, file transfer, remote logon, electronic mail, news, and other services. Often referred to as the Web or the Net, the Internet is based on TCP/IP communications and basically uses the addressing and protocols defined in TCP/IP to provide access to its users. Internet terminology is defined at the Application Protocol level (because that is the level at which most users interact with the Internet), and in the process AS/400-supported functions are identified. Information exchanges on the Internet proceeds as follows

- A client requests connection to a URL through an Internet browser.

- The Internet server containing that URL provides the ability to browse that location through a home page and links, transfers files from the server to the client, or allows electronic commerce such as the requesting of information or ordering of products. In any case, the Internet server writes the information to the client's main storage or disk storage and disconnects from the client while the user takes time to investigate the information received.

Business Functions	Retail Application Set				
Business Management	General Ledger	Accounts Payables	Billing & Accounts Receivables	Cost Accounts	Fixed Assets
(B/M)	Payroll	Human Resources	Lease Management		
Supply Chain	Stock Control	Stock Movement	Forecasting & Replenishment	Inventory Management	Stock Ordering
(S/C)	Distribution Operations	Warehouse Management	EDI Management	Category	
Store Operations	Customer Management	Store Management	Staff Management	Space Management	Inventory
(S/O)	Cash Management	Time & Attendance			
Business Intelligence (B/I)	Data Mining	Data Warehouse	Executive Info System	Geographic Info System	
Market Space (M/S)	Electronic Commerce	Kiosks	Catalog/ Mail Order		

Figure 5.11. Relational mapping of the retail application set against business functions.

Business Partner (Business Function)	All Retail	Apparel	Auto	Books & Music	Mail Order	Home Improve-ment	Consumer Electronics	Pharm. Drugs	General & Mass	Super Market	Video	Wholesale
JDA (B/M, S/C, S/O, B/I)	X											
InfoSystems of N.C. (B/M, S/C, S/O, B/I)						X	X		X	X		
Island Pacific (B/M, S/C, B/I)								X	X	X		
Open Retail Systems (B/M, S/C, S/O, B/I)	X	X				X			X			
Intrepid Systems (B/M, S/C)	X			X								
Nordic Information Systems (B/M, S/C, B/I)	X		X			X	X		X			
Gateway Data Science (S/C, S/O, B/I)	X	X									X	X
BCMS (B/M, S/C, S/O, B/I)	X							X	X			
CSI (B/M, S/C, B/I)	X	X										
Computer General Solutions (B/M, S/C, B/I)		X										
JBA International (B/M, S/C, B/I)		X										

Figure 5.12. AS/400 retail industry solution matrix.

(Continued on next 2 pages.)

Business Partner (Business Function)	All Retail	Apparel	Auto	Books & Music	Mail Order	Home Improvement	Consumer Electronics	Pharm. Drugs	General & Mass	Super Market	Video	Wholesale
Grocery Support Systems (B/M, S/C, S/O, B/I)										X		
Park City (B/M., S/C, B/I)	X											
ADS (S/C, S/O, B/I)	X							X		X		
Worldwide Chain Store Systems (B/M, S/C, DC/warehouse mngt.)	X							X		X		X
American Software (B/M, S/C, DC/ warehouse mngt)		X										
Exeter (S/C; DC/ warehouse mngt.)	X											X
Computer Associates (S/C; DC/warehouse mngt.)	X											
Manhattan Associates (S/C; DC/warehouse mngt.)	X											

Continued on next page

Figure 5.12. AS/400 retail industry solution matrix.

Business Partner (Business Function)	All Retail	Apparel	Auto	Books & Music	Mail Order	Home Improve-ment	Consumer Electronics	Pharm. Drugs	General & Mass	Super Market	Video	Wholesale
E3 (S/C; Forecast/Replenishment)	X											
IBM INFOREM/400 (S/C; Forecast/Replenishment)	X											
Computer Solutions Inc. (M/S; Mail order/catalogue)	X							X				
ASA/Commercialware (M/S; Mail order/catalogue)	X				X							
Lawson (B/M; Financial/HR mngt.)	X											
Software 2000 (B/M; Financial/HR mngt.)	X											
Silvon Software (B/I; Data Warehouse)	X											
SAMAC (B/I; Data Warehouse)	X											
Hoskyns (B/I; Data Warehouse)	X											
I/NET (M/S; Internet)	X											

Figure 5.12. AS/400 retail industry solution matrix.

Continued from previous page

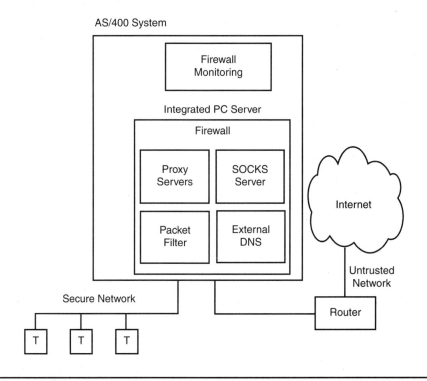

Figure 5.13. Integrated PC server firewall inside the AS/400 system (available on all models except Model 436).

With the AS/400 support for the Internet and the appropriate set of identifiers and passwords, it is possible to access the Web through the AS/400 to obtain information, but as an Internet user, the AS/400 can also be used to develop a program, download that program to your system from a remote site, download the information to execute against that program, and execute the program at a local system. A user has the option of accessing information in any of the files on the AS/400 and having that information HTML formatted on its way to the user's system. The user can have the AS/400 execute the program and only present the output in HTML format to the Web browser, and can develop an application on the AS/400 using CGI/WGS or the Net.Data and have that application downloaded to the browser.

Finally, to make this all work, the Internet connection server requires that the system administrator grant object access to the user profiles under which the server runs and then grant permission to the server to serve specific objects. If the server is on a system with multiple network addresses, it can be configured to serve different files based on the IP address that comes in on a request. Multiple server instances can also be configured by using either a different IP address or a single IP address and different ports for each server instance. As an example, an Internet service provider can configure a single server for multiple Web site customers with different welcome pages, mapping rules, and access control. Both Java and Java applets fit within this scenario.

To complete the discussion of the Internet, let's reconsider the Distributed AS/400 Network Example. Instead of connecting the AS/400 Servers with Wide Area Network communications, let's connect them through the Internet. Each system requires a single communications line with a modem. The system user requires a connection to a service provider like America On-Line, Compuserve, or Prodigy, or to an independent service provider. Assuming maximum security measures have been implemented, data, e-mail, and files as well as programs can be exchanged between the systems at lower costs because there is no charge for leased lines or long-distance telephone services other than the charge for the Internet service provider.

Starting with Version 4 Release 2, IBM will allow you to download PTFs via the Internet.

Electronic Commerce

Electronic commerce encompasses three Internet application enablers, Net.Data, Net.Commerce, and Domino.Merchant.

Net.Data

Net.Data is a CGI program that creates a dialogue with the user of a Web browser. The macro processor provides searches to the DB2 database via SQL queries without the use of programming languages. Responses are provided to the Web browser in HTML. Net.Data is a compatible follow-on version of DB2 WWW Connection building on that tool's database access and reporting capabilities. Net.Data provides a comprehensive Web development environment for the creation of simple dynamic to complex Web-based applications. Net.Data is contained in Internet Connection for AS/400, just as TCP/IP is. TCP/IP Connectivity Utilities/400 is required to use Net.Data. Net.Data includes Web registry and flat file support as built-in functions. These functions increase the ease of creating Web pages. Web registry functions allow macro variables to be stored and retrieved, giving these variables persistence across macro boundaries. A macro variable and its value can be saved into a Web registry by one macro and later retrieved for use in another macro. Flat file functions allow the storage and retrieval of user data into files containing single field records. This single field record can contain multiple pieces of data separated by user-defined delimiters, enabling the performance of such tasks as saving a Net.Data table built in one macro and retrieving the table with a second macro used to create a report. Documentation on Net.Data can be found in Net.Data /Documentation. The term macro as used above identifies a set of short programs which perform specific functions.

Net.Commerce

Net.Commerce for AS/400 enables the building of an electronic storefront on the Web. The storefront can range from a static Web site to a high-volume megasite providing secure links to thousands of consumers. Net.Commerce comes with a sample storefront that can be customized to provide catalogs and search engines. Features include virtual shopping carts, credit validation, and recovery mechanisms in case of network, software, or hardware failure. There is a capability to check on order status, e-mail notification of back-ordered item arrival, and frequent buyer discount programs.

Net.Commerce uses Net.Data as a database, which means it is compatible with DB2/400- and ODBC-based databases. Management components are Site Manager, Store Manager, and Template Designer. Security functions include Internet Secure Server, Frameworks, and Secure Electronic Transaction (SET). The AS/400 does not at this time fully support SET requirements, but will by V4R3.

Domino.Merchant

Domino.Merchant is supported by the AS/400 at Version 4 Release 1. Domino.Merchant is a Lotus product that provides a set of functions similar to those of Net.Commerce. Domino.Merchant separates site design from creation and management. Templates are used to enable development and publication of site pages, using text, graphics, and multimedia. Any Web browser can be used to design the store. Reviewers receive finished pages via automatic routing using the workflow capability of Domino.Merchant. Content authoring and updating are controlled and distribution is managed using roles-based access management. User access is controlled through the Domino server's name and address book. Domino.Merchant supports a shopping basket equivalence in which customers accumulate selections, review choices, and place orders and provides links to data sheets and product reviews as additional product information if available. Multiple payment options are supported.

Net.Commerce vs. Domino.Merchant

How should the AS/400 user position Net.Commerce relative to Domino.Merchant? Net.Commerce is a packaged set of integrated software components used to develop flexible and scalable solutions to use electronic sales channels to address the growing e-business market. It is possible to integrate your e-business with existing enterprise applications using API functions. Net.Commerce addresses the needs of larger businesses, providing sophisticated catalog and Web site design for businesses expecting a high volume of traffic.

Domino.Merchant is intended for the smaller business interested in establishing an Internet presence and seeking a low-cost, easy-to-use solution and for Notes/Domino customers with a preference for a Notes-based solution for e-commerce. Domino.Merchant is complemented by Domino collaboration and tools for workflow and pre- and postsales tasks. Catalog creation requires collaborative transactions and workflow for approvals. Ultimately, both products provide an equivalent function, establishment of an Internet storefront.

Net.Question is a text search engine for HTML information that will search any Single-Byte Character Set (SBCS) language. Net.Question's user interface translation is English only and features the ability to build and maintain indexes, perform Boolean searches (AND, OR, NOT), perform proximity and wildcard searches, and perform a free text search with ranked results. Net.Question also provides a spell wizard. Net.Question can be used with Net.Data, Net.Commerce, or Domino.Merchant.

Internet Terminology

The Internet terminology will be discussed in the context of AS/400 functions provided to support a function required to perform useful work with the Internet.

- *HyperText Transfer Protocol (HTTP)* is the protocol between a client and a server that gives World Wide Web browser clients access to AS/400 multimedia objects such as HyperText Markup Language (HTML) documents.

- *HyperText Markup Language (HTML)* is a markup text language that allows hypertext links to be defined. A hypertext link can point to a different position in the same document or to a different document.

- *File Transfer Protocol (FTP)* allows data to be transferred between local and remote host systems. Files may be transferred using either ASCII or binary mode. ASCII mode is used to transfer data sets that contain only text characters. FTP provides functions such as listing the remote directories, changing the current remote directory, creating and removing the remote directories, and transferring one or more files in a single request.

- *AS/400 TCP/IP TELNET* provides client and server support for the TELNET protocol that allows remote logon to hosts within an Internet, and the *AS/400 TCP/IP Simple Network Management Protocol (SNMP)* provides a means for managing an Internet environment. SNMP allows network management by elements, including gateways, routers, and hosts. Network elements act as servers and contain management agents that perform the management functions requested. Network management stations act as clients: They run the management applications that monitor and control the network. SNMP provides a method of communicating between these elements and stations to send and receive information about network resources. The AS/400 can be an agent, but not the SNMP manager in a TCP/IP network.

- *Serial Line Internet Protocol* (SLIP) allows the connection of systems over a pair of modems that are connected through a telephone line. The communication runs over a point-to-point link. X.25 and Frame Relay are other examples of point-to-point TCP/IP communications that AS/400 supports.

- *Multipurpose Internet Mail Extensions (MIME)* is the Internet standard for sending mail with headers containing information describing the contents of the messages to the receiving client. The messages can be video, image, audio, or binary files or text.

- *Simple Mail Transfer Protocol (SMTP)* allows the sending or receiving of electronic mail over a TCP/IP network. SMTP supports the distribution of notes, messages, and final-form text documents. SMTP can be sent with the OfficeVision for OS/400 licensed program. SMTP can be used for sending MIME formatted mail, but it cannot be used to distribute objects or to transfer revisable-form text (RFT) documents.

- The *Post Office Protocol, Version 3 (POP3)* mail server allows AS/400 systems to act as POP servers for any clients that support the POP mail interface. This includes clients running on Windows, OS/2, AIX, and Macintosh. The POP3 server allows for the exchange of mail using the AnyMail/400 framework.

- *Uniform Resource Locators (URLs)* are used by browser clients to make requests of the HTTP server. URLs are identifiers and instructions (e.g., programs) that tell the HTTP server what object to process and how to process it. The following AS/400 objects can be accessed using URLs:

- Source physical files and physical files containing EBCDIC, HTML, or plain text. EBCDIC is the IBM format for defining the contents of a byte, as opposed to ASCII which is the American Standard Committee format.

- Binary objects from file systems other than AS/400 native file system. The binary objects can be multimedia objects, program applets, graphical objects, audio objects, etc.

- Common Gateway Interface program requests.

- DB2 database requests.

- Image map requests.

- *Common Gateway Interface (CGI)* is the standard that specifies the interface between information servers and gateways, and defines the requirements for programs that the HTTP administrator allows browsers to request. The HTTP server recognizes a URL containing a request for a CGI program and calls that program on behalf of the client browser. The CGI specification dictates how the CGI program gets its input and how it will produce any output.

- *Workstation Gateway Server (WGS)* is a TCP/IP application that transforms AS/400 5250 data streams to HTML for dynamic display on Web browsers, allowing AS/400 applications to be run from any workstation that has a Web browser.

- *Anonymous FTP* enables a general access to certain information on a remote host. The remote site determines what information is made available for general access. Such information is considered to be publicly accessible and can be read by anyone. A user may logon to these hosts using the user ID ANONYMOUS. Typically the only operations allowed with this ID are logging on using FTP, listing the contents of a limited set of directories, and retrieving files from these directories and libraries. As a rule, the anonymous user is not allowed to transfer files to the FTP server system, although some systems do provide an incoming directory for anonymous users to send data. Some sites primarily used for archives ask for the user's e-mail address as the password. In Figure 5.13, the anonymous user is never allowed beyond the server system.

6

Application Systems and Your Business

An important first step in bringing Advanced Systems, or any, computers into your business environment is planning. Largely depending on how well you plan, introducing new computer resource(s) can be like pouring either water or gasoline on a fire. Many readers will already have a significant number of computers in their business and will add Application Systems to their computer arsenal, whereas others will be bringing Application Systems in as their first business computer. In either case, the information in this chapter should help you understand how to introduce Advanced Business Systems computers into your particular environment. The chapter starts by discussing what you should consider when looking at Application Systems versus personal computers versus local area networks. Then it covers software selection, followed by some specific Application Systems hardware configurations appropriate for small, medium, and large businesses. In addition, the following topics will be discussed:

- Business decisions

- Implementation management

- Physical planning

- Training

- Ergonomics

- Security

- Technical support

- Service

- Migrating from System/3X to AS/400 systems

- Migrating from AS/400 CISC to AS/400 RISC

This chapter is not a complete guide to introducing Advanced Business Systems into any business, but it does provide a starting point for developing your plan and discussing some important issues.

What Are My Business Computing Needs?

Many businesses today use some type of computer system(s) to help run their business. These businesses must constantly evaluate whether their current system is good enough. Those businesses still using manual methods must determine whether automating their business might help. This book certainly cannot answer the question for you, but it can provide a starting point. Whether your business has millions of dollars worth of computer systems or none at all, the way to begin answering these questions is to forget about computer hardware and software, and look very closely at your business. Too often, businesses buy computer systems and then look for problems to solve. A properly managed computer project should start by careful consideration of the collective business needs of all functional areas within the business. Independently attacking specific business problems can often result in a "dead-end" computer solution that provides no coherent growth strategy for the future.

From the very start, key people from all business areas should be collected into a project team. Since all business areas will be involved, the top management of the business must consistently demonstrate a commitment to the project. Without top management involvement, disagreements among the peer business areas are slow to be resolved and the sense of priority is diminished. Lack of consistent top management commitment at either the investigation or implementation phases of a computer project is a common cause of unsuccessful projects, which can be quite expensive.

The project team should start by reviewing the overall goals of the business (or segment of a larger business) over the next few years. In some cases, these goals will be well known, but in others a great deal of soul-searching will be necessary. These goals should be as specific as possible and should include any business strategies in place to achieve these goals. After the business goals are clearly defined, the project team should look closely at the current day-to-day operations of the business as it is and document the movement of information through the entire organization. Only after the information flow is understood can the team candidly discuss what is good and what is bad about the current way of doing business. Work to identify the sources of problems rather than focusing on symptoms. Understand the interaction between the various areas of the business. Consider the flow of information from one group to another as you trace the business cycle.

Chances are, not every problem that you will uncover can be solved through a computer. For example, a computerized inventory tracking system will not solve inventory problems if just anyone can casually walk into the inventory storeroom and walk out with what he or she needs with no controls. Computers are only a tool for effectively managing a business. They will not manage your business for you. Only after you have examined your current operation with a critical eye can you begin to see if a computer solution makes sense for your business. In the case of small businesses, this type of analysis can be done in a matter of weeks or even days. In larger businesses, it can span months or even years and is typically done on an ongoing basis. Some businesses choose to do the analysis on their own. If you want assistance with solving business problems with computers, there are plenty of places to turn, including consultants and computer manufacturers.

What about Personal Computers?

Although this book is about IBM's midsize computer systems, to make good buying decisions it is important to understand how these differ from personal computers (PCs). The first difference between Application Systems and PCs is that PCs were primarily designed to be used by one person at a time (single user) and Application Systems were initially designed to be simultaneously shared by many users (multiuser) running several applications at the same time. (Single User and Multiuser are contrasted in Chapter 4.) More recently, Application Systems design has been changed to incorporate the server function, which includes downloading operating systems, programs, and data to PCs.

Although there are some environments in which PCs can be used as small multiuser computers, their hardware and software architectures are primarily geared for single-user computing. Because Application Systems are multiuser computers, multiple PC systems must be purchased to serve an equivalent number of users. Furthermore, because all users of an Application System share a single computer, they can share equipment (printers) and information (inventory data). To obtain this sharing of equipment and information, the multiple PCs must be networked together through a Local Area Network (LAN). With the LAN, PCs can also freely share equipment and information as long as the PC programs were written for the LAN environment. So which is best? The PC LAN versus multiuser system debate still rages, and it is clear that both approaches have merit. Here are some things to consider to help make the decision.

Multiuser systems are more mature than LANs simply by virtue of having been around longer. Because PCs were originally used as independent computers, many of the application programs for PCs do not support LAN environments. The definition of the distributed computing environment helped to solve the problem for UNIX and the more recently written personal computer applications, but the second component, the distributed management environment, is really just beginning to achieve some definition. In general, it is much easier to extend the management principles of the multiuser Applications System to a LAN environment for shared data, applications, and security functions than it is to extend a single-user system environment to that same set of shared data, applications, and security functions. The AS/400 development group with its new system management functions for the AS/400 servers and their clients under Client Access Family for AS/400 and

Client Access Family for Windows for AS/400 are working with the Open System Foundation (OSF) to get the SystemView interfaces and constructs identified as the basis for the Distributed Management Environment (DME). Application programs for Application Systems are typically more comprehensive and support the multiuser environment. This means that there are more tried-and-true business applications for Application Systems than there are for PC LANs.

Furthermore, multiuser systems were designed to be just that, whereas PC LANs were more of an afterthought. This often means that a fair amount of technical skill is required to support a PC LAN. Such variables as the number of workstations, the technical support level, and systems management activity determine which approach yields the lowest cost. Do not forget to consider the PC LAN with Application Systems as the server. This can often provide the best of both worlds. Finally, the most important thing to consider is the application program(s) under consideration for each approach, because PCs and Application Systems are not software compatible and application programs written for one will not always run on the other. This distinction is becoming blurred with the recent announced support for the Integrated Language Environment (ILE). For example, application programs written in C may be capable of execution on both the PC and the AS/400, assuming that you have the source code and recompile (because the code is not object compatible). It is possible that there will also be differences in screens and other I/O interfaces. The approach with the best-fitting application program will normally provide the best results.

What about RISC System/6000 Computers?

The RISC System/6000 family of computers is IBM's entry into the "open systems" area, where international standards take precedence over the proprietary innovations of individual companies. RISC System/6000 computers have a split personality in that they can be used as high-function workstations for a single user or as general-purpose multiuser computer systems in typical business environments. Since the AS/400 is not designed for use as a high-function workstation, the RS/6000 is a better choice if the computer is to be used primarily for activities such as computer-aided design and technical publishing.

In the general-purpose multiuser computer system arena, however, there is certainly room for confusion when deciding between the RISC System/6000 and the AS/400 families of computers. To resolve this confusion, let's look at some of the design points of each family. The AS/400 system's architecture includes a built-in relational database. In other words, the AS/400 hardware and operating system have been designed specifically to provide the database function commonly needed in business environments. Most other computer systems (including the RISC System/6000) require separately purchased database programs that sit on top of the operating system to provide users with a relational database. Since the AS/400 system's database is implemented in the hardware and operating system, the performance and elegance of the database implementation are improved. Further, the programmer productivity afforded by the built-in AS/400 database makes it a good system for those writing and maintaining their own business application programs. Finally, AS/400 systems led the way in the implementation of IBM's Systems Application Architecture (SAA).

As was stated in Chapter 3, IBM no longer enforces the SAA architecture across its systems but leaves it to its systems houses to reach agreement on the level of compatibility they will provide. All things being equal, if you need to coexist with a network of other IBM systems, an AS/400 may be indicated both because of the vast AS/400 application portfolio and because the AS/400 with AnyNet/400 and other integrated communications protocols will interface to those systems, whereas those systems may not always talk to each other. It should be noted, however, that AS/400 computers can also participate in the UNIX "open systems" environments (the primary target of RISC System/6000 systems) through OS/400's support of the OSI and TCP/IP communications protocols including SNMP and the X-OPEN standards. Although the RISC System/6000 has no built-in database, relational database programs that add this capability to the system are available. This added database will add an additional workload on the RISC System/6000, but this is only problematic if not considered when selecting which model is needed.

Those migrating programs and data from a UNIX multiuser computer system will find the migration to a RISC System/6000 much more natural than migrating to an AS/400. Those migrating programs and data from System/36 or System/38 computers will find the migration to the AS/400 much more natural than migrating to a RISC System/6000. If you need to coexist with computer systems of many different brands, the open systems foundation on which the RISC System/6000 is built will be a plus, but with the recent announcements, the AS/400 is approaching equivalent capabilities in this environment. Additionally, if you need to coexist in this environment but would like the computer to manage the complex resources provided by the mixed-brand environment, then the AS/400 should be the choice because the RS/6000 does not offer that management capability and requires the business to integrate the various communications and other programs needed to support that management need.

What about System/390 Computers?

The IBM System/390 (and System/370) computer family is also widely used to fill business needs. Like Application Systems, System/390 computers are multiuser computer systems that allow many users to share the system. Some System/390 computers offer the same level of computing power as that provided by all but the smallest Application Systems, but other System/390 computers provide computational power well beyond even the largest Application Systems. Although System/390 and Application Systems can share information, one cannot run object-code application programs written for the other. In some cases you can recompile source-code applications programs that use common languages such as Cobol and ANSI C.

What should you consider when choosing between System/390 computers and Application Systems? Again, the system that can run the application program that best fits your needs has a strong advantage when it comes to making a selection. There are more prewritten business applications for Application Systems than there are for System/390 computers. In the event you intend to write your own custom application programs from scratch, the programmer productivity features of Application Systems are a strong point, and it has been established that the System/390 typically requires a somewhat larger staff to support the system and its applications. However, your business may have already developed the System/390 application programs you would like to use, in which case the System/390 is desirable. Another reason to select a System/390 approach may be that you need more computing power than is available in the Application Systems family. This may often be the case in a highly technical environment, in which the System/390 architecture is a better fit than that of the Application Systems. One final and important consideration is that System/390 computer operators (not necessarily users) require more data processing experience than is needed by the operator of Application Systems.

When Should I Consider Application Systems?

When looking for ways to meet business computing needs, there seems to be an endless series of questions to be answered. Before getting into how to select an Advanced System to meet your needs, let us pause and glance at some other alternatives. Among the alternatives considered were Networked PCs, RS/6000s, and System/390s. Among the reasons identified for choosing AS/400 over the solution offered by the alternatives were multiuser capabilities; range of applications; number of applications; cost of support staffing; integrated solutions resulting from the integration of database, file system, communications, security, and service. Ease of use resulting from integrated system management of not only the system, (but including workstations and intranets as well); ease of program development (for those involved with writing custom applications); and range of system growth (from an entry system supporting as few as 7 users to a Model 650 supporting greater than 10,000 users, with the option of horizontal growth using optically connected local systems to support 32 times the capacity of a single system, all running the same applications without needing to recompile or change data structures across the entire range). Parallel capability exists in the server environment, where an equivalent server model exists for each general-purpose computing model in the product line. All models support connectivity and development on the Internet from simple home pages to storefront management, which is scalable from a single-department-size store to a multi-department store.

Choosing the Software

Application Systems computers become a useful business tool only when they are executing the appropriate software. Although there are many ways of generating a strategy for introducing computers, considering software needs before selecting detailed hardware configurations usually makes sense. The hardware requirements, such as memory size and disk storage space, will in part be based on the needs of the software selected. With the emerging applications providing a scalable Lotus Notes/Domino server, which may be required to grow to several times larger than available today anywhere, a system that can grow to support data warehousing and, through RISC power, analysis of data through data mining introduces scalability as a new consideration in the decision process. The application programs you select must perform the tasks needed by your end users both today and in the foreseeable future. Chapter 3 has already discussed some application programs commonly used with Application Systems.

Selecting the basic type of application program is often fairly simple: An accounting department needs an accounting application program, a secretary needs a word processing application program, and so on. What is more difficult is identifying the specific application program that best fits your particular needs. Is a custom application program preferred, or will a prewritten application program be acceptable? If a prewritten application program is desired, exactly which one is the best for your needs? If a custom application program is desired, who should write it and what should it include? The answers to these questions depend largely on the specifics of a given business environment and thus are beyond the scope of this book. However, a few basics remain the same whether you are selecting a program for a multinational corporation or one for a corner fish market.

First, you must precisely understand the tasks you are trying to put on a computer before pursuing any application program alternatives. A thorough knowledge of these helps you to identify specific requirements your application program must meet. After a detailed understanding of the tasks is obtained, a search can begin through the many prewritten or off-the-shelf application programs. If you can find an appropriate prewritten application program that fits your needs, you can avoid the expense, delay, and ongoing effort associated with custom software development and maintenance. Good prewritten application programs can be quite flexible. However, because everyone typically has slightly different needs and methods even within a given business function, you can bet that any prewritten application will have some features you do not need and will not have other features you will wish it did.

Do not forget to consider the more specialized type of prewritten application program—vertical market applications. **Vertical market ap-**

plication programs address a highly specific segment of users such as lawyers, doctors, distributors, and manufacturers. There are several sources of information about the many prewritten application programs on the market. Of course, computer companies and consultants can help you select particular application programs to fit your needs. There are also many popular computer and trade magazines that periodically conduct extensive reviews of prewritten application programs. These can be excellent and timely sources of information. For specific or highly specialized needs, prewritten application programs may not be adequate. In this case, custom-developed software may be desirable. Although the development and maintenance of custom software is a long-term commitment that is typically expensive, it may be less costly in the long run to pay for the development of custom software than to settle for a prewritten application program that does not do the job. If you do select the custom software route, an important step is to select the proper developer.

Businesses that have their own programming staff can do their own custom program development. If you do not have your own programmers, it will be necessary to seek outside help—that is, an outside software developer. In either case, the developer will have the largest effect on the ultimate success or failure of the custom development activity. The developer's job is not an easy one. In addition to programming expertise, the developer must become an expert in all aspects of your business, must be a good communicator to understand and discuss software requirements, must understand human psychology when defining the user interface for the program, must be a proficient teacher to train the end users on the new program, and, finally, must be dependable and reliable, and therefore available to provide technical support, software maintenance, and any needed modifications.

Choosing Application Systems Hardware

Selecting the proper Application Systems hardware components that will together fit your needs can be confusing. You must select among the Application Systems and their disk configurations, feature cards, peripherals, and so on. Although we cannot possibly cover all needs for all environments in the limited scope of this book, we can examine some business environments—for example, a small retail franchise establishment, a small manufacturing establishment, a medium business, and a large business—and outfit them with the appropriate Application Systems configurations. With the insight provided by outfitting these hypothetical business environments, you will be better prepared to properly select the Application Systems components useful in your environment. Assistance in selecting specific Application Systems configurations is available from IBM or authorized remarketers.

Small Business Environment, Retail—Anatole's Sub Factory

The first hypothetical small business is a submarine sandwich fast food franchise outlet. Jerry is the owner of the franchise located on the south side of Milwaukee in a predominantly Mexican-American neighborhood. As a result, Jerry has found that the demographics of his location require that he market a taco and a chile relleno sub, which are not in high demand at the other Anatole's Sub Factory locations either in Milwaukee or outside of Texas. Also, the demographics make the normal supply methodology for other Anatole Sub Factories invalid, so Jerry has installed a personal computer connected to an AS/400 Advanced Entry Model 150 configuration in addition to the two cash drawer personal computer retail terminals used at his customer checkout locations. The cash drawer terminals, the personal computer, and the Entry Model 150 are connected by a token-ring local area network operating at 16 Mbps. The Entry Model 150 is connected to an AS/400e system 640 located at the Anatole Sub Factory headquarters in Detroit through the Internet by an EIA 232/V.24 line operating at 19.2 Kbps. This configuration is illustrated in Figure 6.1.

Before Jerry installed his own personal computer notebook and began doing his own demographics studies, the franchise manager had been shipping Jerry supplies for his customers on the same basis as had been done for the other franchisees in the Milwaukee area. After installing the personal computer and the Relational Database Facility on the AS/400, Jerry was able to modify the order process with the franchise manager to control the inventory received to more closely match his sales projections. Jerry also became the test marketing site for two new sub sandwiches resulting from his suggestions to Anatole's Sub Factory—an enchilada sub and a tamale sub. Jerry also uses the PC notebook system and the Entry Model 150 to handle his payroll, attendance, cost/revenue projections, and so on. The PC notebook system allows

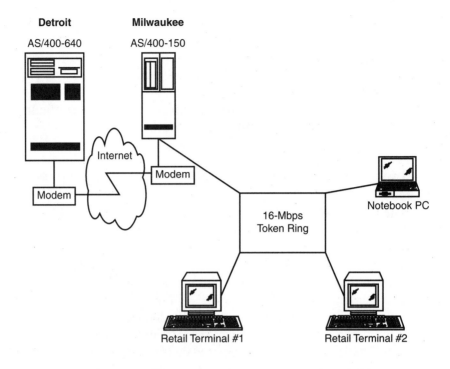

Figure 6.1. Jerry's Anatole Sub Factory—small business retail franchise.

Jerry to take some of the business work home at night, using the Internet interface to download and upload the results to the Model 150 while also being able to make inquiries into Anatole's Sub headquarters for information on how they are processing his inventory and managing the supplying of his franchise.

Small Business Environment, Manufacturing—Bob's Gearbox Co.

The second hypothetical small business is a gearbox manufacturer named Bob's Gearbox Co. Bob's has a standard line of gearboxes and also accepts orders for custom gearboxes. It is a private corporation (owned by Bob, of course) and has 32 employees. Bob has been in business 5 years and has experienced moderate growth. He currently conducts business by noncomputer methods but finds himself needing to streamline his operation as the business grows. Bob is particularly concerned that his profits seem to be shrinking as his sales increase. A study of Bob's business shows that there are two basic causes for this. First, his sales staff often commits to discounted pricing on a gearbox order to capture the business. The trouble is that Bob never really knows what it actually costs him to produce a given gearbox. He uses standard cost estimates to price a customer's order and hopes that the actual cost of building the gearbox is close to this. The second basic problem uncovered in the study is that Bob's inventory is not well managed. The production department is often hampered by not having the right parts and raw materials in inventory. This often causes slips in the delivery of customer orders that hurt customer satisfaction and fuel heated arguments among the marketing manager, the production manager, and the materials manager. Finger pointing is commonplace. The study also showed that 25 percent of the inventory items in stock are obsolete and will never be used.

In this scenario, it is clear that Bob has outgrown his manual methods of doing business. Bob needs a better way to track the actual costs associated with manufacturing his products. This may uncover the fact that his sales staff often sell gearboxes at or below cost. Bob also needs help tracking his inventory. He needs to know when critical parts are getting low and what parts are moving slowly. The deficiencies in Bob's business can be addressed with the proper computer solution.

Let us examine the Application Systems configuration suitable for Bob's Gearbox. Bob will use the Manufacturing Accounting Production Information Control System (MAPICS/DB) to help gain better control over his business. By selecting the appropriate modules (programs) within the MAPICS/DB family of software, Bob can track manufacturing costs more closely (Production Control and Costing, and Product Data Management modules) and better manage his inventory (Inventory Control module). Bob also chooses to take advantage of the computer system to automate the general accounting functions of his business such as payroll, accounts receivable, accounts payable, and general ledger, and he will use the Order Entry and Invoicing module to track and bill customer orders. The Cross-Application Support module is required on all systems. Through a questionnaire, this module allows Bob to customize MAPICS/DB for his particular business environment. Furthermore, the Cross-Application Support module automatically passes information among the various MAPICS/DB modules, making them function as a single system.

Based on the requirements of the software and Bob's business transaction volumes, Bob will get the AS/400e system 600 shown in Figure 6.2. The Model 600 system was selected for its low cost and the Model 600's ability to be first upgraded to higher-performance processors and then replaced by a larger AS/400 system. The standard 4196 MB of disk storage will be expanded to 16,000 MB to provide enough storage for the system software, the MAPICS/DB modules, and associated data. The Model 600 system's ability to expand to 175,400 MB of disk storage will allow for expansion as Bob's business grows. Bob will also expand the standard 64 MB of main storage to 128 MB by adding a 64-MB main storage option. The optional Uninterruptible Power Supply unit will help prevent disruption of the system by power failures—Bob can do without the extra headache. The 7861 Modem will be used to access IBM's Electronic Customer Support (ECS) network.

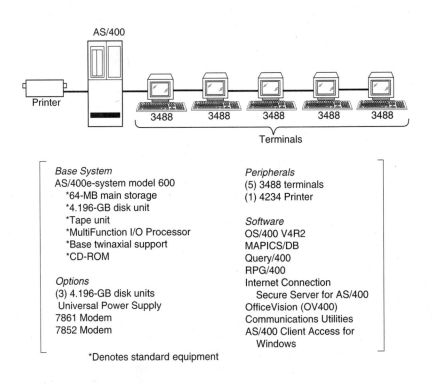

Figure 6.2. Bob's AS/400 Advanced System 400.

The System Console function is performed by a 3489 Modular Display Unit. For the users, four 3488 Displays are provided initially. One display is for the inventory clerk, one is for the purchasing agent, one is for the production department, and one is for Bob so that he can get the management information he needs to make intelligent decisions. The 4234 Printer will be used to produce the various reports provided by MAPICS/DB. The 7-GB cartridge tape unit will allow data stored on disk to be backed up on tape. This will help prevent important business information from getting accidentally lost. Since OS/400 V4R2 is now bundled with the Model 600 hardware, Bob has no need to concern himself with AS/400's operating system. Bob will also get the Query/400 and OfficeVision/400 programs so that he and his staff can generate customized reports and manage schedules as needed.

Bob expects to participate in electronic commerce through the Internet, so he insists on having a 7852 Modem attached. He also figures this will provide him with closer contact with his sales force (whom he plans on providing with notebook computers) through e-mail while they are interacting with customers for his gearboxes. Because he has no programming skills on his staff, Bob anticipates consulting with IBM about setting up his Internet site and storefront.

Medium Business Environment—Johnson & Thornbush

The hypothetical medium-sized business is an advertising agency named Johnson & Thornbush. This company has been in business for 12 years. Their business started with one major account, and today they have 17 active clients. Steve Johnson and Perry Thornbush are both still active in managing the business. The main office has 74 people and is located in Chicago, Illinois. A second office, with 7 people, is located in Fort Lauderdale, Florida, to handle several large accounts in the Southeast. Almost every person at each location has a personal computer (PC) providing personal productivity tools for such tasks as market analysis, trend analysis, word processing, and financial modeling.

Steve Johnson recently sponsored a companywide study to find a way to address the business goals of increasing marketing effectiveness and reducing operating costs. The results of the study revealed that the market analysis being done by one PC user seldom correlated with the market analysis done by another PC user. The cause of the disagreement in information was that there were different versions of the area demographic information residing on the various PC disk units used in the market analysis. Even though one person had responsibility for periodically updating the demographic information and distributing the updates, eventually different versions of the information emerged, making the market analysis inaccurate. Further, as the company's market coverage grows, the demographic information is growing in size and becoming impractical to distribute via diskettes. It is apparent that more sophisticated data management and analysis techniques will become necessary as the firm continues to grow.

Another area needing improvement uncovered in the study was that basic office operations could be streamlined, increasing productivity and thereby reducing operating expense. Mail delays between the two offices were slowing down many day-to-day business operations. Because of busy schedules, it was often difficult to schedule meetings, as the last attendee contacted would often have a conflict. Although the secretarial staff also had PCs and WordPerfect for word processing, turnaround time for even a simple memo was getting longer as the workload increased.

The project team recommended a computer solution that streamlined office functions and centralized the area demographic information. All PCs were to be connected in such a way that they could share information and facilitate business communications. Figure 6.3 shows the system configuration suitable for Johnson & Thornbush. In this solution, the PC users retain their PCs, protecting that investment in hardware, programs, and training, only now all PCs (in Chicago and Fort Lauderdale) are attached to an AS/400 located in Chicago, allowing them to double as PCs and AS/400 workstations. As PCs, they can do everything they could before. As workstations on the AS/400, the PCs allow users to interact with the AS/400, providing some additional capabilities provided by AS/400 programs.

Hardware Configuration

Based on the number of users and the growth being experienced by the business, an AS/400 9406 Model 640 with processor option 2237 is

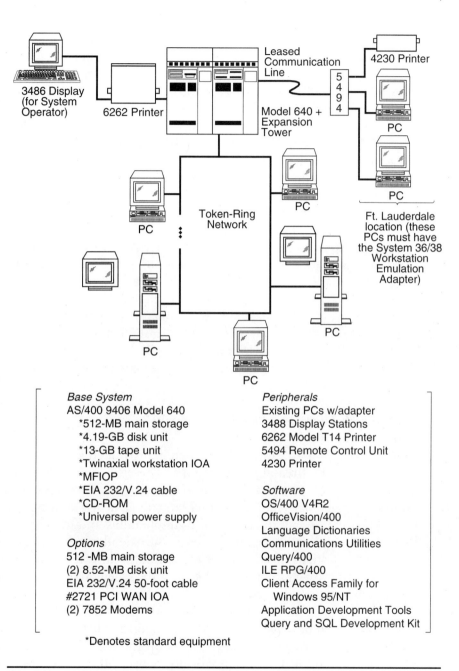

3486 Display
(for System
Operator)

6262 Printer

Leased
Communication
Line

Model 640 +
Expansion
Tower

5
4
9
4

4230 Printer

PC

PC

Ft. Lauderdale
location (these
PCs must have
the System 36/38
Workstation
Emulation
Adapter)

Token-Ring
Network

PC

PC

PC

PC

PC

PC

Base System
AS/400 9406 Model 640
   *512-MB main storage
   *4.19-GB disk unit
   *13-GB tape unit
   *Twinaxial workstation IOA
   *MFIOP
   *EIA 232/V.24 cable
   *CD-ROM
   *Universal power supply

Options
512 -MB main storage
(2) 8.52-MB disk unit
EIA 232/V.24 50-foot cable
#2721 PCI WAN IOA
(2) 7852 Modems

Peripherals
Existing PCs w/adapter
3488 Display Stations
6262 Model T14 Printer
5494 Remote Control Unit
4230 Printer

Software
OS/400 V4R2
OfficeVision/400
Language Dictionaries
Communications Utilities
Query/400
ILE RPG/400
Client Access Family for
   Windows 95/NT
Application Development Tools
Query and SQL Development Kit

*Denotes standard equipment

Figure 6.3. AS/400e system 640 for Johnson & Thornbush.

selected. For now, 1024 MB of main storage should meet the need. Two additional 6713 integrated 8.58-GB disk units will expand the standard 4.19 GB to over 20 GB of disk storage—more than enough for now. The 6390 7.0-GB 8-mm cartridge tape unit provides for efficient backup of the information stored in the AS/400 disk storage. The 16/4-Mbps Token-Ring Network Adapter/HP will allow the AS/400 to participate in a 16-Mbps token-ring network. A 16/4-Mbps Token-Ring Network Adapter/A must also be installed in each of the local PCs, allowing them to participate in the network. The 6262 Printer will provide high-speed printing to all local users.

In Fort Lauderdale a 5494 Remote Workstation Controller is attached to a communications line to Chicago, where the PCs are equipped with the System 36/38 Workstation Adapter/A and attached to the 5494 so they can be used as AS/400 workstations. The smaller 4230 Printer, along with the PC printers they already have, will meet printing needs for the Fort Lauderdale users. Although the PCs will be attached to the 5494 via twinaxial cable for now, a token-ring network could be installed later at the Fort Lauderdale location. The PCs can then be attached to the 5494 via the token-ring network to provide for more efficiency and flexibility as the Fort Lauderdale location grows.

Johnson & Thornbush Software Scenario

The OfficeVision/400 application program provides the basic office functions needed to streamline operations. The electronic mail feature of OfficeVision allows any user to electronically send documents or quick notes to any other user. This eliminates mail delays and reduces the word processing workload, because simple notes and messages can be typed and sent by the users themselves. The calendar management function of the OfficeVision application can automatically schedule a desired meeting by electronically checking the calendars of all attendees and finding a time suitable for all.

Although OfficeVision has a word processing function, those with primarily word processing activities to perform will continue to use the WordPerfect word processing program on the PCs. Since both offices have a heavy word processing workload, using the intelligence in the PCs for this function will provide the highest productivity (lowest response time). This is particularly true in Fort Lauderdale, because AS/400 response time will be reduced by the relatively slow telephone line communications speeds. Furthermore, removing the word processing tasks from the AS/400 provides improved response time for the electronic mail, calendaring, and demographic activities performed on the AS/400 system.

The Client Access Family for Windows program allows AS/400 disk storage to act as the central repository (file server) for the demographic information. In effect, a portion of the AS/400 disk storage appears to be a giant PC disk unit shared by all PCs. With Client Access Family for Windows, all PC users can simultaneously share this single copy of the information, ensuring that all are using the same current data for their marketing analysis. This will result in a more accurate market analysis and thus more effective marketing efforts for the firm's clients.

With the AS/400 Application Development Tools Structure Query Language Development Kit for OS/400, ILE RPG/400, DB2 Query Manager for OS/400(5769-ST1), and AS/400 Query (5769-QU1) —Johnson & Thornbush will develop custom application software over time that will allow the AS/400 to act as a database repository and interact with the PCs in a cooperative processing environment. Through the token-ring network, all of the PCs located in Chicago are attached to the AS/400. The token-ring network was selected for its high-speed information transfer rate and because it could use the twisted-pair wiring already installed throughout much of their building. All of the PCs in Fort Lauderdale will be attached to the AS/400 system as remote workstations through a 5494 Remote Workstation Controller, appropriate modems, and a leased, voice-grade telephone line. This allows every PC, no matter where it is located, to double as an intelligent AS/400 workstation. Whether PC users are in Chicago or Fort Lauderdale, they will have access to the same functions. However, because the Fort Lauderdale PC users are attached via a telephone line, their response time will not be as good (fast) as that of those in Chicago, who are attached over the high-speed token-ring network.

Large Business Environment—Atole Enterprises

The hypothetical large business that will be outfitted with Application Systems is Atole Enterprises. This multinational corporation is a distributor of canned foods and enjoys financial prowess worthy of its

Fortune 500 membership. The many benefits afforded by computers are well known at Atole Enterprises. They have been using computers in their day-to-day operations for many years. The U.S. headquarters is in New York City and currently has a large System/390 computer complex. There are 17 distribution centers located from coast to coast. Each distribution center has its own small System/36 and Atole-written application programs to track orders and local inventory, and to transmit information to the System/390 in New York. System/36s were originally selected for their ease of operation, which minimizes the need for technical skills at each distribution center.

A companywide study sponsored by headquarters came to the following conclusions: Most of the System/36s are fully depreciated and in many cases are not providing enough computing power to meet growing demands. The custom-written application programs written for the System/36s have been around a long time and need major updates to keep the company's competitive edge in customer service. The study therefore recommended that Atole convert the distribution centers from System/36s to AS/400e system 600s with improved application programs. Also, the System/390 located in New York will be right-sized to an AS/400e system 650, which will save significant operating cost over the next 5-year period. In addition, future applications will be developed on the 650 and verified before being shipped to the distribution centers, thus avoiding the need to install a separate Model 600 at the main office. A difficult decision existed between the Advanced 36 Model 436 and the Model 600 systems because of the capability of the Advanced 36 to directly apply the existing System/36 applications, but since the decision had already been made to rewrite the applications, the greatest gain in performance and growth could be attained with the Model 600s. It was decided to get a SSP license for the Model 600 systems during the transition interval related to the application rewrite.

Atole Solution Scenario

The first step in implementing the solution is to install Model 600 systems at the distribution centers. The distribution-center staff will use the migration tools to quickly move the current distribution-center application programs from the System/36 to that AS/400 system, since the Model 600 can execute SSP and OS/400 concurrently. After the initial migration is complete, the headquarters staff on the Model 650 will exploit the programmer productivity features in the AS/400 system to enhance the distribution centers' application programs. It is critical to get the improved application programs ready as soon as possible. Once this is done, each distribution center will download the updated application programs. The headquarters staff will assist each distribution center in performing systems management on the new systems.

Figure 6.4 shows the AS/400 distribution-center configuration that will be used by Atole. The AS/400e system model 600 with processor option 2129 was selected because its performance and capacity best matched the need and because of its continuing upgrade path. The standard Model 600 configuration will be expanded to 8380 MB of disk storage and 256 MB of main storage to provide enough capacity to meet the needs of the distribution centers for an estimated 5 years. In the event of a power failure, the UPS power unit will provide power to sustain critical components while they ride through short power outages and will allow the system to perform an orderly shutdown in case of longer power outages. This will reduce the disruption associated with power failures at the distribution centers.

The 7852 Modem will be used for IBM Electronic Customer Support (ECS), which will derive from the base 9720 PCI WAN/Twinaxial IOA which will support up to 28 twinaxial attached workstations in addition to the ECS communications line. In this case, however, Atole chooses to provide the ECS for each distribution center from the headquarters location; that is, headquarters will maintain a help desk and a technical question-and-answer database pertaining to their custom software in addition to the IBM question-and-answer database. They will be the first line of support for the distribution centers. A second communications line is provided by the 2721 PCI Two-Line Wan IOA and 0331 EIA 232/V.24 50-foot cable and the 7852 Modem. This leased line will be used to communicate with the Model 650 at headquarters to consolidate information needed from each distribution center much as before. This will allow for communications at 33,600 bps.

The NetView program running on the AS/400e system 650 will work with the 7852 Modems to manage the communications network. Further, the SystemView System Manager for OS/400 program will be loaded on the central site's AS/400 to allow the retrained S/390 personnel to perform change and problem management for the remote AS/400 systems. Atole will use 3487 Display Stations as color terminals to allow their custom application programs to exploit color to associate and highlight information on the screen. This will result in improved ease of use.

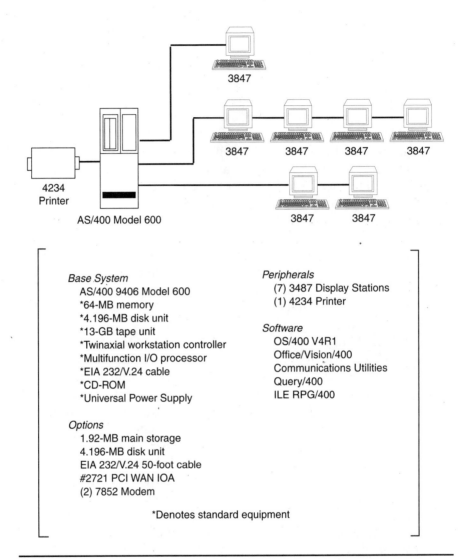

Figure 6.4. AS/400 distribution center configuration that will be used by Atole.

Each distribution center will have a 4234 Printer to produce reports and correspondence-quality documents. The standard streaming tape drive provided with every 9406 Model 650 will be used to back up disk storage. Backup will only be performed to the Model 650 at the central headquarters site.

The AS/400 software needed, in addition to OS/400, includes IBM's Communications Utilities, Query, and ILE RPG/400. IBM's Communications Utilities provides some additional communications functions between the AS/400s. Query/400 will allow local distribution center management to develop their own custom reports, giving them more flexibility. Finally, OfficeVision/400 will facilitate communications between headquarters staff and each distribution center.

Server Selection

The medium business environment of Johnson & Thornbush could equally well have used an AS/400e server S30. Performance within the locally connected personal computers would have been improved with no degradation at the remote site. In fact, performance would appear to improve if the process of maintaining the database concurrent between the two server systems were managed properly. Figure 6.5 illustrates the preferred configuration for Johnson & Thornbush in a server-based implementation. Note that the 5494 Remote Workstation Controller has been replaced with a LAN-configured AS/400 Advanced Entry Model 150. This transformation is possible because the servers are specifically set up to manage LAN-connected personal computers.

The only non-LAN-connected terminals on either of the systems are the system console and the printers. If the 9720 Base PCI WAN/Twinaxial IOA feature had been chosen using an additional communications line, both the console and printers could have been LAN connected. It is worthwhile for the business that has almost all its terminals as personal computers to consider the server configurations because specially priced packages to meet those configurations are available. Figure 6.6 illustrates the Johnson & Thornbush system configuration as it would appear if implemented as a network configuration. In a network computing configuration, the leased line connecting the two modems in Figure 6.5 would be replaced by an Internet cloud, which would give each group of users (those on the Model 640 and those on the Model 150) access not only to each other's groupings, but to all the information on the Internet. Of course, it would cost more to provide security—including a

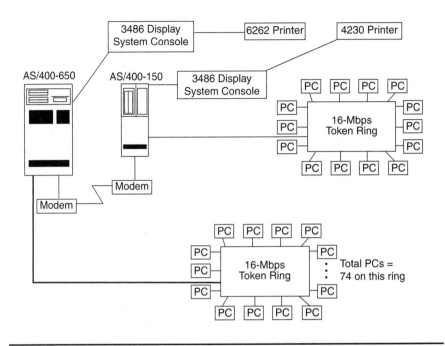

Figure 6.5.   Johnson & Thornbush configuration as a set of servers.

firewall, an encryption card to send corporate information encrypted, and the Internet Connection Secure Server software on each system.

The Competitive View of 64-Bit Processing

One other aspect needs to be considered before deciding which computer system does the best job in the long term for your business. That consideration is the turmoil associated with getting your applications to execute as the industry migrates from 16-bit and 32-bit processing to 64-bit processing. As described in "RISC PowerPC AS Microprocessors" the AS/400 is based on a 64-bit RISC processor. So are DEC's Alpha and HP's Precision architecture–based systems and Microsoft's NT architecture. In the case of DEC and HP, the processor is 64 bit, but the applications that exist are 16 bit and 32 bit, and because they were processor centric (written with a direct relation to the processor that they were intended to execute on), they must be rewritten to perform in

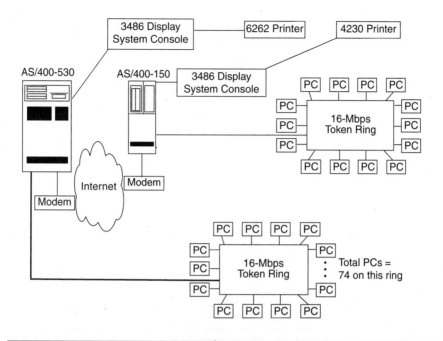

Figure 6.6. Johnson & Thornbush system configuration in a network computing environment.

a 64-bit manner on the 64-bit processors. This is not to say that those applications will not run on the 64-bit processors from those vendors, but that they will run as 16-bit or 32-bit applications, dissipating the value of the 64-bit processors they are using.

The NT Architecture defined by Microsoft has the same problem except that rather than being processor centric, it is API centric and the 16-bit and 32-bit applications must be rewritten to match to the interfaces of a 64-bit world before they can leverage the hardware when it becomes available from Intel, Motorola, Sun, or whoever provides it. The IBM AS/400, because of the Technology-Independent Machine Interface (TIMI), can take applications written for 16-bit or 32-bit environments and translate them to a 64-bit environment. This translation is intrinsic in the AS/400 system and has happened with each release of new processing hardware, which did not effect the applications that executed from previous releases. Figure 6.7 illustrates the impact of the architectural decision upon the applications for these companies as it relates to the movement to 64-bit processing.

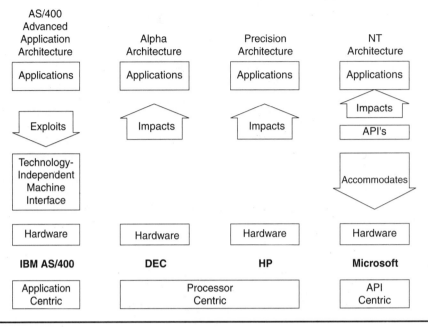

Figure 6.7. Positioning 64-bit processing, a competitive view.

The Business Decisions

In addition to selecting the hardware and software to solve identified business problems, you must also consider financial questions before you install your computer solution. Two important areas that must be addressed are cost justification and the lease or buy decision.

Cost Justification

All businesses are the same in one respect: They exist to make a profit. In the final analysis, the only reason for a business to buy a computer is to increase profits. In other words, the computer system must be **cost justified**. There are two parts to the cost justification analysis: costs and benefits. The price you pay to the computer company is easily identified early in the project. What many people fail to consider are the costs of owning a computer system beyond the original price paid. The costs of operating the computer installation after you buy it should also be considered over several years. Some costs that should be considered beyond the price tag are identified next.

Costs

Hardware Maintenance

This is usually a monthly or annual fee you pay that basically is an extended warranty for the computer hardware. There are various alternatives, but the basic deal is that if your computer system breaks down, the service company will come out and effect repairs at no charge. You do not have to put your system on a maintenance contract, but if you do not you will have to pay an hourly fee and parts costs when your system breaks down. Since this parts/labor billing approach can be extremely expensive, most businesses choose to put their system on a maintenance contract.

Software Maintenance

In some cases, you will have to pay the software supplier a fee to get fixes and updates to your programs. Users who have been purchasing applications that use two-digit year designations in date codes should consult "Year 2000 Challenge," because they may be approaching an expensive software maintenance job unless they are using or have updated to OS/400 Version 3 Release 2 or Version 3 Release 7 or later. IBM is making Version 3 Release 1 and Version 3 Release 6 suitable for development of year 2000–ready applications through the PTF process. Those with this concern should contact their IBM Technical Support Center.

Technical Support

Technical support provides answers to your questions and resolves any technical problems in either the hardware or software. This kind of support ranges from providing a telephone number to having permanently assigned personnel from the computer company on your premises. Sometimes this support is provided free of charge; other times it is on a fee basis. In Chapter 4 and earlier in this chapter ("What about Personal Computers?"), we discussed the relative positioning of the AS/400 and personal computers relative to systems management. Whether you are operating a large, medium, or small business, if you have more than one computer functioning within that business, you have a system management concern. That system management concern has a very real cost associated with it. It is difficult to associate a dollar value because each system configuration is different, but estimates of the cost do exist. Whether you hire someone directly to deal with the concern, do it yourself, or get technical support from an external company, you must pay that cost. Estimates indicate that for 3 to 40 computers or terminals the cost is one full-time person and increases with the addition of one full-time person for each added 40 computers or terminals.

Facilities

It is often necessary for you to modify your building to accommodate a computer system. These modifications might include adding additional air conditioning, running cables between workstations and the computer, or modifying the electrical power services available. Fortunately, the costs of such building modifications are relatively low with Application Systems as compared with large computers, which often require water cooling and raised floors. The new packaging reduces these costs for new installations, because only the largest systems require two-phase service to operate.

Education/Training

The people who will be using the new computer system will need education. The computer operator(s) will need to understand how to manage the day-to-day operations of the computer. The users of the computer system will have to understand the application programs. It may also be necessary to train your own programmer(s) to write custom application programs for your business. Fortunately, Application Systems are easier to operate and use than larger computer systems. However, some education is still necessary. Many different types of education are available, some of which are discussed later in this chapter.

Communications Line Costs

If your computer system is attached to remote workstations or other remote computers, you will incur communications line costs. There are many different communications services available today, and these costs should be considered in your justification.

Environmental Costs

Environmental costs are the costs to operate the system over a period of time. It has been calculated that the difference in operational costs for an existing System/36 Model D24 and an Advanced 36 over a period of 60 months is $20,220. This difference results from the reduced heat load on air conditioning systems, reduced cost in electrical requirements, and reduced cost of a maintenance agreement. That cost reduction will pretty much pay for the new system, and you will reap the benefit of improved performance that increases the efficiency of your workers.

Enhancing Applications

Anytime you either downsize or modify your computer installation to modernize it to be more compatible with emerging technology it is to be expected that you will have to pay the cost of updating your applications or purchasing new applications to operate within that new environment. This is dealt with in greater detail in the discussion of application development in Chapter 4, but the one thing you can trust is that your host-centric applications will not operate in a distributed client/server-centric environment.

Benefits

On the brighter side, the computer is being purchased to solve identified business problems and/or address new business opportunities. You will receive benefits after the computer system is installed (or else why install it). Although it is fairly easy to identify and quantify the costs associated with a computer system, it is often difficult to do the same for the benefits. This does not mean that benefits are any less real than costs; it simply means that they require more work to uncover. Benefits are also more specific to your business, so it would be impossible to list all of them here, but we can consider some common benefits associated with the application of computer systems to basic business functions.

Improved Business Cycle

The basic cycle of most businesses has the same components: The business buys goods/equipment, takes customer orders for goods or services, makes deliveries, and bills the customer. The classic application of computer systems to these areas produces improvements in the basic business cycle that result in real dollar savings. These savings can result from such basic things as collecting accounts receivable more quickly and taking better advantage of accounts payable discount terms.

Inventory Reduction

Many carrying costs are associated with a business inventory. These include items such as warehouse space, insurance, taxes, and interest expense. The proper application of computers can reduce the level of inventory that must be kept on hand, thus reducing carrying costs.

Improved Productivity

Given the proper tools, anyone in any part of a business can do his or her job more efficiently. This allows a business to get the same amount of work done more quickly or with less people. Excess time can then be redirected to performing other tasks that help meet the business objectives. Further, as natural attrition reduces the work force, it may not be necessary to hire replacements, allowing for a reduction of the work force over time.

Improved Quality

By providing more timely or better organized information to personnel, businesses can often improve the quality of the services and/or products they provide. This is particularly true in manufacturing environments, in which computers can be applied to everything from design simulations to statistical quality control. It has also been found that providing the needed information in a more timely fashion (reduced wait time) results in fewer errors being made by the users, increasing productivity.

Improved Customer Service

By allowing a business to respond to customer orders, questions, and special requests, computer systems can improve customer service. These improvements can involve quickly responding to requests for price quotations and accurately quoting/meeting delivery dates.

Competitive Advantage

The items that have been discussed contribute to reducing costs, improving quality, and improving customer service, so they all work to improve the competitive posture of the business. The flexibility provided by a computer system can also help improve your competitiveness by allowing you to more quickly respond to changing market demands. The business additionally has the opportunity to use advanced software technology products such as , multimedia, telephony, and so on to increase revenues.

This list of general benefits is in no way comprehensive. Every business can add to the list based on its current position and business objectives. Once benefits have been identified, however, you have still not finished. You should try to quantify the benefits in dollars and cents where possible, to help focus on the areas with the largest payoff first.

Quantified benefits also help when comparing computer investments with any other capital projects under consideration. However, quantifying benefits can be difficult and subject to judgment. Unlike the price of a computer, which can be looked up in a catalog, benefits must be calculated according to expected results. For example, if you feel that inventory can be reduced by 10 percent by installing an inventory management application program, you would multiply 10 percent of your inventory value times the carrying costs to determine the annual benefit. This is not very difficult, but other areas are more difficult to quantify accurately. For example, if an engineer's productivity is increased by 15 percent, then you might multiply the annual salary and benefit costs by 15 percent, yielding the annual savings. In this case, some would argue that because the engineer is still paid full salary, nothing is saved. However, if the time is devoted to developing a product to enter a new market, for example, the actual benefit may be much higher than 15 percent of the engineer's salary. You will have to decide what a benefit is worth to your business.

Other benefits that are typically difficult to quantify and thus are often overlooked when tallying savings include increased sales (resulting from improved customer service) and lower employee turnover (resulting from improved working conditions and pride). The fact that these benefits (and others like them) are difficult to quantify does not make them any less valuable, but it does mean that they are often overlooked. After the costs and benefits have been quantified, you can begin to evaluate the proposed computer project against other capital projects.

Two often-used guidelines with which to measure a proposed computer system are

1. The *payback period*, in which the time to recover the investment from accrued benefits is calculated.

2. The *net present value*, in which the cash flows are calculated and then discounted based on the cost of money and risk associated with the project.

Although this type of analysis can be valuable, do not overlook other aspects of the capital project such as its strategic value and its effect on customer perceived quality and professionalism. Classic accounting techniques are easy to defend but do not always reveal the entire picture.

Lease or Buy?

Just when you think you are through analyzing all the software and hardware alternatives, you are faced with a whole new set of questions concerning the acquisition method you will use. Several methods are commonly used to acquire a computer system. The most obvious alternative is to simply pay cash for the computer system—**outright purchase**. This is the least expensive way to acquire a computer system. However, it has a direct and usually substantial impact on the business's cash flow and capital position.

The next acquisition alternative is to finance the purchase price over a period of time, just as you would finance a new house. In this case, you simply make a down payment, typically 10 percent, and take out a loan for the balance. The loan and interest are repaid through monthly payments (over a period of from 2 to 5 years typically). Since you must pay back the interest on the loan, this is a more expensive alternative than a cash purchase, but it can reduce cash flow requirements. In either case the title of the computer system passes to the business, as do any tax benefits such as depreciation.

The purchaser of a computer also has the ability to sell the computer when it is replaced or no longer required, thus recovering the **residual value** of the computer system.

Another acquisition alternative is the **term lease**. In this alternative, the lessor (computer owner) grants use of a computer system to the lessee (the using company), which in turn agrees to make lease payments for some specified period of time or **term**. The term of a lease can be any length, but typically runs from 2 to 5 years. If the lessee decides to terminate the lease before the end of the term, there is usually a termination fee, which can be substantial. Some of the advantages offered by the term lease alternative include the conservation of business capital and lines of credit, which can then be used to finance other investments.

Two commonly found lease types are a **capital lease** and an **operating lease**. Capital leases are rent-to-own, in which, at the end of the term, you can purchase the computer system for a relatively small fee (e.g., 5 or 10 percent of the original cost). With a capital lease, the lessee is considered the owner and gets the tax benefits of ownership. Capital leases are much like a financed purchase, the major difference being that a capital lease does not require the user to make a down payment as does a financed purchase. Operating leases are real leases in which there is no discounted purchase option at the end of the lease term. The lessor is considered to be the owner and thus retains the tax benefits of ownership. Because of this, the lessee typically makes a lower payment than with the capital lease alternative.

A final acquisition alternative is to rent the computer system month by month. This provides the most flexibility, because this kind of arrangement typically requires only 1 to 3 months' notice to discontinue. Of course, you usually must pay higher rental payments to get this flexibility, and because the payment is usually not fixed, you are subject to increases.

The acquisition of computer software is a whole different story. Typically, you will not have the option to buy software. Most companies **license** software. A software license grants the licensee the right to use the software under the conditions specified in the document supplied by the software company, called the **license agreement**. Typically, these licenses allow the licensee to use the software on a specified computer system for a specified fee. Three common ways to pay for this license agreement are **one-time charge, lease,** or **monthly charge.** With the one-time charge, the licensee pays a set price and retains the right to use the software indefinitely. The price can be paid in cash or financed. The leasing alternative is really just another way to finance the one-time charge with no down payment. Finally, the monthly charge is like renting the software month to month indefinitely.

Although some basic lease/purchase alternatives have been introduced in this section, the rules governing these various alternatives are complex and subject to change. The effects on a company's cash flow, income statements, balance sheets, taxes, and so on can also be strongly affected by these various acquisition alternatives. You should consult the proper professionals to determine the best alternative for your situation.

Education

The discussions in the chapter so far should assist you in selecting the appropriate software and hardware to fit your needs. However, no matter what computer hardware and software you select, they will require people to interact with them. To maximize efficiency, these people or users must be educated in the use of the computer system itself as well as its software. Proper education is critical to the success of any computer automation project. Inadequate education prevents reaping the productivity benefits afforded by moving a task to the computer.

The first goal of education is to make users (and system operators) proficient at using the computer hardware and software they need to do their jobs. Another important goal achievable through education is to make the users' interaction with the computer system an enjoyable experience. If using the computer is enjoyable, users will be more highly motivated. However, if using the computer is a frustrating struggle because the users have inadequate education, they will be less productive or perhaps will avoid the computer altogether. AS/400-specific education is available from IBM Education and Training, IBM's training subsidiary, as well as from other non-IBM companies.

The IBM Education and Training educational offerings come in the following forms:

- *Classroom courses* are traditional lectures/discussions led by an IBM instructor. These forums provide for direct interaction between students and instructors. Hands-on, in-class exercises are often part of a classroom course. Public courses are held regularly at IBM facilities. Alternately, private courses can be arranged and held either at IBM locations or customer locations.

- *Personalized learning series* courses are basically duplicates of the classroom courses except in a self-study format. The student is provided with transcriptions of the classroom course lectures in electronic form. The transcribed lectures are loaded on an AS/400 system using a CD-ROM and read on the user's display screen. Also provided is a booklet containing the foils (illustrations) normally presented in the classroom lectures. An additional offering in the self-study format is a set of diskettes containing the self-study courses for the AS/400 that may be loaded on to a personal computer and studied from there.

- *Discover/education series* courses cover additional AS/400-related topics in a format identical to the online education provided as standard with AS/400 systems.

- *Learning centers* are educational facilities that allow students to come in and use the educational materials just discussed (for a fee) without having to buy them. They also sell these educational offerings.

There is also a set of self-study courses shipped with every AS/400 system. Those courses are listed in Figure 6.8.

Ergonomics

No plan would be complete without addressing the human needs that directly affect the day-to-day productivity of computer users—**ergonom-**

Course ID	Type of Course	Course Description
PS586	Self-study	AS/400 Getting to Know Your System
PS587	Self-study	AS/400 Administrator-Work Management and Basic Tuning
PS588	Self-study	AS/400 Administrator-Security Planning and Implementation
PS589	Self-study	AS/400 Administrator-Availability and Recovery Management
PS590	Self-study	AS/400 Administrator Library
PS682	Self-study	Lotus Notes R4 System Administration I: Extending A Notes
PS684	Self-study	Lotus Notes System Admin II: Cross Certificates and Multiple ...
PS685	Self-study	Lotus Notes R4 System Admin II: Server Activity and Performance
DE204	Self-study	AS/400 Basic Education Series
DE205	Self-study	AS/400 Implementation Series
DE206	Self-study	Office Vision/400 Support Series
DE208	Self-study	AS/400 Implementation for Entry Systems
DE209	Software	AS/400 Overview and Introductory Topics
PS153	Software	AS/400 Implementation and Operation Series
PS154	Software	COBOL/400 and SQL/400 Programming Series
PS155	Software	RPG/400 and SQL/400 Programming Series
PS156	Software	AS/400 Library
PS163	Software	AS/400 System Using the S/36 Environment
PS164	Self-study	AS/400 System for the Experienced S/38 Implementer
PS274	Self-study	SQL/400 Programming Workshop

Additional information on each of these courses can be obtained by accessing the Internet at *http://www.training.ibm.com/ibmedu/news/400f96.htm.*

Figure 6.8. Listing of self-study courses available for the AS/400 on CD-ROM.

ics. Ergonomics is a science dedicated to investigating the designs for effective interaction between devices and human beings. Human beings have many physiological and psychological characteristics that should be considered when designing computers, software, desks, lighting, chairs, and so on. Attention to ergonomics increases effectiveness, work quality, health and safety, and job satisfaction.

Application Systems workstations have been designed with careful attention to ergonomics. Everything from the power switch location to the length of the keyboard cable was scrutinized. Much effort is also expended fine-tuning the ergonomics of most application programs. To get the most out of your Application Systems, you must also provide an ergonomic environment for the users. Organizations such as the American Optometric Association (AOA) and the New York Committee for Occupational Safety and Health (NYCOSH) as well as IBM have probed deeply into the relationship between the computer and the user. Items such as desks, chairs, lighting, noise, and the like are important to productivity. Some of these steps are inexpensive and easily accomplished. Others may be expensive and accomplished gradually over time. Let us explore some specific steps that will help improve the ergonomics in your environment.

Comfort for the Eyes

The eyes, like any other part of the human body, can get tired as a result of intensive use. This fatigue, called eyestrain, is not new to people who work long hours reading material. With the increase in computer use over recent years, however, we have seen an increase in eyestrain. Although eyestrain is only a temporary condition, it can cause users to feel tired and irritated, particularly if they continue to work under the pressures of deadlines. The eyes function most naturally at distances greater than or equal to arm's length. After all, throughout the majority of history, the eyes were used to pick fruit, not read contracts. When the eyes focus on anything closer than arm's reach, be it a computer terminal or newspaper, they are forced to look inward toward the nose. This is extra work for the muscles that move your eye within its socket, resulting in fatigue. To reduce this effect of fatigue, the computer user should take breaks and go to an area in which the tendency is to focus on more distant objects.

Another factor contributing to eye fatigue results from the work done by a muscle in the eye that re-forms the eye's lens to maintain sharp focus. Frequent changes in the distance at which objects are viewed (such as a computer display and a paper on your desk) make the focusing muscles effectively do "push-ups." This also leads to tired eyes. To help prevent these eye "push-ups," it is desirable to put any paper that is frequently referenced during a computer session at the same distance and orientation as the computer screen. A clip-type holder used by secretaries to hold documents as they are typing works well for this. Poor image quality can cause the eyes to constantly change focus in a futile attempt to correct the image. Application Systems terminals provide a high-quality image that helps to minimize eyestrain. As if all this were not enough, there is still another contributor to eye fatigue commonly found in offices, namely, improper lighting. The eye adjusts to all of the light in the field of vision. Unwanted light reflections called glare can appear in the user's field of vision, causing nonuniform light intensities. If the light intensity varies widely, the iris in the eye will continuously expand and contract to adjust for the light-level variance. To reduce the glare in the user's environment, Application Systems displays have an antiglare screen.

Similarly, the workstation (desk, table, etc.) surface should have antiglare or nonreflective surfaces. Windows are big culprits in causing glare, but almost everyone likes windows. You can reduce the amount of glare caused by windows by positioning your computer display screen at right angles to any window. You can also use curtains or (preferably) horizontal blinds to direct the light away from the screen. Diffused office lighting will provide fewer "hot spots" and tend to provide the most uniform light and soften harsh shadows. For using computer displays, 30 to 50 foot-candles of ambient light is optimum. The goal is to have the screen brightness three or four times the ambient light. Since typical offices were originally designed to work with paper, not video displays, there is usually more light than this in an office. This may be difficult to change, depending on the type of lighting used. You can try using fewer or lower-intensity bulbs or fluorescent tubes. Another possibility is to install dimmer switches.

Workstation Comfort

The workstation furniture shared by the computer and the user can also affect productivity. For this reason, attention should be given to the details of the user's workstation; that is, the chair and desk/table to be used. A properly designed chair can help reduce back problems and make the user more comfortable and more productive. An improperly designed chair can lead to reduced alertness and shorter concentration spans. A user may not even be aware of being uncomfortable, yet may unconsciously but constantly seek a more comfortable position.

What makes a chair a good chair? First, because a chair is typically used by many different people during its life with a company, it should be adjustable. The height of the seat pan should adjust from around 16 to 22 inches and should allow the feet to rest flat on the floor. Weight should be distributed through the buttocks, not the thighs. The front of the seat pan should roll off smoothly as in the **waterfall** design to provide for proper blood flow in the legs. A 20-mm compression is about firm enough. Backrests should adjust up or down over a 2-inch range and backward or forward between 80 and 120 degrees for good support. Both the seat pans and the backrests should be upholstered and covered in a material that absorbs perspiration.

If mobility is required, wheels or casters are recommended unless the floor is slippery, making the chair unstable. Hard casters should be used for soft floors and vice versa. A five-legged chair will provide stability and prevent tipping. Seats should swivel if lateral movement is required. Once the users are seated, their relationship with the computer display and keyboard directly affects comfort and thus productivity. The computer display should be positioned properly, with the top of the computer display 10 degrees below eye level and the center of the display at about 20 degrees below eye level and between 14 and 20 inches away. A tilt/swivel stand under the display allows the user to adjust the display angle as desired. Users should avoid bifocal lenses because they force the head to be tipped back while reading the screen.

This can lead to discomfort in the back and shoulders. The keyboard should also be in a comfortable position. Application Systems' separate keyboard, attached by a flexible cable, allows the user to position the keyboard as desired. The keyboard height should be such that the elbow is bent at about 90 degrees when typing. Finally, provide sufficient desk space for documents used during the computer session.

What about Noise?

Noise is not conducive to efficiency. Irregular noise is more distracting than constant noise. Unfortunately, irregular noise is common in the office environment, resulting from nearby conversations, telephones, printers, copy machines, and many other things. If possible, isolate noise sources such as impact printers and copy machines by placing them in isolated areas or separate rooms. Noise can also be reduced by installing doors, carpets, and other sound-insulating materials.

Security

In many business environments, computer systems are the very backbone of business operations. This makes the information stored on the computers a corporate asset at least as valuable as cash. Because of the new methods of accessing the data on your business computer (Internet, intranet), it is necessary to rethink the security aspects of your system. One of the items that distinguishes the AS/400 family from most other computer systems families is the flexibility of its security features. System security has three important objectives:

- Confidentiality

  - Protecting against disclosing information to unauthorized people.

  - Restricting access to confidential information.

  - Protecting against curious system users and outsiders.

- Integrity

  - Protecting against unauthorized changes to data.

  - Restricting manipulation of data to authorized programs.

  - Providing assurance that data is trustworthy.

- Availability

  - Preventing accidental changes or destruction of data.

  - Protecting against attempts by outsiders to abuse or destroy system resources.

System security is often associated with external threats, such as hackers or business rivals. The intent of these paragraphs is not to minimize the external exposure but to present a more balanced approach to system security. More damage can be caused by the accidental depression of the wrong key at the wrong time. A well-designed security system will provide protection against system accidents by authorized system users.

As with an application, good results from the system security functions cannot be obtained without good planning. Setting up security in small pieces without planning can be confusing and difficult to maintain and to audit. Planning does not imply designing the security for every file, program, and device in advance. Planning *does* imply establishing an overall approach to security on the system and communicating that approach to application designers, programmers, and system users. The following questions need to be considered when planning the security on your system and deciding how much security is needed:

- Is there a company policy or standard that requires a certain level of security?

- Do the company auditors require some level of security?

- How important is your system and the data on it to your business?

- How important is the error protection provided by the security features?

- What are your company security requirements for the future?

Like a business's cash, computer information must be protected from loss or theft. Let us look at how this vital information can be protected.

Loss Prevention

An ever-present hazard when dealing with information (with or without computers) is the possibility that the information will be lost. This loss can occur in many different ways. A computer system's breakdown, such as a disk unit failure, can result in lost information; operator error can cause data to be accidentally corrupted, resulting in lost information; or a disaster (such as a fire or flood) can result in a loss of vital business information. For this reason, **recovery** from the loss of vital business information must be addressed.

One way to deal with the risk of losing vital information is to make backup copies of computer information at regular intervals (e.g., daily). Multiple backup copies should be made on a revolving basis and kept in a place safe from damage or loss. Three copies will allow at least one copy to be kept in safe storage at all times and provide for different levels of backup. In the event of an information loss, the computer system can be restored to the point at which the most recent backup copy was made. Application Systems' operating systems and the various tape devices discussed in Chapter 2 are designed for these kinds of **save/restore** operations. Any changes to information after the point of the last backup will have to be re-created after the backup copy is used to restore the system. This may involve manually reentering the transactions since the last backup or exploiting OS/400 features such as journaling and checksum (see Chapter 4) or the integrated RAID controller (see Chapter 2).

Any good disaster recovery plan will also consider how the business will operate in the event the current computer system is destroyed. Many companies, including IBM, offer disaster recovery services that essentially provide you with emergency access to a similarly configured computer system located elsewhere. Usually, a test allowance is part of the deal so that you can run disaster recovery drills to ensure readiness. The "AS/400 Backup and Recovery Guide" (SC41-8079), available from IBM, is a good reference when planning your backup strategy.

Theft Prevention

Theft prevention deals with protecting sensitive information from unauthorized disclosure. These security requirements vary widely from environment to environment. Consider your particular needs early in your planning. Application Systems provide various levels of security that help deter unauthorized access. All Applications Systems are now designed to meet the C2 level of security, although the current rating is specifically for Version 2 Release 3, Version 3 Release 0.5, and Version 3 Release 1 of OS/400, Source Entry Utility, Query/400, SAA Structured Query Language/400, and Common Cryptographic Architecture Services/400. The AS/400 is the first system to achieve a C2 security rating for a system (hardware and operating system) with an integrated full-function database. The requirements for the C2 level of security are defined by the United States Department of Defense (DoD) in the Trusted Computing Systems Evaluation Criteria (TCSEC).

AS/400 security is integrated into the computer system hardware along with the associated operating system. Depending on the needs of the user environment, one of five levels of security can be activated. The first level is basically no security at all. People can access the system and can do anything they wish. The second level of security requires the user to enter a password before access is granted to the system. After the proper password is entered, the user can perform any task. The third level of security is user access control, which is just like the second level except that the user can be restricted to various functions as well. A security officer is usually assigned to manage the security of the system. The fourth level of security adds operating system integrity by restricting the use of certain operating system functions and unsupported interfaces. The fifth level enhances the integrity protection provided at the fourth level and is designed to meet the requirements of C2-level security.

For sensitive environments, you may wish to consider restricting access to the area in which the Application Systems itself is located. It may also be necessary to restrict access to the area(s) in which workstations are located. These needs should be considered early in a computer automation project. For additional discussion of security subjects and AS/400 security capabilities obtain "Tips and Tools for Securing Your AS/400" (SC41-3300-00) from your local IBM branch or IBM representative.

Internet Connection Secure Server for AS/400

Internet Connection Secure Server for AS/400 (5769-NCI/NCE) replaces HTTP Server. Among the differences from HTTP Server are the ability to name a user profile from which HTML is served and a different profile from which CGI-bin (Common Gateway Interface-binary) programs are run. This allows the authorization of different profiles to different Web applications and data, providing assurance that the correct data is served to applications. The capability for basic authentication (a user must provide at least some type of identification and password) before allowing access to certain data has been added. With basic authentication come the concept of an "Internet user," who may be allowed to see certain data but is not a real AS/400 user, complete with an AS/400 user profile and password (allowing access to all publically authorized objects). The Internet users are managed using a validation list: When an application requires user authentication, the information is requested on the browser, returned to the Internet Connection Secure Server and verified using the data in the validation list defined for the Web application. The validation list is one-way encrypted, making it secure. CGI applications can use AS/400 Activation Groups in their AS/400 Web Server solutions.

The AS/400 Secure Web Server is enabled by the IBM Internet Connection Secure Server (ICSS) for AS/400. ICSS provides the security to send proprietary or confidential information over the Internet and corporate intranets, enabling online transactions including electronic commerce to be performed. The security level comes from the Secure Sockets Layer (SSL) protocol, which provides end-to-end security. Data transferred between a server and a client is encrypted to ensure privacy. Before the data transmission starts, the identity of the server is authenticated by the client through the use of a certificate (digital ID). In a data transfer operation, the Web browser authenticates the identity of the AS/400 server and then the encrypted data is transferred.

Two different encryption algorithms are supported by ICSS: 5769-NC1 supports 128-bit data encryption capability, and ICSS_5769-NE1 supports 40-bit encryption capability. Although 128-bit encryption cannot be exported outside the United States and Canada; 40-bit encryption can be exported to other countries.

ICSS includes a Digital Certificate Manager (described next) to enable the creation of your own corporate certificate authority for your intranet or Internet sites. The certificate authority can sign certificates for clients and servers and download the needed certificates into users' browsers.

Digital Certificate Manager

The SET level of Internet security involves the use of **digital certificates**. A digital certificate is a file of information that when used with PKCS (**Public Key Cryptography Standard**) cryptography can serve to authenticate that the respondent to a certificate request is exactly who they claim to be. It is the "fingerprint" of the digital world, to ensure that sensitive information is going to exactly the trusted receiver expected. The X.509 certificates are supported on AS/400. A user wishing to exchange secure data with a server applies to an authorized certificate issuer (**certificate authority**) for a digital certificate to be issued to the user's ID and password. The Certificate Authority (CA) "signs" a digital certificate to verify its authenticity. It is the CA's public key that lets a certificate requestor unwrap it to verify its veracity. Certificate authorities are the "Notary Publics" of the digital signature world.

After receipt of a certificate the user exchanges that certificate with the secure server with which secure information exchange is desired. Upon receipt of the certificate and the user ID and password, the secure server sends the user the encryption algorithm to be used and the key to be used. The **Public Key Cryptography Standard** (PKCS) system uses an asymmetrical encryption algorithm such that one key (the private key) encrypts the data and a second key (the public key) un-encrypts it. This solves the problem of symmetrical encryption (the same key is used to encrypt and un-encrypt a file of how to provide the key to the remote user across the unencrypted line) related to making the key itself available to both end-users.

The AS/400 has the capability to serve as a Digital Certificate Manager at V4R2. This means that the AS/400 can set up an intranet certificate authority, sign client and server certificates, distribute client certificates via a Web browser, and provide support for MD5 and SHA-1 hash algorithms.

Firewalls

IBM suggests the use of firewalls where any connection to the Internet may possibly occur. The firewall may be formed using a separate system or the Integrated PC Server (IPCS) discussed in Chapter 2. A **firewall** controls the access and flow of information between a secure (trusted) network and an unsecure (un-trusted) network. Usually a combination of hardware and software provides firewall function. Firewalls can provide the following benefits when your network is connected to the Internet:

- Controlled access to internal systems.

- Concentrated security administration.

- Enhanced privacy and secrecy of your network configuration.

- Enforcement of your security policy.

- Protection of vulnerable services, such as network file systems.

- Improved system availability by blocking denial-of-service attacks.

- Statistics of network use and misuse.

- Protection of your organization's reputation as secure and reliable.

Some common firewall functions are traffic blocking, acting as a network gateway, and domain name serving. **Traffic blocking** blocks unwanted traffic between the secure and the unsecure networks. The **network gateway** function hides both the Internet Protocol (IP) addresses and domain names of your **internal network** from the Internet. The **domain name serving** function makes it appear to the Internet that the firewall name is the source of all outbound traffic and also manages the routing of inbound traffic to the appropriate Intranet addresses. It is critical that other domain servers cannot use your firewall to resolve your intranet domain names.

Most firewalls involve a separate system with separate programming. The AS/400 firewall is implemented using the Integrated PC Server (IPCS) internal to the AS/400 Server system. This allows processor separation without requiring an additional system. Security functions running on the IPCS are separate from applications running on the AS/400 processor. The software used by the firewall is on a read-only disk, eliminating the possibility of a virus being introduced and preventing modification of programs that carry out the communications security functions. Communication between the main processor and the firewall is over an internal system bus immune from sniffing programs on local area networks. The firewall can be disabled by the main processor when it detects tampering, independent of the state of the firewall. Installation of firewall software is the same as for any other AS/400 software. The administrator is guided through the initial install and configuration. The firewall is administered by a Web browser on the internal (secure) network. The Secure Sockets Layer (SSL) protocol can be used to protect the administration session. Authentication of the administrator is with OS/400 security support.

IBM Firewall for AS/400 (5769-FW1) is an application gateway firewall using Internet Protocol (IP) packet filtering to prevent undesirable traffic from reaching the internal network. Packets may be filtered by source IP address, protocol, port number, direction, and network interface. RealAudio is supported through dynamic packet filtering technology. An HTTPs proxy server provides Web access to servers on the Internet without revealing the name or address on the browser, and can cache Web pages for better response time. All internal users have a single mail domain with hidden internal e-mail addresses. Various levels of logging are supported, ranging from logging all traffic to logging only exceptions. Figure 6.9 illustrates the firewall environment on an AS/400 system.

Service

Although every effort has been made to make Application Systems as reliable as possible, some computers will fail. If yours does, you must have a way of getting it fixed. All Application Systems come with a 1-year warranty that provides free on-site repairs from IBM's service division 7 days a week, 24 hours a day. Each of the various terminals and printers associated with Application Systems has its own warranty terms and periods ranging from 3 months to 3 years. After the warranty period, you become responsible for maintenance of the system.

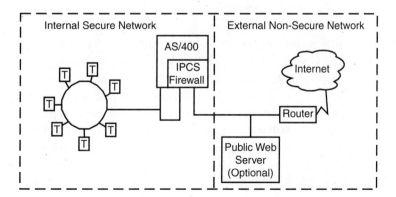

Figure 6.9. The firewall environment.

IBM and other companies offer service agreements that, for a fee, provide postwarranty on-site service just like that provided during the warranty. Various maintenance discounts are available, depending on the level of system management procedures you are willing to implement in your business. Appendix A contains a listing of some of the many IBM Service offerings. If your system fails and you do not have any type of service contract, you will have to pay for parts and labor, which can become extremely expensive. For this reason, most people choose to keep their systems on maintenance after warranty.

Year 2000 Challenge

The AS/400 Division is the first organization in the computer industry to receive the Information Technology Association of America's (ITAA) ITAA*2000 certification, the industry's first Year 2000–readiness certification program. The certification recognizes AS/400 Advanced Series systems, Advanced 36 included, using OS/400 Version 3 Release 2, Version 3 Release 7, and Version 4 Releases 1 and 2 as being Year 2000 ready now. In addition, these systems have some powerful tools for getting the rest of your applications ready. More information is available on the IBM AS/400 Partners in Development Year 2000 home page at *http://www.softmall.ibm.com/as400/year2000.html*.

Migrating from System/3X to AS/400

Some businesses may be replacing System/34, System/36, or System/38 computer(s) with an AS/400. AS/400 has been designed to ease the migration of most programs and data from these earlier System/3X computer systems to AS/400. OS/400 functions plus available tools provide a guided and highly automated procedure for these types of migrations. Although programming skills are still required to guide the migration activities, the tools reduce the manual work of analyzing, documenting, saving, and restoring application programs. Programs are migrated to either the AS/400 System/36 Environment or the AS/400 System/38 Environment discussed in Chapter 4. If desired, the programs can be further adapted to take advantage of new AS/400 functions at your own pace after the migration is complete. Now let us look at some topics related to migrating from S/3X to AS/400:

- Sizing a replacement AS/400

- Migrating System/3X I/O devices to the AS/400

- Migrating programs and data from the System/36

- Migrating programs and data from the System/38

- Migrating programs and data from the System/34

Sizing a Replacement AS/400

Whether AS/400 will be your first computer system or you will be replacing a System/36 or System/38, you will have to choose the appropriate size AS/400. "Size" refers to the processor speed and capacity, which by model depend on memory size and amount of disk storage. There are many things to consider when choosing the size AS/400 needed in a given situation. If you are migrating from a System/3X, you can use that system as a starting point for your sizing activity. Here, you know your current memory size, disk storage size, and so on. If you are migrating programs and data from a System/36 to an AS/400, you will need more disk storage and main storage capacity on the AS/400 system than you needed on the System/36 for several reasons: First, the AS/400's operating system (OS/400) takes up significantly more disk space than that of the System/36 (SSP). Further, the AS/400 automatically generates extra program debugging and external data definition information during the migration process that are not present in the System/36. Finally, the "blanks" in programs are not compressed as they were on the System/36.

The net effect of these factors is that load members (object code) will need about 7 times more disk storage (this can be reduced to a factor of 2.5 by removing the extra debugging information after migration), source members will require about 3.6 times more disk storage, and data files will require about 1.2 times the space. Mail logs and data dictionaries are approximately the same size on the AS/400 as they are on a System/36. You will also need more main storage when migrating to the AS/400 from a System/36 because the more powerful (and more complex) OS/400 requires more main storage to operate, keeps more information about the current jobs resident in main storage, and uses larger control blocks. The bright side of these facts is that the number of disk storage operations (each of which takes a long time in the context of a computer system) is reduced because more information is in main storage and ready for immediate use.

Those migrating from the System/38 to the AS/400 will also need more disk storage and main storage capacity than they did with the System/38 for similar reasons. In this case, more disk storage space is necessary mostly because of the increased requirements of OS/400. More main storage is needed because more information about each task remains resident in memory. More information in main storage has been a traditional advantage of the System/38 because it makes for better system performance. The AS/400 takes further advantage of the same concept. Whether you are migrating from a System/36 or a System/38, you must also select the correct AS/400 processor model. The performance section of Chapter 1 will give you a rough idea of the relative performance of the various computer systems of interest.

To refine your model selection, you must start by examining your current computer system very closely. Tools like the **Systems Management Facility (SMF)** and the **System/38 Performance Measurement Tools** can be used to determine the workload on your current system. The capacity planner portion of the AS/400 Performance Tools (discussed in Chapter 5) can help analyze your current system to determine which AS/400 model is appropriate. An IBM document that will help in using these sizing tools and determining AS/400 disk storage requirements is the "AS/400 Performance and Capacity Planning Newsletter" (GC21-8175). If you are adding additional functions (programs and data) or more users to the new AS/400 system, you must also consider the effect of these new requirements on performance, memory, and disk storage requirements. IBM personnel have tools and resources available to them to help you size the appropriate AS/400 system.

Migrating System/3X I/O Devices to the AS/400

Most of the twinaxially attached input/output devices, such as terminals and printers, are supported on AS/400 systems. One of the design points of AS/400 was to protect current investments in I/O devices. Not all System/3X I/O devices, however, can be supported by AS/400. These include some old terminals and disk storage devices. These older devices should therefore stay with the System/3X system being replaced, whether it is sold, redistributed, or otherwise disposed of. Information stored on System/3X tape or diskettes can be read by a properly configured AS/400 system. However, because AS/400s do not come standard with a diskette drive, it is possible that System/3X users who use diskettes as the backup media (no tape drive) may not be able to exchange information with a particular AS/400. Furthermore, because AS/400 does not support a diskette magazine (a System/3X device that holds a group of diskettes), diskettes must be fed to an AS/400 one at a time.

Transferring large amounts of information one diskette at a time is time-consuming at best and often impractical. For situations like this, the **0059 Transition Data Link** provides an alternative method to move information between a System/3X and an AS/400. The 0059 allows for the direct attachment of an AS/400 system with a System/3X as shown in Figure 6.10. A twinaxial cable, like that used to attach workstations, attaches the 0059 to the workstation controller of each computer system. With this configuration, information can be transferred at twinaxial

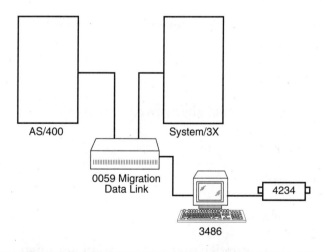

Figure 6.10. The 0059 migration data link can be used to transfer information between AS/400 and System/3X computers. It can also be used to provide workstations with access to both systems.

cable speeds, resulting in efficient information transfer. Dedicating multiple workstation addresses to the 0059 data transfer function (up to seven) can further improve information transfer performance. The 0059 can also be used to attach workstations to both computer systems during migration activities. This allows the user of a single terminal to switch from one system to another by simply striking a key. Although printers can also be attached via the 0059, they can be accessed only by one system or the other, not by both.

Migrating Programs and Data from the System/36

With the announcement of compatible operation for SSP programs on all models of the AS/400 Advanced Series RISC-based systems (Models 6XX and SXX), the migration of System/36 programs and data just got easier. Those who are considering that upgrade must first create a logical SSP machine (Advanced 36 models already contain that logical SSP machine, but other AS/400 models must be licensed to use the SSP as an operating system) and then load the application programs and data as described in the previous paragraph. The following can be migrated from a System/36 to an AS/400:

- Source members for programs, screen formats, messages, and menus

- Procedures

- Data files and alternative indexes

- Libraries

- Folders

- Data dictionaries

- Security and master configuration information

You can also migrate the following items (e.g., files, folders, directories) used by System/36 SSP and licensed programs:

- Advanced Printer Function (APF)

- Business Graphics Utilities/36 (BGU/36)

- Data File Utility (DFU) programs

- Distributed Data Management (DDM)

- Multiple Session Remote Job Entry (MSRJE)

- PC Support/36

- Personal Services/36

- Query/36

Migrating Programs and Data from the System/38

The migrating of System/38 programs and data is accomplished using the same basic steps as migrating from the System/36. You first load the System/38 Migration Aid on the System/38. You can then analyze and select the objects (data, libraries, files, and programs) to be migrated. The purpose of this step is to look for things that must be changed to work properly on an AS/400 system. You can select objects to be migrated by libraries, categories, and other groupings, or you can choose to migrate the entire system. The System/38 objects to be migrated are then transferred to the AS/400 through diskette, tape, or a communications link. Once on the AS/400 system, facilities are available to make the necessary changes to System/38 objects.

Personal Services/38 documents and virtual disks are automatically converted to be usable by AS/400. Unlike System/36 programs, System/38 programs can be transported to AS/400 as object code that is automatically adapted (reencapsulated) to run on AS/400 without recompiling. This is true for programs written in RPG III, COBOL '74, PL/1, BASIC, or Command Language (CL). Because a few things are supported on System/38 but not on AS/400 (96-column cards and diskette magazines), consideration must be given to programs using those items. As with System/36 migration, menus provide guidance throughout the migration process and reports show the status of migration activities. Since AS/400's architecture is based on that of the System/38, the migration of programs and data is more direct than when migrating from the System/36, this is true whether the processor architecture is IMPI or RISC. For the same reason, you do not pay a significant performance penalty when running System/38 programs as you do when you run System/36 programs (except when the System/36 programs are run on a licensed SSP operating system). The following can be migrated from the System/38:

- User profiles

- Most system configuration descriptions.

- User libraries, including library QGPL (General Purpose Library)

- Objects in user libraries, except for

  - Printer Images

  - Documents

  - Document lists

  - Edit descriptions

  - User-defined message queues

  - Card files

  - Many of the system values

Another migration aid, called the **System/38 Utilities,** runs on the AS/400 and provides support for programs written using the System/38 Data File Utility and Query/38. The Text Management/38 functions of this tool also provide word processing capabilities to AS/400 users not using OfficeVision/400. The AS/400 document that discusses the details of this migration is "Migrating from System/38 Planning Guide" (GC21-9624).

Migrating Programs and Data from the System/34

Users of the IBM System/34, a predecessor to the System/36, can also migrate many of their programs to AS/400 systems. As with the System/36, System/34 programs and data are first saved to diskettes and then restored on an AS/400. Optionally, the **System/34 to System/36 Migration Aid** (5727-MA1) can be used to identify missing source members and provide an audit trail during this process. System/34 programs can be modified if necessary, recompiled, and run in OS/400's System/36 Environment. As with the System/36, BASIC subroutines must be converted to source code. The migration of System/34 Data File Utility routines, security, and configuration members is a manual process. A technical newsletter, "System/34 to AS/400 Migration Tips" (GC21-8161), is helpful in such migrations.

Migrating C, D, E, and F 9402, 9404, and 9406 Models to the Advanced Series

Most of the I/O processing adapters used on the old models will be usable on the new system unit package. In some cases, disk units and tape units in particular, I/O devices will require repackaging to properly adapt to the new system unit package. The 9402 and 9404 base and expansion towers must be replaced. The 9406 system unit racks are convertible to expansion/extension racks with the removal of the system unit. The 9406 rack-mounted devices and expansion/extension units may be attached to the new system units. In the new system units, processors, expansion memory cards, MultiFunction I/O Processor cards, and battery backup units are unique to the Version 4 Release 1 and 2 hardware. In general, B-level hardware cannot be migrated.

Migrating Advanced Series 20X/30X System Units to Advanced Series 40X/50X System Units: CISC to RISC

Because the RISC processor and memory interface has changed relative to the CISC processor/memory interface, it is necessary to change the backplane to migrate the system units. The processors and memory from the CISC models must be replaced, and no net-priced exchange of memory cards is supported. All of the I/O and IOPs are preserved and can be used with the new models. All of the expansion units can be migrated. The new method for preserving the contents of main storage does not make it necessary to change the batteries. For migrating programs and data from the CISC-based system to the RISC-based system, it is recommended that the user obtain a copy of the "AS/400 Road Map for Changing to PowerPC Technology" (SA41-4150-01) and follow its suggestions religiously.

Version 4 Release 2 4XX/5XX Performance Impact

In addition to the changes in OS/400 for Version 4 Releases 1 and 2 that affected performance, the algorithm for computing CPW has been changed to more closely reflect the way the systems are being used. The algorithm changed so that when the interactive CPU utilization threshold is crossed, only the interactive work on the system will slow down. Batch/client server work will continue to perform at the higher performance rating. At V3R7 when interactive CPU utilization threshold is crossed, all work on the system slows down, both interactive and batch/client server work. Figure 6.11 shows the performance improvement of the AS/400 Model 4XX and 5XX systems, and Figure 6.12 shows the performance improvement of the 4XS and 5XS server models as a result of these actions.

Other performance improvements included:

- Improved IOPs

- 30% Web server improvements

- Save/restore improvements

- Query performance on N-way processors

- 3590 Tape Drive at full rated speed with 1063 Optical Bus

Model/Feat. Code	V3R6 CPW Value	V3R7 CPW Value	% Increase Over V3R6	V4R1 CPW Value	% Increase Over V3R7
400/2130	12.3	13.8	12	13.8	0
400/2131	18.3	20.6	13	20.6	0
400/2132	24.5	27.0	10	27.0	0
400/2133	30.6	33.3	9	35.0	5
500/2140	18.7	21.4	14	21.4	0
500/2141	26.9	30.7	14	21.4	0
500/2142	38.3	43.9	15	43.9	0
510/2143	66.7	77.7	16	81.6	5
510/2144	85.0	104.2	23	111.5	7
530/2150	107.1	131.1	22	148	13
530/2151	132.5	162.7	23	188.2	16
530/2152	198.7	278.8	40	319.0	14
530/2153	299.0	459.3	54	598.0650	30
530/2162	349.8	509.9	46	650.0	27

Figure 6.11. AS/400 Advanced System—V4R2 Performance for V3R6 general-purpose-based processors as a result of V4R2 actions.

Model/Feature Code	V3R6 CPW Value	V3R7 CPW Value	% Increase Over V3R6	V4R1 CPW Value	% Increase Over V3R7
40S/2109	24.5/8.4	27.0/9.4	10/12	27.0/9.4	0/0
40S/2110	30.6/12.3	33.3/13.8	9/12	35.0/14.5	5/5
40S/2111	52.9/18.3	59.8/20.6	13/13	63.0/21.6	5/5
40S/2112	77.3/26.9	87.3/30.7	13/14	91.0/32.2	5/5
50S/2120	66.7/18.7	77.7/21.4	16/14	81.6/22.5	5/5
50S/2121	85.0/26.9	104.2/30.7	23/14	111.5/32.8	7/7
50S/2122	106.8/26.9	130.7/30.7	23/14	138.0/32.8	5/7
53S/2154	132.5/26.9	162.7/30.7	23/14	188.2/32.8	16/7
53S/2155	198.7/26.9	278.8/30.7	40/14	319.0/32.8	16/7
53S/2156	299.0/26.9	459.3/30.7	54/14	598.0/32.8	30/7
53S/2157	349.8/26.9	509.9/30.7	46/14	650.0/32.8	27/7

Figure 6.12. AS/400 Advanced Server V4R2 Performance for V3R6 Server-based Processors as a result of V4R2 actions.

System Performance Tables for AS/400 Systems

System Performance of AS/400 systems prior to V3R6 are presented to allow comparison to the V4R2 performance capabilities for those older systems. Figures 6.13 through Figure 6.16 illustrate the performance capabilities of all previous AS/400 system and processor models.

Model Group	Feature Code	Memory Capacity (MB, min-max)	Disk Capacity (GB, min-max)	Relative Performance Ratings (RPR, B10=1.0) Internal Processor C/S Interactive	Relative System Performance Metric (CPW Value) C/S Interactive
9402	S01	8-56	1.96-3.9	5.9-1.9	17.1-5.5
	100	16-56	1.0-7.9	5.9-1.9	17.1-5.5
9404	135	32-384	1.0-27.5	10.9-3.3	32.3-9.6
	140	64-512	1.0-47.2	22.5-4.0 (2)*	65.6-11.6 (2)*
20S	2010	16-128	1-23.6	5.9-1.9	17.1-5.5
2FS	2010	16-128	1-7.8	5.9-1.9	17.1-5.5
2SS	2010	16-128	1-7.8	5.9-1.9	17.1-5.5
2SG	2010	16-128	1-7.8	5.9-1.9	17.1-5.5
30S	2411	32-384	1-86.5	10.9-3.3	32.3-9.6
	2412	64-832	1-86.5	23.5-4.0 (2)*	68.5-11.6 (2)*
40S	2109	32-224	1.96-23.6	8.3-2.6	24.5-8.4
	2110	32-224	1.96-23.6	10.6-3.8	30.6-12.3
50S	2120	64-1024	1.96-318.7	19.7-5.7	66.7-18.7
	2121	64-1024	1.96-318.7	26.6-8.3	85.0-26.9
53S	2154	512-4096	1.96-520	43.4-8.3	132.5-26.9
	2155	512-4096	1.96-520	66.6-8.3 (2)*	198.7-26.9 (2)*
	2156	512-4096	1.96-520	101.4-8.3 (4)*	299.0-26.9 (4)*

The number in parentheses shows the number of CPUs contained in that model.

Figure 6.13. Relative performance of AS/400 Advanced Servers CISC and RISC models.

Model Group	Feature Code	Memory Capacity (MB, min-max)	Disk Capacity (GB, min-max)	Relative Performance Ratings (RPR, B10=1.0)		Relative System Performance Metric (CPWValue)
				Internal Processor	System (RAMP-C)	
9401	P02	8-16	1.0-2.1	2.5	2.1	7.3
	P03-2114	8-24	1.03-2.99	2.5	2.5	7.3
	P03-2115	8-40	1.96-3.93	3.3	3.3	9.6
	150-2169/70	32-96	4-16			10.9
	PO3-2117	8-56	1.96-3.93	5.8	3.9	16.8
9402	C04	8-12	0.6-1.3	1.0	1.1	3.1
	C06	8-16	0.6-1.3	1.3	1.3	3.6
	D02	8-16	0.8-1.2	1.3	1.3	3.8
	D04	8-16	0.8-1.6	1.5	1.5	4.4
	E02	8-24	1.0-2.0	1.5	1.5	4.5
	D06	8-20	0.8-1.6	1.9	1.9	5.5
	E04	8-24	1.0-4.0	1.9	1.9	5.5
	F02	8-24	1.0-2.1	1.9	1.9	5.5
	F04	8-24	1.0-4.1	2.5	2.5	7.3
	E06	8-40	1.0-7.9	2.5	2.6	7.3
	F06	8-40	1.0-8.2	3.3	3.3	9.6
9404	B10	4-16	0.6-1.9	1.0	1.0	2.9
	C10	8-20	0.6-1.9	1.3	1.3	3.9
	B20	4-28	0.6-3.8	1.7	1.7	5.1
	C20	8-32	0.6-3.8	1.8	1.8	5.3
	D10	8-32	0.8-4.8	1.8	1.9	5.3
	C25	8-40	0.6-3.8	2.1	2.2	6.1
	D20	8-40	0.8-4.8	2.3	2.4	6.8
	E10	8-40	1.0-19.7	2.6	2.6	7.6
	D25	16-64	0.8-6.4	3.3	3.4	9.7
	F10	8-72	1.0-20.6	3.3	3.4	9.6
	E20	8-72	1.0-19.7	3.3	3.5	9.7
	F20	16-80	1.0-20.6	4.0	4.2	11.6
	E25	16-80	1.0-19.7	4.0	4.2	11.8
	F25	16-80	1.0-20.6	4.7	4.8	13.7

Figure 6.14. Relative performance of AS/400 Systems (9401, 9402, and 9404 models).

Feature Code	MemoryCapacity (MB, min-max)	Disk Capacity (GB, min-max)	Relative Performance Ratings (RPR, B10=1.0)		Relative System Performance Metric (CPW Value)
			Internal Processor	System (RAMP-C)	
B30	4-36	0.6-13.7	1.3	1.4	3.8
B35	8-40	0.6-13.7	1.5	1.6	4.6
B40	8-40	0.6-13.7	1.8	2.0	5.2
B45	8-40	0.6-13.7	2.3	2.3	6.5
D35	8-72	1.3-67.0	2.5	2.6	7.4
B50	16-48	0.6-27.4	3.3	3.2	9.3
E35	8-72	1.3-67.0	3.3	3.4	9.7
D45	16-80	1.3-67.0	3.7	3.7	10.8
D50	32-128	1.3-98.0	4.5	4.8	13.3
E45	16-80	1.3-67.0	4.7	4.8	13.8
F35	16-80	2.0-67.0	4.7	4.8	13.7
B60	32-96	0.654.8	5.1	5.2	15.1
F45	16-80	2.0-67.0	5.9	6.0	17.1
E50	32-128	1.3-98.0	6.2	6.4	18.1
B70	32-192	0.6-54.8	6.8	7.0	20.0
D60	64-192	1.3-146	8.1	8.3	23.9
F50	64-192	2.0-114	9.5	10.2	27.8
E60	64-192	1.3-146	9.7	10.2	28.1
D70	64-256	1.3-146	10.9	11.2	32.3
E70	64-256	1.3-146	13.5	14.2	39.2
F60	128-384	2.0-146	13.7	14.7	40.0
D80	64-384	2.0-146	19.0 (2)[*]	19.8	56.6 (2)[*]
F70	128-512	2.0-256	18.9	21.0	57.0
E80	64-512	1.3-256	23.8 (2)[*]	25.2	69.4 (2)[*]
E90	64-1024	1.3-256	32.6 (3)[*]	34.4	96.7 (3)[*]
F80	128-768	2.0-256	33.5 (2)[*]	36.5	97.1 (2)[*]
E95	64-1152	1.3-256	40.2 (4)[*]	42.1	116.6 (4)[*]
F90	128-1024	2.0-256	43.8 (3)[*]	50.5	127.7 (3)[*]
F95	128-1280	2.0-256	51.0 (4)[*]	59.0	148.8 (4)[*]
F97	128-1536	2.0-256	61.2 (4)[*]	71.5	177.4 (4)[*]

The number in parentheses shows the number of CPUs contained in that model.

Figure 6.15. Relative performance of AS/400 System 9406 models.

Model Group	Feature Code	Memory Capacity (MB, min-max)	Disk Capacity (GB, min-max)	Relative Performance Ratings (RPR, B10=1.0)		Relative System Performance Metric (CPW Value)
				Internal Processor	System (RAMP-C)	
CISC Models						
200	2030	8-24	1.03-23.6	2.5	2.5	7.3
	2031	8-56	1.03-23.6	4.0	4.0	11.6
	2032	16-128	1.03-23.6	5.8	6.2	16.8
300	2040	8-72	1.03-117.4	4.0	4.2	11.6
	2041	16-80	1.03-117.4	5.8	6.0	16.8
	2042	32-160	1.03-117.4	7.2	7.5	21.1
310	2043	64-832	1.03-159.3	10.9	12.0	33.8
	2044	64-832	1.03-159.3	19.0 (2)*	20.2	56.5 (2)*
320	2050	128-1536	1.03-259.6	23.2	25.7	67.5
	2051	128-1536	1.03-259.6	41.3 (2)*	45.8	120.3 (2)*
	2052	128-1536	1.03-259.6	61.2 (4)*	71.5	177.4 (4)*
PowerPC Models						
400	2130	32-160	1.96-23.6	3.8	4.1	12.3
	2131	32-224	1.96-23.6	5.7	6.1	18.3
	2132	32-224	1.96-23.6	8.3	8.7	24.5
	2133	32-224	1.96-23.6	10.6	10.9	30.6
436	2102	32-224	1.96-23.6	1.0 (SSP mode)	4.8 (OS/ 400 mode)	14.4 (OS/ 400 mode)
	2104	32-224	1.96-23.6	1.3 (SSP mode)	6.1 (OS/ 400 mode)	18.3 (OS/ 400 mode)
	2106	64-256	1.96-23.6	2.4 (SSP mode)	8.7 (OS/ 400 mode)	24.5 (OS/ 400 mode)
500	2140	64-768	1.96-151	5.7	6.4	18.7
	2141	64-768	1.96-151	8.3	9.3	26.9
	2142	64-1024	1.96-151	11.4	12.6	38.3
510	2143	256-1024	1.96-318.7	19.7	21.6	66.7
	2144	256-1024	1.96-318.7	26.6	28.5	85.0
530	2150	512-4096	1.96-520	32.9	37.4	107.1
	2151	512-4096	1.96-520	43.4	48.9	132.5
	2152	512-4096	1.96-520	66.6 (2)*	74.0	198.7 (2)*
	2153	512-4096	1.96-520	101.4 (4)*	119.2	299.0 (4)*

The number in parentheses shows the number of CPUs contained in that model.

Figure 6-16. Relative performance of AS/400 Advanced System (CISC and PowerPC RISC models).

Other performance improvements included:

- Improved IOPs

  - 30% Web server improvements

    - Save/restore improvements

    - Query performance on *N*-way processors

- 3590 Tape Drive at full rated speed with 1063 Optical Bus

Appendix A

AS/400 System Support Services

The following listing identifies and briefly describes the system support services available for the AS/400 family of systems as well as the older S/36 and S/38. It is adapted with IBM's permission from IBM document G325-0740-03.

- **AS/400 PerformanceEdge** provides standard maintenance agreement services with 24-hour telephone access to technical hardware support, on-site access to IBM customer engineers, plus AS/400 Service Director, PM/400-subset, and AS/400 Forum.

- **AS/400 and AS/400 Advanced 36 Support Line** provides prime shift 2-hour response, access via IBMLink, management activity reports detailing usage, additional contacts option, and software defect and usage questions answered by Rochester specialists.

- **AS/400 and AS/400 Advanced 36 Associate** will assign a specific support representative who possesses in-depth knowledge of your account and system, is your advocate to pursue technical concerns and questions beyond the limits of the Support Line service, and will call you back within an hour during prime shift.

- **AS/400 and AS/400 Advanced 36 Consult Line** provides you access to experts in such areas as availability and recovery; systems management; communications, including multiple platforms, personal computers, and LANs; cooperative processing; client/server applications; system migration; rightsizing; database design; application design; and other areas to meet your needs.

- **PM/400** performs many of the resource-intensive manual operations required to record and track system throughput and response. It helps you maintain optimal system performance and plan future capacity requirements with minimal resources, and it provides reports by schedule or on demand.

- **AS/400 Forum** provides access to the cumulative experiences of the AS/400 community from which you can share technical ideas, tips, and techniques of other midrange professionals. In addition, you have access to a software tools repository for downloading both source and object code.

- **AS/400 Alert** will make you aware of critical software and hardware fixes, which could cause system interruptions and expensive system downtime. System availability can be improved by anticipating and preventing problems before they occur.

- **AS/400 VitalSign** is a systems administration assessment that evaluates your existing system administration practices and provides comments and recommendations specific to your business and IS operations. This is done by collecting information from your system and using an interactive questionnaire to gather customer input.

- **AS/400 Recovery Express** provides an entry-level recovery service from IBM Business Recovery Services. This service is provided to assist customers in responding to an unplanned interruption of critical information processing (disaster) at a specified location due to causes beyond the customer's control.

- **AS/400 SiteManager** alerts you to small problems before they become disasters. It monitors your hardware, business applications, and systems environment, and alerts you to problem conditions 365 days a year, day and night.

- **AS/400 RemoteInstall** provides a remote installation service to keep you current on the latest releases and software fixes (PTFs).

- **IBM HouseCall** provides scheduled assistance at your location for basic, task-oriented services. Specialists trained on each hardware platform are available to work at your place of business.

- **AS/400 Support Solutions** supplements your technical staff with AS/400 experts to provide, either on site or remotely, services such as performance and capacity planning, cooperative processing, client/server, client series, application design reviews/application development, recovery readiness exams, installation services, availability and recovery audits, security audits, or voice integration programs.

- **AS/400 SysMigration** provides an IBM specialist to assist in moving data and applications from existing systems to new systems using tape to restore.

- **AS/400 SoftInstall** provides customers with expert planning, verification, installation, and education for all new OS/400 releases. This service offering is used for all new OS/400 releases. This service offering is used for all release-to-release upgrades.

- **AS/400 Advanced 36 Installation** provides IBM specialists who will assist customers with the installation of their new Advanced 36 system.

- **AS/400 SmoothStart** provides an IBM specialist on site with customers to assist with the installation of their new AS/400 system.

- **AS/400 GigMigration** provides an IBM specialist to assist with the DASD data migration from an existing system to a new configuration.

- **AS/400 Gopher Client Internet Installation** provides an IBM specialist to assist customers in connecting their AS/400 to the Internet.

- **AS/400 Novell Client Works** provides an IBM specialist to enable customers to successfully install and configure Client/Access 400 (or PC Support) on PCs that must access Novell servers at the same time.

- **AS/400 OMEGAMON/400 Installation** provides an IBM specialist to assist in getting this software in production and running quickly.

- **AS/400 Version 3, Release 6 System Transition Services (SysTransition)** provides an IBM specialist to plan, transition, and verify the transition of your current IMPI-based system to the new AS/400 RISC-based PowerPC processor. This service is comprised of three offerings: (1) Upgrade Assistant, (2) System Transition, and (3) Total Project Management.

- **SmoothStart Service for Lotus Notes** provides planning, installation, and configuration of Lotus Notes for the AS/400 FSIOP Server, and also provides on-site installation training.

- **Integration Services for OS/400 for Novell Netware** provides installation of OS/400 software features and PTFs, integration of Novell Netware into your OS/400 Operating System, and integration of the new AS/400 server into your new or existing Novel Network.

- **AS/400 Security Review** provides an IBM specialist to assist the customer in running the OS/400 provided security tool to analyze their system security procedures.

- **SmoothStart Service for Web Server/400 from I/Net, Inc.** provides the install, configure, and tailor the I/Net Web Server/400 to allow your business to be connected to the World Wide Web.

- **Planning for Internet Connection for AS/400** is a planning service to provide information and guidance to determine which are the best functions of your AS/400 to offer Internet users.

- **SmoothStart Service for Internet Connection for AS/400** provides for the AS/400 HTTP Web Server to be installed and configured.

Gain visibility on the Internet with your own home page, and reach your clients around the world through Web servers.

- **AS/400 BRMS Installation Services** provides an IBM specialist to assist with the planning and implementation of the plan to install and operate Backup Recovery Media Services.

Appendix B

User Groups

In addition to the methods of gaining AS/400 education identified in Chapter 7, AS/400 technical conferences are conducted every year by IBM and other companies. Yet another educational forum is provided by user groups. **Guide, Share,** and **Common** are the user groups most easily recognizable to users of IBM equipment. Guide and Share are user groups associated with the enterprise- or mainframe-sized systems and are of interest to those readers who will network their AS/400 with a mainframe system. Common is a large association of IBM users of small and midrange systems. Like Guide and Share, it is a member-run organization, although IBM provides considerable support. Common has two national conferences each year in the United States (April and October), as well as one in Europe each May, run by European Common. There is a large MAPICS user group within Common, and each conference has many sessions on using the various functions in MAPICS, and others on upcoming enhancements. You can contact Common at:

Common
401 North Michigan Avenue
Chicago, IL 60611-4267
Phone: (312) 644-6610
Fax: (312) 565-4658

Common also has user groups in other countries that meet at various times each year: Common Peru, Common Australasia, and Common Europe. Information on the times for meetings of these groups located outside of the United States may be obtained from the Common location identified earlier.

Share and Guide are primarily related to mainframe systems functions. However, because the relationship between mainframe systems and the midrange systems covered by the AS/400 is no longer obvious, contacts for those user groups are provided to enable the potentially needed information exchange.

Share can be contacted by either mail or phone at:

Share U.S.
401 N. Michigan Ave.
Chicago, IL 60611-4267
Phone: (312) 822-0932
Fax: (312) 321-6869

Guide or G.U.I.D.E. user groups can be reached at:

Guide International Corporation
401 N. Michigan Ave.
Chicago, IL 60611-4267
Phone: (312) 644-6610
G.U.I.D.E. Headquarters
c/o Schindler Information, Ltd.
CH-6030
Ebikon, Switzerland
Phone: +44-41-33-28-27

Index

Reader Feedback Sheet

Your comments and suggestions are very important in shaping future publications. Please email us at *moreinfo@maxpress.com* or photocopy this page, jot down your thoughts, and fax it to (850) 934-9981 or mail it to:

Maximum Press

Attn: Jim Hoskins

605 Silverthorn Road

Gulf Breeze, FL 32561

_____

_____

_____

_____

_____

_____

_____

_____

_____

_____

_____

_____

_____

_____

_____

_____

_____

_____

_____

*Exploring IBM's Bold
Internet Strategy*
by Jim Hoskins and
Vince Lupiano
$34.95
ISBN: 1-885068-16-6

*Building Intranets
with Lotus Notes &
Domino*
by Steve Krantz
$32.95
ISBN: 1-885068-10-7

*Exploring IBM
Technology and Products*
edited by Jim Hoskins
232 pages, paper
$54.95
ISBN: 1-885068-29-8

*Exploring IBM's
New Age Mainframes
Fifth Edition*
by John L. Young
512 pages, illustrations
$39.95
ISBN: 1-885068-05-0

*Marketing on the
Internet, Third Edition*
by Jan Zimmerman
445 pages, illustrations
$34.95
ISBN: 1-885068-09-3

*Exploring IBM
Client/Server Computing*
by David Bolthouse
471 pages, illustrations
$32.95
ISBN: 1-885068-04-2

*Exploring IBM
RS/6000 Computers,
Eighth Edition*
by Jim Hoskins and
Dave Pinkerton
423 pages, illustrations
$39.95
ISBN: 1-885068-14-x

*Exploring IBM
AS/400 Computers,
Eighth Edition*
by Jim Hoskins and
Roger Dimmick
502 pages, illustrations
$39.95
ISBN: 1-885068-13-1

To purchase a Maximum Press book, visit your local bookstore
or call 1-800-989-6733 (US) or 1-850-934-0819 (International)
or visit our homepage: *www.maxpress.com*

What About
ProductManager?
by David Curtis
200 pages, illustrations
$34.95
ISBN: 0-9633214-4-7

What About
MAPICS/DB?
by Ken Blackshaw
221 pages, illustrations
$29.95
ISBN: 0-9633214-2-0

Dr. Livingstone's
On-line Shopping
Safari Guidebook
by Frank Fiore
501 pages, illustrations
$24.95
ISBN: 1-885068-07-7

Exploring the
IBM AS/400
Advanced 36,
Second Edition
by Jim Hoskins and
Roger Dimmick
105 pages, illustrations
$26.95
ISBN: 1-885068-11-5

Exploring the
PowerPC
Revolution!
Second Edition
by Jim Hoskins and
Jack Blackledge
165 pages, illustrations
$22.95
ISBN: 1-885068-02-6

Exploring IBM
Personal
Computers,
A Business,
Ninth Edition
by Jim Hoskins and
Bill Wilson,
360 pages, illustrations
$34.95
ISBN: 1-885068-12-3

Real World
Client/Server
by Steve Krantz
344 pages, illustrations
$29.95
ISBN: 0-9633214-7-1

Exploring IBM
Print on Demand
Technology
by Jim Wallace
122 pages, illustrations
$22.95
ISBN: 1-885068-06-9

To purchase a Maximum Press book, visit your local bookstore
or call 1-800-989-6733 (US/Canada) or 1-609-769-8008 (International)
or visit our homepage: *www.maxpress.com*